PATRIOTS TO BUSINESS

BUSINESS STRATEGIES FOR ENTREPRENEURS

DISCOVER HOW YOU CAN BECOME A SUCCESSFUL ENTREPRENEUR YOURSELF!

JASON MILLER

Copyright © 2017 Jason Miller

All rights reserved. No part of this book may be reproduced, stored, or transmitted by any means—whether auditory, graphic, mechanical, or electronic—without written permission of both publisher and author, except in the case of brief excerpts used in critical articles and reviews. Unauthorized reproduction of any part of this work is illegal and is punishable by law.

I would like to personally thank you for making the time to read this book and appreciate that you respect the work that went into creating it. I genuinely hope this book changes your life.

FIRST EDITION

ISBN: 978-1-365-91609-0 (hc)
ISBN: 978-1-365-91607-6 (sc)

Because of the dynamic nature of the Internet, any web addresses or links contained in this book may have changed since publication and may no longer be valid. The views expressed in this work are solely those of the author and do not necessarily reflect the views of the publisher, and the publisher hereby disclaims any responsibility for them.

Any people depicted in stock imagery provided by Thinkstock are models and such images are being used for illustrative purposes only.

Certain stock imagery © Thinkstock.

Contents

Famous Quotes about Entrepreneurship vii
Dedication ix
Acknowledgement. xi
Special Shout Outs xiii
Foreword xv
The Patriot Philosophy xxi
What the Wealthy Hide. xxv

Chapter 1: Getting This Party Started 1
- My Story and How I Got Started In Business 1
- My Experience Coupled With Masterminds 5
- Getting Your Own Business Started "Warm Up". . .7
- Productivity in a New Business. 55
- Becoming the Leading Authority 77

Chapter 2: Making Some Important Connections
and Implementing. 85
- Outsourcing in Your Business. 85
- Launching a Website for Your Business. 105
- Joint Venture Mastery 110
- EBook Marketing. 115
- Knocking Out Your Competition
  (USP Formula) 126

Chapter 3: The Commission Business and
Cashing In Big 136
- Business by Commission -
  Boosting Affiliate Sales. 136
- Private Label Content Cash 143
- Autoresponder Methodology 156
- Social Media Marketing for Cash 163
- Viral Marketing Strategy 205

Chapter 4: It's all about the Customer Base 229
- Knowing Thy Customers 229
- Effective Marketing to
  Build Your Customer Base 231
- 7 Fundamentals in Our Own Business 233
- Being the CEO of Your Own Life. 238
- Getting Outside Your Comfort Zone 240

Chapter 5: The Awesome Discovery Process. 243
- Ditching All the Excuses 243
- The Missing Ingredients. 245
- Online or Brick and Mortar Business 248
- Measuring Up In a Business Venture. 251
- Discovering Your Why 254

Chapter 6: Getting This Puppy Kick Started 257
- The Art of Personal Branding. 257
- Developing Who Your Ideal Customer Is 259
- Branding Yourself with Video. 263
- "Old School" Mindset and
  How It Hurts Your Future 266
- Pushing Content like a Big Dog 267

Chapter 7: Some Little Tidd Bits of Information 272
- Spending 15K for Access 272
- List Building and Its Importance 275
- The Online Magic Formula 277
- The Death of Multi-Level Marketing 279
- Making a Hobby into a Business. 281

Chapter 8: Some of my Pretty Cool Secrets and Tips . . .284
- Email or Direct Mail Marketing. 284
- Our Simple Facebook Secret. 286
- The Price of Scaling Your Business 288
- Finding a Profitable Business Model Online . . .289
- What Story are You Telling. 292

Chapter 9: Important Tips to Drive You Further 295
- The Affiliate Marketing Fairytale 295
- The Importance of Honesty and Integrity. 297
- Taking Charge of Your Website Traffic 300
- Out of Control Content Marketing 302
- Innovations That Drive Your Business Faster. . .305

Chapter 10: Mobile Connectivity and a Little Humor . .310
- Today's Mobile World 310
- Mobile-Optimization. 313
- Advanced Affiliate Marketing. 314
- Puppy, Monkey, Baby Acid Trip 316
- Elements of a Successful Sales Letter. 318

Chapter 11: Social Media Growth and
Secrets to Success. 321
- High-Quality Blogs .321
- Thinking Twitter 323

- Grow Your Audience Online. 325
- My Best Kept Solo Ad Marketing Secrets 327
- Filthy Rich – Think Like the Wealthy. 338

Chapter 12: Some 8 Figure Business Tips. 362
- Ultimate Traffic Parts 1-3 -
  Prospect to Customer. 362
- Ultimate Traffic Part II - Prospect to
  Customer Prime the buyer's greed glands 428
- Ultimate Traffic Part III -
  Prospect to Customer 492
- Big Wealth and the Law of Attraction. 556
- Exploit Business Opportunities
  like the Wealthy. 570
- Financial Empowerment -
  Earning the Greenbacks 583
- Wrapping It Up!! 598

Famous Quotes about Entrepreneurship

"My biggest motivation? Just to keep challenging myself. I see life almost like one long University education that I never had — everyday I'm learning something new."
-Richard Branson, CEO
Virgin Mobile

"Your time is limited, so don't waste it living someone else's life. Don't be trapped by dogma – which is living with the results of other people's thinking. Don't let the noise of other's opinions drown out your own inner voice. And most important, have the courage to follow your heart and intuition. They somehow already know what you truly want to become. Everything else is secondary."
– Steve Jobs, Co-founder, CEO
Chairman Apple Inc.

"Twenty years from now you will be more disappointed by the things that you didn't do than by the ones you did do. So throw off the bowlines. Sail away from the safe harbor. Catch the trade winds in your sails. Explore. Dream. Discover."
-Mark Twain

"*Every time you state what you want or believe, you're the first to hear it. It's a message to both you and others about what you think is possible. Don't put a ceiling on yourself.*"

– Oprah Winfrey, media proprietor

"*Entrepreneurship is living a few years of your life like most people won't so you can spend the rest of your life like most people cant.*"

-Warren G. Tracy's student

"*Don't be afraid to assert yourself, have confidence in your abilities and don't let the bastards get you down.*"

– Michael Bloomberg founder Bloomberg L.P.

Dedication

This book is dedicated to all aspiring entrepreneurs that are, "Stepping Outside The Box" within their own lives, and was designed to help those that are willing to step outside their comfort zone and become the CEO of their own lives.

I would further like to dedicate this book to the military members and family members (my brothers and sisters) that have paid the ultimate sacrifice. The world is forever in your debt.

I wrote this book to bring forward new possibilities in your life as an entrepreneur. I want to give you the encouragement, tips, tricks and strategies I have used as an entrepreneur. I encourage you to think big and allow your creative imagination to skyrocket you to new heights in your life.

"Risk more than others think is safe. Dream more than others think is practical."

–Howard Schultz, Starbucks CEO

Acknowledgement

I would like to personally thank my mentors that have helped me make this book possible and have influenced my decision-making process as an entrepreneur. I appreciate each of you and you know exactly who you are. Thank you for the valuable time, input and feedback that you have provided me as a business owner and entrepreneur.

Without your guidance, counsel and occasional tough love, our business would not be where it is today.

My family is forever in your debt and we appreciate you very much!

Special Shout Outs

To my wife Erika – I wouldn't be where I am without you… You are a very special woman and I love you!

To my three wonderful children, Briana, Haylee and Barrett. I Love all of you!

To my ultimate mentor and great friend T.J. Rohleder – You have been an inspiration and the best mentor one could ever ask for. Thank you for all of your mentorship and guidance.

A very Special thank you to Chris and Susan Beesley, Chris Cobb, Tom Still, Dr. Kevin Williams, T.J. Rohleder, Norbert Orlewicz, Matt Lloyd and all of our mentors that have helped us succeed.

To my family – All of you have influenced my life in one way or another. Specifically my father Terry. Thanks for raising me tough and resilient and being there for me.

To every Soldier that I have ever served with.. "Those of You I Respect" You know who you are! I Salute You! Thank you for your service!

Foreword

Are You The Patriot of Your Own Life?
It's Not a Sheeps Game!

Many people sit around a table and talk about being free of life's hustle and chaos. Many people are in love with the dream of being the "Patriot" or by definition, the "Protector" of their own lives and what they do. Here is a fact… Most will never achieve it! "Pay Attention" I want to tell you a story that involves true "Patriotism"! It was five months into a tour in Afghanistan, boiled by the sun and desensitized by the nature of my employment. Standing feet from my armored vehicle, I watched my leader stab the ground with his 8" knife. The length of his blade I assume provided a small comfort, putting his hand at least a few inches farther from the possible IED. I remembered that moment not for the heroic act of putting himself in harms way, but rather from the shock of moments earlier he had told me that my life was worth more than his and to stand down upon finding what looked very familiar in shape to IED's we had seen before.

I reflect upon this time not in the way that I assume most do; to me it was a microcosm of human behavior, the nature of man exposed in extreme situation so that even the slightest of personalities became exaggerated. I noticed in a very brief time the pendulum of personalities; rocking between war-hardened patriots and humans who just wanted to feel human again.

A Patriot Has Intention

Leading off, I would like to make it clear that a Patriot is not always the one who puts himself in harms way, or thrusts the responsibility in one direction or another. Often the "True Patriot" is a normal human being with a common objective. The Patriots we often have (love them or hate them) have a reason to be the leader. In the first look at what makes a leader, it's important to note that there has to be a reason to lead. Anyone can call themselves the leader (often people do). To be a leader, however, there certainly has to be a cause to lead. In this case I am telling you as an entrepreneur to be the "Patriot" or "Leader" of yourself. Breaking these chains is very important.

Being a Patriot Supports a Common Goal

I often divulge in my writings and talks that "intentions" are the glue that holds our lives together. It is intention that focuses our efforts and aligns them in a singular direction. Being a Patriot in your own life follows the same simple concept. "If you have intention, you have a place to go and thus a reason to lead yourself." In the action of becoming a Patriot in your own life start by finding your intention. This can happen by asking yourself the question: "what am I intending in my life?". Find the answer to that and then you'll have all the reason you need to lead yourself and not work for other "Small Minded Monkeys" and make them millionaires.

A Leader at Any Level

I've seen it far too often, the micro-mutinies of employees in many different organizations. You know how it goes, standing around in a circle, bitching about how things are being done and how they should be done differently. Well, I've got some chilling news for those people; that's sheep's talk! Whenever you complain about your leadership you are effectively saying "I'm not being led the way I want to be led" or "my leader is not leading me the way I wish to be led". Its victimization of yourself to think that way. By living with the sheep's mindset, it's easy to lose perspective and feel a loss of control. When you lose control over your perspective, you begin to feel that life gives you the cards and you play them as they come. This is why I chose to step away from the employee model and run my own company. Essentially becoming the "CEO" and "Patriot" of my own life!

Consider Yourself Self-Employed

"When you accept complete responsibility for your life, you begin to view yourself as self-employed, no matter who signs your paycheck. You see yourself as the president of your own personal service corporation. You see yourself as an entrepreneur heading a company with one employee: you. You see yourself as responsible for selling one product, your personal services, in a competitive marketplace. You see yourself as completely responsible for every element of your work, for production, quality control, training, development, communication, strategy, productivity improvement, and finances. You refuse to make excuses. Instead, you make progress.

Your personal company, or any company, can increase its profits in one or more of three ways. First, the company can increase its sales and revenues, holding costs constant. Second, the company can decrease its costs, holding sales and revenues constant. Third, the company can do something else altogether, where one or both of the first two are possible. As the president of your own company, you have these three options".

The Application of Self-Leadership

Self-leadership does not involve blindly disregarding the objective of the organization you belong to. This could be your own company to! It simply means finding what is important to you and applying your best qualities to anything you take on.

"Effective self-leadership involves achieving an equilibrium between focusing on the cohesiveness of a work group and/or organization and focusing on the value and identity of each individual employee. Thus, self-leadership does not require entirely autonomous behavior without regard to the team or organization. Nor does it require that the identity and value of each individual employee be entirely put aside in favor of the work group or organization. Rather, an effective self-leadership perspective would encourage individuals to find their own personal identity and mode of contribution as part of an establishment, a group or an organization that produces synergistic performance".

Promote Yourself to CEO

The last thing I want to touch on is where you sit in your board-room of life. Imagine your life is the product, the grand creation of intention and design. In order to enable its success and fulfilment in the market place "your mind", it has to be planned with much simplicity, desirability and usefulness. Once you've settled on what this life should look like, promote yourself immediately. You are and always should be the "Chief Executive Officer" in your own life. Your life is the company and you need to lead it so that it can grow and develop. Remember, you can always change directions, seek new opportunities and should always be investing back into "Yourself". So take charge of your life… Become that "Patriot Protector", "Leader" and "Self Employed" entrepreneur that you know is hiding deep inside! Consider this book your shortcut to success in this new endeavor you have yet to find in your life. Embrace it and most of all Dream, Believe and Achieve excellence!

Jason T. Miller

Jason T. Miller (U.S. Army, Retired) Founder, Jump Start Marketing Concepts Founder, Patriots to Business

The Patriot Philosophy

To achieve greatness at multiple levels of your endeavors you have to have the spirit of an entrepreneur. The spirit of an entrepreneur is what will get you through the hard times when running your own business. Follow these simple tips as you get started and use them as a guide to your success. The word spirit should be your guide:

Self-sufficient and disciplined
Passionate
Integrity
Respected by others
Imagination
Tools for success

This simple guide should point you in the right direction for mindset in your business.

You must be ***self-sufficient and disciplined*** in everything you do. Whether it's setting your hours of operations as an entrepreneur or deciding how much family time you want to spend daily, be self-sufficient and disciplined with your choices. You are now accountable to yourself!

Do something that you are ***passionate*** about. Find your passion in life and work your business and your lifestyle around it. If you are passionate about what you do than it won't feel like work. It will be fun and you will enjoy doing it every day. You can also share your passion with your family and make it a family business like my family and I have done.

Always maintain your *integrity* in your business. It's something you can't get back. Once it's gone, it's gone. Be honest with your customers and don't be afraid to admit that you did something wrong. Mistakes happen in business, own them and move on.

Be *respected by others* in your community, with your customers, employees, family and other leaders in your field. Respect goes a long way with the people that surround you. They are the ones that will help you take your business to the next level.

Don't be afraid to have an *imagination* like a kid. Some of your best ideas will come with creative thinking and being a dreamer. No idea is too big or too small to try. Be inventive, innovative and adaptive by letting your imagination take you to new levels. The only unsuccessful idea is the one you never tried!

Always seek the best *tools* that will set you up for maximum success. Having the right tools, systems and processes in your business endeavors will allow you to make breakthroughs that you never thought possible.

Having the right mindset in your business and the SPIRIT to succeed is critical to your success. Just as important is the ability to operate as a business. You have to be the PATRIOT (The Protector) of your own business and business ventures. Know how your business operates from start to finish. Know your products and customers on an intimate level and you will achieve greatness.

Planning with consistency
Actions that create revenue
Train, mentor and coach
Reinvent yourself often
Integrate your systems
Operate with consistency
Turn your ideas into profit

This simple guide should point you in the right direction for operating your business.

Always ***plan with consistency*** in your business. If you are consistent with your budget, your products, inventory and customers you will see success in your operation. Always be planning the next big thing and thinking about how you can tweak your business to net more profit.

Take ***actions that create revenue*** in your business. Often times entrepreneurs get tied up with doing little tasks that can easily be outsourced or completely done away with all together. Focus on revenue generating processes in your business that effect your bottom line in a positive way. Do this every single day!

Be the leader and ***train, mentor and coach***. This could be employees that work for you or your customers that you serve. Step up and be the professional leader that you are. The world will not brand you as a leader or an expert. You just have to own it and become it yourself.

Always be prepared to ***reinvent yourself often***. Don't get tied to a specific idea on an emotional level. If it doesn't work than scrap it and move on. Reinvent yourself again and continue to make forward progress. Don't be so stubborn and married to a failed idea that it ends up putting your business into bankruptcy.

Have systems in your business that you can ***integrate*** with ease. Systems are what keep you going and automation is a wonderful thing. Do your homework and ensure that the systems you use will work for your business.

Operate with consistency. A business as an entrepreneur is all about finding what works and then washing, rinsing and repeating. Find what works and then maintain the consistency required to simply repeat the success you have found over and over again.

Turn every idea you have into profit. Be a thinker and be inventive with the things that you do. Aspire to remain on the cutting edge in your field and develop new ideas that produce profit. Remember, the greatest ideas in the world have changed all of our lives. On the same note, an idea is useless without execution!

Use these two acronyms above as a road map in your business. These simple tips and strategic ways of thinking will assist you in your path to "Breaching the Wall" and taking the needed steps to your own success.

What the Wealthy Hide

I want you to see some of the things that the rich marketers try to keep away from the poor marketers.

As you read these things, you will find out that there is not much that people do not know... The rich marketers try to reach new products earlier and try to dominate.

If you want to make the transition from being a poor marketer to being a rich marketer, then these are the points that you should read quite closely.

Many of those who today are well-known entrepreneurs, successful and mega rich have one thing in common with each other. Each of them was at one stage poor students or bankrupt business people who refused to give up.

They started with a dream, an idea that began as a spark and that spark of an idea grew into the multimillion-dollar companies with which their names are synonymous. What created the success for them? What was the key to their success when so many others have failed? Pay attention!!

1. They had a dream and they lived that dream and did not give up on that dream. That dream was a big dream and it drove them. They believed their dream even when failure looked them in the face.

2. They learned from mistakes and turned mistakes into success. They used failure as a learning tool to enable them to consider how to do things better next time.
3. They started small and gradually built up. Their focus was on building a niche and being the best in that niche. They did not allow their focus to become too big too quickly. This is the sure recipe for success.
4. Their focus was not on the income but on the product and building a loyal base of supporters through the product (or service) they were offering. Networking was the key, it produced the market, and it produced the opportunity for expansion. They did not need to do it alone. Others bought into their dream.
5. They explored and utilized every available marketing strategy to build their dreams, with the focus firmly on building social networks to develop strong customer focused and customer driven products and services. Therefore, the products sold themselves.
6. They invested time and energy into the development of businesses that eventually produced income with little or no effort on their part.
7. They explored and understood social and economic trends to ensure they understood where the market was going and historically what to expect, understanding that history often repeats itself.

8. They focused their time, energy, and resources on the outcomes of their research, and invested accordingly, rather than following the crowd.
9. Although at times they did hesitate, they kept the dream and did not allow setbacks to destroy the dream, but having learned from the setback, they allowed themselves to continue the dream and take risks.
10. As they took risks, they did not lose sight of their objective to create successful businesses and have an income source that did not rely totally on their involvement to be successful.

Those who have failed in business are those who have allowed the current economic climate to drive their business decisions. They have failed to do their research. They do not understand the rise and fall of the markets and the wealth cycles. This has prevented them from taking full advantage of investments and portfolios that create income and lose what income they have earned. They have accumulated debt rather than focusing on escaping the debt cycle and failed to see the money market for what it is.

They have succumbed to their failures and been scared off by them and they have given into the market trend that suggests that you cannot make money in today's economic climate as a business person.

Robert Kiyosaki has the last word:

"The size of your success is measured by the strength of your desire, the size of your dream and how you handle disappointment along the way."

Chapter 1

Getting This Party Started

My Story and How I Got Started In Business

My name is Jason Miller and I grew up in a small town on the border of Montana and North Dakota. I grew up on a farm as a hard working kid raising crops and tending livestock with my family.

We were a small farm operation that just made enough to live a comfortable life. My parents worked very hard to provide for my sister and me, but it was certainly a tough road and a lot of hard work for them. We were not poor by any means, but we fell in a common category like many, we lived comfortably.

There were certainly no luxury cars and fancy houses and certainly no beachfront property for a summer vacation home. But this taught me a valuable life lesson growing up.... Appreciate the things you do have.

My family has a long bloodline of military service and has served in many of the wars we have fought. Following a time honored tradition, I joined the military at the ripe age of 17 and shipped off for basic training upon graduation from high school.

Upon completion of all my training as a new Infantryman I was assigned to my first duty station. I spent the first part of my career in a light Infantry Recon Platoon as a Scout Sniper and Spotter.

I have made many moves over the course of my 20+ year career in the military. I have seen many things and have been to many places both good and bad just like many of my fellow brothers and sisters at arms. Then my life changed. I met my beautiful wife Erika who was also in the military.

We instantly related being in the military and because of our common goals and desires for a future of personal, professional and financial independence. We moved from place to place as we all do in the military and realized that there has to be more.

After my wife got out of the military she found it very difficult to start a career. She would just begin to climb the ladder of success just in time for us to make that next move to another duty station. So she did what many military spouses do and went to college. She now has two Masters Degrees, but has never fully been able to utilize her education because of moving every 3-4 years.

Like many, she has worked in jobs not careers. My wife and I have always had that sense that there was something better out there waiting for us. We have discussed many times the possibilities of starting our own business full-time and giving up the hectic life of the military. At the time I was well over the 10-year journey of my military career so it made sense to stick it out and get my 20 year retirement.

So fast-forward to 2014 - I deployed to Afghanistan and spent some time there assisting the Afghan Army rebuild and take control of their country. It was there that I had an absolute epiphany as I was sitting on my makeshift bed inside a sweatbox plywood room that was about the size of a prison cell. This is where the initial seeds were planted in my mind to take action and start our own online business. I knew I was quickly approaching retirement and needed to figure out a plan for our next chapter in life.

So there I was on the crappy make shift bed with crappy internet service searching for opportunities to make money with an online business. I did the research but ultimately set it aside as an idea upon redeployment home.

When I returned home and settled back into normal life, Erika and I began to reengage the discussion of starting our sustainable online business. I remembered the research I did on many business models when I was deployed, so we did more research and decided to give it a shot.

This was an opportunity for me to do when I retired and also an opportunity for my wife to have a meaningful career working from home. We decided to become an unstoppable team and start our own online business.

We wanted to create a lasting income that would allow us to spend more time together as a family and not have to live the normal 9-5 lifestyle dealing with traffic day-in and day-out and having to report to a "boss." We wanted to become the CEO's of our own lives by taking our years of military experience and pouring it into a solid business model.

Our goal has always been to earn a full time income online and be the CEOs of our own lives. So we jumped in feet first and 100 miles an hour. We started attending business training, which was very relatable since training is second nature for us "military types." The training and business summits that we attended were easy to get through because it walked us through the initial process of setting up our online business step by step.

We reached out to industry leaders for mentorship to help walk us through the things we didn't fully understand.

The one thing that set us apart was our consistent drive to succeed at anything we do. The military has deeply instilled this attribute in both of us. This has served us well in our business ventures and has helped us reach new heights in our lives.

My wife and I will never have to work "normal" employee jobs ever again. Our military careers have been a driving factor in our success because of that sheer will to succeed. Like many, I enjoyed the last 20+ years of my military career. It has been exciting, rewarding and has taken care of my family in many ways that the outside world cannot relate to.

However, we have now found a new start and a new journey down another path in our lives as successful entrepreneurs helping others find their success in life.

Now, to be honest, business up to this point was not completely new. In 2001 I started my first eBay business online. I nurtured this business for almost 14 years and it was also very successful. Running a multiple six figure eBay business is not an easy task. Imagine shipping thousands of items from your home without a central storage and shipping facility!

eBay was a fun and exciting business but it grew out of control. I often tell people we got too big for our britches in the physical products niche. Then we found the power of digital products and the ability to license products as affiliate marketers.

This really changed the game and is how we have been able to build a sustainable online business today. Coupled with our own digital learning products of our own, we can license other company's products and sell them for a cut of the final cost of the sale.

Now that we are established in the industry, we have been able to create multiple six figure quarterly sales in our business through cultivating multiple income streams. In this book I will show you some of my best tips and tricks to help you do the very same thing! Read every page of this book and feel free to reach out to us on our website anytime!

My Experience Coupled With Masterminds

Experience? Is experience really necessary to start a business? Well, I would say to a degree that the answer is yes. Do you really need a Master's degree in business? Absolutely not! When I started my first business back in the late 90's and early 2000's I had -0- business experience. I later went on to get my degree in business management which I can tell you has contributed a big goose egg to the success of my companies.

Experience is best had through two things:

- Trial and error by self-teaching
- Attending summits, seminars and masterminds

The best experience you will ever get in business will be to get in there, get dirty and experience failure alongside success. You will experience both and it does not matter what business you are in. The one thing business is not is butterflies and pixie dust. Many business owners will not share their very rough times. The fact is that all businesses go through ups and downs and left and rights!

Self-study will be so important to your success. Study other successful people and model what they are doing. Often time's people try to recreate the wheel. This normally ends up in a massive failure. A small percentage of people who do start-ups with their own ideas actually succeed!

This is why you need to take a hard long look at what your options are and how you can exploit a business opportunity that makes sense for you. Formal education is great but doing things through exploration are lifelong learning events. I have spent many years self-learning. In our online business one of the best learning tools out there is YouTube. I always tell people that I have my second degree from YouTube! This is a great way to learn and consume information in a very quick way.

Second is the power of Masterminds. These business building summits are great for many reasons. They are a great place to learn business strategies from 7 and 8 figure business owners that have "Figured it out" for lack of better terms. It also gives you the opportunity to meet people like you and share business ideas and help each other.

I actually met my very first mentor at a Mastermind and he helped me take my business from a hundred dollars a day to over one thousand dollars a day in a very short period of time. The power of a mentor and or coach is massive.

Lastly, attending these Masterminds can help position you within the Niche you are working in. You may be able to offer your services to some of the people attending. You may even be able to do Joint Venture deals with some of the other attendees of the Mastermind or summit.

So, do not count out this avenue for your new or existing business. Now, attendance to these summits or masterminds can be extremely expensive. With airfare and tickets to the event you can easily exceed $10K for tickets. Sounds scary but it's all a tax deduction so don't let this stop you from attending an event that could possibly take your business to an entirely different level.

Getting Your Own Business Started "Warm Up"

This section is all about getting started. Deciding what niche you plan to break into is the first step and you will want to research this heavily before starting any opportunity. Once you have a nice list of niche ideas, section two will help you analyze the list of niches and "prune" it down to only the most profitable niches.

We hope this information will aid you in your Internet marketing journeys. You may want to use it as a resource guide whenever you're looking to expand your business, so keep it on your desk or somewhere it'll be easy to find. At the end of this book we will provide you with many resources that you can use when setting up your business. Its taken years and lots of experience to learn these methods and resources that are compiled in this book.

Niche ideas are all around you, offline and online. I'm about to share with you 21 resources and ways to get good ideas for niches. Get out a pad and a pen and make a list of potential niches because you're about to discover literally thousands of them. I want you to write down the ones you resonate with. Sure there are profitable niches everywhere, but the niche you choose should be something you're at least interested in or already know about.

You don't need to be an absolute expert in a niche to break into it. However, it helps to have interest in it since you'll be doing business in that niche every day. If a niche bores you to death, then not only will it be hard to get motivated to do any work, but your lack of passion will show to potential customers and website visitors. Another thing to consider is to choose only a niche that you feel comfortable with. For example, Gambling niches are very profitable, but you may or may not feel comfortable with it.

The same goes for any other niche you may not be comfortable with such as Pay Day Loans. It's lucrative, but if you can't sleep well at night promoting Pay Day loan offers, then don't touch that niche even with a 50 foot pole.

For hobby niche ideas, check out Magazines.com and browse the various categories. If there's enough interest in a subject that there's a popular magazine based around it, then you may have a profitable niche on your hands! Also, if you happen to have a subscription to any of the magazines at magazines.com, then you can find great niche ideas by checking out the paid ads inside the magazines.

You can search CPA (Cost Per Action) offers that will give you plenty of niche ideas at Offer Vault. One of the best parts about Offer Vault is that you don't even have to search for anything to get profitable niche ideas. Right when you land on the site, you'll see the offers that are paying the highest per lead.

You can get good physical product niche ideas by checking out the Amazon Best Sellers list. You can browse the best-selling products in any category. Another thing you may want to take a look at for niche ideas is the Table of Contents of best-selling books by using the "Look Inside" feature on Amazon.com. There are sub-niches galore to be discovered inside the tables of contents of these books.

The National Enquirer has the most expensive ad space of any print publication, so pay attention to the ads you see inside each issue you read. If advertisers are paying that kind of money to run their ads, then the offers they're running must be hot. Take a look at what they're advertising in these mega expensive advertisements because where there are hot offers, there are hot niche ideas.

You can get some great niche ideas by checking out eBay Pulse, which will tell you the most popular searches and trends on eBay. You can also browse categories and stores on eBay to spark niche ideas. The categories section is one of the most in-depth I've seen, so give it a look and see what niches are out there.

I'm sure you've seen the "For Dummies" books over the years. If a subject has profit potential, then they make a book about it. What most internet marketers don't know is that Dummies.com is an excellent place to get niche ideas by browsing the various "For Dummies" books.

One great way to find out what people are talking about on forums is by using a forum search engine like BoardReader. You can type in a topic like "Weight Loss" and find out what people are talking about in various forum threads. Pay attention to the problems they're talking about and get niches ideas from them, because people pay for solutions to problems.

Flippa is a massive marketplace for buying and selling websites. As you look through the marketplace, pay attention to the expensive sites and ones that are making a profit because if those sites are making a profit, then why can't you have a site in the same niche that makes a profit as well? You can actually reverse engineer these websites in a way, to find out how their links were built, what type of content they have, and who their audience is by using a tool like Quantcast.

If you're a digital products marketer then you no doubt already know about ClickBank and the ClickBank Marketplace. Besides internet marketing related products, the CB Marketplace is a great place to find niches based on Gravity. Each product in the marketplace has a Gravity Score (Grav), which is a measurement of how many affiliates have had success promoting a product, so you can find some profitable niches by looking at the products with the highest Gravity.

JVZoo is a newer affiliate network, but growing by leaps and bounds. I predict it will become one of the major affiliate networks for digital goods across all niches, so you should join and take a look at the products in the marketplace. The best part about JVZoo is you can see the $ Per Click (the Earnings Per Click) of each product, so the higher the EPC, the higher converting it is. Products with the highest EPCs may give you good ideas for niches that have high converting products.

You can find niche ideas by also browsing the Pay Dot Com marketplace. Pay Dot Com is another digital products affiliate network like ClickBank and JVZoo, bigger than JVZoo yet smaller than ClickBank. The best niche ideas you can get from Pay Dot Com will come from the Top Sellers section.

You may or may not be a fan of infomercials, but nonetheless, they are great for conjuring up niche ideas! When you see an infomercial running multiple times, then chances are that infomercial is profitable. Try to figure out who the ideal customer is for that product. You can actually promote many of these products you see in infomercials in CPA networks like Wolf Storm Media.

You'll get a good idea of what topics are hot at any given moment by using Google Trends. It's also a good idea to type in subjects such as "weight loss" into Google Trends, because you'll find related news articles. You can get some great niche ideas from those news articles. Just beware that trends come and go, obviously, so you may not want to base an entire business on trends.

When you're looking to find out what kind of problems people are having and what solutions they're looking for, Yahoo! Answers can be an almost magical tool.

If you have no idea what you're looking for, then you can browse categories to find potential niche ideas.

If you have a question in mind, then type it into the search box to see what related questions people are asking, and try to find the most pressing problems.

Shopping.com is where consumers go to compare products. You'll get niche ideas by exploring their list of Most Popular Products and Popular Pages. Here's one I found that I never would've thought of on my own: Wedding Corsages.

Yahoo! Shopping can give you great ideas for profitable niches with their Shopping Insider articles. Looking at the front page right now I'm getting ideas like Prom Styles and Valentine's Day Gifts. Browse articles by category and you'll end up with a good list of possible niches.

Although Ezinearticles.com got drilled by Google's Panda update, it is still a massive resource for niche ideas for you to take a look at. You'll get niche ideas by browsing different categories and seeing what these authors are writing about. If a particular author has many posts, pay attention to what subjects he or she is writing about because nobody writes that many articles for no reason. There may be profit potential.

The Google Keyword tool can be used to find sub-niches galore. (Do a Google search for "Google Keyword Tool"). When you have a keyword like "weight loss," type it into the Google Keyword tool, then select "only show ideas closely related to my search terms."

You'll start to see long-tail keywords related to the keyword that will begin to dig deeper and find sub-niches.

AdSense Sandbox is a fun site that will show you AdSense ads that are running on sites related to the subject you submit. When you see the ads that are running and what products and services are being promoted, you should start getting good niche ideas.

Pay close attention to the similarities of products, you may be onto something if you see the same type of product over and over again.

If you're looking for niche ideas related to Health in particular, then Bottom Line Publications is an excellent resource. When you go to the site, browse the subjects of their books and newsletters because they are big-time direct marketers. If these niches are responsive to their direct marketing tactics, then they may be responsive to yours as well.

Mixrank will show you PPC ads that are running in various niches when you submit an advertiser, keyword, or publisher into the field.

The best part is Mixrank will tell you how long an ad has been running. The longer an ad has been running, generally the more profitable that offer is, so you can see how you can get some niche ideas that are more likely to be profitable. There's a free and a paid version, but the paid version is unnecessary with what we're trying to accomplish here.

Part 2: Pruning your list of niches

By now you should have a monster list of potentially profitable niches if you went through each resource. No worries if your list is small from only using a couple of the resources. Now we're going to take your list and "prune it." We'll prune it down to the niches of your liking by analyzing them. We're not going to analyze them by using exact data or an exact science.

No niche is perfect, but there are many things to consider when deciding to do internet marketing in a niche. The most important part of this process is finding out the things that appeal most to YOU when it comes to each niche. Use the following 21 Questions when determining whether a niche is for you or not. Some of the questions are about the profit potential of a niche. Other questions are about how easy it's going to be for you to reach your target audience on a daily basis.

Then there are questions about how fast you can grow and become a force in any given niche market. If a niche doesn't sit with you after asking these 21 questions then delete it from your list. By the end you will have a handful of niches left to choose from.

Keep in mind that there are more questions than just these 21 questions you can consider when selecting a niche. These happen to be the questions that are important to us based on our experience with internet marketing. Besides having a general interest in a niche and being comfortable with it ethically, I want a niche to have profit potential, potential to generate easy traffic, and potential for fast growth.

Question #1: Are there multiple products in the niche?

The first question you want to ask yourself is, are there a lot of good products? You want to know this because you may quickly run out of good products to offer to your website visitors or e-mail list subscribers. If you're running AdSense or selling ad space on your website or selling ad space in your e-mail newsletter, then that's one thing. But if you're going to be depending on making commissions, then it's vital to have multiple offers you can promote.

Question #2: How big is the problem your prospect is having?

If it's not a hobby niche, how big is the problem the prospects are having? Is the problem they're having big enough that they'd be willing to part with their hard earned money to get a solution? Maybe someone would be willing to pay for pain relief, but they wouldn't be willing to pay to solve a lesser problem.

Question #3: Are there potential JV partners in the niche for explosive growth?

Here's something not many marketers consider when selecting a niche. Are there potential Joint Venture partners already in the niche? Are all of them so big that they would never consider doing a JV deal with you? Or are they so small that it wouldn't matter if they did a JV deal with you? There's no faster way to grow a business than by using Joint Venture deals, so it's something to consider.

Question #4: Does it make sense to build a list in the niche or not?

Are other internet marketers in the niche building an e-mail subscriber list? Would it make sense to build a list in the niche? You may or may not want to get into a niche where it's a must to build a list in order to make nice profits. Take a look around at the competitors and see if they have opt-in forms on their websites or not. Join their lists and see what it would be like to market in that niche.

Question #5: How expensive is available ad inventory in the niche?

One major thing you have to consider before getting into a new niche is how easy it will be to reach your target audience. If you're looking to pay for traffic, then you'll want to see how expensive the ad inventory is for that market. For example, you'll find the costs vary when bidding on keywords and URLs using CPV networks like LeadImpact and also when bidding on PPC keywords with Google AdWords.

Question #6: Will it be easy to generate free traffic in this niche?

If you're looking at going the free traffic route, then take a look around at how easy (or hard) it would be to reach your target prospects in a particular niche using free methods.

You can use the Google Keyword Tool to discover generally how competitive keywords are in a niche. Also try to do some digging around and find out if your competitors are successfully using other free sources like YouTube, Twitter, and Facebook. If they can do it, then why not you?

Question #7: Are there high end products or services at $1,000 or more in the niche?

Are there products or services being sold at $1,000, $5,000, or even $10,000 in a niche?

Not many niches have customers who actively spend $1,000 or more on a single product or service. If you can find many offers in your niche in those price ranges, then that's a good sign that you can make easy money in your niche. Because in a niche where high end products are being sold often, you'll find it's easier to make 1 sale at $1,000 than 100 sales at $10.

Question #8: Are there continuity programs like membership sites in the niche?

It's easier to make dependable income when there are continuity programs in a niche. I'm talking about membership sites, subscriptions, etc. They are especially lucrative when there are services that customers need and will keep paying for month after month.

Webhosting and auto-responder services come to mind.

Question #9: How fast do vendors pay out in the niche and do they pay out at all?

When vendors don't pay out fast or if they don't pay at all, then that can cripple your business in itself. That's why I recommend staying away from any affiliate programs that aren't on networks like ClickBank, for the most part. There are exceptions to the rule.

Many product vendors wait up to 90 days to pay out commissions, and many don't pay out at all because either they're dirty or they're not responsible enough with their money.

If the only available affiliate programs in your niche aren't on affiliate networks then my advice is to avoid them like the plague. There are exceptions to this just choose carefully.

Question #10: Are exact match domains available in the niche?

While this isn't a must, it can give you an edge when it comes to free traffic from Google.

An exact match domain is a domain name (.com preferably) that matches a keyword you want to rank for in Google. One easy way to find whether there are exact match domains available in your niche is to take your keyword list and copy and paste it into GoDaddy Bulk Domain Register. You can use that feature on GoDaddy to find out whether there are exact match domains available without actually buying the domains through GoDaddy.

Question #11: Could you create a product in this niche?

Having your own product gives you maximum leverage in a niche. You can create cross promotion deals with JV partners and you can sit back and let your affiliate army crush your offer with traffic all day long. If it's a physical product you must create in a niche, then that may be something you can't do. As for digital products, if you don't have the expertise in a niche, then there may be Private Label Rights material available on the web that you can use to aid you in creating a respectable product.

Question #12: Will it be easy to build your authority in the niche?

Having your own product is honestly the ultimate way to build authority in a niche.

Another way is by having JV partners who has customers associate you with, so you're borrowing your JV partner's credibility in a way. A popular blog can also give you authority in a niche. Are there already authority blogs in the niche you're looking at? If so, then you may also be able to have one yourself.

Question #13: Do you already have knowledge of this niche?

It's much easier to enter a niche when you already have knowledge or expertise in it.

You don't have to be an expert, but being an intermediate is enough to share what you know information-wise. If you have a burning desire to learn more about a niche, then that can help in entering a niche as well. In that role you're more of a reporter than an authority figure.

Question #14: Are people spending money in this niche?

Many hobbies are popular and solutions for problems are searched for all over the net, but that doesn't mean they spend money on it. In this case you'll need to verify whether there are buyers in the niche or not by checking out bestseller lists using the resources we talked about earlier. We will include a resource page at the end of this book. It's easy to make the mistake of choosing a popular yet unprofitable niche, so make sure you "do your homework" on this.

Question #15: Is coaching being sold in the niche?

Everyone knows there's good money to be made in coaching, whether internet marketing coaching, life coaching, etc. Coaching packages are sold for thousands of dollars, so if you're a good lead generator then you can either sell your own coaching packages or generate leads for coaches who do sell packages. They can afford to spend more on leads you generate for them because they're charging high prices.

Question #16: Are there pay per lead offers in this niche?

Promoting Pay Per Lead Offers can be much more profitable than Pay Per Sale Offers, which you may be accustomed to. It's easier to get someone to fill out a form than buy something. If there are Pay Per Lead Offers in the niche, then you may have an easier time converting your traffic into money.

Question #17: Will it be easy to stand out from the crowd in this niche?

Some niches have a crazy amount of competition, but that doesn't mean you should be scared to enter them. Is there a way you can stand out from the crowd in a competitive niche? Think about it, because standing out can help you stomp your competition into the ground. This has a lot to do with positioning. Maybe you have expertise in a sub-niche that you can share that will put you head and shoulders above your competition.

Question #18: Are there webinars or teleseminars in the niche?

Webinars and teleseminars generate sales like crazy, but not every niche is responsive to them. In any niche you need a vehicle to make money, so if there are webinars and teleseminars in a niche, then chances are you can do the same thing or promote them as an affiliate. While the average conversion rate of a sales letter online is roughly 1%, webinars and teleseminars convert generally around 10% or more.

Question #19: Are there call centers in this niche?

What converts even higher than webinars and teleseminars, is one-on-one phone selling, so keep an eye out for it in the niche you're assessing. Just beware that many call centers are dirty. However, just using the phone to sell will increase your conversion rates to as much as 50% depending on how the lead was generated. If there are call centers in a niche, then you can also use the power of the telephone to close more sales.

Question #20: Is this niche related to Health, Wealth, or Relationships?

If the niche you're looking at is related to Health, Wealth, or Relationships, then you may have a mass market on your hands. Health, Wealth, and Relationships-related products and services are known to be cash cows. Also, the traffic potential is generally higher when related to Health, Wealth, and Relationships.

Question #21: Are there many searches in Google in this niche?

Take a look at the Google Keyword Tool (type "Google Keyword Tool" into Google to find it). If you see low traffic levels for keywords in your niche, then it doesn't make much sense to choose this niche. Sure the competition is likely low. However, there's usually a reason for that. There is a lack of customers.

Part 3: Broad brush of traffic

Now, let's just do a broad brush on traffic. There are some nice new advertising sources in this book for you to discover and some of them are huge. Others are smaller yet legit.

I'm talking about Solo Ads, PPC, PPV, as well as some untraditional types of advertising like paying for blog posts. I hope you'll find many new ad networks and places to buy ads from that you didn't previously know about.

It's important to note that you're not going to need all of these sources. You could spend millions of dollars with just one or a handful of these select sources. Think of these traffic sources we discuss as a mini guide to the available ad inventory out there that you may have not known about. Crack it open whenever you're looking to buy some traffic.

Before we get started with these ad sources, I also wanted to tell you that you can get a world-class education in buying traffic for free.

One way is to join a CPA network such as Wolf Storm Media and take their free trainings. Another way is to learn all you can from the actual ad network sites that you'll discover here. It's also vital to get some ads running and track everything using a program such as ClickMagick. You honestly don't need a $2,000 course to learn about internet advertising because the best way to learn is to get out there and do it.

While you can learn the basics from someone else, the real learning comes from your experience. When you're tweaking ads, when you're tweaking your bids, when you're crunching your numbers and looking at your metrics and adjusting... That's when you're REALLY learning! So take everything you learn from others like a grain of salt.

Take these advertising sources, go out there, and generate all the traffic your little heart desires.

JV Rocket and "Tier 1 Solo Ads"

With JV Rocket you can buy a solo ad that will go out to a double opt-in list of 226,000 subscribers for the price of $2,500. Your ad goes out to customers who have purchased ClickBank products in the Make Money niche such as Get Google Ads Free, Health Biz in a Box, Forced Money, and Top Secret Magic Code. You'll also reach affiliates for ClickBank products such as Get Google Ads Free, Health Biz in a Box, Forced Money, Top Secret Magic Code, Cash Making Power Sites, Top Secret Fat Loss Secret, and Top Secret Car Secret.

Many of the top Internet Marketing and Make Money niche gurus are using JV Rocket to build their lists and also to directly mail to their hot offers. $2,500 is a nice chunk of money to risk, so before testing a JV Rocket you'll want to make sure you have tested sales material. You'll also want to be sure that your offer would be a good match for the type of customers who would buy the type of products I just mentioned above.

This doesn't mean that your offers must be similar, but it does mean that the same demographic would order your product. The downside of this solo ad source is that there are no guaranteed amount of visitors you'll get. The upside is that if you have an offer that's on fire and would work well with these type of customers then JV Rocket can be a goldmine. Just remember, as with all of these ad sources in this book, you're responsible for your business and the risks you take with buying advertising.

Profiting from paid advertising is simple, but not easy. Here's what I mean. It would be easy to blow through $10,000 on JV Rockets. The inventory is there waiting for you to order anytime you want. However, it would be wise to test your sales funnel out buying solo ads on a small scale at $30,

$100, or $300 a pop from "Tier 2 Solo Ad" vendors such as the ones on Safe-Swaps.com, SoloAdDirectory.com, or Directory of Ezines.

After you have a tested and proven funnel that works well with the solo ads you've purchased on a small scale, then you may want to consider going big time and ordering what I call "Tier 1 Solo Ads" such as JV Rocket.

JV Rocket isn't the only Tier 1 Solo Advertising available. Here are some more in various niches: Arcamax (General Consumer List), Newsmax, Self Growth, and Nextmark.

LeadImpact and Top CPV Networks Technically TrafficVance is a better quality CPV network than LeadImpact in my opinion, but the barrier to entry with TrafficVance is $1,000.

With LeadImpact, on the other hand, you only need $100 to get started using their massive network. I find it much easier to generate mass targeted traffic with LeadImpact than the other major CPV networks with a low barrier to entry such as Direct CPV and Media Traffic. LeadImpact allows you to buy traffic on a Per View basis. You're essentially buying something similar to popups.

Paying "Per View" means a small window will open on their screen and it will lead to your webpage. Your webpage must fit inside that window. You can bid on keywords or URLs using LeadImpact. When bidding on a keyword, website content will match your keyword and trigger your pop up. When bidding on a URL, visiting that URL will trigger your popup. Depending on your Geo Targeting and the Category/Sub-Category of your offer, the lowest bid you can start with will be as low as .015 to .017.

The downside of LeadImpact is that I don't personally like how they have the minimum bidding set up. For some

Sub-Categories you might have a minimum bid of .015 and for others it may be .025.

One cent may not seem like a big difference but when you multiply that 1,000+ times per day, it starts to add up. Small squeeze pages seem to do very well with LeadImpact. They can be your own squeeze pages or a Pay-Per-Lead (PPL) offer in a CPA network.

I find there's not as much inventory in the Make Money and Internet Marketing niches, but there's a ton in large markets that are multiple times bigger.

For example, you can generate a serious amount of traffic on a daily basis to Pay-Per-Lead online gaming offers. Same goes for Weight Loss, Health, and Financial niches.

To find PPL offers to promote, try a CPA offers search engine such as Offer Vault.

With Plenty of Fish ads, you can reach 20,000,000 users on a CPM basis. In case you're not familiar with "CPM," it simply means "Cost per 1,000 impressions of your ad." You'll also be bidding for ad inventory on a CPM basis. The minimum buy is just $25, so you can cheaply give POF Ads a nice test run for as low as $25.

It takes 24 hours or less for your ads to be approved. Image ad sizes include 110x80px, 300x250px, 160x600px and 120x600. Besides the insanely low point of entry at $25 minimum, there's something else about POF Ads that makes your traffic highly targeted.

In-depth demographics targeting is available. You can target prospects based on:

- Country, State/Province, Zipcode
- Age, Gender
- Education, Profession

- Has Children, Games and Puzzles
- Body Type, Drinking Habits
- Looking to Marry Soon, Ethnicity
- Height, Income, Marital Status
- Religion, Smoking Habits, Hair Color

Your ads are so ultra-targeted that they're not even shown to POF visitors who aren't logged in. Your ad is displayed above the fold as well. With POF Ads you can really go to town with specific dating offers. For instance, imagine targeting Christians who are looking to date. You can put a Christian Singles offer in front of them.

Do you see how powerful POF Ads can be? Because you have access to so many demographics, your ads don't even have to be about dating. They can be about something totally unrelated, but targeted to the demographic you choose.

There are many CPA offers out there related to dating if that's what you want to explore.

Or this is a perfect time for you to start your Dating or Relationships niche empire by generating leads from Plenty Of Fish to your own subscriber list. ClickBank products such as The Magic of Making Up may also do well with POF Ads.

7Search.com is one of my favorite of the "Tier 2 PPC" networks, search engines, and the like. Google, Yahoo, MSN, and Facebook are considered "Tier 1 PPC" in my book. Everything else is Tier 2 PPC the way I see it. The great thing about 7Search is you don't have to worry about Quality Score or other headaches. You set up a landing page, you bid on keywords, and you tweak your campaigns until they're profitable.

If you're looking to generate Biz Opp leads, then you may want to check out Ad Hitz.

With Ad Hitz, you can do Site Specific Targeting (recommended) on some biz opp sites that get serious traffic, such as MyBrowserCash.com that gets 23,1411 unique visitors per day and ClickSense.com that gets 281,360 unique visitors per day.

Now, if you're looking for serious Internet Marketing niche leads, then Ad Hitz may or may not be for you. These leads you generate will be the type that hang out on pay to click sites and probably paid survey sites. This doesn't necessarily mean that these prospects are "low quality" or not serious about business, but it does mean that they're clueless about what you and I know about. So I think it's important to not take advantage of these clueless prospects. Instead, you should show them the light.

For serious Internet Marketing leads who are already more advanced, you'll want to buy an ad at the top of WarriorForum.com or run Warrior Special Offers. There are over 450,000 members on Warrior Forum and growing.

Another option for generating serious Business leads in general is by using LinkedIn Ads. You won't necessarily generate all internet marketing leads there, but there are 130,000,000 business-minded members on LinkedIn to advertise to. 40,000,000 are US based. With LinkedIn Ads you don't have to pay on a PPC basis because they also offer inventory on a CPM basis (cost per 1,000 impressions). It's your choice.

PayPerPost, Blog Ads, and ReviewMe

You may want to consider blog advertising. This is where your website or your product is promoted on real blogs. PayPerPost is one of them and they connect you with real bloggers out there who are willing to do a write up about your product or site for a fee.

Besides generating the direct traffic from your links, you'll also be building links, except you won't be building links on fly-by-night blog networks that get de-indexed from the search engines in the blink of an eye.

You have complete control over how much you'll spend on a post when you create your listing called an "Opportunity." You also get to select the categories and the Geo Targeting. Blog Ads is another option for advertising on blogs, but it's not contextual like PayPerPost. Here you're buying actual ad space on a time basis. What I mean is you're not buying on a PPC or CPM basis like some of the other sources we've talked about.

You're buying ads based on the amount of time they'll run on the blog.

It's just like buying ad space direct from a webmaster at a fixed rate, only you're doing it through the Blog Ads network. The pricing is set up similar to Text-Link-Ads. Price doesn't go up or down based on the amount of impressions or click through on your ad.

ReviewMe is another option with blog advertising and it can work well to create buzz for your new product or service. You can browse the different blogs at ReviewMe.com and purchase a review of your product or service.

You'll also get the link back to your site, but just keep in mind that these bloggers will do an honest review for you and that review will be permanent. You can also create a listing for what you're looking for if you're looking to be found by bloggers who are looking to review products or services similar to your own.

AbestWeb, CB, JV Zoo, W+, PDC, DigiResults

If you're advertising to get affiliates, then you'll want to run some ads on AbestWeb, the world's largest affiliate marketing forum. Super affiliates galore hang out on this forum and have their eyes open for hot offers to promote all the time. They can generate traffic all day long, but they don't always have offers that convert, so if your offer is appealing enough to them, then just one super affiliate you get from running an ad can be worth much more than what you paid for the ad. Check out the different advertising options at AbestWeb website. They have all kinds of inventory from banner ads to e-mail blasts to their members.

Getting your digital product listed in the ClickBank Marketplace is also a great way to pick up affiliates who can drive traffic to your site all day and night on a commission basis. With ClickBank, you're technically buying traffic, but it's no risk because you're only paying when someone makes a sale.

Other options have emerged as well including JV Zoo, WSO Pro, PayDotCom, and DigiResults. Honestly, I'm a fan of all those programs just listed. Instead of being paid by ClickBank, you're paid directly upon each sale with PayPal. However, the marketplaces aren't even close to as old or as big as ClickBank. So there are a lot more affiliates waiting in the ClickBank marketplace to see your offer to promote than the others, but you don't get instant PayPal payments.

You can also pick up some affiliates by listing your product in the Warrior Forum Affiliate Programs Database for a small fee. There are more ways to get super affiliates to promote for you. One is by busting your butt putting together a massive product launch and getting listed on sites like JV Notify Pro and Warrior JV. Another way is to simply get the attention of super affiliates by running your offer on networks.

If you throw $10,000 at advertising your offer, then chances are super affiliates are going to see it, and they are always looking for one thing: offers that convert.

StumbleUpon Ads, PR Web, and Direct CPV

If you know how StumbleUpon works, it's where users click the "Stumble" button and they are sent from webpage to webpage checking out pages that have been "Stumbled" by other users and are related to their favorite topics. With StumbleUpon Paid Discovery, your webpage becomes part of that Stumbling process. Users land on your landing page while Stumbling through websites and you pay per view. My opinion is it's a bit pricey at this point, but I also think it's a great way for companies to spread brand awareness and it's also potentially good for viral marketing.

Using PR Web is another way to launch a viral marketing or brand awareness campaign.

To tell you the truth, it's also possible to generate a lot of direct traffic as well. Not to mention you can get some serious offline traffic if your press release gets picked up by a newspaper. PR Web allows you to distribute a press release to the far corners of the internet, depending on the package you choose. The important thing to remember when writing the press release is making it newsworthy, so you could technically do a press release for virtually anything that's happening with your website, product, or business.

Whenever you launch a new website, for example, you can create a press release and submit it to PR Web.

You can also do this when you put out a new product. Although Direct CPV was already briefly mentioned in the

CPV section, I never pointed out that you can use their Run of Network (normally referred to as RON) traffic for brand awareness and getting viral marketing campaigns off the ground. Run of Network traffic is untargeted and it runs to all available inventory on the network, so it's an insanely high amount of traffic.

You could blow through thousands of dollars very fast, so be careful with it.

Don't expect to get any good measurable results with Run of Network traffic on Direct CPV. But it is possible to use to get thousands of views on a YouTube video in one day, for instance. Just don't expect to use this type of traffic as you would other types.

More advertising networks and ad sources

Bravenet Media, MyAds, Her Agency, Indie Click, Batanga, 24/7 Media, BuySellAds, Adfish, Crisp Ads, ExoClick, Adtegrity, Intermarkets, HIRO, Casale Media, Banner Space, Ad On Network, Advertising.com, Yahoo Media Services, AdBuyer.com, Kitara Media, Flux Advertising, Burst Media, Kontera, Clicksor, Pepperjam, TrafficJunky

Opt-Media, Mirago, Miva, Ad Magnet, AdBlade, Tribal Fusion, Pulse360, Marchex, Domain Gateway, AdMarketplace, AdEngage, Chitika, Traffic Taxi, Yes Mail, AdReady, Bidvertizer, Zedo, WeatherBug, Epic Advertising, PCH Games, Popup Traffic, Bardzo Media, ADXDirect, Contextweb, AdBrite

Ok, so these are just some ideas to get your brain muscles working as we continue on.

Part 4: List building

So moving forward and also another area were we want to get your brain muscle working a bit is list building. A lot of the same things that we were discovering in 2009 still work today, but some don't work as well.

What you're about to get is a combination of new and old list building tactics that I've gathered since 2008 up until now. Just to be clear... I'm going to only share what's working RIGHT NOW. When I go over the older tactics I'm going to talk about how well they work RIGHT NOW and how I'm using them TODAY. What I'm going to share with you is not just the tactics themselves, but some I'm going to point out to you and tell you which ones have built me the most subscribers, for example, and which ones are working the best for me right now.

I don't want you to look at this as if it's Just a book of information, I want you to look at it as if it's life changing knowledge because it doesn't matter if it's written on a napkin. It doesn't matter if it's on audio. It doesn't matter if it's on video. It doesn't matter if it's in a PDF. It doesn't matter if someone is teaching it to you one-on-one over the phone or one-on-one through a webinar or through group coaching; it's all information, and this powerful information is the most powerful information that I've discovered through experience.

List building has been the key to our success over the years and we have a lot of people to thank for that, but we mostly have to thank ourselves because we've gone out of our way to explore all of these realms of list building. The first thing you need to know is that business and making sales depends on fresh lead flow. What I mean is you want constant leads coming in. If I were you, I would start aiming to generate something like 250 subscribers per day.

You might be thinking, that's a lot of subscribers, or it's going to be too expensive. Well, there are great paid lead sources; there are also very good free ones that you can use to build up your list to generate 250 or more subscribers per day. Once you hit 250 subscribers per day or more, then it's all a matter of focusing on converting them and then just doing the list building stuff you're doing over and over and over and getting the same results all the time.

Converting them is another thing and I am not going to cover converting leads into sales, it's all about generating lead flow. As I was telling you, I can't stress this enough that the bulk of your money that you make is going to come from the people who are the newest on your list. THE FRESHEST. The older a lead gets, the less responsive they become, generally, especially if you're an affiliate.

Now if you're a product creator and you do classes and such, you may find that some of your older subscribers are the most profitable subscribers you have because they're your own customers who enroll in all of your classes; all of your $1,000 classes and whatnot.

As an affiliate, it's different; you don't have that retention. When you're a product creator, it's easier to keep the retention of your list for some reason.

I've found this to be true and that's one of the reasons why I'm starting to create more and more products now, although over the years I've been mainly just an affiliate. If you are just an affiliate, again, your normal focus should be fresh leads and keeping your leads coming in on a daily basis. That's at least 250 leads a day.

If you're a product creator, you may not need as high of a lead flow, but why not do both? Why not be a creator that keeps retouching the list and also generate 250 subscribers or more to your list? Let's go ahead and get into this because I have tons and tons of list building methods and strategies to cover for you now.

Public and private JV giveaways

The first one is JV giveaways. JV giveaways haven't changed much as far as public JV giveaways go. You can go to newjvgiveaways.com anytime you want and jump in on any JV giveaways. But what has surfaced since 2011 is something called the private giveaway. There are a lot of little private giveaways taking place that you can be part of all over the internet. You can go to people who are just as big as you are online, and even bigger, and start a private JV giveaway with them.

What I mean is you can get 5 to 10 or more people in on a private giveaway, where no one else can join and be a contributor. This means that the people who are on there, who are contributors, are responsible for generating all the traffic to the giveaway and there is a WordPress plug-in that you can use to host your own private giveaways called WP Venture. So go do a search on Google for WP Venture and it's being sold on the Warrior Forum for chump change, as a Warrior Special Offer.

A giveaway is where a group of contributors come together and submit their gifts. People who come and join the giveaway as members are going to opt in to different giveaways and this will add subscribers to your list. If you've been around for a while, you no doubt know what JV giveaways are, and I'm not going to dwell on what JV giveaways are or how they can build good business for you because you can go to a place like newjvgiveaways.com and find out all you need to know about giveaways freely on the net.

But just the fact that I'm pointing you in that direction is pretty valuable because if you're just starting out and you have no money to spend on ads, getting giveaways is a really good way to start, because you can add that first 10, 50, 100 subscribers on your list fairly quickly. Some of these giveaways get up to 30,000 subscribers joining; not to your list, but to the actual giveaway. What happens is the host of the giveaway is going to get the most subscribers.

They're putting the giveaway with all the contributors and setting the dates, and then once the giveaway is live, all the contributors send traffic to the JV giveaway main page, but the host is going to get all the subscribers onto their list. Then the member who just joined will probably see a one-time offer or some kind of offer before they go and see all the different gifts that that contributors have.

So when you're a contributor and you promote one of these JV giveaways through your own link, you often make sales right there before they even get to the gifts. That's one thing about it. My point is if you're just starting out and you don't have much money to buy traffic, then this may be one that you want to master. The truth is, if you became just a master of one of these methods, then you'll generate all the leads you'll ever need.

Let me say that again. If you become the master of just one of these methods I'm going to share with you then you will generate all the leads you'll ever need. So why not do something like JV giveaways? You can do public ones, you can do private ones, and you can host ones and make the real money. I've hosted a couple and that's where I generated the most leads. You could generate 10,000 leads in one day, 20,000 leads in one day from contributors blasting traffic to your own giveaway.

So just think about that. If you were to jump headfirst into the world of JV giveaways as a contributor to start off with, then one day you may be able to host your own JV giveaways.

Solo ads

The next list building tactic I want to talk about is solo ads. When I'm actively running solo ads, I'm usually able to generate hundreds of leads per day right now. This may change down the road, but as of right now. Solo ads are cheap, they're effective and very easy because you don't have to worry about landing page quality score or paying per click and keeping an eye on your ads and paying by the click.

What you're getting is an ad that goes out to a subscriber list, so whenever you buy a solo ad; let's say you buy a solo ad for $600 for 1,000 clicks to your site, you pay 60 cents per click to your site and you know exactly how many clicks are going to come to your site and the guy who sends you a solo ad sends an ad out to his email list, which recommends your freebie or your website.

So they're transferring their authority over to you, in a way, that's what makes it the most effective way of generating traffic right now, in my opinion. Because the ads are still cheap, it's very effective for anybody who has the money to risk on it. One place you can find a lot of great solo ad deals is by getting on Skype and talking to different solo ad sellers.

I realize it's not going to be easy just to find a solo ad seller, or any solo ad sellers if you have no clue about the world of solo ads right now, but once you find some solo ad sellers, you want to start connecting with them on Skype and getting into the world of solo ads because you can meet so many different solo ad sellers who will give you great deals on Skype that they don't give outside of Skype. You can find solo ads at one place called udimi.com or soloadsx.com. That's where I would go if I were going to go and look for solo ads right now. The key to have profitable solo ads is your sales funnel.

You want to have the squeeze page that generates the free leads that gives away something. Then you have an upsell from there, which will be a one-time offer for something that's in the $17-$49 price point, then you want to have upsells from there so you can afford to pay for your solo ads.

Now you may also want to promote things on the download page for your freebies that you're giving away. That way you can come close to breaking even or you can profit directly right away from that solo ad before you even get the subscribers on your list. Although many solo ads I haven't profited from right up front, I made a profit on the backend from promoting strictly to the subscriber list. That's something you have to think about.

A lot of companies in advertising are willing to pay a lot of money upfront and even lose money on the front end because they know they're going to make money on the backend with their follow up marketing, which is what email marketing is all about.

Ad swaps

So let's move on to ad swaps. Ad swaps are where you send out an ad to your list promoting someone else's squeeze page and then someone else does the same for you to their list. So it's similar to solo ads except for no one is buying anything; you're just trading off ads. The place where everybody has moved to these days is called safe-swaps.com.

There used to be a site called IMadswaps.com, which was like an ad swap forums. There are other forums that kind of emerged in the last few years and they've pretty much slowed down because of safe-swaps.com. The thing about ad swaps is that it is getting less effective because seeing that it emerged around 2009, that's when everyone was discovering ad swaps and starting to do it. Now people are over-mailing their lists with ad swaps.

They're doing way more ad swaps so they're getting less responses from the subscribers.

Retention rates are going down, click thru rates are going down, but if you still want to generate hundreds of leads per day, you still can do that. The key to profiting from ad swaps is the same key to profiting with solo ads, which is your sales funnel. So if you've got a good sales funnel, you can use it for your ad swaps.

Also, ad swaps are a great way to test your sales funnel before you start buying something like solo ads. You're probably going to get less quality leads from ad swaps than you are solo ads, yet it's still a good indication of whether your sales funnel will convert traffic into sales, and that's what's necessary to profit with ad swaps, because you're not promoting anything that's going to be making money directly to your list; you're promoting someone else's squeeze page, so you're relying on the traffic coming from the JV partner's list to your sales funnel.

Depending on your sales funnel, you can do ad swaps every single day if you want to, become the master of ad swaps and just tweak your sales funnel and have very good business there. You don't want to overcomplicate marketing. This kind of thinking is really profitable if you could get super focused. Think about how simple this business is right here. You put together a sales funnel. You do ad swaps every day. You test your sales funnel every day until you're converting the maximum amount of visitors who land on your page.

That in itself is a business no matter what anyone says. So that's what I try to do in my business... SIMPLIFY.

I have a daily routine that I try to simplify down more and more every day until it's just brain dead stupid, and lately, it has been solo ads because I've found that I'm getting the best returns on solo ads. But if I didn't have any money, I would start off with JV giveaways just to generate 100 subscribers or so, then I would move to safe-swaps.com and I would start ad swapping. That's what I would do if I didn't have any money.

Click banking

There's also another thing I would want to do if I didn't have any money and I had a small list. This goes out to the small list owners, people who are just starting their lists and what not. If you have a list of 100 people or 1,000 people, you could start doing what's called click banking. It has nothing to do with ClickBank.com but what it is, is you go to a marketer with a huge list and you say, "I will send you 100 clicks or 1,000 clicks over the course of this month (clicks mean visitors) and what you will do is return those clicks all at once after I'm done."

So what happens is the big marketer with a big list will give you a tracking link to use on all your emails. You'll work hard to build up your traffic to them through that link, and then when you're ready to cash in your clicks you go to them and say, "I'd like to cash in my clicks," and then they send you clicks; they send you as many as you have sent them.

This is real similar to ad swaps, as you can see, but it works out well for small list owners because you can just focus on sending traffic to one big marketer without having to set up all kinds of ad swap deals.

For example, if you have an email follow up series, the first couple of days of your email follow up series could be sending the new people on your list to another marketer who you are click banking with. Now this isn't the greatest advice for product creators.

I don't think that ad swaps or click banking is a great idea for product creators because if you're a product creator, then you can have so much longevity on your own list by just promoting your own products. If you're a product creator, you might want to just focus on paid methods and getting affiliates to promote your stuff, but that's just my opinion and that's what I've seen from experience.

As an affiliate marketer, who doesn't have a ton of products to promote to the list all month, who doesn't crank out many products, it's all about fresh lead flow, like I was saying in the beginning of this chapter. Things like ad swaps and click banking are the mother load of free, fresh lead flow.

Free WSOs

Now let's get into another method, which is something I've been doing since 2013 or so, which is running free WSO's. I'm talking about freebies that I give away on the Warrior Forum, which is WarriorForum.com and WSO stands for Warrior Special Offers. So I will give away products on the Warrior Special Offers forum in exchange for opt-ins.

One thing that I've noticed between the Warrior Forum and the leads you may get from ad swaps, click banking, and solo ads is that Warrior Forum traffic is used to buying lower priced products. So your funnel may be a lot different for free WSO's than it will be with ad swaps, click banking, or solo ads. For one of my funnels they get a freebie on the squeeze page, then the OTO after that is a $10 offer, then the OTO after that is another $10 offer.

So you can see I'm keeping it at $10 or less because I know they buy $10 or less things, whereas with ad swaps, click banking, and solo ads I'll have a freebie, a $9 offer, then to a $97 OTO and then it will go up from there. Good luck trying to sell a $97 to Warrior Forum members because it's not going to happen, unless you have a done-for-you service or something that's worth 25x $97 price points.

It's just a different world there, but the good thing about running free WSO's is that's a business in itself, if you want it to be because you can run free WSO's and then you can promote WSO's as an affiliate to promote programs like offers through WSO Pro, which is at WarriorPlus.com or JVzoo. com or DigiResults.com.

Do you remember how I was talking about making a business just by focusing on one thing? Well this is a business for you too. Think about this. This is all you need to do is to run free WSO's.

You can have six or seven free WSO's for six or seven different freebies that you create and you can rotate those once a day so that you're launching a new WSO a day, but it's giving away one of your six or seven freebies. You can generate your list like that and your sales funnel will get you close to breaking even or making a profit right away on the front end, then on the backend you can promote WSO's as an affiliate to your list you've built.

I've been known to have multiple free WSO's that I rotate on a daily basis and I've done that model before. You see... I get bored with certain things in marketing and then I try different models. I just simplify things and just go at them with a very narrow focus. Right now I might be buying a lot of solo ads and doing what I described in the Solo Ads section, but just months ago, I was buying a lot of free WSO's and trying to get as many leads as I could with that and just promoting WSO's every day and making plenty of money. So once you get that narrow focus and simplify everything, everything becomes clear and you can make a lot of money just focusing on that.

PPV/CPV list building

Another way to generate hundreds of leads per day is through something called Pay Per View or Cost Per View advertising. I have a friend who does around 1,000 leads a day. I've only generated 50 leads or so per day with it, but it's on autopilot. So you can go to a site like leadimpact.com and you can buy cost per view or pay per view advertising.

It's a little different from other types of advertising in that you're paying per view of your page, you're not paying per click on an ad. It's actually more like a pop up, so you're paying for these ads to pop up on people's sites, and it's run through software, so it's different than someone, say going to Google and seeing pay per click ads. You can advertise on any URL on the internet as long as the user has the software installed on their computer. So this allows you to bid on different URL's online. Now can't you see how this could be popular and profitable? Because you could bid on your competitor's URL's. You could bid on so many different URL's it's not even funny. You could bid on PPC URL's even.

So for people who are spending gobs and gobs of money on PPC, you can take those URL's that they're using for their landing pages, plug it into lead impact and then be bidding for ad space for those URL's through the software. One place to learn more about PPV and CPV is cpvden.com. It can be a nice little lead flow generator that's different from the other lead flow sources you might be generating leads from right now.

What you need to know about also is you can generate tons and tons of traffic for a lot less money, but the traffic won't be as responsive because they didn't click thru to your ad. Because they didn't click through to your ad it's kind of like an annoying pop up that comes in their face but it's all legal and they know they're getting pop ups in exchange for using the software that they're using.

It's an agreement they made before downloading the software that they're using on their computer. Say a company, like leadimpact.com, let's say they say, "You can use this software, which has huge value in exchange for being able to run an ad on your computer 5 times per day." So instead of charging for the software each month, they get the software for free, but they have to see ads and this is where your ads can get in front of their face. You can get in front of millions of people for .017 cents each time your ad is shown; that's a fraction of a penny.

But like I said, with other forms of advertising you may get a high opt-in rate on your squeeze page such as 10% and on some ad sources, 10% is very good. On some ad sources, 10% is horrible. On some ad sources, like solo ads, for example 30% is very good, depending on whether they actually send your solo ad or not because 60% may be considered good on there, as well.

But with PPV advertising, we're talking 1-2% could be good, just depending on how much money you're spending, how much money you're making up front and how much money you're making on the backend. But because you can get traffic so cheap, it doesn't mean that the traffic is created equal to other advertising sources.

Because they haven't clicked through any targeted advertising, the traffic responsiveness will be lower as far as opting into your squeeze page goes.

The point is... all that matters is your ROI, not your opt-in rate... because your opt-in rate is always going to be different depending on where your traffic is coming from.

Bartering for leads

Bartering for leads is a really great way to generate the highest quality leads you can generate besides having your own product and having an affiliate program. In actuality, it is almost the same or identical to that, except for you are NOT selling your own product. Here's how it works... What you want to do is go to a marketer who does product launches, who is bigger than you online. They don't have to be huge; you could just go to someone who does WSO's, for example.

If you go to someone who does WSO's often, you can say this, "I'll do customer service for your launch," or "I'll write the sales page for your launch," or "I'll create bonuses for your launch," or "I'll help create the products for your launch," or "I'll help create buzz using social media for your launch," or "I'll help get JV's on board for your launch" or, "I'll do (something) for your launch in exchange for leads." So you're not asking for money, you're asking for leads.

You're not asking for them export leads to you; we're talking about just placing some kind of bonus of yours on their download page that customers have to opt-in for, which you get the lead for. For example, this one time I did one of these bartering for leads deals with a top marketer, and for his bonuses on his actual sales page, I advertised my bonuses that they're going to have to opt-in for. So on the download page there was a link to my squeeze page, which allowed them to opt-in to download the bonuses. On the page after the squeeze page was the download page for the bonuses.

I didn't send them through any kind of sales funnel, but the thing is, you get a list of red-hot buyers when you do this. I'm talking about scorching hot buyers. That first week of having that list you want to promote your highest converting thing, do a webinar or do something that you made money within the past because this is the time to sell them while they're the hottest and they're buyers (you have gained trust by them listening or watching your bonus, depending on what the product is, so they will be responsive).

Actually, the way I came up with the bonus for these kinds of launches is I would just use private label rights. So I use private label rights material that was a video course that I didn't even record, but I had rights to give away as a bonus to a paid product. So that's something to think about. One of my best tactics was solo ads, one was ad swaps, and at one point click banking. I did click banking on a big scale. Bartering for leads was a huge, huge tactic that I've done before. It's not a current phase I'm going through but it works like a charm. It's not going anywhere. It will always be effective.

It's a very simple tactic where you barter your skills with a product launcher who adds your bonus to their download page and the customers have to opt-in for it. It's not like relying on Google for leads because they can slap that away somehow for you. And it's not getting less effective like ad swaps are for example.

Your own affiliate program

Another way to generate red-hot quality leads is by having your own affiliate program. Now I'm going to tell you that I've mainly generated leads through using Rapid Action Profits. I know that a lot of people in recent days have moved on to other scripts, such as Warriorplus.com, WSO Pro or JVZoo.com or DigiResults.com, but I like trusty old Rapid Action Profits. It may cost $197, whereas I bought it for something like $297. It's always being updated so it's not out of date with technology or anything, but the reason why I like Rapid Action Profits over any other is two-fold.

For one, I only have to pay a fee one time to use it. So I pay my $197 for the script and I use it over and over and over. A lot of these other sites, you may not have an upfront fee, but they take out fees for every sale you make so you end up paying a lot more than you would pay with that one-time fee to RapidActionProfits.com. Or there may be, like with WSO Pro, you have to pay a fee every time you want to start a WSO with.

I'd rather have a script like Rapid Action Profits so I can use it over and over and over. This is just my personal opinion and preference. Also, I think there is a lot of wisdom in what I'm about to tell you with Rapid Action Profits vs. the other solutions.

The other solutions are like affiliate networks, so when you're recruiting affiliates to actually promote your product, they may end up promoting someone else's product, but with Rapid Action Profits, you have complete control over the situation. So once you show people your affiliate program, there's only an option to promote you. Therefore, whenever I launch a product on Rapid Action Products, at the bottom of the screen I have a link that says, "Affiliates make 100%

commissions." They click there and then they sign up for my affiliate program through Rapid Action Profits.

They can now get their link and they can then sell the product. If I use the other programs, and I have a link at the bottom that says, "Sign up here to promote my product," and then they go to some affiliate network, they'll probably end up promoting some other product that they find. They may get lost in the sea of products trying to find mine; they give up and don't promote any product at all.

The best kind of affiliate program that attracts affiliates is to have an instant PayPal commission affiliate program like the ones I've been talking about. You can also use something like ClickBank, but you can't give away 100% commissions from ClickBank. With these other programs, you can give away 100% commissions, which is really attractive on the front end to affiliates, and then you can give 50% commission on the one-time offer, for example. You're making money off sales, but you are attracting affiliates that you don't have to ethically bride much to promote for you. If you're giving away 100% commissions, in my mind, you're not going to owe any other affiliates back for promoting you because you gave away 100% commissions.

Those leads that you get right away are going to be red-hot leads.

Exit popups

Another way to add about 10% opt-in rate to any website you have is by adding an exit pop up script. You've probably seen these and they're pretty annoying. You can get one at exitsplash.com. When someone tries to leave the page, a pop up will come up that says, "Here's a quick chance to get this freebie," or whatever ad you want there. This can add 10%

more opt-in rate to your page or to any website you send traffic to. Actually, depending on how aggressive you want to be, you can have multiple exit pop ups that lead to different squeeze pages.

What I've noticed in the past, doing a very aggressive launch's with a marketer and bartering leads, seeing he wanted to go balls-to-the-wall, I decided that it would probably be most profitable to do a squeeze page for one offer that pops up once. If they don't take that offer, have a squeeze page that pops up for another offer. If they don't take that offer then another squeeze will pop up for another offer. So it will be three squeeze pages popping up in a row for different offers. You will be surprised at how many leads that added onto the product launchers list.

Just think about this, the first squeeze page pops up and they get 10% opt-in rate on that; they've just got 10% of the traffic to sign up on their list. But if they don't take that, and another one pops up and they get 7% on that, well that's an extra 7% tacked on. If they don't take that one though, and they see the third squeeze page up, then maybe 5% tops into that list and all together you've got what, 22% of the people getting on your sales page or site opting into your list. That's almost as good as a decent converting squeeze page. I'll take 22% from a lot of different ad sources depending on the source.

But I will tell you this, that I believe exit pop ups are getting less effective over time because they've been used so much. It's similar to "ad blindness."

What will likely happen is that people will stop using exit pop ups and then wait a little while and then they will start using them again and they will be just as effective as they were before. That's my prediction and that happens to a lot of things where trends and tactics come and go. Tactics will work well, then they stop working as well as they have and everyone stops using them. Then someone starts using them again and talking about how profitable it is to use it and everyone all of a sudden is using it again.

Reverse Opt-in form

Another way to generate about 10% of your website traffic to your list on a sales page is using a reverse opt-in form. This is where someone clicks on the "Add to Cart" button or an "Order Now" button and then you have a page between your sales page and your order form. That page in between will be a Step 1 of 2 order confirmation form. So at the top is will say, "Step 1 of 2 Order Confirmation," then they'll have to put in their email address to continue. This is a Reverse Opt-in Page.

You want to grab the email address here so that everybody who buys your product is added to your list. Also, the people who chicken out on your product, you'll have them on your list and they can also be very high quality subscribers to have on your list. So you might find that the majority of people who actually opt in to that form won't even order, but you'll end up generating a lot more subscribers from your sales page by doing that.

So you can see how all these leads will add up if you're promoting to a squeeze page or a sales page. You will see how all these leads add up by promoting to a sales page by using all the factors we're talking about here. Because if you're getting 22% opt in rates from doing exit pop ups and you're getting 10% from doing reverse opt in forms, then you are generating an extra 33% of people to your subscriber list during a launch.

That's something to think about because when you have all these affiliates hammering your page, a lot of their traffic might not want to buy the product that you have, but there will be people who buy products you are selling later on as an affiliate or as your own product.

Buying ad space direct from webmasters

The next tactic I want to talk about is buying ad space directly from webmasters. This can be done as easily as going to different webmasters who have, say forums in your market, and asking how much it would cost to run an ad on the top of their page. First of all you're going to them and asking, "How much is your AdSense ad making you on a daily basis?" Chances are you're going to have more money to spend than they're making on this ad from AdSense.

So, say they say, "Well I'm generating 200 people to my site every day, but I'm only making $3.00 in AdSense per day." Well, if you had an ad that has a 10% click thru rate, then you can generate those people to your page for the same amount of money or more, so tell them that you want to take a test run on their page by advertising their ad in place of their Google ad.

You can pay them by PayPal and with a deal like this, "Will you run this ad one day and we'll see how much money I make," and you'll give them $5 instead of the $3.00 he makes from AdSense, for example. Then you see what happens when you run your ad on their site for that day and see how many opt ins you get, how much in sales in commissions you make from your sales funnel, and this will determine whether it's profitable or not.

If it's profitable then you can say, "Well I would like to rent that ad space from you on a monthly basis, for the rest of this month for x amount of dollars," or whatever is equivalent to $5.00 a day, or whatever you're testing. If you go to some real busy forum, for example, and you do the same thing – and if we're talking about bigger numbers here, maybe you will do a $50 test run for one day. You measure the results and see what happens and if it works out well, then what you need to do is just tell them that you want to run an ad that month for x amount of dollars. And that's traffic you don't have to touch. That's just autopilot traffic hitting your page.

You can run it on a weekly basis or anything that you can afford, but the point is these webmasters want to make more money on their sites because they're probably not making as much as you can give them using the advertising that they're running. They're making piss poor profits from AdSense, for example.

Actually, in the internet marketing space, WarriorForum.com has an option to run an ad at the top of the forum for $100 a day, and they run something like eight different spaces on there a day and yours would rotate with eight different advertisers. That's a good way to test something in the internet marketing niche.

If you want to test an ad out and see how internet marketers would respond before you go and promote something on internet marketing, then use the tactic of contacting vendors and webmasters directly and you could run a $100 ad and see what happens. Chances are you could get at least $100 clicks of traffic, or you may get 50 to 100 opt-ins. You may get one sale at $100 that makes you break even. You never know.

You never know until you try, but what I like about this media buying approach is that it's very easy traffic that you don't have to work toward, you just have to monitor your metrics.

Nested squeeze page on a blog

Here's a tactic for generating a lot of leads from a blog. I actually built my first list of 1,000 subscribers this way in the weight loss niche before I even got into the internet marketing niche. It's so easy. You take a blog and maybe your blog is generating 100, 200, 300 visitors per day because you're cranking content out on a daily basis. Even if you don't try to target certain keywords on your site, it's pretty easy to start generating 200 to 300 visitors per day just by cranking out content and ranking it for long tail search terms without even trying to, and actually only doing it.

So what you do is, take your squeeze page in your niche, and you nest it at the top and center of that blog. So before they actually see the blog site at the top of the page, they should see your squeeze page as it is. You can nest it up there using an image and an opt in box, if you want. That's if you don't want the test of the squeeze page to interfere with any other on page SEO that's happening. You'll be surprised at the opt-in rate you can get from that.

Let's say your site isn't really an interactive site as much as you want it to be; it's really difficult to get a site with a lot of interactivity. Maybe your site just has a lot of traffic coming to it and doesn't really have people interacting, so it doesn't really matter if you put your squeeze page up there or not. One of the best ways to generate leads form a blog is to nest a squeeze page front and center.

Another way is by using Robert Plank's WordPress Plug-Ins. One is called Action Opt-In. This is where you can put an opt-in bar on your side bar that you go opt-in to. Once they opt-in to it, the form will disappear and say, "Thanks for subscribing," and keep the people on the blog they're on. One is Action Pop-Up, which is a fade in window that fades into your site and asks for the opt-in there in exchange for a freebie or whatever you're offering. The other is Action Comments, where if someone comments on your blog, they check a check box and it automatically subscribes them to your list.

You can get all three, I believe, in one purchase from Robert Plank if you go to Actionoptin.com or search on Google for Action Opt-In and you'll probably find it. He's always updating that.

Integrated cross-promotions

The next way I want to talk about generating leads is using integrated cross-promotions. I think Mark Joyner coined the term integrated marketing. Well integrated cross-promotions are different kinds of cross promos that you have with your joint venture partners other than ad swaps, click banking, or anything like JV giveaways.

These are different because these are integrated into your marketing on autopilot, so you should think about the different parts of your marketing systems that you can integrate some kind of joint venture link to.

For example, on your download page, you might have a banner that leads to one of your JV partner's squeeze pages and they have the same for you on their download page. That would be an example of an integrated cross-promotion. So instead of monetizing that part of your download page with an offer, what you'll do is do an integrated cross-promotion with one of your joint venture partners.

Another way is to cross promote your joint venture partner in your follow up series. So in your email follow up series, maybe your fifth email in the follow up series will promote their squeeze page and their fifth email in their follow up series will promote your squeeze page.

Another way is through P.S.'s of your emails that you send out. So when you're sending out an email to your list, you can make a deal with one of your joint venture partners to always promote their squeeze page in their P.S. and they have to do the same for you.

That's one way to do it. Think about the power of integrated cross-promotion. You're generating subscribers on autopilot by doing this. You can add tons per day to your list or more, all on autopilot, by doing this a set of joint venture partners or with just one, but just think about this; let's say you have 10 joint venture partners and you're going to do integrated joint venture cross-promotions with your follow up series of emails.

Say all 10 of you are in all 10 of your first follow up series emails, you all promote each other, well visitors would be flying all over the place and going onto your list if you do that.

Viral PDF reports

The next tactic I want to talk about is using viral PDF reports. So let's say you write a little report that can be 2 to 5 pages long, as long as it's rock solid content; it's going to be for a free report anyway, and you create a PDF report out of it. Well, inside the PDF report, you want to say that this is free to distribute.

Also inside of your PDF report, you want to have a link at the end that leads to your squeeze page or an entire ad that leads to your squeeze page. What I've found in the past is that other people started using my reports to build their lists with. So they would actually give my reports away to their squeeze pages and I would generate those subscribers under my list, the ones who actually read the report and then clicked thru at the end.

The ones who read the reports and clicked through to the end and discovered you that way, end up being some of the highest quality leads you'll get because they've just read one of your reports, and they clicked through at the end to get your freebie, and you've got them on your list.

If you're not sure how to do this, you can go to OpenOffice online. You can just type into Google, "OpenOffice" and download OpenOffice Writer. You're going to open up OpenOffice Writer and write your report. It's kind of like Microsoft Word. Then you're going to click "File" and export as a PDF. Once you do that, you have a PDF that you can give away, and you have clickable links inside the PDF and that will become your viral report. It's a little different than rebrandable reports.

If you have your own affiliate program, you can give affiliates a way to give cool content to their list and to promote you at the same time by offering a viral brandable rewritable report. This is a little bit different, a little more simplistic, and if you give enough of these reports away that are viral reports, you may see them circulating all over the place and generating leads from all over the internet.

Affiliate list cross-promotions

The last thing I want to tell you for now about list building is using affiliate list cross-promotions. This is very simple. Let's say you have your own offer on Rapid Action Profits and you've built an affiliate list, which is just a list of affiliates who promote your products. What you do is go to other product owners who have affiliate lists and say, "I will tell my affiliate list about your affiliate program if you do the same for yours."

You might pick up some really good affiliates like that. They might pick up a few and once you pick up affiliates, that means more traffic heading into your paid offer, which means more people on your list of high quality. This is one of those tactics that kind of makes you want to slap yourself in the head.

Productivity in a New Business

In this chapter we will discuss insightful tips to motivate, encourage and energize you to become a successful entrepreneur and attain your goals. Success in any aspect of your life is a result of planning out your goals and utilizing your creativity. The entrepreneurial life is a blessing and perfect personal growth opportunity that allows you the flexibility of working your professional life around your personal life instead of having to work your personal life around your professional life, as it often is when you're working for someone else.

Operating and growing as a work-from-home entrepreneur takes some serious self-discipline. While any business run from home poses some challenges, there are unique challenges that face those that are running the bulk of their business online. Taking business online is an easy concept for many people to get started with, but not always seen as a regular and devoted business. Many online entrepreneurs are trying to 'fit in' their online business into a busy life and not making the complete commitment to the business.

Although the ability to work from home provides a great deal of benefits that effect much more than just your work life, the challenges that come up can make the idea of working from home an extremely difficult endeavor. Business needs to be taken seriously to succeed. Even if you only have 10 hours a week to work your business, you need to be consistent, plan out your progress, stay focused and remember all the other parts of your life that need attention too!

Gaining the right kind of knowledge and putting that knowledge into practice will set you up for a happy and productive work life that will wonderfully mesh with your personal life. Read the following tips and advice with a determined mind that will see each idea as an opportunity to try new activities and open the door to a clearer picture of how you can use your time wisely to run an online business from the comfort of your home.

Planning - Tips to organize your business

Being a productive entrepreneur takes a great deal of planning, but don't let this discourage you if planning and organization hasn't been your strong point. Most of the planning gets done occasionally to whenever-you-deem-it-necessary and once you learn some effective methods of planning then it will become a natural task for the operation of your business. The following tips will help in creating goals and implementing strategies to see them realized along with maintaining the motivation to keep yourself on track.

Set short-term and long-term goals

Goal setting is effective in every area of your life. Giving yourself a clear picture of what you really want in life - in the immediate future and years down the road - is an excellent way to keep yourself motivated and energized to take action. Start the process by asking yourself:

"What do I really want to do with my life?"

Don't allow limitations of time and money distort your answer. Just assume that there is nothing that can stop you from eventually achieving and having what you truly want.

These goals do have to be written down and kept somewhere you can look at regularly. Put your goals into concise sentences using the "SMART" system as outlined below:

Specific: State exactly what you want to achieve. Can you break a larger task down into smaller items?

Measurable: Establish clear definitions to help you measure if your reaching your goal.

Action Oriented: Describe your goals using action verbs, and outline the exact steps you will take to accomplish your goal.

Realistic: Give yourself the opportunity to succeed by setting goals you'll actually accomplish. Be sure to consider obstacles you may need to overcome.

Time-Bound: How much time do you have to complete the task? Decide exactly when you'll start and finish your goal.

Brainstorm strategies to achieve your goals

Once you've defined some short-term and long-term goals you'll want a list of possible strategies to achieve the results you're looking for. Create a list of strategy options that encompass various alternatives you could use to deliver the results you're looking for. Move beyond your comfort zone and think of any wild idea that comes to mind - you want a large list of ideas to work with. Keep this whole list to refer to in the future, but pick a few ideas from the list to schedule in and add to your To Do list now.

Strive for greatness and don't compromise

I'm sure you've heard of many stories about people achieving great success online. Perhaps you've even thought that they had something you didn't or were in a better position to start with than you. Or maybe you even discredited the story, as some marketing ploy and their 'rags to riches' story wasn't true at all. While there are a lot of schemers out there, there are also a lot of people that have genuinely focused on a goal and worked hard and smart to achieve it. You can do it too.

You can achieve whatever great things you put your mind to. When you're adding value to other people's lives, it's just a matter of making a plan, getting organized and never giving up until you can make your mark in whatever area is meant for you. Don't just settle for affiliate sales (although these sales are a nice bonus) and earning money from the success of others. That's what being an employee is all about and if you're interested in working online than you have already made the decision to be your own boss. Find your niche, explore the opportunities and don't settle for a mediocre business that doesn't have a soul. Don't compromise on your opportunity for greatness!

Counteract procrastination

Procrastination is one very bad habit. It affects most self-employed people from time-to-time due to the fact that there's not always someone expecting you to produce something. It's fueled by fear, lack of confidence, and disorganization. Putting things off is a sure way to produce an ineffective business. Beat procrastination by building up new habits that make you get tasks done, like scheduling in time to do the things you've put off.

Habit breaking and making takes about 21 days to take effect, so keep this in mind as you're struggling to stop your learned habit of procrastination and creating a new habit of getting things done.

Grow from the accountability effect

Create accountability in your work life by joining or creating a group of like-minded entrepreneurs where you share plans, ideas and goals in weekly, bi-weekly, or monthly meetings. You can also gain this same effect with a one-on-one accountability relationship. This type of set-up creates an inner desire to report back the results of your objectives and gives you that little extra incentive to get your plan in action. Additional benefits of being accountable to others are: gaining inspiration from the insights of others, being in the position to assist others in their business focus, and developing deep and trusting relationships.

Use the power of your mind to your benefit

The human mind is an extremely powerful tool in your business and we're not talking about intellect. The sub-conscience mind is your motivator, your dreamer and your source of productivity. It can also be your discouragement, your criticizer, and your source of inactivity. Used properly, the power available in your mind will have an extraordinary effect on your life and your business. Keep your thoughts positive, keep them creative and, most importantly, keep away the damaging and defeating thoughts that are passed on by your environment!

Create flexible schedules and adaptable to do lists

Unless you're the type of person that loves to stick to a specific routine and can adhere to a strict schedule, then you'll really want to cut yourself a bit of slack and create schedules and to do lists that allow for shifting of times, and deferring tasks. Working from home can involve work time getting delayed from the original plan and projects taking longer than anticipated. Just be aware of not letting work always get put on the back burner, which is very easy to do in a home office. Working from home does allow for a different approach to planning and scheduling.

When creating a schedule for a day, week, or month in advance (whatever is the best process for you) don't schedule the whole day hour for hour. For example, plan for marketing tasks Monday morning, website maintenance Tuesday afternoon, social media tasks Thursday evening, etc. Plan the time you have to conduct business, block it out for the morning, afternoon or evening instead of 9-11am.

Use online resources to create a schedule

It only seems appropriate that your online business should use online resources. This is effective, as you can keep focused on what you need to do with a click into a browser instead of switching your focus to paper, another program or another device. This is also great for anybody that happens to use more than one computer or device for their work as you can quickly access your schedule, as long as you've got an internet connection, which is necessary for your business anyway.

Google Calendar is a great option for this. You can sync Google Calendar with an iPhone or Android device and set it up to notify you in different ways of upcoming entries in your schedule. Create a strict or casual schedule - whatever you feel is best for you - and if you tend to like the paper approach you can print off your schedule as well. As with most Google products, it's quite customizable to your preferences.

Use online resources to create a to do list

All the little jobs that you want to do or need to get done should be written down on a list. This list will be comprised of thoughts and ideas that pop into your head; tasks to do to move toward your goals and regular tasks that you need to do in the operation of your business. Using an online program for this has the same benefits as using an online calendar.

Trello is a flexible and user-friendly option for organizing your ideas and projects in one area. You can create many boards and different organizations, which is very helpful when you want to start a new project in your business. A board consists of a 3-column listing of "To Do" "Doing" and "Done" (which you can change the names of) and you can add in comments, checklists, due dates, files and customize to your liking in several different ways. You can also share a Board or Organization with other people, so you can collaborate with others on a project and see what's been done, who has done it and what needs to be done. It's also beneficial to share your task list with someone that can simply check up on your progress to add that bit of accountability motivation.

Make it official and make a business plan

Many home businesses never get the benefit of a well thought out approach to operations and expectations. Although business plans are especially popular for those who are in search or financing, every person that would like to make money with their business should have spent the time creating some type of business plan. You don't need to focus on the financial details as much as a traditional plan would, but you want to create a plan of how your business will operate and what the products and/or services are. A business plan makes you think about various parts of running a business and clarifies its viability in the marketplace. It may also force you to think of a more viable business venture if your original idea does not look as good written down as it did in your head. The Internet is full of great resources to assist you in creating an effective business plan.

See each day as a fresh start to your business

Don't let any setbacks from yesterday or any point in the past allow you to judge your effectiveness for today. Only focus on what did work and what has been going well for you so far and leave all the negative stuff behind you. Each day will have a new plan of attack that you use to your advantage in building your business. Frustration and defeating thoughts are BIG productivity stealers and have no place in growth of a business.

Create a small routine to get you "in the mood" to work

If you were leaving home to go to work, you would have a transition period of getting ready for work at home and traveling to a location and then settling into your work space. When working within your home, you need to create some type of routine that becomes a sub-conscience signal for your brain to get focused on work. As an example, you might prepare yourself a drink (coffee, tea, smoothie), bring it into your work area, turn on some non-vocal music, then read a book on personal and/or professional development for 15 minutes.

Make a today list

Similar to a To Do List, a Today List is an informal yet intentional way of thinking about what you want to accomplish in your day. Get yourself a pad of sticky notes of whatever size you would like to be able write down daily tasks. You may want to consult a 'master' To Do list or some type of schedule that you have created to be aware of what your overall tasks are. Write down short, to the point notes of what you plan to accomplish in your day then stick this somewhere where you can easily glance at it throughout the day.

You can add to this list as the day goes on as you might think of a phone call you need to make or new task that comes up. The most important part of this exercise is the conscience thinking about your day and writing down your intentions as you begin working. This little list should get chucked at the end of the day and don't make any judgments on yourself about whether you did what you had planned to at the beginning of the day or not. Start a new list at the beginning of a new working day. If there are tasks that you want to remember to do that didn't get done from your Today List then just transfer them to your schedule or business To Do List.

Do the small but essential tasks first

Attending to email, making phone calls or updating your social media accounts may be possible essentials that need daily attention. They are also things that can be distracting if you are returning to them throughout your working time.

This is why it is effective to do these jobs to begin with and possibly to finish off with as well. You will likely have other responsibilities that fit into this category, depending on the type of business you run - think of all those little things you do that take focus away from other jobs.

Don't get caught up on getting everything perfect

Many precious hours can be wasted on spending too much time perfecting something. Although you want to portray a certain level of professionalism, don't be overly concerned with getting the perfect look, the perfect words or the perfect plan. You can always add something on your To Do list if you're not really satisfied with how it initially worked out. This allows you to at least complete the task at hand and move on to other productive tasks.

Effectiveness: Tips to getting results!

To be productive you must approach your business with a specific mindset that is relaxed, determined and open. It is most helpful to create processes and delegate when needed and keep focused on the task at hand while avoiding distractions that take that focus away. Being effective at everything you do and with the thinking you do is a major contributor to a productive and prosperous business. Use these following ideas to get the most out of your workday.

Keep your desktop free of clutter

At the end of office time for the day put everything in its place, which can be a combination of drawer's shelves, wall files, filing cabinets and any other organizing elements you are utilizing. Clutter in your environment, clutters your mind and can lead to inefficient practices from disorganization. Keep this great little saying in mind: "Everything has its place and there's a place for everything. If there's not a place for it then you don't need it!"

Create a space to put papers that you need to deal with eventually

This may be a box (sized slightly larger than standard letter sized paper and 3-4 inches in height) on your desk, a set of stackable organizer inboxes, or a multi-pocket/single pocket wall file (great for freeing up desktop space.) Unless you feel that you need the separation, don't create one space for work and one for home. Consider this a one-stop drop for anything you can deal with later and schedule a regular time that you attend to these papers. Don't let it pile too high so that you feel daunted by the effort to go through it.

Create systems for your business

The most efficiently run businesses are made up of a regulated and unique group of tasks that are created once and repeated again and again and again. If you've been in business for any length of time you probably have a few systems in place already, even if you don't realize it. Make the time to write down a step-by-step guide to the mechanics of your business; what you do in your home office that affects your business. This process will not only help you in defining and organizing the tasks you do (or should do) as an entrepreneur, but will also allow you to have someone else keep your business running if you're unavailable for various reasons, which moves us on to the next tip...

Outsource business tasks that you don't need to personally do

Every entrepreneur has "stuff" to do that isn't part of their skill set and isn't enjoyable to them. Generally, finances don't allow them to pay others for essential business tasks, especially when starting up, yet many people will find that as soon as they offload those unappealing chores they become more efficient at other jobs and their business really starts to flourish. In our multi-communication society, outsourcing business projects is easier than ever and definitely has various benefits to hiring an employee. You can find freelance professionals that are eager to do any project you may have through a variety of avenues. Whether you post a job on one of the many freelance bidding sites (Elance, Upwork (formerly o'Desk), Freelancer, to name a few), search for a virtual assistant online or through your local resources, or just have a friend or family member complete some work, you can put yourself in a position to achieve more with less time.

Pay attention to business tasks during your business time

This may seem like it's an opposite of being productive. After all, with our technology at the level that it is we can have the devices and access to our business 24/7. And why not attend to a few emails or phone calls if time permits during non-business hours? First of all, because those business matters won't really have your full attention if you're out shopping or visiting with friends, and secondly, just as you should give your business your full attention, you should also give the other areas of your life your full attention. This advice may not be for everyone, but perhaps it's just something for you to think about for now.

Be devoted to just one project at a time

Whether it is work or personal, remove all other programs and browsers that aren't related to what you're working on. As well, clear your desk/ working space of anything that is not related to the task at hand.

Set boundaries of when you answer emails and telephone calls

Keep in mind that these various forms of communication are for your convenience and not for the convenience of others. You can't be as focused and efficient when you're letting distractions always take you away from the task at hand. Schedule in a period of time once or twice a day to respond to and initiate conversations, whether it be through email, texting, phone calls or any other form of communication with customers, business associates and personal contacts.

Use the Pomodoro technique

This technique was created in the 1980's by Francesco Cirillo, which assists in achieving greater focus and better time management. It's a fairly simple concept of breaking down your workday into blocks of 25 minutes and builds on that main practice to teach more in-depth techniques of blocking out distractions, accurately estimating the length of time to do a task, and other organizational tips. You may not want to be a true 'Pomodoro' follower, but reading the details about this technique will definitely provide you with some insightful ideas to better manage your home business.

Schedule closed-door and quiet periods of time

While it can be good to be accessible to family members if needed, you may need to make at least a couple of 'no interruptions' times in your week. Some tasks just need your full-uninterrupted attention and if you can do them without any chance of an interruption, then you will be able to produce much better results. Not everyone will need to use this tactic, but if you find that you're less productive due to minor interruptions then stand-up for yourself and your business and make your family aware of the times you have set aside to complete your high concentration tasks that may also mean a quieter time for everyone in the house.

Do productivity checks

This will be a great new habit to foster that will help to keep you focused and stopping lots of those time-wasting activities. Every hour or two check in with yourself asking "Is this the best use of my time?" Set an alarm to go off, set up Google Calendar to send a notification to your desktop or simply stick a note on the wall in your direct sight with this question on it. Eventually you will get in the habit of asking this question regularly without external prompts and not get into unproductive work to begin with.

Don't get lost in multi-tasking

Creating an environment that is extremely efficient involves a sustained time of focused work. It can be difficult to really get focused when, each day, you're switching from one activity to another, just to get things done. Being able to schedule your time so that you complete a months' worth of blog posts in one day or set up some email broadcasts for the next two weeks allows your brain to really get into the one project and produce better work in less time than if you broke up the same kind of job over several days.

Always generate a growing sense of optimism

Expect that good things are going to be plentiful. Have the sense that life will bring good rather than bad outcomes and that when you encounter less than ideal situations you will be able to overcome it. Living your life with an optimistic mindset will allow you to see the possibilities and take advantage of opportunities that come out of hardship.

Create your business around your passion

The most successful people have attested to the fact that their passion for their business drove them to be innovative, determined and keep focused on their tasks. Be sure that your business focus is somehow connected to something you're passionate about and you'll find that staying motivated and productive feels much easier.

Schedule your more challenging work during your prime time

Are you a morning person, or does your energy rev up after 6pm? Determine when you are at your peak performance and schedule the more difficult work, or the stuff you are not so keen on doing, during these times. The routine tasks and more enjoyed activities can then be scheduled for the other times of the day.

Incorporate a reward system for a job well done

Although you've got "the big picture" incentive of having an awesome online business for long-term motivation, it's useful to create some short-term incentives to help you get through a challenging undertaking or detailed project. Gear the incentive to your own preference of what you see as a reward.

Balance – Tips to Energize Your Work Life!

Use the following tips and advice to create a better-rounded life. Working from home affords you the luxury of taking longer breaks, creating a unique home life and fulfilling your desires related to every part of your life while running a successful business. Your life goal should be to have a prosperous life, and although this can mean financial prosperity, it more importantly points to prosperity in all areas of your life that will result in an increase in your enthusiasm for your business. Strive for balance and creating harmony between work and life. The following tips focus on creating balance in your life that will directly influence your business.

Always be learning and growing

Always have a book on the go. Reading is a vital component to self-development, which you should be making time for on a regular basis. This is to enrich both your personal development and your professional development. Just making time to fit 15 minutes of reading in will benefit you greatly in all areas of your life, which will directly result in better results in your business.

Schedule your time for business matters, don't impose on your personal time

Don't let all the "to dos" get in the way of your personal life. Working from home can end up with some people working all the time, which sort of defeats the purpose of being self-employed. Make that schedule for business tasks and work within that schedule. There can be the occasional exceptions of course, but when you find that you're not sticking to the flexible schedule that you had created, you either need to re-think your time or be more disciplined in your approach to working time.

Don't aim to please everyone

Be clear on what your motives and intentions are and don't let someone else's opinion sway your informed decision. This relates to people in your personal life and in your business. Whether it's customers that want more time from you or quicker responses, or a spouse that feels your online pursuits are taking up too much time or doesn't understand your passion, don't let the opinions of others change your business process when you know that's what you want. Don't be completely close-minded either. Hear people out and consider their opinion, then stand up for what you feel is right.

Share your work schedule with your family

Posting a print out of your weekly schedule on the fridge, office door or other visible area will let your family members know when you have planned to work and even what kind of work you'll be doing. This helps to avoid someone in your house planning something that requires or requests your involvement during your work hours and allows you to share a bit of your business life with your family.

Discuss your business challenges and accomplishments with family and friends

Have one or two people that you can regularly talk to about what's happening with your business. Especially when you're first starting out, it can be discouraging to feel like you don't have anyone to share the achievements and the frustrations with. Even though you can connect with many other people online in the same situation as you (which you should do) it's much more effective to get to vent and share with someone you already have an established relationship with.

Take at least a 15-minute break every 2 hours of work

When you're mainly focusing on your computer screen, you can get fatigued much more quickly than if you are moving around. After sitting at your computer for 2 hours, get up and get a drink, have a stretch, take a walk, anything that gets you on your feet and not staring at a screen. You'll find yourself more focused and refreshed after a short break.

Use the freedom of your work-from-home lifestyle to have getaway breaks

If you're working a number of hours in your home business then take breaks where you can possibly do some personal errands or leave the house for an hour or two to take in some physical activity or meet up with someone. Shifting your focus for a longer length of time and creating a day that is filled with a variety of activities provides a greater feeling of satisfaction with your day, as you've been able to give attention to several areas of your life.

Take a reading break

If you haven't made the time in any other part of your day to devote to your personal growth through reading then take a reading break. Find yourself a comfortable spot to lounge in, go outside if possible or just locate yourself in a different spot than where you were working. It's good to get a change of scenery and fit in the always-important element of learning.

Use your work break to give attention to the other areas of your life

The most effective kind of break to take is a break that has you giving attention to some other areas of your life. Using your time wisely in this way will create a more productive life and not just center on a more productive work life. As the points above described more specific things you can do with your essential break, it is important to keep in mind that making your work break a short and sweet time to see family or a lengthy outing to experience various other things is an integral aspect to creating a balanced life that will have a direct result on the productivity in your business.

Be nutritionally conscience

Eating right is essential on so many levels, but you will find you are so much more motivated and productive if you're feeding your body the right kind of fuel. Get educated on what the best diet is for you and eat a variety of foods that are providing your body with the appropriate nutrients that it needs to function at an optimum level. Try to eat with the focus that food is for the proper functioning of your body and not just for your taste buds. Of course, moderation is the key and having little treats now and then is acceptable, but make the majority of meals and snacks about providing your body the right fuel.

Engage in fun and rejuvenating physical activity

Physical activity is a great energizer and provides your whole body with overall feeling of satisfaction. Although any type of exercise is beneficial, it is an added bonus when you can get some exercise while having fun and possibly spending some quality time with family or friends. A few examples of this type of invigorating exercise is biking, brisk walking, playing sports, skipping, jumping on a trampoline and rock climbing - just to name a few of your options. Even if you just take a regular trip to the gym and give your body a workout, you'll reap the rewards of physical activity. The overall point here is that exercise can and should be integrated into your life and it doesn't have to be some rigorous workout in the gym. There's a whole world of possibilities.

Nourish your spiritual side

You are a spiritual being that needs to regularly nourish that aspect of yourself. If you don't feel drawn to an organized faith or religion, just be connected to the spiritual nourishment of nature. Realize that there is more to life than just what you see and think about and take time every day to become aware of your inner spirit through mediation, communing with nature, or learning about various spiritual aspects of humanity.

Make time for face-to-face socialization

Get connected face-to-face with people in all aspects of your life, whether they are family, friends, business associates or casual acquaintances. Try to make brief encounters and lengthy visits a chance to really connect with someone and not just a passing of time. You never know what may come of a conversation where you are truly in the moment and making the most of your time with someone.

Schedule in time to nurture the most important relationships

Just being around your spouse or your children, or any other vital people in your life, isn't going to be an effective way to value that relationship. You have to spend quality time with the people you love and this is easily left out if you're not aware of the lack of connection you may have. If you find you're not connecting with those special people in your life on an intimate level then schedule in a weekly 'date' where you spend time with one another and get a chance to openly talk.

Be an ongoing source of inspiration for others

Being an encouragement to other people to have great aspirations, be persistent in achieving their goals and being open to new opportunities creates a greater sense of ownership in all you are planning to achieve in your business and personal life. Keep the momentum by reaching out to other people that you know personally and that you connect with through online sources. When you are constantly inspiring others you will be building a habit of determination and success that will lead you to living your life to its fullest potential.

Live the life of a successful online entrepreneur!
Surround yourself with empowering messages and people and avoid negative voices and mediocre minds. All the challenges that are faced by those working their business from home are eventually overcome by getting rid of those ineffective habits and renewing their life with a set of new productive habits that are the building blocks to a successful and well-balanced life. Building an online business is an achievable feat for anyone - you don't need to start off with special skills or have a lot of money in the bank and you don't need to have everything figured out. Learn as you go and be open to change, especially the change that needs to take place in your mind to think and execute plans like a determined entrepreneur.

Take risks and try new things that have the potential to get you in a position of growth and wisdom. Gain knowledge wherever and whenever you can to keep motivated and informed. Planning out various aspects of your business, being effective in your approach and having a life that is balanced in all areas will provide you a clear path to complete life of fulfillment.

Don't count on the success of your business niche, count on the success of you. If you focus the right attention and determined attitude to keep at it and don't get stuck in a rut or a process that doesn't work, then you'll always be able to roll with the punches and keep on keeping on.

Becoming the Leading Authority

One of the most important things you can do for your online business is to become an authority in your market. People underestimate the value of a recognized brand, but when they finally take action and begin building authority in their market, they are shocked by how much it impacts their business.

When you have secured authority in your market, you will:

- Generate unlimited traffic to your site
- Drive conversion rates through the roof
- Gain access to endless joint venture opportunities
- Increase prices for all your products
- Grow a massive, targeted mailing list
- Command attention and recognition.

Authority equates to more money, because when people recognize you as a leader in your market, there is very little resistance when purchasing your products and services.

Since you have more at stake (your reputation and credibility), even new customers who research you feel far more comfortable buying from someone that other people recommend, and trust. So, how can you quickly become an authority in your market and outsell the competition? This chapter outlines 7 power steps to becoming a trusted authority in your market, by building a world class brand, all your own.

Complete market domination

Building a brand and becoming a leader in your market isn't nearly as difficult as you may think, but it involves a very strict focus. Rather than trying to be everything to everyone, you need to begin with one market at a time. You then work towards complete market domination by saturating the market with YOUR brand. To do this, you will need to first choose your niche. Consider this carefully because when you tie your brand to one topic or market, you will forever be linked as an authority in that specific field.

Consider:

- What are you experienced with?
- What are you most interested in?
- What do you feel you can offer that's unique and valuable?
- What do you want to be known for?

Once you have chosen your niche, it's time to begin a full market assault. You will need to set up a website, squeeze page and social media accounts to begin weaving your brand message throughout your industry. While this can take a bit of time, once you have the brand-building tools in place, it will be easy to replicate for other niche markets.

Your website is key to building your brand and authority. You can set it up a number of different ways, including by using Wordpress as the foundation for your entire network. Just make sure that you optimize it based on your audience, and offer high quality content, tools and resources.

Here's our top recommended resource for help in building a full featured Wordpress blog wpunraveled.com. Part of building authority in your market requires going above and beyond what other marketers in your field are doing. You want to stand out and offer your audience genuinely helpful information and tools that showcase your commitment to providing value. Regardless of the niche market you are involved in, your brand begins with offering tremendous value. You will quickly become the "go to" person in your market if you give more than your competitor's give, and you are transparent with your intentions to help your audience, nurture relationships with your customers, and provide exceptional value throughout every campaign, beginning with your website. When adding content to your website, consider outsourcing to professionals so that you're able to deliver the best quality material possible.

Consider creating "pillar content" within your authority-building campaigns. Pillar content forms the foundation for your website and is considered your very best material. Pillar content is usually in the form of tutorials, step-by-step lessons, guides and "how to" based products and offers long-term appeal. You should accompany this with downloadable material where visitors can opt into your mailing list in order to receive free products and information. Always be on the lookout for ways to build authority by developing your very own mailing list!

Just keep in mind that the quality of your content is the driving force behind being able to create a brand recognized for value and authority. Your objective is to become an expert in your market, and so everything you do needs to emphasis your ability to deliver solid, high quality content.

Siphon credibility from authority figures

One of the easiest ways of building authority in your market is to siphon credibility from established leaders. They have already done the hard work in building relationships with their peers and customers, and in solidifying their place in your niche, so by associating yourself to them, you can siphon instant authority that will go towards building your own brand! You can begin by targeting 5-10 leaders in your market, paying close attention to any outlet in which you can become visibly active.

For example, one easy way of siphoning credibility is to begin communicating with their audience through forums, websites and blogs. Leave valuable feedback including tips that will help their visitors, and through direct association and by providing value, you'll be able to garner attention instantly! Another powerful technique is to interview the experts, and then offer this as a unique product on your own website! By interviewing experts, not only are you able to develop a unique, high quality product absolutely free (and very quickly), but you are able to associate yourself with the authority in your market!

People love interviews, because it gives them insight into how an authority thinks, what they've done to be successful and what your audience can do to achieve the same success.

Trade content for credibility

Another easy way of building authority in your market by borrowing credibility by association is to become a guest blogger. You can submit quality content that features your website links for distribution amongst authority blogs and websites.

Marketers and authority figures are always on the lookout for quality content that they can publish on their website. Their objective is to cater to their audience, while minimizing their workload and so by offering to guest write on their site, you both win!

You can also submit your content into content syndication networks and outlets that will circulate your articles throughout some of the leading websites and communities in your niche market. Run a quick search for content syndication channels in your niche, and then begin contacting all of the top leaders. Make sure that you have at least 2-3 high quality, full length articles to submit and that they are 100% unique. Authority blogs and websites do not want to post rehashed content or material that can be found anywhere else, so you need to be sure that your content provides exceptional value!

Create your own product line

You can also piggyback off of the success of authorities in your market by creating auxiliary products and special offers around THEIR products. For example, choose 2-3 leaders in your field and identify what it is that they are offering their customers. Analyze their websites and products and then create your very own special offer around their main product. Do NOT copy their product, but instead, create an offer that ties into their brand, and offers additional value to customers. Then, give it away on your website! Not only will you be able to generate traffic quickly, but you can offer the download through the back-end of your mailing list, so you can build a massive list of your own!

Then, take it a step further by creating additional products that you can sell to your new audience. The objective is to swipe traffic and credibility from leading authorities, and then turn that traffic into your very own customer base. You will do this faster and easier when you're able to offer a full product line of your own. Start by developing a single product, and then expand your sales system to include one time offers and back-end products. If you need to outsource the creation of your product, consider the following resources:

WarriorForum.com (especially valuable for finding writers, designers and copywriters).

Guru.com (great place for expert writers) Fiverr.com (great place for cheap content that you can use to build your list – blog posts, articles, etc)

Note: You can use high quality private label content as bonus products and value enhancers, from places like QuickStartPLR.com however your primary products should all be original and exclusive to your brand.

Brand yourself

From day one, every marketing campaign, website, and product that you create should carry your brand messaging, identifying yourself as an authority in your market.

Create a signature for use on all blogs, websites and forums that you participate in and include direct links to all platforms that you are a part of including:

- Your money pages (sales pages)
- Websites
- Blogs
- Hubs
- Social Media Accounts
- Articles
- Syndicated Content

You want to saturate your name and URL everywhere you can so that people begin to recognize it. Include a sign off in every email, every forum, and on every social media site that you participate in. Forums are a great vehicle for building your brand and generating mass exposure for free, so search out the top 2-3 forums in your niche and get active!

Link your offers to established products

Another simple way of siphoning authority from existing leaders is to write comprehensive, full-scale reviews of their products. At the end of your review, offer a free resource that ties into the core product, and offers extended value. For example, if an authority in your market is selling a guide to making money with Wordpress, you could write up a review outlining the key benefits of purchasing their product, while also offering a free set of Wordpress themes that will help customers minimize their workload.

Not only will you make money from promoting the product as an affiliate, but you will gain authority and recognition by offering a quality bonus for free! You can begin building your website on Wordpress, instantly. Not only will this save you time, but Wordpress is absolutely free. Once you have created your website and developed (or outsource) expert written content, you will want to implement affiliate links, a shopping cart for your own products as well as thank you pages and more. You can do all of this easily with WPSalesBuddy.com a robust Wordpress based plugin that will instantly create secure download pages, subscription links, shopping cart links and more.

Build a membership site

Nothing speaks of authority as a membership site does! When you build a subscription-based website, not only are you able to secure your place in your market faster, but you'll be able to generate a passive, recurring income from your niche market.

Nearly every authority figure offers a membership program of some kind because it's the most powerful way of building relationships in your market, and securing your foothold as a leader in your field. Membership sites go beyond just the exchange of information and resources. Your membership site can easily become a full-scale community, where you are recognized as the leader instantly, while being able to tap into an ever-growing customer base that can ultimately maximize your profits faster than anything else.

Start off with a simple membership program that offers monthly content, tools and resources and then expand your outreach by creating upgrades and additional products that tie into your membership theme. The easiest way to build a dynamic, full featured membership program while also building your list, offering unlimited one time offers, back-end products and more is through ClickFunnels, the leader in membership software. You can find out more at clickfunnels.com

Final tips

Building authority in your market will dramatically increase your overall income, while setting you up for long-term success. Once you've established authority in your market, it's extremely easy to dominate nearly any niche just by spreading your authority throughout. Here is to dominating your market and maximizing your income for life!

Chapter 2

Making Some Important Connections and Implementing

Outsourcing in Your Business

If you're a business owner, you already know how burdensome and stressful it can seem to get everything you want accomplished on many rushed and hurried days. For Internet business owners, they may find themselves over their heads at times when it comes to getting everything they need for their business completed in a timely fashion.

Today's Internet business owners are a diverse bunch; however, many of them are one-person operations—that is, there is no "staff" or "employees" to speak of. This is where outsourcing some of the work that needs to be done can really come in handy—and provide you with more free time to get other things done. Outsourcing simply means that you delegate various work and tasks to other people for a set amount of pay, usually in the form of a one-time payment.

Since business online is booming, the need for more quality people to assist business owners with various tasks is stronger than ever. It can be hard to find good people you can trust to get the job done. In fact, today over half of all Internet businesses use the services from outsourcing resources and websites to help them accomplish their business goals. There are many significant benefits to outsourcing work.

Perhaps the most obvious one is the low and fair cost. You can outsource work to others on a case-by-case basis, so you are only paying for the satisfactory completion of very specific assignments. This is much more cost effective than if you were to hire a full time staff of employees. Staff requires salaries or hourly pay plus benefits, not to mention the overhead of a building to keep them all in.

Outsourcing work can come from all over the world, and you can find eligible candidates through a large number of different helpful websites. Most people who perform freelance work are familiar with the client's needs and the pay rate, so don't be afraid to be very vocal about what you want done, and what you are willing to pay for it. This new modern method of getting help from outside sources is a great way to network. In addition, it is a real time saver that is often worth its weight in gold.

You may wonder just what type of work can be done through outsourcing. Some of the most common tasks include graphic design, web page design, script writing (web), content writing, editing, copywriting, coding, software creation, eBooks, and even customized music for your website.

The possibilities are limitless today. If you only need one logo created for your website, for example, you can enlist the help of a freelance graphic artist and then pay him or her a one-time fee for the logo. It makes running a virtual business that much easier.

Remember, when looking for someone to do a job for your business, be sure to ask for some kind of credentials, like a portfolio or a reference. Think of it as doing an interview via email for a new employee. You don't want to pay someone simply because they SAY they can do the job.

If you enter into some kind of payment agreement and then you're not happy with their work, you may be in a legal bind, so be certain the person you choose to do the assignment is qualified and able to produce what you are looking for.

Outsourcing has increased almost exponentially over the last few years. This means as a business owner, the resources for finding great talent have increased as well. You can use several different websites to "recruit" the help you need. In some cases, all you need to do is post the need for the job, a thorough job description of what needs to be done, and a price you're willing to pay for it upon completion.

People then bid on the job and submit your qualifications, and you can decide who you'd like to "hire" by either the price they bid or the background information they provide. A great advantage to using these types of sites is that in many cases the website will guarantee you're happy with the job before you pay. This ensures that you get exactly what you need without incurring any extra costs.

Time is so precious to so many business owners, it is no wonder more and more of them are looking to outsource various tasks. It is also much less expensive than hiring someone to work for them full time. You can choose the job you need done and how soon you need it completed.

Outsourcing also gives you the freedom you need to make a budget for each task. How much or how little you are willing to pay is completely up to you, and then those who are interested in doing the job will contact you through either direct email or through the post you create on a number of outsourcing websites. You can control how much money you're willing to spend, which gives you great flexibility.

Outsourcing as an investment

If you own an Internet business, surely you know there are many costs involved. Aside from the common cost of web hosting, domains and company email addresses, there are many other expenditures you need to consider. Even with an online business, you need to be as professional as possible. Business cards are great for networking when attending conferences or meeting people face to face.

You also need to consider the cost of faxes, copies (as well as printer ink), a cell phone and service, and a land line if you need one. Don't forget the smaller costs of pens and other office supplies. As far as larger costs go, you can incur anything from inventory to shipping costs, as well as the price of providing whatever service it is you are offering your customers and clients.

With all of these costs to consider, outsourcing may initially look like just another mark on your general ledger. Keep in mind that when you use outsourcing, in most cases you will only need to pay for the services you receive on an individual basis. Most people who run traditional brick-and-mortar businesses typically have much more financial overhead. They must pay for a building to lease or buy, utility bills, phone book listings, as well as the salary they must pay their employees. With outsourcing, this overhead can be cut significantly.

Outsourcing should be looked at as more of an investment versus an overhead cost. This is because the services you use will be something that your business can keep forever. For example, if you're selling eBooks, having one person write an eBook for you at a one-time price can bring you a lifetime of residual income. A graphic designer will usually take a flat fee per design, while your logo sticks with the business for life, and provides you with branding. People who provide content for your website are giving you text that people will read and see on your website for as long as you wish to keep it there.

Of course, the best thing about outsourcing is the fact that you will have much more time to focus on other aspects of your business. As they say, time is money and the more time you have to attend meetings, procure more inventory, and focus on marketing, the more money you'll generate. With the help of outsourcing, you are investing in your business. You can take more time to actually get the things done you need to do without worrying about where the extra help will come from. In today's web based world, the resources to find reliable people for outsourcing is quite expansive.

Some of your associates or competitors might initially scoff at the idea of outsourcing, but in the long run they'll be literally amazed at how much time and money you have saved. You will get projects and issues with your website completed while freeing up time to get other things done.

Those who scoff might still be running around worried about how they are going to get everything accomplished for the day so that their business can progress. Be proud of the fact that you're finding and using an extremely valuable resource that will give you back much more than just finished jobs. Outsourcing provides you with peace of mind and another tick on your checklist.

You should view outsourcing as an investment, since it will save you time and money, and will provide your business with the things you need in order to be successful. Think of every job you pay for as another item done on your to do list, and you can feel more relaxed knowing you've put the work needed into capable hands. It is not so much something you have simply spent money on, but instead something that will bring you a return on your investment.

The best places to outsource

The Web offers many different places to find good outsourcing assistance. Here are a few of the most commonly used websites and some of the feature they offer, so you can make an informed decision about where to find good people and resources for outsourcing work:

1. scriptlance.com- This website allows you to post a number of different jobs for outsourcing. Some of the categories include web design, graphic design, SEO writing, content writing, tool development for your website, and even administrative support as it is needed.

    You can post the job type and exactly what you need and eligible bidders can then bid on your job. It is up to you to decide whom you'd like to choose to complete the job, and then you may give them allotted time fame for completion. You may post your budget as well, so that bidders know how much you're willing to pay for a completed task.

2. rentacoder.com- The website does exactly what the name says: it allows you to "rent" a coder to help you with the development of your website. This site only allows qualified web coders to apply and bid on jobs, so you can be sure you're getting high quality work. The coders are notified of new jobs posted, so the task goes out to thousands of

people at one time. The bidders do not get paid until you approve the work, which provides a great motivating factor. If you run into problems, rentacoder has a staff of people who can assist you with either getting in touch with the coder you've chosen or help you moderate issues if a problem arises.

3. upwork.com – This site is extremely thorough, and it allows all of its freelancers to take a wide variety of skills tests. These tests can vary from typing speed to grammar, web coding to office terminology fluency and comprehension. Each test that a user passes is then added to their score, so that business owners can see how well each person did on specific tests.

   This is a great way to gauge how well someone will be able to complete a task for you, and a good resource for finding high quality work. Upwork allows you to post your needed project in a kind of bulletin board style, where all users can see it by category, and then bid on the job.

4. elance.com- One of the web's most popular choices for outsourcing, this site has a plethora of different projects you can post or view. Everything from marketing to legal, freelance writing to web programming is covered. This is a one-stop shop for all of your outsourcing needs.

   The site has helpful forums, video tutorials, and is registered with Verisign and the Better Business Bureau, so you know your investment is protected, and that you will receive quality work from elance members.

5. sitepoint.com- This website provides a wide range of helpful information for Internet business owners. It has many great features including helpful forums and articles. There are also helpful tips for business owners in regards to marketing your website, and how to get more people to see your website. It is an invaluable resource for both you and those looking to outsource their talents.

A list of things you can outsource

People often think of outsourcing jobs as moving a call center to India or shipping manufacturing jobs overseas. But the term outsourcing can also simply mean using someone else's help to get a job accomplished and completed. Here is a list of different things you can outsource simply by finding qualified people online:

- eBooks
- SEO Content
- Music Composition
- Graphic design and logo design
- Web content
- Website programming and coding
- Web tool development
- Chat room and forums moderators and monitors
- Live Help assistants
- Schedule maintenance
- Virtual assistants/secretaries
- Report writing

- Telephone help
- Copywriting and editing
- Publishing assistance
- Ebay listings
- Article compositions and rewrites
- Legal assistance
- Court document research
- Photography

These are just a few examples of the many different jobs you can find online through outsourcing resources. There are thousands of qualified people who actually make their living freelancing on the web. With the help of outsourcing sites, you can connect with high quality people who can provide you and your business with the essentials it needs to succeed.

Just because you own a business does not necessarily mean you can do it all yourself. Sometimes help is needed with certain tasks, and this is where outsourcing comes in. Through networking, many people often find a reliable source for outsourcing and a great person who eventually can provide them with the help they need on an assignment basis, without having to pay them an annual salary.

Brainstorm and come up with a comprehensive list of different things you will need to outsource. Think about your budget ahead of time, and allot a proper amount to each task. Remember that this is an investment, and that high quality work will definitely pay for itself. You don't want to pay for too many tasks at once, so prioritize your needs and decide which things you need accomplished, and how soon. Just about anything you can think of can be outsourced. It's all a matter of properly wording the job you need done, so that people know exactly what you're looking for. Try and list one job at a time, and see how it turns out. Use each website for one different job, just so you can get a feel for their fees and layout, and for what kind of quality people they are providing.

If you feel overwhelmed, just determine which task needs to be completed the soonest. Then, decide on how you want to post the listing. Wait for qualified bidders to contact you, and then make a decision on which you would like to complete it. Remember that they must adhere to the time frame that you set, and that the work must be to your liking before you pay for it.

You can always ask the person to make changed and edit things as needed, until it meets your requirements. Most people are more than happy to adjust their work to give you what you need so that they can get paid, so do not be afraid to ask them to make changes until you get exactly what you want. Remember, it is your money and your business, so you deserve the best. What to Look for in a Freelancer, Ghostwriter, Designer, etc.

If you're new to outsourcing, you want to be sure you choose someone to complete the job that is qualified. There are several things you need to look for in this type of person, since you cannot make a face-to-face connection with them, and almost all of your communication with be via email or on the web. The first thing you can do is ask the person to provide you with a portfolio.

For example, if you're in need of a graphic designer, have him or her send you some examples of the work they have done in the past for other companies. Another option is to give them a "test" example that has a quick turnaround time. This will allow them to prove to you their capabilities, as well as their ability to meet deadlines. How quick they respond also shows you how serious they are about assisting you, and how eager they are to do a good job.

For freelance writers you can ask someone to provide you with a few writing samples. Writing samples give you good insight into how well a person expresses his or her self. Read over the sample articles carefully so you can get a feel for how this person writes. If you feel like their style matches what you're looking for, then odds are they will do a good job writing your web content or your SEO content that you need.

If you feel so inclined, you can also ask the person for references. Many people who freelance have been doing so for some time, and have probably built up a list of clients who can vouch for their work. References are a great way to ensure you're getting someone who can do the job well.

If you are searching for freelance web coders, ask for a few examples of some sites they have done and what exactly it is that they accomplished for the site. If you are using one of the previously mentioned websites or another site, many of them have ratings on each freelancer. Previous completed projects are shown, as well as feedback from other people who have used them to do a job.

This can provide great insight on the person's record, timeliness, and accuracy, as well as buyer satisfaction. It takes some time to build up positive feedback, so this is a good indicator of their track record as well. It is much like the feedback you see on eBay: it provides you with an inside look at how others have dealt with the person in the past on other jobs.

No freelancer you speak with should have any problems providing you with a record of their past work. They understand that this is how you will make a final decision on who you choose to complete the tasks you need to get done. If you feel any sense of doubt or hesitation, do not hire someone just because you may feel a little bit guilty.

Many times, freelancers get turned down for jobs, but they can always move on to another one. If you think the person is not capable of giving you the high quality of work you expect within a certain amount of time, politely let them know you have chosen someone else to finish the job, and move on to the next person.

Getting a freelance job is much like auditioning for a part in a play. The person must show their skills and talents to you, and then you as the director has to make a final decision based on what you see. It also depends on the type of work you need done. For example, you cannot afford errors when it comes to getting some coding done for your website. An eBook or content provider may not need to have as stringent guidelines.

Ultimately, the choice is up to you, so review all work carefully. Ask for portfolios, writing samples, references, and even resumes, depending on the thoroughness of the job. You can usually tell who will do a good job for you, so follow your instincts and intuition.

Think of using someone in outsourcing just like hiring someone to work in your office. You want them to be honest, trustworthy, accurate, and efficient. Only you can make this final call, but by using the various resources and websites available for freelancers, you have a better chance at finding someone you really want to use time and time again.

Remember that you can always just use people for one small project and then move on to someone else if you're not happy with the results or the work.

In outsourcing, nothing is written in stone in regards to the buyer. You are in control, since you set the budget, the requirements, and the needs you have in regards to what it will take to get the job done.

The Internet is full of extremely talented, gifted, and organized people who have a real passion for what they do. You might choose one person for a job, and then move on to a different person for the same or similar job later down the line. Outsourcing is great because you do not have to be tied down to one person to do the jobs you need done. It's a wonderful way to network and find new talent as well. Use the outsourcing websites to make contacts and get together a team of virtual employees who can help you get things finished while freeing up your time to focus on other things.

As a business owner, you already have a definite goal in mind. Use your goals to project that same attitude onto the freelancers you choose, so they fully understand what it is you need completed. Look for people with a positive and friendly attitude, and people who respond to your communications on a fairly quick basis.

Those who can keep to deadlines are those you will want to keep for a longer period of time. Make connections, and ask those you hire to do jobs for referrals for other assignments. They may know someone else who can assist you with other goals such as graphic design or eBooks.

What should be included in a project?

If you've finally made a decision on what you need, and have chosen someone to complete the assignment or project, or if you're in the infant stages of listing your project, be sure you thoroughly state your needs. For example, if you need content written, list the topics the content will be about. Include the number of words you need as well as the number of articles written. Be sure to list the price that you are willing to pay for the articles, whether as a completed set, per word, or per article. This way, eligible candidates know ahead of time exactly what you are looking for, and how much you're willing to pay.

For coding jobs, show candidates an example of your site. Let them know in as much detail as possible the type of coding you will need and what needs to be done. For all listings, be as thorough as possible in regards to what your business is about. State the type of business you have, the attitude you're looking for, and the tone. What you say in your "help wanted" listing is crucial, since this will be what people look at in order to decide whether or not they want to assist you with the project.

Devise an outline of each project you need completed. Write it down clearly, and know exactly what you want to see accomplished, as well as your goals and timeframe for completion. Then, pass these requirements on to the person you choose to do the job.

This will help them get a very clear concise picture of what it is you're exactly looking for. If you try hard to make it as simple yet detailed as you can, the odds are in your favor that the person you pick to finish the project will do it to your liking and your specs. Remember, a project is only as good as the person who created it, so by giving very simple yet clear instructions, you'll see much better results.

If you need an eBook written, let people know exactly what you need in regards to the subject and the length of the book. If you need it written in chapters, specify that. If you need the person writing the eBook to state all references they use, be sure to list that as well. By being as specific as possible, you can assure that the project will be completed per your needs and that the person competing it will do the job to the best of his or her ability. This also saves time, since the candidate knows exactly what's needed in advance and this leaves little room for errors or time-consuming editing. When a job is done right the first time, it eliminates the back and forth of emailing, and saves you time from having to go over the submitted project and list all of the corrections needed.

All projects that are completed should include exactly what you've asked for, and in what format, so state this ahead of time. For example, if you need SEO content in Word format, the person needs to turn it in this way. If your eBook should be in PDF format this would apply as well, or a picture that you require to be in Adobe Photoshop format or JPG format. By being specific about the file format ahead of time, you are saving both yourself and the freelancer you've hired a lot of unnecessary headaches. As stated before, be as clear and detailed as to what you need as possible, so there is less room for error and for edits.

Thinking ahead of the curve will save you lots of time and money when it comes to outsourcing. By being open and honest, as well as upfront about what you need, you are helping to ensure you will get only the best people to complete your projects. Do not be afraid to turn work back over to the freelancer and have them fix any errors or problems. After all, this is your money and your business and anyone in freelancing already knows that it is their job to return high quality work to you. Make sure you are very clear about what you want and need in advance and this will help you avoid problems later on.

Anything you pay money for as a business owner, whether it is a service offered by others such as web hosting, or an assignment you've given to someone to be outsourced, should be done to your utmost satisfaction. By using websites that hire or use highly qualified people, you are making sure you get the best of the best. After all, this is your time, your money, and your business.

All projects you receive should be completely finished and next to perfect before you pay for them. Don't just accept second best. Never pay for a service or project unless it is finished, correct, and thorough. You can be sure this will happen if you already have a picture in your mind about what you want the project to look like or consist of. Knowing this in advance gives everyone a better edge to be successful.

Ways to get your project at a cheaper price

Since it is your money that you'll be spending out of pocket for various outsourced projects, you want to be sure you are getting the best deal and the best price possible. Negotiation is usually a good way to start. Set a limit in advance about the maximum amount of money you will be willing to spend, and try your best not to go over it.

Often, freelancers are willing to negotiate prices, since this is the bulk of their income, and freelance work can be hard to come by. If you ask for a project and the person does not like the amount you want to pay, see if you can get them to add a few extra things to the project, such as an extra graphic or an additional article. Often people will take the price you offer upon agreement to do just a little bit of extra work. Bartering for services is another idea to help you get a good price on your outsourcing needs. For example, you can offer the person who wants to do the job a free service that you offer in exchange for the completed project. You can offer them web related referrals in exchange as well. Many times, you can trade services instead of paying out cash and this is an excellent money saver.

Negotiate your project price carefully, however. Many people will turn a job down in the long run if the pay rate is too low. Think carefully about how you want to negotiate, and make sure both of you are communicating clearly and often to avoid any misunderstanding.

Another way to get your project done at a cheaper price is to "buy in bulk." For example, let's say you need 15 articles written. Instead of paying for each individual article, you can offer to pay a flat fee for all 15 articles at once for a lesser price. Many people understand the concept of doing a list of projects for a flat fee, and this enables you to get more for your money. A lot of the freelance bidding websites will let you post projects on a multiple or bulk basis. You can get more accomplished at a much cheaper cost this way.

Advertise work you need done on free job boards. Sometimes you can find a local person who can help you for a low fee. Usually these people are easy to work with since they're close and they may do the work for a discount for you since you can simply pick it up or call them on the phone through a local call.

Negotiate prices with everyone you come in contact with unless they are willing to do the job you need completed at a lower price than you've budgeted yourself for. Many people opt to pay new freelancers that they've hired a lower fee for the first few assignments, but if they like the work they do, as they progress they often increase the pay rate.

Brainstorm other ways you can get the things you need done without spending a pretty penny. Look for people who are able to do more than one job at a time for you, and are experts in many different fields. This way, you may be able to get them to finish projects for you at a reduced cost.

They might be able to finish two or more projects at one time, for one flat fee or rate. Buying your jobs in bulk is a great way to save money. Think about the different ways you can get more work done for less bucks. It will be an invaluable tool for you to make more time for yourself and your business, thus making you more money in the long run.

With so many things happening today in business at the speed of light, you do not always have time to cover all of your bases. However if you neglect certain aspects of your job or your business, you could end up shooting yourself in the foot. This is where outsourcing comes in.

By choosing an outside person or source to assist you with your business needs, you are making a very smart move. Not only will you save loads of time, but also you're getting things done without spending the excess overhead. This is invaluable for small businesses. Assigning projects to willing professionals at a set rate allows you to stay within your budget while still allowing you to get important aspects of your business up and running.

The Internet now provides so many wonderful resources for outsourcing that the possibilities are endless. By looking for websites that offer qualified people and a structured method of payment, you can maximize your time and look for people who will get things done for you in a timely and professional manner. In many cases you will find someone who you can count on permanently, who will accept projects from you on an individual basis as often as you need them.

Outsourcing can also offer you new ways of thinking about your business that you might not have thought of before. You may end up finding a good group of people who can assist you with new ideas, great graphics, website content, and other brainstorming concepts that can bring your business to a whole new level.

By enlisting the help of others through outsourcing, you are really broadening your horizons with a fresh outlook and a new method of getting things done. You may also find that you really like outsourcing your projects to others, and that it will help you to organize other aspects of your business, giving you more time for networking, meetings and focusing on expansion in other ways.

There is a wide, wide range of talent online today with so many skilled and experienced freelancers that you will be surprised by how much truly reliable and outstanding talent is out there. Choosing your group of people personally gives you the freedom to make choices on whom you want to work with you and your business.

It also opens up the doors to a new opportunity to accomplish goals in a much more timely fashion. Make a list of the things you need done, and then check out the number of helpful websites available today that offer a group of experienced freelancers who can handle any task. Outsourcing may seem like an overhead expense at first, but in essence it is really a solid investment in your business and its future.

At first, the term outsourcing might invoke feelings of uneasiness or uncertainty about the quality of work you will receive. Rest assured, by using certified websites like elance.com, rentacoder.com, and many others, you can find helpful people who are willing to assist you in any way you need. The work gets done on time, and it's quality work with a guarantee before you make payment.

Both sides benefit, making it a win-win situation for you and the other parties involved. Don't be afraid to enlist the help of others if you feel like you're becoming overwhelmed with the number of tasks you need completed. By outsourcing, you can be sure your tasks are completed on time and to your satisfaction, all while freeing up more time for you to focus on other things.

Even the most ardent business owners run into issues, deadlines, and overwhelming tasks they need to get done. Enlisting the help of a freelance worker through outsourcing is an excellent way to ensure you get the job done in the timeframe you have allotted, and you can also be sure it will be done to your satisfaction.

Have no fear; outsourcing online today is one of the most effective ways that small Internet businesses get things completed. Don't be afraid to explore and try out different small tasks through outsourcing, just to get a feel for how the process works. Eventually you will be surprised at how easy it is to use others to assist you with your tasks.

Thinking of outsourcing as an investment has proven to be a great way for businesses to get things accomplished that may have otherwise been on the backburner for months. With the help of others, you will find that the job you thought could or would never get done is getting finished in a matter of days.

You will be amazed at how helpful outsourcing others can be if you find the right people. Set goals, set standards and know what you're looking for. Decide on how much you're willing to budget, and then put your project out there for others to see. You will be able to find reliable, accurate, and professional people who can help you get your business on track by providing services and finishing tasks you may have never had the time to finish yourself.

Launching a Website for Your Business

Launching a website is a process. Many people seem to think you can simply create a website and upload it and it will magically start making money, but that's just not true. Even if you have a large email list at your disposal, sometimes that's not enough to make a website successful.

In this chapter, you're going to uncover the major steps it takes to launch a website successfully. These tips are geared specifically toward product launches, but they can certainly apply to any type of website launch including blogs. You will want to start your pre-launch campaign at least 2-4 weeks before launch. Any longer than that and the buzz will wane before launch, and any closer to launch and you won't have enough time for the buzz to spread. An important part of launching a website or product is planning, so be sure to plan your launch strategy out day by day before launch. This will help keep your organized and right on point.

Pre-launch buzz

Perhaps the most important phase in a website launch is the building of buzz before the launch. If you release a website without first building buzz, the launch probably isn't going to go very well. You may have heard the common marketing idea that it takes at least three times of hearing a marketing message before the average person responds. The first time they hear it, they will often ignore it. The second time, they may be slightly interested, but they quickly forget. The third time they hear it, it finally begins to sink in and they will remember it and act on it if they are interested.

Building pre-launch buzz takes advantage of this by inundating potential visitors with your message before the site launches. Not only does it help get the word out about the launch, but it gets people excited about the site before it even launches. There are many ways to create pre-launch buzz. We're going to look at a few of them in this report, but it's a good idea to think of some of your own, too. Originality is important.

Videos

Videos are great for creating buzz, because they can be interesting, they can grab attention, and they're easy for people to share. If your video is interesting enough or helpful enough, people will start sharing it with their friends and family. This is called "going viral". Viral videos have the potential to reach thousands of people, sometimes millions, quickly and easily, with very little work. When you create a video, make sure it really speaks to your audience. You can't just make a sales video. It should provide real value to prospective visitors or buyers, and it should obviously be related directly to your niche or your product.

Giveaways

Giveaways have a lot of power to generate buzz. People love free stuff, and they'll go to incredible lengths to potentially get it. If you can set up a special script, you can open a giveaway that gives people another entry into the giveaway for every person they refer. This helps spread the word quickly.

Contests

In addition to standard giveaways, you can also hold contests to generate buzz. There are so many types of contests you could hold that could really get people excited. You should get creative when planning your contest, and try to tie it into your niche. Let's say you're launching a weight loss product. You could hold a trivia contest and give away free copies of your product to the top 5 winners. You could ask people to send in "before" shots of themselves, or create videos and submit them to YouTube about why they want a free copy of your product. Get creative with your contest and how it ties in with your product or website and it will be very rewarding!

Live webinars

A webinar is a seminar that is held online. They are usually educational in nature, and they can be very powerful if you really make people believe the information you'll be giving will be valuable to them.

Traffic

Creating marketing pieces for pre-launch buzz is important, but they can't do you any good if no one sees them. You need a lot of traffic to get the buzz going. Many types of traffic aren't suitable for the pre-launch phase, because they take too long to bring in. You need immediate, instantaneous traffic, because you need to ensure the traffic comes in when you need it – before launch. We're going to take a look at some of the different sources of traffic that work well for launches.

Social marketing

Sites like Twitter and Facebook are great for creating buzz, because they are in real-time. As soon as you post something, it is visible to everyone who is following you. Obviously, you will need a targeted list of followers for this to be effective. If you have 10,000 followers who aren't targeted, your response will likely be negligible. If you have 500 followers who are very well-targeted to your niche, your response could be phenomenal!

Don't forget to ask your followers to re-tweet or repost your messages. This will help you reach people who aren't following you.

Email

If you have an email list, you will obviously want to use it for sending out your pre-launch messages. But what if you don't have a list of your own? You can make use of other people's lists! You can buy a message in a newsletter very cheaply, or you can buy a solo mailing that will be much more effective, but it will cost a lot more. I highly recommend solo mailings, because you want your message to be the sole focus. If you buy a spot in a newsletter, your message could get lost in the shuffle. If you can afford it, I recommend buying solo emails from several of the most high-traffic newsletters in your niche.

Joint ventures

If you have your own list, you can multiply its potential by offering to do joint ventures with other people who own lists in your niche. Let them know you're planning to launch a new website or product, and that you're looking to generate as much buzz as possible before the launch. Let them know the launch date, as well as the anticipated date for beginning the pre-launch phase. That way, they can schedule your mailing so it won't conflict with anything else they need to mail out around that time. Ask them to email out for you, and in exchange you will mail your list about something for them in the future. It's the perfect win-win situation if both parties have comparably sized email lists.

Affiliates

What if you can't afford a solo mailing and you don't have your own email list? If you are launching a product, you can have affiliates do the mailing for you without paying them up front! You may need to have a special script made in order to track pre-launch traffic. Since you won't be able to have affiliates send traffic directly to an affiliate link before the site launches officially, you will have to set things up to track affiliate clicks before the product can even be bought. This will mean you will need to set up a cookie that won't expire before launch, or you will need another tracking method. You may want to offer pre-launch affiliates a special commission. If your normal commission if 50%, you might offer affiliates who promote during the pre-launch phase a 65% commission. This will be an incentive to get them to promote you before you're ready to take orders.

Pay per click

Pay-per-click traffic is great for generating pre-launch buzz, but you have to use it wisely. Since you won't be taking payments immediately, you will need to use the traffic to build a list that you can announce to on launch day. Be prepared to spend quite a bit of money up front, and you may not make it back right away.

Joint Venture Mastery

Joint ventures are a great way to promote your product without having to spend a lot of money up front on traffic. You can leverage your own resources to multiply your own promotional efforts, and you can benefit others by helping them with their own promotions. Profitable joint ventures are a win-win situation for both parties. Done correctly, a joint venture can be extremely beneficial for everyone involved.

In this chapter, you're going to discover what a joint venture really is, how to use them profitably, and how to find people who would love to be your joint venture partner.

Remember, a joint venture should be beneficial to both parties. Make sure you focus equal time on making your joint venture partners happy, and they will reward you with more traffic than you could ever get on your own!

What is a joint venture?

A joint venture is a mutually beneficial relationship in which one party promotes the product of another party, and in return the party whose product is promoted agrees to similarly reciprocate. In some ways, being a JV partner is like being an affiliate. You're promoting someone else's product in exchange for compensation, but instead of being paid in cash, you are paid by having your own product promoted in return.

Usually, joint ventures involve email lists. This isn't always true, but in the majority of cases it is. In the next section, we're going to take a look at some of the different types of joint ventures.

All JVs should be equally beneficial to both parties. If one party benefits far more than the other party, it can't be mutually beneficial and you probably won't be able to JV with that person again in the future. Build relationships, not money!

Types of joint ventures

There are many different ways to develop mutually beneficial joint ventures. We're going to look at a few of the ways you can build the most effective joint ventures.

Email joint ventures

The most common type of joint venture is when two parties who have email lists of similar sizes agree to email their own lists for each other. Let's say you have an email list of about 5,000 people and you meet someone who has a list of around 7,000 people.

Chances are good that a good portion of your list will not be on their list and vice versa. That means each of you could reach many more people by cooperating and sending emails out for each other. Email joint ventures work well as long as lists are within about 50% of each other.

If you have a list of 10,000 people, you could JV with someone with 15,000 people or someone with 12,500 people, but not 20,000 people or 5,000 people. If one party has more than 50% more subscribers, both parties may not feel satisfied. You can JV with anyone who will agree to JV with you, but it's a good idea to make sure all of your JVs are as mutually beneficial as possible to keep the relationship preserved for the future.

Traffic exchanges

If you don't have an email list, but you do have a website or blog with significant traffic, you can do a traffic exchange with someone else in your niche with similar traffic.

Generally, the traffic you send to your JV partner won't be exactly on par with what they send you. Even if both websites have the same amount of traffic, visitors aren't likely to respond evenly to different offers. As long as both parties understand going into the business relationship that there is no way to guarantee equal response, traffic exchanges can definitely be beneficial. Just do your best to make sure you reciprocate as evenly as possible and both parties should be relatively satisfied.

Cross promotions

When you release a product, you can form a partnership with someone who has a product that complements your product well. Let's say your product is a book about losing weight with a low-calorie diet. You could do a cross promotion with someone who offers a calorie counter software program. They could promote your program as the best weight loss program to work with their software, and you could promote their software as the best software to use to keep track of calories with people who are using your weight loss system.

Cross promotions are another type of mutually beneficial relationship that can work really well. Again, both parties need to understand that the response they receive or the money they make may not be perfectly aligned with the other party's outcome. There is no way to ensure a perfectly even reciprocation, but that doesn't mean both parties can't be happy.

Finding JV partners

Perhaps the hardest part of joint venturing is finding people to form JV partnerships with. It can be very difficult to find JV partners, especially if you don't already have a big name in your niche. When you contact potential JV partners, you need to make sure to let them know what's in it for them. Don't talk extensively about yourself. Don't talk extensively about your product. Talk about what you can do for them. You need to make sure you let them know why they should JV with you. While it is important to tell them a bit about yourself and your product, you should focus on why it would be beneficial for them. Now, let's take a look at a few ways to find potential JV partners. There are many other ways, but we're just going to take a look at some of the easiest and most popular ways to find potential JV partners.

Contacting potential JV partners

One of the easiest ways to find JV partners is to locate people in your niche that have large email lists or high-traffic websites or blogs and contact them. Many websites have contact forms or pages you can use. You may be able to find email addresses or telephone numbers. If not, you can check WHOIS.net. You may be able to get contact information that way.

Forums

Webmaster forums and JV forums are great for finding potential JV partners. There are forums dedicated specifically to JVs, and general webmasters forums can also be helpful.

Try these:

- warriorforum.com
- digitalpoint.com
- jvnotifypro.com

JV brokers

Try these:

- jointventurebroker.net
- williecrawford.com
- Master Joint Ventures

Tracking results

In order to ensure that your joint ventures are as profitable as possible, you need a way to track the results you get from each partner. You want to ensure that your partners are living up to their part of the bargain, and you want to make sure you know how well they performed in case you JV with them at a later date. Instead of having JV partners send traffic directly to your domain, you should have them send traffic through a special link so you can track results. This could be somewhat like an affiliate link. If you have software that can track it, this can work well.

If you don't have special software that can track results, you can have traffic sent through a simple script. You can easily get a PHP script that will let you redirect traffic through a special link and will track the traffic that goes through each link. Just find a link cloaking script that tracks traffic and you'll be able to easily measure the results you get from each partner. You may also be able to track sales by setting up a system like Google's Website Optimizer.

EBook Marketing

An eBook is one way to get an individual's ideas online either for free or for a reasonable price tag. Basically the term eBook refers to the electronic form of publication of any information. The information can be on a vast and almost infinite variety of topics and the information can also be sources from other online postings.

EBook basics

Most eBooks use the PDF format but there are also other formats that can be used without many problems while producing the same results. The individual would have to ensure the electronic format used is compatible otherwise the information would not be able to be accessed easily therefore defeating the purpose of the posting.

The basics

The process of successfully churning out an eBook is not very difficult and with a little bit of knowledge and research one should be able to come up with a presentable piece worth posting. For the more experienced and serious eBook authors this is a very lucrative revenue-earning platform. The following are some tips on how to get started:

Ensure one has a word processor that saves information in PDF formats. Google Docs, which is free, Microsoft Word, which is not available for free, and Open Office, which is also free, can get the job done adequately.

The next step, which for most can be quite challenging is to be able to come up with material that is worth sharing or selling. This material has to be original in its content in order to be able to draw the attention of the target audience and to also create a sense of expertise and trustworthiness for the author. Copied works are usually not favorably look upon.

Print or save the written material in PDF. Deciding on a set amount of words would also be wise as material that is too lengthy can be off putting for some.

Decide how your eBook will be used

There are several different ways to use an eBook compilation online today. Some of these are specifically designed as marketable revenue earning product while other are the contributions of individuals who just want to share information with others and yet others who write eBooks as a way to indulge in a writing passion that they have.

The point

Whatever the reasons may be the eBooks that are produced will usually be done in a fashion that best suits its purpose for creation

Those who choose to create eBooks for the purpose of establishing steady revenue earning platforms will definitely be more serious and conscientious about its content and design as compared to those who simply do so for the sheer pleasure of being able to share their views and knowledge.

The one that chooses to do so as an earning tool will focus more on getting the information that is the most relevant, recent and fact based. Being a tangible asset the eBooks are something that can be tapped for its profit churning capabilities at any given place and time.

The sale of such eBooks can be done individually whereby the author has to actively promote his or her eBooks to parties interested in purchasing them or the other option would be to sign on with an already established entity that specializes in churning out eBooks to others for a fee.

EBooks can also be designed to create an individual's presence within a specified platform. The individual would then be perceived as an authority on the subject matter being produced through the eBook, thus creating a need for the said individual to be needed for their contributions.

Creating eBooks is considered a big business entity for today's information hungry world. Almost anyone can create an eBook when armed with the adequate amount of corresponding information.

Decide on formats relative to how your eBook will be used

Deciding on the format most suitable for the types of various possible uses of the eBook is most important to ensuring its effectiveness. It is considered by those who are better informed as an essential point to consider when it comes to electronic publishing styles.

Formatting

The format eventually chosen after the relevant considerations have been made will determine the nature of the digital package in which it is distributed. There are many new formats that are available and many more new ones being developed. Currently there are tools available to facilitate the repackaging of existing formats into other acceptable or customs designed formats for alternative use.

This is of course very useful when the decision is made to commit to one style early on in the designing phase of the eBook exercise.

Considering the compatibility of the target audience in accessing and browsing through the content of the eBook is important. If the target audience intended is unable to access the information posted on the eBook through the chosen format then the eBook would not be worth anything to them besides of course the more obvious element of frustration they would experience when trying to access the said information.

Creating ways to ease the installation and use for the intended target audience is also another important point to consider. Here too if the installation process is lengthy and tedious the definite existence of the user unfriendly aspect of the design would be off putting and frustrating.

Therefore it is necessary to look into the installation requirements so that one that is easy can be tailored to fit the accessibility of the eBook.

The supporting tools that maybe required in order for the special features to be viewed without any interruptions must also be well chosen. There is nothing more annoying for the user than to have these interruptions marring the general experience of the eBook browsing.

Choose a relevant topic

As eBooks are predominantly designed for a specific target audience there should ideally be some thought put into the topic matter to be featured in it.

The content provided in the eBook should ideally reflect the information, solutions, problem encounters and other related material that would be useful to the reader focused that the particular subject.

Therefore choosing topic to write about should be done with some thought and care to ensure the choice made is interesting, attention grabbing and competitive in the eBook arena of current times.

Suggestions

The following are some suggestions of how to choose relevant topics:

Determining and understanding the reasons for writing the eBook should be clearly established even before the exercise to write begins. Questions such as is it being written for monetary gain, promotional reasons, expansion of knowledge, creating an online presence or any of the other motivating reasons should be addressed.

Conducting a thorough market research exercise to determine what is currently causing a "buzz" and the online keywords that are popularly used is also another way to determine a suitable choice topic to write on.

Considering a topic that has a personal connection to the individual is also something that can be explored as such material is often well received as others are able to relate to such personal style content.

"How to" eBooks are another popular option to choose to write on. However if one decides to do this kind of eBook the information contained in the book should be both of sound and substantiated material. A lot of research and thought needs to be put into this style of content.

Having a brainstorming session with colleagues, friends, family and basically anyone who is willing to listen or already connected to the eBook scene, to come up with topics is also a viable way to get ideas.

Put your eBook together

There are several software's available in the market today to assist in the exercise of eBook compiling. Some may seem complicated while others may seem too technical so the following points are designed to create an easy step by step guide for putting together a simple eBook presentation.

Put it together

Following the eBook compiler options the individual would have to assign a suitable title for the intended eBook listing and then enter the content about the page while setting the eBook's window parameters.

Using the eBook compiler files the next step would be to select the eBook folder and set up the order of the files and assign a startup page.

For security reasons the individual would be expected to set up the user password with a combination of serial numbers for the intended eBook posting.

The toolbar usage would require the eBook compiler toolbar icon to be keyed in. the individual would have to select the buttons, assign the captions for the chosen buttons and icons for the toolbar corresponding actions.

The eBook compiler bookmarks is where the individual would insert bookmarks or links that would be displayed at the navigational page of the eBook design content.

Generating the branding capabilities through the e-brander with the selection parameters can be done in the eBook compiler branding phase.

The compilation stage of the process requires the individual to create and save the eBook.

Using other time saving tips when compiling the eBook is also encouraged. Another eBook compiler tip that is rather useful in the pop up tool tips points.

This tool is accessed whenever the individual places the cursor over any area that requires some sort of action. The tool tip information will then appear informing the viewer of the next course of action that needs to be taken to proceed smoothly.

This is better that having to revert to the manual and wasting a substantial amount to precious time and energy.

Arrange the ads in your eBook

Though not widely accepted at the moment arranging ads for eBooks is fast gaining some level of popularity. The revenue earner is nowhere near phenomenal yet it would be something interesting and beneficial to consider.

Ads

The popular question that is currently hotly debated is whether or not eBooks should feature ads and if so how much should the authors receive in terms of revenue percentages.

Some eBook designers are now including platforms for advertising applications to facilitate revenue earning possibilities. Though it is still considered unfamiliar territory there are visible concerted efforts made to tap into this possibility for the future.

Attracting advertisers to the eBooks is an ongoing exercise but unlike other media there is some level of ambiguity when it comes to the accurate projection of sales derived from eBooks.

Some advertising can be comfortably applied to the particular device or brand author with a proven track record for sales to the digital versions made.

Then there is the possibility of garnering smaller advertising revenue projections which might be available to a target based audience for specific content. However meaningful projections of sales percentages which are to be based on corresponding advertising costs may prove to be rather difficult. There are also those that are quite against the idea of including ads in the eBook style of publications as it is currently perceived to be somewhat annoying and cumbersome.

Those who choose not to be interrupted by such ads basically download applications that stop such interruptions adequately thus defeating the overall intentions of advertising in the first place.

There is also the issue of interactive availability and color screen help when it comes to viewing the ad on an eBook. To date both these issues though being addressed by the relevant experts it has reached a level where the eBook user gets optimum quality visual effects.

Decide what extras to include in your eBook Package

Designing an eBook is no longer just that. There should be other beneficial element added to the general makeup of the eBook to make it more competitive. Exploring the various possibilities would be advantageous and definitely create the platform for more interest and revenue earnings.

The extras

The first and important step to take would be to ensure the material posted is done in a PDF format although HTML versions are also acceptable though not as accommodating. Apart from the revenue earning potential there is also the fact that eBooks present opportunities that ordinary printed information lacks.

Without restrictions in place such as using incompatible formats, the viewer should be able to access many platforms from the actual article posted.

From the viewers point of view, finding and accessing information should be made easy and quick therefore making the text "clickable" would be advantageous.

Being able to click on a particular chapter, title or any segment and then having it immediately pop up is something that would be time and energy saving thus be looked upon favorably.

Providing further extras such as facilitating a link on the eBook that opens a web page or even starts an email is also a good idea. With this facility the viewer can easily make other references from different sources and also access web links.

The email pop up can be used to get immediate feedback from the viewer which would help the host to address any shortcomings.

Making recommendations on other products, services or businesses can also be done in the eBook. When the viewer clicks through to the site where the new information is being posted the affiliate program can then bring in extra revenue to the host.

Market your eBook depending on its use

Having a great eBook but marketing it without any real direction will bring about less than desirable results. Knowing the eBook contents and matching it with the target audience that will find the content suitable for their needs is an important factor to look into if the desired success rate is to be achieved.

Marketing

Creating a market that is well served with the particular eBook is always a good idea and putting the relevant tools into practice to ensure this end will allow the eBook to be sold according to its particular niche market. Once this is established more viewers will be interested in making a firm purchase. Understanding that the eBook creator may not always be an authority on the current needs of the viewing public is a humble place to start.

Doing some research or arming one's self with supporting information before the niche market is approached for the purpose of getting the eBook well received should be done at the very onset of deciding the marketing strategy.

Conducting surveys, keeping abreast with current comments on blogs, reading material from popular forums or any other information that can shed light on the perceptions toward the content of the eBook in the market will assist the eBook owner to make better judgments on who would be best served by viewing the said eBook.

This would then enable the owner to focus the attention on this group to promote the book to. Understanding the customer is basically looking for real solutions when they source for eBook will also assist in being able to promote the eBook according to its use. The target audience should be able to connect with the material in the eBook if it is to achieve any level of success.

Launching your product

The following are some tips which should ensure a successful launch strategy:

Putting it together

Offering a pre-launch discount or even freebies to all those on the individual's emailing list would be a good way to start the attention grabbing campaign for the launch of the eBook. This action will also contribute to the loyalty status of those on the email list.

Making the launch more attractive by adding features that include bonus earning potential for committed buyers is also encouraged. Most people will be more inclined to make a commitment if there is something else to be gained besides the intended product itself.

Hiring outside help with the proper tools and knowledge on how to make a successful launch is something that should be considered especially if previous launches did not live up to expectations. Sometimes this is not only cost effective but also a less stressful option.

Making a good first impression is sometimes the only way to ensure a successful launch. It is therefore in the best interest of the eBook design to have an attention grabbing cover design. It may even be necessary to hire a professional who would have a better idea on what is sellable.

Keeping track of every aspect of a launch is also necessary and using good supportive tools that can ensure this would be an advantage. If the monitoring system chosen is adequate there is will less stress for the individual as everything would be visible and accessible at a moment's notice. If there are any problems detected within the launching process it can be addressed immediately and effectively.

Wrapping Up

There are a lot of things one can do to ensure the eBooks are well received. Some may take a little more time and effort than others but ultimately they all are designed to garner as much attention and revenue to the launch of the eBook.

Knocking Out Your Competition (USP Formula)

Have you been struggling to compete and stand out in your market? Are you fighting your way through a never-ending crowd of merchants, feeling as though you'll never be able to generate the exposure that your business needs in order to survive?

If so, chances are that the reason why you haven't been able to generate the kind of business you'd been hoping for is because you're not giving people a reason to buy from you!

In today's market, it's easy to slip into the huddle of new businesses that are cropping up within your market. In fact it's dangerously easy to end up being nothing more than a "me, too!" business owner where your voice is drowned out by the sound of every other similar business in your industry.

And in today's market, the ONLY way that you'll ever be able to build a business that stands on its own and is successful over the long-haul is by discarding the safety of the "me, too!' space and separating from the crowd.

And my friend, the only way to do this is with a USP.

...a what?

USP stands for Unique Selling Proposition (or Position) and it can literally make or break your business because it tells your target audience exactly why you are different, what you bring to the table and why they should choose you, over the competition.

Without a USP, your product slinks into the shadows, barely able to compete in the marketplace.

It doesn't stand out nor does it leave an everlasting impression in the minds of your prospects. In fact, without a USP it's virtually impossible to create a unique brand that will be instantly associated to value because you haven't defined what makes your business special. People will never recognize you as being any different from your competition.

The great news is that your business, or product already has a USP. It's simply your job to define what that is and implement it into your marketing message so that your target audience knows exactly what you are offering, how they will benefit and most importantly, why they should go to your company or business, rather than the competition.

So, where do you begin? How can you figure out what your U.S.P is and how to deliver your message to your audience of potential customers?

It all begins by evaluating your business, your products and your offers.

- How can what you offer improve someone's life?
- How can it help your customer in some way?
- Why do they need it?
- Why should they purchase from you rather than the competition?
- What are you offering that other people aren't?

Evaluating your product – your business and your offers objectively, from a third person perspective is incredibly important. It's the only real way to determine your strengths and your weaknesses so that you can improve your business, reach out to your global audience and give them a genuine reason to come to you. And when you do this, you will never struggle in the market again because your USP will be the leading force that drives in non-stop business for many years to come.

Knowing your customer base

Before you can create your USP for your business, you need to know your target audience – your customer base. What is most important to them? How can you truly connect to your target audience? What is their greatest challenge and how can you help them overcome it?

The more you know your audience, the easier it will be to develop a USP that hits home with them – that provokes a positive response and really shows your customer base that you know what they need.

When creating your USP, think from your customers perspective so that rather than identifying what YOU may feel is most important about your product, you turn it around - and focus on what THEY want to know and feel is most important to them.

Dan Kennedy's method for identifying a USP is in answering the question, "Why should I choose to do business with you versus your competitor?".

The very reason why you created a product in the first place could hold the key to defining your USP. Think about how your product is different than others on the marketplace, how does it add more value? How does it address a question, concern or simplify a process, such as reducing a learning curve, saving your customers time or money.

Your product USP is the driving force behind defining value and creating a recognizable brand in your market. There are businesses who have so carefully highlighted their USP that they are able to charge DOUBLE what their competitors charge, and still sell out every single time simply because their USP adds perceived value to their products or services!

One of the most well-known examples of an effective USP is Dominos Pizza. The business, struggling and close to filing Chapter 11 needed a quick turnaround. Hence, the USP, "Fresh, hot pizza delivered in 30 minutes or less or it's free" was coined.

Then there's Burger King who, competing against the McDonalds franchise giant had to stand out from the 'pre-made fast food service, and successfully did so by coining the USP, "Have it your way" where customers are able to customize their meals based on their preferences. They put customers in control, and the USP was successful at helping them stand out.

Other competitors in the pizza delivery business jumped on board, integrating powerful USP's into their marketing campaigns, including Papa John's restaurant whose USP promises "better ingredients, better pizza".

All of these businesses had existing competition yet became successful national franchises that are instantly recognized in their industry. They did this with the help of a powerful USP that made a clear promise and working to align your brand with delivering on that promise.

Your USP will differentiate you from your competition; more than any other aspect of a marketing campaign ever will, but you need to make sure your USP is not only memorable, but believable.

Using Federal Express as an example, their USP is "when it absolutely, positively has to be there overnight", emphasizing their guarantee of prompt delivery service. "Absolutely, positively" reinforces that promise, adding extra punch to their USP while ensuring they can follow through.

You want your USP to clearly define your brand, separate you from the competition and be believable.

In today's marketplace, your business will struggle to stand out from the crowd without a USP to give that extra boost it needs, so that it instantly offers an added incentive for prospects who are making the decision between purchasing your product or your competitors.

Take your time when developing your USP. Think of ways that you can add unique flare to your product, how you can use your USP to demonstrate value, to illustrate performance, and to showcase the distinctive benefits of your product.

Your USP should be described in a couple of sentences. You want to keep it short and to the point so that it lends "stickiness" to your campaigns and becomes quickly (and permanently) associated to your brand.

Once you have defined your USP, you want to include it in every single marketing campaign. From newsletters, ezine advertisements, social media marketing, forum marketing, PPC advertisements, to your website itself.

Creating a successful U.S.P

USP's are far more than just catchy taglines associated to your company, product or brand. They are reinforcement tools that help you establish credibility in your market while shaping the foundation of your business.

When it comes to creating a USP for your information product, think of the different ways that you can stand out from the competition, including:

Enhanced Training Tools, Additional Support Options, Extended Guarantee, Price Discounts, Better Service, Faster delivery/ turnaround time/completion, Additional Bonuses & Special Offers

All of these are common components of what forms a strong USP. Your objective is to evaluate your product, and come up with a powerful unique selling proposition that you can integrate into your marketing campaigns.

The easiest way to come up with a powerful USP is to think about how you would describe your product if asked by a complete stranger that you met at a seminar. You are given 10 minutes to describe your product in enough detail to sell a copy right on the spot.

What would you feel is most important to say about your business or offer within a 10-minute span of time?

This exercise will help get your creative juices flowing, while helping to verbalize the benefits of your product. Call a friend or family member if you have to, and let them ask you questions about your product.

Not only will this help you to evaluate your product objectively, but you can often gain better insight as to what questions and concerns potential customers may have based on the questions you are asked.

If you have an existing channel of communication with your customer base, either through social media sites, community forums or perhaps even through a newsletter, ask for their feedback.

Offer a handful of customers a free copy of your product and let THEM evaluate it, providing important feedback based on what they felt were the most positive aspects of your product, as well as what could possibly use a bit of improvement.

Many times, your customers are the best sources for developing your USP because they know your product better than even you do. After all, you created it for them and you can gain a lot of incredibly valuable information just by letting them try it out, and sharing their thoughts and ideas as to what the most powerful benefit of your product is.

Evaluating feedback from your customer base will also help you to develop a USP that carries a message that matches your market.

For example, if you develop an information product USP that defines your product as "Advanced Training for Beginners", you'll struggle to transfer positive branding if the majority of your market have virtually no experience and are looking for a product that teaches them the fundamentals of web design before considering advanced techniques. In other words, your USP message doesn't match your market.

So, survey your market, pay attention to feedback, and take a hands-on approach to closely monitoring the questions, concerns and problems that your market is facing. Then, develop a USP that speaks directly to the core of what they are most interested in.

When you have evaluated your product, its competition and have decided on a USP for your product, you need to lead your USP by example.

This means that you might have to make changes to the way you do business, or how you present your product on your sales page, within marketing campaigns and in branding your product.

If your USP is "10 Minute Training for $10k per month", you want to make sure that your product is designed to provide quick access to bite size information that your customer base can instantly apply to their online business.

Make sure your product and USP match up, in every way. If you offer extended support in your USP, or you define your brand by being 'unique or exclusive', you need to make sure that your product offers a new perspective, a unique approach or a different way of doing something.

Price based U.S.P

If your product fails to carry a USP, the only way people will differentiate your product from a competitors' is on price alone.

Think about this in regards to your own buying decisions. If you were to visit your local computer shop with the intention of purchasing an external hard drive, knowing little about brands or features, and were presented with two similar products to choose from, which would you buy?

In the absence of any other differentiating factor, the lowest price becomes the deciding factor.

You never want to compete on a price based USP, because it leaves you little control over your markets decision whether to purchase from you or a competitor.

Instead, you need to develop a Unique Selling Proposition that uniquely separates you from other products in the marketplace, and do so in such a way that it would be difficult for a competitor to replicate that.

Also keep in mind that your USP not only helps you stand apart but becomes part of your brand, so even if a competitor replicates your USP, if you've done your job at associating that unique selling proposition to your product, they'll struggle to compete.

Integrating your U.S.P

When you've decided on a USP for your product, you need to begin weaving into your marketing message.

This includes:

- Business Cards
- Your Sales Pages
- Squeeze Pages
- Print Advertising
- Social Media Advertising

Wherever you advertise or promote your business, your USP needs to become a permanent part of that marketing message. You want your customers to identify you by your USP, and to solidify your place in the market by leveraging your USP to build instant recognition.

Your USP is more than just a tagline; it represents your brand and your commitment to fulfilling on your promise. You want your USP to communicate a positive benefit, to leave an everlasting impression with your target audience, and to nurture positive association to every other product you create.

One thing to keep in mind is that your USP can and sometimes, should, change if your market does. Of the examples from earlier, Domino's Pizza and Federal Express no longer use the original USP that was designed to give their businesses that extra push in the market.

Eventually their competitors started incorporating similar USP's into their own marketing campaigns and before too long, their USP's became ineffective.

After all, a USP is designed to help your business or product stand out in the marketplace, but if everyone else is using a similar USP, it can actually hinder your chances at building a recognized and unique brand. So they changed it, and you just might have to as well.

Your USP can help turbo charge your marketing efforts, but always be open to changing your USP as the market demand shifts, or as new competition enters the arena.

Chapter 3

The Commission Business and Cashing in Big

Business by Commission - Boosting Affiliate Sales

You've joined the affiliate marketing industry, and you're excited about the opportunity to finally carve out a successful business online.

Perhaps you've already started making money in affiliate marketing, or you're a complete beginner - either way, it makes no difference because this chapter will show you exactly how you can maximize your income in this ever-growing arena.

Affiliate marketing is considered one of the easiest start-up businesses online, because rather than having to produce your own product you can start making money instantly - just by promoting other people's releases. However, in affiliate marketing, there's one key difference between struggling affiliates and super affiliates. That difference is the effort that they put into building profitable campaigns!

Super affiliates go the extra mile to provide exceptional value. They want their customers to be satisfied because after all, they are potentially lifetime customers.

Keep in mind that just because you are referring a customer to another merchant, rather than through your own product, they are still associating their purchase to you. You become the middleman, and once you've established trust within your audience, you'll be able to outsell any other affiliate marketer.

This chapter will give you the information you need to maximize sales quickly and easily. Whether you're brand new to affiliate marketing, or you've got some experience under your belt, these strategies will increase your overall profits.

Enhancing value = Increased profit

When potential customers consider purchasing products, one of the first things that they ask themselves is, "what is the value of this product?" For many, the answer lies in how the product directly improves their lives, or provides support or answers to their questions.

For others, especially seasoned buyers, they are constantly on the lookout for something else - Added Value.

Experienced buyers understand the dynamics of affiliate marketing, even if they are not involved in the industry themselves. They know that you are referring them to products because you earn a commission for doing so, and in return, they expect to be rewarded for purchasing from you, rather than another affiliate.

This is when bonus products that enhance value become so incredibly important. Bonus items can directly maximize your chances of making the sale, while building authority in your market as an affiliate that can be trusted.

You see, when you create bonus products that enhance the overall value of a product, you are giving your customers something more at absolutely no cost. You leave them very little reason not to purchase, while standing out from the crowd of affiliates who offer nothing more in return.

As to the types of bonus products you can offer, consider how they tie into the core product. You want your bonuses to add value, to serve as auxiliary components to the main product.

For example, if you were promoting a guide to blogging, you could offer a package of "ready-made" blog templates, blog content, or perhaps other tools and resources.

Just the same, your bonus could extend the training cycle, covering information not included in the main product.

For example, if you were selling a guide to work at home jobs, you could offer a bonus product that offered information on setting up a home office, or creating a winning resume. Your bonus could also offer similar material, but in another format.

Since people prefer to learn in many different ways, you could offer a variety of material types, such as reports/eBooks, video training, webinars, transcripts, or audio lessons based around the core product's topic.

Plan out your bonuses carefully, making sure that they represent clear and distinct value. You should always assign a value price to all of your bonus items. Getting Started Online, "How To" Modules, Website Basics, Social Networking and more.

Transforming content into cash

One of the easiest ways to siphon in customers and squeeze out more money from your affiliate campaigns is to become the leading "content authority" in your market.

This means that you have to over-deliver. You become second in command to the product developer, the original merchant, and position yourself, as an "authority affiliate" who people know will provide more value than anyone else will.

It's the winning formula to maximizing profit quickly, while actually having to do very little in exchange

One way of bundling in tons of extra value is to build your bonus around PLR (private label content). By doing this, you instantly eliminate two important factors:

1. You don't have to pay a fortune to outsource content to freelancers.
2. You don't have to spend any time creating content yourself.

Private label content also comes in many different forms, so you'll have greater access to tons of content that your customers want, such as:

Complete tutorial guides

People love full sized collections of tutorials and guides, and you can easily compile your own by bundling together a variety of PLR based reports, guides, and eBooks.

Done for you tools

If you can eliminate the learning curve and workload for your customers, you can easily make more money with every affiliate campaign.

Create a 'done for you' package around the product you are promoting, and include as many different tools and resources as possible, each one designed to save customers time.

Extended training

Even the greatest product on the market leaves room for improvement, and by compiling extra training tools out of private label content, you can extend the level of training to give customers a well-rounded system, designed to maximize their results.

One thing to be careful of is to only buy private label rights from authorized resellers and from quality developers. You can download as much private label content as you'll ever need at master-resale-rights.com including 500 full-length videos that you can repackage into 'auxiliary training tools' for your bonus!

Building your business from other people's work

So, you are about to make money promoting a product from another merchant. Why not leverage the value of every customer by thinking beyond the front-end commission?

You can maximize your income instantly by taking things a step further and focusing on building YOUR business while promoting other people's products. You do this by building a targeted mailing list of your own!

You probably already know the importance of having a mailing list in any business online. It will give you instant access to a built-in customer base, help you solidify your place in the market and build a recognized brand. But did you know that even as an affiliate marketer, you can start building your own list without a product of your own?

You now understand the importance of creating bonus products as part of your affiliate marketing campaign, but here's where things get interesting. Rather than just offer a bonus as part of their purchase, you can offer additional FREE bonuses in exchange for their subscription to your list.

Sounds simple? That's because it is. You build a squeeze page around every product and topic you plan to promote, and on the squeeze page you highlight the key benefits of joining your list, including the free bonus items that will become available instantly after each visitor subscribes to your list.

Just make sure that your bonus ties in directly with the product you are promoting, so that you can build an individual mailing list for every market. This will make it easier to segment later on, so you can effectively target your core customers.

Your bonus offers can be anything imaginable, provided it adds direct value with the main product, including:

- Audio/Video Guides
- Ebooks & Reports
- Software & Graphics
- PLR Products (offer resell rights to your customers and give THEM a bonus they can offer their customers as well!)
- eCourses
- Templates & Web Design elements

One critical part of the process is to "circulate" your bonus items. You don't want to offer the same item on your squeeze page for more than a few months before switching it up to offer something else.

That way, you don't have to worry about losing potential subscribers simply because they've seen the same bonus on another squeeze page.

Use private label as the foundation for all of your bonus products, and you'll be able to create new offers quickly and easily, every few months. Keeping your offers fresh!

Final tips

Packing value into your affiliate campaigns is easy, even if you've never done it before. It will help you stand out in the marketplace, and will maximize your affiliate income instantly, just by giving more to your customers than they will find anywhere else.

When you position yourself as a super affiliate who has genuine interest in offering your customers extended value, you will never struggle to motivate customers to purchase through you. They would be silly not to!

Part of your affiliate plan of action should include creating your own creative media and material, so that you aren't using the same banners and graphics as everyone else. Plus, by creating your own banners and material you can customize it around your website theme, color scheme and preferences.

Get super high quality sales page graphics from iSalesGraphics.com

You don't need any design experience or technical "know-how" to get started. You can simply create instant graphics using this powerful website. All that's left is for you to take action and apply these strategies to your affiliate campaigns.

Focus on building a full inventory of bonus items that you can implement into existing campaigns and new ones that highlight clear value and motivate your customer base into taking action.

If YOU take action, they will too!

Private Label Content Cash

Does this sound anything like you? You are surprised to discover that you have a massive collection of un-used private label content stored haphazardly throughout your computer's hard drive.

When you purchased it you were sure you'd earn your investment back quickly, because the PLR was advertised in such a way that it seemed like a great idea to use on your websites, in products and for creating content for your online marketing campaigns.

After all, private label content not only saves time, but because you don't need to hire-out someone to create custom content, you get to save a lot of money!

Then somewhere along the way, you simply forgot all about it, or you just haven't managed to monetize all of that private label content that you purchased.

Maybe you don't have a large collection of private label content now, but you've been seriously considering purchasing some of the newer releases available online.

Regardless if you're are new to private label buying or if you've already got more private label content than you know what to do with, this chapter will show you how to monetize private label content instantly, so that you're able to make more money from every PLR package you own or buy!

So without further delay, let me show you exactly how to get started!

The real value of PLR

I'm sure that I don't have to tell you that private label content is only as valuable as its quality. There are hundreds of PLR distributors online, some of which write their own content while others outsource cheap article content and package it up together in order to sell it with PLR rights.

When it comes to buying PLR, you truly get what you pay for. If you find yourself being attracted to the advertisements offering "thousands of PLR articles with unrestricted rights for $5.00", you'll want to reconsider your purchase.

Private label content should be written as if it were not intended to be PLR at all. In other words, if YOU wouldn't want to read it, and if you don't find the information valuable, helpful or comprehensive, your customers won't either.

Apart from the quality of the content and material itself, you also want to consider the different licenses that are attached to PLR releases.

For the most part, you will want to avoid "unrestricted rights" because it entitles all buyers to distribute the content in virtually any way they wish, including re-selling the content cheaper, or giving it away. This kind of license may provide extended freedom, but it will also be saturated throughout your niche. This sort of content will be de-valued in a matter of days, due to its saturation throughout your niche.

To protect your investment, consider purchasing PLR that comes with either limited options and licenses (sold to fewer people with clear restrictions in place) or extended PLR, where PLR rights are given only to the buyers (not passed onto their customers and so on).

That way, you can avoid buying PLR that will be passed on to thousands of people, making it easier to sell to your customers with personal, non-transferable rights - just like any other high quality product you release.

Many different private label developers online offer high quality content with limited rights.

You can explore one of the leading PLR communities at EnterpriseMembers.com where you can create a free account and gain access to brand new, all-inclusive private label packages. You can also explore premium PLR releases at Master-Resale-Rights.com

How to monetize PLR – Today!

When it comes to making money with private label rights, there are many different options available to you.

You could:

- Rebrand the content as your own and sell with personal rights.
- Use the content to build quality authority-type websites and blogs.
- Power up auto responder systems or create a newsletter for your niche.
- Offer smaller segments of content as free downloadable reports.
- Create incentive offers for squeeze and landing pages.
- You can also resell PLR content 'as is', or you could:
- Hire an affordable freelancer to "tweak" the content and make it your own.
- Compile multiple PLR products into one longer, full featured package.
- Create training packages - "how to" guides and courses that include a variety of training material derived from various PLR content sources (reports, worksheets, eBooks, etc).

How you monetize PLR will depend on your target audience, your niche, and your overall goals but one thing remains the same - you can start making money from PLR TODAY even if you've never done it before!

Quick start "prep"

Before you can monetize PLR, you need to complete a few simple steps that will not only help you make more money, but will drastically improve the quality of the PLR that you distribute under your brand.

Edit content

Even if the content is professional and well written, you will want to touch up the content in a few different ways including:

Inject your personal message

You want your customers to feel as though the content was written for them, so it's important that the information contained within the PLR release represents your personal message and voice. Touch up the content by adding in your own introduction, or add a "Note From: Your Name" at the beginning of each guide.

Inject your brand

If you are planning to use PLR to create information-style products for your business, it's important that each release carries a strong brand message. It's important to remain consistent with every product you release under your company and this may include font styling's, color schemes, layouts, templates and even chapter titles or headlines. Run through each PLR product quickly and make sure that it reflects your company and the impression you wish to make.

Inject your links

Regardless if you plan to monetize PLR content or use it in giveaways, incentive offers or lead-in free products that capture attention and push your marketing message out to your audience, it's important that you include direct links to your websites and blogs.

Every PLR product could be used as a lead generation tool or a traffic magnet, so take the time to add in relevant links that direct readers to other useful resources.

Inject your sign off

Consider creating your own 'sign off signature' and add it to all of the PLR products you intend to use, in both your product line and marketing campaigns. This may be as simple as your full name, a slogan, message of encouragement or a logo.

When editing content, you will also want to consider restructuring chapters and re-titling Table of Contents to make it your own. Since PLR is sold to multiple buyers, changing things up just a bit will help prevent refund requests from customer's identifying the material as PLR (or as being sold by other people).

Sometimes spending just a few minutes editing, tweaking, and improving the content and layout, can do wonders at adding incredible value to the PLR products you purchase, and in transforming each one into a product that you can call your own!

Instant monetization strategies

Once you have edited the content so that it better reflects your message and brand, the next step is to determine how you plan to use the content.

- Do you want to create your own PLR store?
- Do you want to upload PLR based products and sell them directly from your website?
- Do you want to use PLR products as incentive offers on lead capture pages?

Depending on how you plan to use or monetize PLR content – we will outline the next steps you need to take. To help you get started, here are a few ways that I instantly monetize every private label package I purchase:

Setting up a store

Creating a digital store that offers PLR content is exceptionally easy, especially with the power of Wordpress.

There are many different templates to choose from that will help you create a full featured storefront in a matter of a few minutes. You can use a series of powerful plugins to handle the delivery and order processing.

One of the easiest plugins that comes bundled with everything you need to set up a fully loaded e-commerce shop is found at getshopped.org

Get Shopped offers a full payment gateway while providing instant protection for all digital products, making it easy to set up a digital storefront in minutes.

If you already use a payment processor or product protection service such as e-junkie.com or DLGuard.com, you can easily integrate payment links into a blog-based eCommerce shop and let your preferred processor handle payments and delivery. If you aren't currently using a digital delivery system, you may want to take a look into digitaldeliveryapp.com , a fully loaded payment processing and delivery system that will automatically process orders, deliver digital files and even subscription based offers.

When looking for a commerce friendly template for your Wordpress storefront, I recommend choosing a 2-column theme that is clean and simple. You want potential customers to find the kind of products they are looking for quickly and easily, without having to fumble through a complicated navigation system, so keep your blog free of clutter, and limit ads to just 2 or 3.

You can browse through 20 of the best Wordpress eCommerce themes from webdesignledger.com/resources/20-best-wordpress-ecommerce-themes or run a quick search through Google for "WP eCommerce Themes". While you can pay for a premium theme, there really isn't a need to as there are hundreds of free templates and themes that will work just fine!

You will also want to give customers the option to search through your inventory for specific product types or by category. You can download free plugins that will enable on-site search from wordpress.org/extend/plugins/wp-e-commerce/ where you will also find hundreds of other free eCommerce plugins that will further enhance your storefront options and capabilities.

Just remember that every time you enable a plugin, you run the risk of slowing down page loads, so start with only the essential plugins needed to provide your customers with a positive shopping experience.

When creating a digital storefront based around PLR products, you will want to create categories for all of the different product types and formats that you are offering.

For example, if you have PLR reports, you would create a category called "PLR Report", or you could break it down even further and create categories and sub-categories around specific topics, markets, or niches. Just do all that you can to make it easy for customers to find exactly what they are looking for.

Keep in mind that the keywords you use within your category titles will also help your website rank within the major search engines!

Build an automatic sales machine

If you are interested in making fast cash with a "done for you" website, you will want to look into Automated Sales Websites that will do everything for you, including:

- Upload fresh content every month.
- Handle all orders and delivery.
- Generate professional sales pages instantly.

These are fully automated stores that not only create the sales system for you, but they will deliver the products to your customers every single month, leaving you free to focus on other aspects of your business!

One of the easiest, most powerful solutions available to you is found at MarketingEbooksClub.com where you'll be able to gain instant access to your very own sales site that includes:

- Customized website and sales page

- Instant products! (You will have your very own special reports to sell instantly!)
- Monthly updates - all set up on autopilot, leaving you nothing to do!

Plus, all of the products come automatically branded with your links, encouraging customers to return to the site time and time again!

Check it out at MarketingEbooksClub.com and set up your own PLR based store right now, without ever having to lift a finger. This is true automation!

Build a PLR powered membership site

You can monetize PLR very easily with a membership-site model. Here's how it works:

You build a simple subscription based website that offers customers access to content on a weekly or monthly basis (I always stick with monthly because from my experience they are easier to sell)

You repackage PLR content either into "personal use products" or if you are planning on reselling the PLR rights, you will want to decide on one type of package and stick to it.

Example: You could build a membership site that offers PLR to reports that come with squeeze pages, or to a business in a box package that includes everything from a sales page to an eBook. Just the same, you could start a PLR article website that offers direct access to 50 articles a month, with PLR rights.

Whatever you decide to offer is what you will need to stick with, as members will expect the same content type (and amount) every month.

Membership PLR sites usually go above and beyond by offering bonuses, extra content, freebies and incentives that keep members subscribed to the site. Since there are so many different avenues in which a customer can purchase PLR content, you want to give subscribers a clear reason as to why they should stick with you.

You can create strong benefits easily just by offering more - for less, or by hiring a freelance writer to create small packages of custom content that are only available to your members!

Your membership site may need a specific focus, depending on what you plan to offer. If you are offering PLR rights to content, you should decide whether you are covering a wide market (such as marketing or design), or a more specific niche market (weight loss, PLR, etc). One of the easiest ways to set up a powerful membership website is with www.MemberSpeed.com

I've been using MemberSpeed for years and have been absolutely satisfied with it, not to mention how happy my members are simply because it's not only easy to use but you can really customize your website around what is most important to your customers.

In addition, MemberSpeed can be easily enhanced with plugins giving you the opportunity to expand your membership offer, build up a strong back-end, monetize through many different channels and much, much more. It truly is one of the most powerful, feature-rich and SIMPLE membership systems online.

Selling PLR – No cost set up

If you can't afford to purchase membership scripts, download delivery clients or you just want to start off at the lowest cost possible, there are a few different ways to build a bare-bones website that sells PLR or PLR based products. For a Membership PLR site, if you can't afford DLG, then here's how you do it:

- Log into PayPal and click Merchant Services at the top.
- Click the Buy Now Button.
- Choose Subscriptions from the drop down menu.
- Give it an item name and customize your button - however, you want it to look.
- Enter the billing amount for each cycle, and choose what a "cycle" is

Skip the Track Inventory Feature and enter any checkout page specifics you want for your subscribers and then create your button!

PayPal will handle your subscriptions, but you'll be responsible for manually delivering via email the monthly deliverables to each PLR buyer – and make sure you do it with a BCC (Blind Carbon Copy) so that you're not showing every buyer's email address to the group.

If you don't have a website, consider using a Squidoo lens (Squidoo.com) or some other web 2.0 portal such as Blogger.com – although I caution you that with free sites, you don't own the page – and it can get deleted in the blink of an eye without warning, so only use it as long as you absolutely HAVE to.

You can set up your Squidoo lens with the introduction as your short sales copy, and then use Link Lists or whatever type of module (text, etc) that you want to showcase the different product categories that you offer.

Essential tools

Regardless how you plan to monetize PLR content, whether you choose to create a PLR based store or you are planning to simply create information products from existing PLR content, you will want to create a web presence all your own. To do this, you need a professional hosting account.

One of the most affordable options (and the easiest to use) is available at HostGator.com

I choose HostGator for a few reasons including the fact that they're affordable (one of the lower-cost hosting options online), reliable; have 24/7 customer support and they're VERY easy to use!

You can start out with a Hatchling Plan, but it only allows one site. It's $8.95/month. I like to use the Baby Plan for $9.95/month because it allows unlimited sites.

You will also need a domain name. One of the easiest ways to uncover great keyword-based domains is by using the free domain search tool available at InstantDomain.com

When you log into your Host Gator account, scroll to the domains area and click Add-On Domains. You will enter the domain name without the http://www part – just yourdomain.com and then hit your Tab button – it will automatically fill in the rest before you choose a password and click Add Domain.

Step 1: Register a domain name that represents your offer, the type of website you are creating and the kind or products available to customers (example: highqualityplr.com, weightlossplr.com etc)

Step 2: Secure a hosting account with HostGator.com (or another provider). Link your domains to your hosting account via name servers.

Step 3: Use "Fantastico" to automatically install Wordpress if you plan to use it as the foundation for your website or eCommerce store. Fantastico comes bundled with all HostGator hosting accounts and is a simple script that allows the instant installation of many different scripts including Wordpress.

Step 4: Set up your FTP Client to connect to your hosting account so that you can upload files, products and customize your website with templates, themes, or plugins.

Step 5: Integrate your product delivery and download system. You can use a service like E-junkie.com, DL Guard, or Paypal directly. If you plan to create a membership-based website, purchase a copy of MemberSpeed.com

Step 6: Upload your products into categories (if building a PLR based store) and use keyword-based titles to attract traffic from the major search engines. If you are planning to monetize PLR by reselling the product only, now is the time to touch up sales copy, integrate payment links and test out your sales system. Keep in mind that you can purchase PLR packages that come with pre-written sales pages and simply tighten them up! This will save you a ton of time and money.

Step 7: Make Money!
Tools & Resources
Rebranding Tools:

- ViralPDF.com

Membership Software:

- MemberSpeed.com

High Quality PLR Packages:

- Master-Resale-Rights.com

Exclusive Membership:

- EnterpriseMembers.com

Autoresponder Methodology

When it comes to making money in email marketing, there is one tool that is **essential to your success**. In fact, it's one of the **ONLY** tools that you need to start building targeted email lists in your niche market.

Of course, we're talking about autoresponders.

With an autoresponder, you're able to **automate the entire process** of building and monetizing your email lists. In addition, using this automation system, you can begin to build valuable relationships with your subscribers, enforcing a positive brand message with every email.

Without an autoresponder, you'll be stuck manually emailing a database of leads and as you can imagine, not only is that extremely time consuming but managing your list would be a complete nightmare!

You know yourself that the only way to truly maximize your income online, while minimizing your workload is in your ability to streamline your business and automate as many tasks as possible.

In order to do this, you need to be able to communicate with your audience on complete autopilot so that your time is free to spend on growing your business and your brand.

So, how can you begin to automate your list building while being able to maximize your list profits instantly? This special report outlines the key essentials to setting up a powerful autoresponder campaign that will drive in leads and affectively build a positive brand in your market.

In this Chapter we'll show you what autoresponder services are available, what your options are, and how to make the best decision based on your overall goals.

Why you need an autoresponder

If you're serious about your online business, you know that in order to be successful and develop a business based on long-term profitability, you need to free up your time and resources so they can be better spent expanding your business.

There are only so many hours in the day and in order to dominate your market and expand your sales system, your time should be spent creating new products, enhancing your websites with additional monetization channels, and on promoting your business.

So, that leaves a very important task unfinished.

Building your list and relationships with subscribers

This is why autoresponders are such an important part of your business. With an autoresponder, you can instantly greet new subscribers and begin the relationship-building phase, without having to spend any time doing it! Your autoresponder will take care of everything for you!

As you probably know, the top leaders and authorities in your market make their money because of ONE main component that helps them stand out and make more money than ever before.

They rely on the *relationships they've developed* to further their business and maximize their income. They've worked hard to build valuable relationships with their subscribers and customers and they've done this through the use of autoresponders. Without an autoresponder they simply would NEVER have the time to expand their business!

Imagine marketing to a group of 1,000 customers by emailing each one individually. It would take hours and hours just to touch base with your subscribers and at the end of the day, chances are only a small fraction of your direct emails would ever make it to their inbox!

Now, consider the advantage of using an autoresponder service that can contact your entire subscriber base within minutes – all with a click of the mouse (or set it up on COMPLETE auto pilot and it will automatically email your subscribers on predetermined times or dates!).

Not only will you be able to stay in constant communication with your subscribers, but you'll finally be able to take advantage of *"automation monetization",* by combining content based emails, which offer valuable free information, along with promotional based campaigns that trigger an avalanche of orders!

Securing your autoresponder marketing system

You should now understand the importance of an autoresponder when used as part of your marketing strategy. So, the next step is to choose your autoresponder service provider.

While there are many different options available to you in terms of the type of autoresponder you use, it's recommended that you choose a professional account that is hosted by a third party company.

Here's why:

Should you choose to host your own autoresponder software, you are opening yourself up to many potential problems, including:

Spam complaints

You will have to be on the look-out for spam complaints that come in both directly, and to your ISP. Since you're hosting your own autoresponder, if a subscriber feels that you are emailing them without consent, they may contact both your hosting provider and your Internet service provider leaving you at risk of losing your accounts.

Ensuring compliance

By hosting your autoresponder with a professional service you are guaranteed that your emails are compliant with the SPAM-CAN act of 2003.

Higher Delivery Rates

Professional autoresponder companies are experts at ensuring high delivery so that your emails make their way to your subscriber's inbox. If you host an autoresponder on your own, you may find that your delivery rates are very low, or that your emails wind up in peoples spam folders, where they do you no good.

Extended features

The majority of professional autoresponder providers offer a variety of important tools and resources that make it easy for you to tweak your campaigns and maximize open rates, and response rates (which equate to more money for you!).

Included with most professional autoresponder providers are tools such as the ability to split test, monitor performance, as well as the ability to segment and target different parts of your overall list. These are all important features in order to maximize your email marketing results.

There are many other reasons why a professional autoresponder service is the best choice for your email marketing, including:

Unlimited mailing lists

With a professional autoresponder provider, you'll be able to create an unlimited number of campaigns and mailing lists, giving you the opportunity to target specific segments of your market as well as venture into as many different niches as you wish!

Advanced segmenting

If you really want to maximize response rates, you'll want to segment your lists so that you're able to connect with specific subscriber groups. For example, if you were promoting a product geared towards beginners, you could target only those who have indicated that they are new to the business. You do this through "list segmenting", which utilizes demographics to categorize subscribers and break them down into specific, identifiable groups.

Siphon trust & credibility

Many of your potential subscribers may not feel comfortable joining a mailing list that is managed or handled by an unknown source. People don't want their sensitive or personal information shared or distributed beyond their consent and so by hosting your mailing list with a professional and well-known autoresponder provider, you won't have to worry about potential subscribers being concerned about how their information is stored. Another consideration is whether you should pay for an autoresponder service or take advantage of free account offers.

The upside to this is that you can start building your email lists instantly without any start-up costs involved, however the downside is that with the majority of free autoresponder offers, your messages will carry third-party ads that may hinder your ability to monetize your own campaigns.

In addition, you'll put yourself at risk of not being taken seriously as subscribers will see that you are using free services, rather than a professional autoresponder account. When it comes to making money online with email marketing, it's always wise to invest in your financial future by securing a professional autoresponder account.

So, which provider should you choose?

In the next segment, we'll take a look at the different options available to you so that you can choose the best fit for your business and budget.

Top autoresponder providers

Choosing an autoresponder provider is an important decision because once you've begun to build a mailing list, it's not always easy to transfer your contacts over to a new provider.

While the majority of professional autoresponder providers offer the option to "export" your database of leads and then "import" them into a new autoresponder account, all of your subscribers will have to re-confirm their desire to be on your mailing list and as you can imagine, for this reason alone it won't be easy to transfer everyone over.

So, with this in mind you'll want to spend some time evaluating the top autoresponder providers online so you can make the very best choice for your future in email marketing.

To get started, we will take a closer look at how autoresponder providers differ and what they have to offer.

Keep in mind that autoresponder pricing works on a tier based structure, where you pay based on the number of subscribers you have so as your list grows, you can expect your monthly charges to change.

Get Response, available at GetResponse.com was founded in 1998 and is a leader in autoresponder marketing. You can get in for free by taking advantage of their new account option, however for just $9.95 a month, you'll be able to grow a list of up to 250 contacts.

Aweber, available at aweber.com was also founded in 1998 and has a solid reputation within the email marketing arena as being a quality and reliable tool for marketers. With high delivery rates and extended features that include segmenting and split testing, you'll have access to all of the tools you need to maximize performance.

Constant Contact, available at ConstantContact.com offer a free trial for the first 60 days, giving you the opportunity to experience their service and guarantee of customer satisfaction with no upfront costs involved. You can then upgrade your account based on your subscriber units for as little as $15 a month.

iContact, available at iContact.com offers a wide range of features with a low monthly budget plan for beginner marketers with smaller lists. You can easily upgrade in the event your list grows quickly for as little as $9.95 a month.

Autoresponse Plus, available at AutoresponsePlus.com offers a full scale autoresponder script that you can host on your own services for a one-time payment of just $197.00. With this script you're able to install your own autoresponder portal, with additional features included such as social media integration and link tracking.

Moving forward

Your next step is to secure a professional autoresponder account of your own, so that you can begin to build and monetize your email lists.

Spend some time browsing through the feature overview lists on the top autoresponder provider websites and choose the provider that best suits your needs. Then, once you've secured your own autoresponder account, you'll be able to finally join the ranks of successful email marketers!

Social Media Marketing for Cash

In case you're wondering whether social media could be useful for your business, the verdict is yes: social media is a great way to drive repeat business and attract new customers. Whether or not you're just starting out, this guide will help you sort out what is needed to get the business moving, and if you implement the steps outlined here, you should be able to see a positive change within a short period of time.

Social media has changed the way people connect, discover, share information and conduct business- but you already know this so let's get to the good stuff. Here's what you need to know:

- Social media – this is the technology people use to connect, share ideas and experiences. Businesses tap into this infrastructure to connect with customers and grow their brands.
- Social networks – such as Twitter, Facebook, LinkedIn, etc.; these are the places where social interaction take place.
- Social media marketing – using this technology to build relationships that build awareness, customers trust and of course, repeat business.

Any of this make sense? It should, because social media is basically just word-of-mouth powered by technology. Over 75% of people are highly likely to share content they like online with their friends, family or coworkers; and 49% do this on a weekly basis.

Social media for your business

Both large and small businesses use social media to do the following:

- Promote the name of the brand and business
- Tell people about their products and services
- Find out what people think about their brand
- Attract new customers
- Build stronger relationships with existing customers

What are the advantages of social media to your business?

There are a myriad of advantages to using social media in business. These include:

- Broader reach—you're able to reach millions of people through a single popular social media platform.
- Localized, targeted marketing—it's essential to target your niche specifically in order for the message to have its intended effect; and social media facilitates this.
- Low-to-zero cost—majority of popular platforms are free to use, and the ones that cost money won't stretch your budget thin.
- Quick and simple setup—It only takes a short time to setup an account and post information- and anyone can do it.
- Personalized communication—social media allows businesses to send personalized messages to customers and help them with common problem such as implementation.

The setup

How do businesses use social media effectively? It all starts with goals. If you set your goals right and know from the start what you expect to achieve from your marketing efforts, it shouldn't be too difficult to organize and implement a winning strategy. These are some of the ways established brands use social media to expand their reach:

- Spreading the word–show your customers who you are, what you can do and more importantly, how your product or service can benefit the prospect.
- Drive sales–you can do this by offering existing customers special offers or starting a promotion. Just make sure they like it well enough to share it with their own social circles.
- Provide people great customer service–this is essential to any business but social media makes it much easier to engage with customers and find out what it is they need from you. Find out what they are saying about you and establish a good feedback loop.
- Keep them coming back–when you set in place an effective system and build strong relationships with your customers, they will always come back.

Key networks

Different types of social networks work for different marketing purposes. The key is to find a central position that takes into account as many platforms as possible, without saturating the message. Some of the main platforms include:

- Facebook – a website that allows you to have conversations with your customers and post photos, videos and news about new products and features.
- Twitter – a micro-blogging website that you can use to send and receive short messages as well as post photos.
- Youtube – the most popular video hosting website. This should be used when posting promotional

videos and the videos should be linked to other social media networks.
- Photo-sharing – these are websites that allow you to store, organize and share photo collections with customers. If you're not entirely familiar with social media and don't know how you could use it to grow your business, this chapter was written for you. The specifics may seem complicated at first but it's all worth learning more.

How to get started with social media

When using social media to grow a business, the worst action is no action, and the worst problem is invisibility- not bad perception. If you're part of the conversation you can always massage what people are saying about your brand; but if nobody knows about you, then you have no chance of growth. What this means is that you need to get involved: not only to exploit the many business opportunities available for your business, but also to develop a winning reputation.

It's a good idea to start by developing a plan that takes into account the social trends that characterize social media interaction today and organize a framework that will help make your conversations popular and relevant. But with all this mass of social networking sites and tools available today, how does one navigate through it all to set up a strategy that works?

Here are ten steps to get you started:

Setup goals

Think about what you hope to achieve from the social interaction. Are you doing it to generate direct sales, offer better customer service, or better yet, develop stronger relationships with your clients? Your answers to these questions will determine how you go about setting goals.

Consider your resources

It's going to take more than a clever idea to set up a marketing plan that works: you need people working for you. Someone has to set up the social media accounts, engage with customers and respond to questions, create compelling content, etc.

Know your audience well

Find out where your audience spends time, what conversations they are involved with, who influences them, and what kind of information they're looking for from you. In order to provide your audience what they want, you first have to understand who they are, how they think, and what they want from you.

Come up with good content

Once you find out what your audience is into, you can then work on giving them something to talk about and possibly share. Conversations have to keep going and this means creating lots of good content for the audience. Try to create a variety of different types of content that can be shared.

Consider quality

While the pressure of creating content is certainly understandable, you cannot resolve to create a bunch of pointless topics for the sake of interaction; people will get tire of it. The goal here is to build actual customers, and that won't happen if you're not offering useful information and products/services.

It's tempting to promote your products every two minutes on every social platform available to you but you may need to do something not self-promotional so that you don't come off overly self-absorbed or too salesy.

Find time every day to look up what's going on in social circles and engage with your customers to find out what the general vibe is about your brand.

Learn the culture of social networks. What are your competitors doing and what does that teach you? Learn more about social trends and find out where companies or brands have gone wrong with marketing strategies so that you don't make similar mistakes.

Acquire brand ambassadors by observing the most active people in the social networks and encourage them to sell your brand. So which social platforms should I concentrate on? Most large brands operate dozens of social media accounts but they have more people working on that so you might not be able to start big. Besides, you want to learn how to use each website perfectly to get your message across and this might take more time if you embarked on creating 20 social media accounts at once. Focus your attention where it matters and learn everything about those websites and how larger businesses use them to promote their own brands.

Facebook

When it comes to this, the numbers don't lie; you want the websites with the highest number of active users in order to get a broader reach. Facebook alone will get you access to a social network with over a billion users worldwide. If Facebook were a country somewhere off the coast of California, it would be the third largest in the world in terms of population. Features such as Like, Timeline, Newsfeed, Apps, Cover Photo, and Mobile Upload; these will be useful as you gradually build a connection with your prospects, so learn the lingo and get to work.

Twitter

You get up to 140 characters when sending out messages to your subscribers and you can include links, videos and photos as well. Adding images and videos expands the message because the words are somewhat limited and you need to communicate more effectively than 140 characters can articulate.

If you have an existing Twitter account for your brand but have let it drop off lately, you might want to take a fresh look at what Twitter's offering. Features such as real-time marketing and multi-screen usage will be useful to your marketing efforts. In the world of micro-blogging, Twitter stands as the most powerful tool you can use for business. Other popular micro-blogging sites include Plurk, FriendFeed and Tumblr.

Present your brand

Your social media accounts form the foundation of your marketing efforts. They give you the chance to tell the world about your business and so they need to be well defined. Create a web presence people find appealing and distinct; that way people recognize your brand across multiple platforms.

In order to present the brand more confidently, you have to fill up and complete the profile, and make sure people know your bio, the actual location of the business and the address to the official company website. When creating a social network for your business, start with these people:

- Customers
- Business partners, suppliers and contractors
- Relevant trade organizations for your industry
- Local businesses in your neighborhood

Work up a time schedule for social media

You could end up spending hours each day trying to keep up top speed with what's going on online so if you want to manage your time better, create a time management structure to keep your time online useful and strategic. One way to do this is to find out what time your customers start responding to your feeds, and take a couple of hours to engage.

A social media marketing plan for your business

Effective social media strategies require proper planning and execution. If you're new to this and expect to see results from a few blog posts and random updates, you might find the whole endeavor very disappointing. Serious marketers know that in order to harness the full potential of social media one has to incorporate at least these three elements:

- Listening to the audience
- Sharing relevant messages
- Enabling the audience to share the message

So what is it that you're supposed to share? Good content. You can't have effective social media marketing without good content. The entire marketing plan originates from a solid content creation strategy. The good thing about useful content is that it gets people to appreciate your brand and share; and the sharing is what builds your brand.

This works whether you're a small business or a large multinational and it costs very little to set up so the budget shouldn't be a major factor when setting up. Ever heard that saying that goes "failing to plan is planning to fail?" It's very true when it comes to marketing because creating a well-detailed social media strategy is just as crucial as having a rock-solid business plan.

In order to attract, engage and ideally convert fans and followers into customers, employ this strategy.

What should I aim to achieve from social media?

This depends entirely on what type of business you're in. you may want to use it to gain exposure for your brand or simply to interact with customers because it's good for business. Remember, if you're just winging it your audience will know and that's not good for you. Try to understand your customers' goals and find out how to connect with that. One way to do this is to find out how you can use social media to solve your customers' problems.

Who should set up the company's social media account?

For smaller companies it would be better to delegate the task to a staff member who has experience implementing effective social media campaigns. Larger companies give the job to qualified workers in the marketing department and if the budget allows, some may choose to hire a consultant or firm.

Should I create accounts on all social media platforms when starting out?

As a starting point, it would probably be better to operate with a presence on one or two social networks and a blog. The network you choose will be determined by where your audience hangs out; so survey your customers and find out what their most popular platform is. The more the business grows the more social networks you can get into.

What's the best social network for a small business?

Whether you're operating a large or small business, you can never go wrong with a Twitter account. The platform is easy to learn and it gives your business a voice in the micro-blogging world. Another crucial network to be on is Google+- if only to boost your site's search engine rankings. If however, you have a B2B firm, social networks such as Slideshare and LinkedIn would be great places to reach influencers, and you wouldn't go wrong with Facebook and Pinterest.

What's the right frequency to post updates?

Two-five posts each day should be enough. Remember your followers visit social media websites at different times, and a single post each day couldn't possibly be enough simply due to differences in timing. To reach more people, stagger the posts consistently throughout the day.

What type of content should I post?

Again, the purpose of your marketing campaign will determine what you post. But also, the platform you're using matters to a certain extent. For instance, Pinterest and Instagram are inherently visual, so striking, memorable images detailing your products and services would be ideal if you're operating such accounts.

Company events and a few behind-the-scenes photos are great for connecting with audiences on these networks. But you may also post text updates on Facebook and have them trend well, especially if you're posing a question or giving out relevant information. When using Twitter, try to keep a balance between tweets and re-tweets. Curate a diverse mix of content (photos, links, tips, short videos, thoughtful questions, etc.) across different platforms in order to keep things fresh and interesting.

Is social media a good platform to provide customer service?

Social media has over time become one of the most popular platforms for businesses to interact with potential and existing customers. You can use all the popular platforms to respond to customer questions and complaints, order status enquires, etc.

How exactly does one convert followers into customers?

There aren't any surefire tactics to get fan's dollars, however some tricks seem to work better than others. For example, Facebook ads are a simple, affordable way to expand your fan base, boost engagement and collect sales leads. It's entirely up to you to convert those leads. One of the best ways to go about converting leads is to implement a cross-platform contest that integrates all the popular platforms and perhaps offer sweepstakes that resonate well with the audience and draws in potential customers.

For instance, in order to drive consumers to your online store, you could send a simple tweet that describes an ongoing contest on your Facebook account, and drop a link to the rules of the contest and the entry form on your online store.

How do people go about measuring the success of their marketing efforts?

It's very important to make sure you always track your marketing metrics so as to establish which tactics are working and which aren't. Some platforms come with their own metrics; Facebook for instance gives you administrator access where you can check out page insights data and use the data to evaluate what's working and plan your future posts.

LinkedIn offers similar analytics which are essential for business pages. Google analytics can be used to measure the effectiveness of social media campaigns and see how your strategy's driving your traffic to your online store.

Biggest mistake to avoid

You can't afford not to have a social media plan, so create one and stick to it. Remember social media is constantly evolving and in order to stay ahead you have to be prepared to adapt and redefine your strategy as needed. If you do this every few months you will identify which tactics are redundant and in the process work out the best plan for your business.

Most organizations begin their social efforts by listening and engaging with their customers across different platforms but at some point they have to look at the staffing required to carry out an effective campaign and ask what it is they're really getting from social interaction. In order to maintain a social business strategy that binds desperate efforts together to create a long-term plan that keeps the business growing, significant time and resources have to be set aside.

How to build brand awareness using social media

So you've already built a pretty impressive social media engagement campaign for your business; but how do you know you're doing it successfully? Keep in mind the number of followers you have doesn't always determine the effectiveness of the campaign- it's about how many people in your circles who actively respond. There's a wide range of responses you could get from social media aside from the usual customer questions and complaints. Aside from the comments, blogs, dialogue and re-tweets, look into this:

- Humanize the brand
- Manage perceived reputation
- Generate leads
- Create a few brand advocates
- Resolve problems with customers
- Handle crises effectively

It doesn't matter where the conversation is at:
Whether you're on Facebook, Twitter or your blog, there are a number of ways you can generate good conversations. These conversations will solidify your relationships and fans will experience a more direct connection with your business, which is what your aim is.

Engagement for creating awareness

One common purpose of social media is to create a public profile. Consider Canadian Olympian Sarah Wells; she started a campaign on Twitter where she hoped to engage Olympic fans and raise awareness of her quest for the gold, and possibly gain a significant number of followers. Just days into the campaign, Sarah had hit the 400 follower mark owing to the strength and enthusiasm of her friends and family. It's one example of an effective grassroots social media campaign.

The benefits of creating brand awareness

One of the many benefits include measurability. Consider these key awareness metrics:

- Share of conversation–this is about how often you get mentioned in context of the conversations that are relevant to you.
- Share of voice–how often are you covered or mentioned in comparison to your competition?
- Mention sper time period–this describes how many times audiences discuss your brand in a given time period. It gives you a sense of overall chatter and awareness.
- Potential reach–followers, fans or eyeballs; this is seen as potential reach because those people won't pay attention to you simultaneously.
- In bound links–an indicator of audiences that are aware of you and are talking about you. To get a better sense of which types of media drive consistent attention to your brand, look at all the active social media accounts.

Offer people choices

Perhaps Twitter does not reflect your communication style and you prefer Facebook instead. Learn how your audiences like to communicate and give them different choices by creating more than one social media platform for dialogue. Ensure that you post the same information-perhaps in different contexts- across all platforms in order to get a response. Tools such as Hootsuite will save you a lot of time when you want to manage and schedule posts across all platforms.

Whatever channel you like most, remember to give the audiences a 360° look at your company and brand. Use a communication style that's consistent with the brand so as to avoid confusion. You will be able to build those strong meaningful relationships with your audience if you learn how to initiate smart dialogue across all platforms.

Generally speaking, people enjoy being part of a business or brand that is actively building an engaging community and multiple studies have revealed that customers prefer to purchase from businesses that have active social media pages. That emotional connection with prospects is what builds a positive business reputation.

Recognize community strength as a powerful force for a brand and employ all the features of social media in creating a massive community of happy and loyal customers.

Lessons in brand awareness

Branding tactics keep changing and marketers have had to learn an entirely new playbook- a playbook that keeps evolving with new social platforms and technologies to make it all work. Learn what you can from larger brands that have successfully implemented their social media campaigns and established themselves as trendsetters. Each one of those large companies dominating social media today started small. YouTube was started by two friends in a small room above a pizza place and M&S begun as a market stall so don't let the competitiveness wear you out; little can still get pretty big.

Lesson 1: Think like a publisher

Innocent founder Richard Reed adopted the publisher model of marketing by publishing multiple recipe books as a way to expand their growth. It has had a tremendous impact on the company's overall reach and also, it changed the general perception about the company- people don't see Innocent as a brand trying to sell products for cash; they're seen as a healthy company that encourages people to live healthier lives.

They also have a blog on which they post content that helps people make decisions that impact their lives positively, and this enables the company to engage with large audiences. In addition, 10% of Innocent's profits go to charity, so the blog is also used to show how they are making a difference the world over.

Lesson 2: Find your tone of voice

When you find a tone that works for your audience, stick to it and maintain it when creating content for all your platforms. You are marketing to people; not robots, so start by creating buyer personas and learning what their goals are and what types of challenges they face. It will help you get a better understanding of who your audience is and that way you can adjust your tone of voice to one that they can relate to.

Lesson 3: Make your content shareable

When you create valuable and engaging content it makes you a great resource to your audience. Give your prospects what they need and it will help create an organic audience who engages with your company and follows you across multiple platforms. Always consider how shareable your content is. Just ask yourself whether or not you would find it engaging enough if you were the audience, and whether you would consider sharing it with your own circles. If the answer is no, then you need to go back to the drawing board and figure out where you went wrong.

Lesson 4: Create headlines that attract people

When you're trying to come up with something that will get you maximum exposure, you have to nail the headline. Most successful brands come up with dozens of possible headlines for each piece of content then settle on the one they believe would get the best response. If you can come up with something that grabs people's attention, it will expand your brand's reach and make your content that much more popular.

Lesson 5: Never be boring

This goes without saying but you'll be surprised how many brands keep posting the same dull material on social channels. In order to ensure that your customers don't opt out of your social networks, you will have to come up with content that's not just interesting and shareable but remarkable. The only way this could happen is by making sure you don't create the same content as everyone else in the industry. Make the brand stand out in a way that makes it unique and original.

Want to show off the personality of your brand, do something quirky and experiment with info-graphics, videos and other visual content and see what you come up with. Keep in mind that 90% of all information transmitted to the brain is in fact visual, and the brain processes visuals 60,000 times faster than plain text.

Lesson 6: If possible, hire journalists

Whether they're working in-house or for a large traditional media outlet, journalists have the same job; figuring out how to come up with the next interesting story that will make people want to read about. The best journalists asks questions and challenge common assumptions, and not just in terms of what business your company is into, but also other people in the same industry. That's how great content comes about and people can't help but share it.

How to get more engagement from your followers

As we mentioned previously, follower count is worthless in and of itself and if you believe that follower count is a badge of honor or some sort of powerful status symbol, then you've got the whole thing wrong.

But that being said, getting more followers is good for you and here's a good reason why:

The more followers you get, the more engagement you have. It's an obvious benefit to have a large number of people following you because then there's the likelihood that someone will see one or two things they like and share it. It's a math game: if more people see the content, more people will interact and share it. This means more likes, more re-tweets and comments, etc.

Such growth can provide you with excellent feedback for future discussions. If for instance one particular subject of discussion happens to get more interaction, then it could inspire you to create more content around the subject in order to keep the conversation going. On the other hand, if a customer asks a question about your brand, it could inspire you to write a new blog post.

People absolutely love to share content they find interesting and engaging. Want your brand name to be recognized the world over? It won't matter if your initial plan was to simply generate more sales for your business; social media opens up a bigger aspect of business success: brand recognition. When you set up a good campaign, you will have the opportunity to not only increase sales, but also create brand awareness and a strong sense of loyalty from customers. Let's look at ways you can increase engagement across the two most important social platforms for your business.

Twitter offers you a great platform for engagement but how much do you really know about Twitter?

Let's look at a few statistics you could find useful to your campaign:

- Engagement for brands is higher by17% on weekends. Clearly not many people realize this, which is why only 19% of brands actually send out tweets over the weekends. Are you trying to get your audience to engage more but don't feel like working over the weekend? You could use Buffer to schedule the tweets and have them sent out while you stay cozy at home.
- Tweets with images and links get twice the engagement so work on creating photo stories that will get people talking.

- Keep your tweets relatively short. Statistics show that tweets with more than 100 characters spark fewer conversations, so work within that 100-character limit. If you've got links in the posts, it shouldn't go over 120 characters.
- The fastest-growing demographic on Twitter is 55-64 years old. If your brand accommodates the senior crowd, then it would help to reach out to the new users who are more than willing to try out new discussions and check out brands.
- Hashtags inspire more engagement. But that being said, keep the engagement at a minimum: 1 or 2 hashtags will increase engagement by up to 21% but too many hashtags will kill the conversation before it starts.
- Target mobile users. Mobile users make up 6.66% of user-generated tweets that mention specific brands so it would be a good idea to link out to usernames of people you mention on Twitter and add in a hashtag.
- Mobile Twitter user's are 181% more likely to login during their commute. When sending out content, think about where most of your audience could be at that time. If it's morning on a workday, then they might be commuting to the office, and it's a good time to start engaging with them; that way you can have their attention for the rest of the day. Find something interesting to occupy them in their morning commutes and they will make it a habit to check out your posts each morning.
- You want more engagement? Ask people to re-tweet. You may have heard that the best way to

get your content re-tweeted is to ask for it: well statistics show that spelling out the word "re-tweet" actually increases the chances of it happening by 23 times, as opposed to abbreviating with "RT".
- Include more links in your tweets. Just like images, links are more likely to cause an effect; however, unlike images, which directly boost engagement, links tend to increase the number of re- tweets.
- Now let's look at Facebook and what makes a good engagement campaign in that platform. There are a few effective strategies you could implement in order to get your followers talking.
- Create open loops on some of your posts. An open loop is where you give a hint to what's in a new post. It's actually quite simple; let's say for example you want to post an article about "Why All Business Should Use Social Media", you could just put in something like "Great post, useful guidelines", or something similar, but it wouldn't get that much attention. But if you said something like "The second point is insane! I need to implement it right now", or something similar, you would get a better response because people will want to know what the excitement is about.
- Mix up the content a little bit. If people have gotten used to you publishing blog posts every day, it's going to get boring pretty fast, so every once in a while get them off guard and publish video series, images, podcasts, slide-show presentations, etc.
- Use older content that new audiences might have not seen yet. If you have some good material from a

while back and you've accrued a significant number of new people on Facebook, consider posting one or two good stories at least once in a while. Because a larger part of your audience is new, this will add value. And for the rest of audience who might have seen the post the first time but forgot about it, this would be a great way to spark new discussions.

- Check out Facebook insights to find out which posts your followers liked the most and if you find that people respond more to a specific type of post, then you want to work on perfecting that format and find more related topics to discuss.

- Add more apps to your page. There are a variety of apps available for you depending on what industry you're in and how you want to engage with your audience so head over to the apps section, shop around and find an app that makes sense for the followers.

- Upload videos to your Facebook page and stop copying and pasting YouTube video URLs. There's nothing particularly wrong about pasting video links to other sites on YouTube, but statistics have shown that these types of videos get significantly less engagement than when users upload the videos directly. When you upload videos alongside cool posts, it allows people to interact without having to leave the page. It's a little trick which requires more effort but it can get you more engagement in the long run.

That's where you need to start if you want to get more engagement on Facebook and Twitter. Hopefully this gives you some perspective on how audiences operate on other social networks. Companies have been investing more money in paid content distribution on Facebook and that's certainly a viable option for when you want more targeted ad campaigns and great content, but if that's not part of your strategy, you can still achieve solid engagement with these strategies.

How to get more fans to your Facebook page

Has your Facebook page growth been stalled? Now might be a good time to start evaluating your Facebook strategy, see what's working and what isn't, and cut out whatever's stalling growth. Let's start with the basics: a lot of people get impressive engagement on their personal Facebook profiles and while that's a good get in itself, it's still important to set up a business page.

If you're creating a products, offering a programs or services, your business page will allow you to create an image that will allow you to become an authority on the subject and once you get to that place, you can then discuss your business freely. It should be your goal to become that go-to authority in your niche and that's why you need to have a business page.

Set up a marketing plan to get you more fans

Start with these three phases when putting together the plan:

- Attraction-this means finding different ways to grow your fan base depending on what they're in too. Learn as much as you can about your audience and create a persona of your typical fan. That way

you know how to center the campaign around them.
- Promotion—come up with strategic posts and keep them short and to-the-point.
- Sales—one of the best ways to get audience feedback for when you want to sell products and services is to ask questions. You'll find out what your audience wants and develop something they will spend money on.

Now in the next step you can use the following tips to really grow your fan base.

Connect with fellow page managers

So let's say you run a small ice cream store and have already set up a Facebook page with a decent following: try to make a live connection with the pizza parlor across the street if they attract the same clientele. Talk to the owner and invite them to do a little cross promotion on Facebook, where you can share posts with your audiences and forge stronger connections.

Share content

This works across all social platforms because when people see and share your content, it has a direct impact on your sales. Have you considered taking original photos and using them as part of your content on Facebook? It could be a simple behind-the-scenes picture at your workplace, a thought provoking image or an inspirational picture: whatever you decide to post should serve to get people sharing. Just make sure to follow copyright laws when downloading pictures online.

Tag your Facebook page on your personal profile

The goal here is to make sure your prospects can access your page easily. Pages aren't getting too much attention these days so you need to come out and make sure to tag your business page so that people can like it right from your update.

Link the page to your profile

It's a simple thing to do but a lot of businesses get it wrong. If users can search and find your personal Facebook page, then you want to make it so that your business page is just as easily accessible.

Include Facebook in your email signature

Do you send out emails every day? This is not a complicated trick: just a reminder to include a link to your Facebook page in your email signature. Use a mail program that allows you to customize your email signature and put in clickable icons.

Comment on different pages

This is yet another great way to get more people to notice you on Facebook. Find out which other pages your audience could be having conversations and get involved. Like complementary Facebook pages as your own, and then keep an eye on your home page feed and respond to the posts.

Run contests

Lots of businesses do this just to get more likes on their page. It will cost you to run a contest but hopefully you've set aside a marketing budget for this campaign. All the contests have to be run through Facebook aps but they don't cost too much and they're relatively easy to set up.

Set up a QR code for your business card and use the link for your Facebook page

Websites such as QRStuff and QR Code offer the codes for free so set up the codes on any of your business cards so that people can find you.

Use a sponsored like story to generate more fans on Facebook

There are many ways to advertise on Facebook these days and one popular option is the sponsored like story which advertises your page to your fans' social networks, basically notifying their own friends about your page and showcasing that the user's friend already likes your page.

Include a like box on your site

If your website gets a good amount of traffic, you should be able to get a fair number of likes on your page. Track where the likes are coming from and find ways to win more fans from those avenues.

Use blog feeds

Apps such as RSS Graffiti and NetworkedBlogs can be used to import posts from your blog and right into your Facebook page. Make sure the posts are useful to your audience and keep it engaging so as to enhance interaction.

By now you've probably heard that offering your Facebook fans something extra can be an effective way to grow the number of fans you have. It's simple, you come up with an offer you know people will love, spend time promoting it through all your social channels, and in the process, get more people coming in on your official Facebook page.

For many businesses, special offers are a regular component of their marketing strategy. Things like special discounts, coupons and giveaways are used to attract new customers and reward the most loyal. But sometimes creating this type of campaign is not as effective as one would hope, and prospects remain unmoved.

In such cases, a downloadable content campaign would be a great solution. If for instance you run a restaurant, you could offer your followers a recipe for the upcoming season. Likewise if you're a marketing consultant you could offer a white paper with helpful tips for prospects and clients to enhance their marketing efforts. It is a way to showcase your expertise and also build familiarity and trust, which will be crucial to your own growth.

Examples of businesses using social media successfully

Are you experiencing the success you thought you'd have with social media? Or could it be that your business has seen little-to-no growth even after rolling out a bunch of campaigns to get the brand noticed? If you've had some bad luck with social media, then you're certainly not alone because many companies, both large and small, experience some sort difficulty achieving their marketing goals at some point, but what sets some of them aside is the fact that they learn fast, and adapt.

Look at some of the tactics used by companies that employ effective social media strategies: don't focus too much on their target audience, because that's hardly relevant. These tactics will work on just about any audience if done right.

Martell home builders

This is an Atlantic Canadian custom home building company which in the past relied on realtors to keep the business afloat. This however changed once they decided to embrace social media and they finally developed an effective direct-to-consumer strategy which kicked out the middleman and allowed them to bring in the business.

This all started with the creation of a blogging strategy that mainly focused on giving homeowners and would-be homeowner's valuable tips about home ownerships and they were able to capture the attention of countless homebuyers. Posts such as "Home Staging Tips and Techniques" were particularly useful to their audience and today, the company gets 86% of their total leads from consumers.

An important point here to note is that multiple studies have revealed that people respond more to blog subscription via email as opposed to RSS feed. Martel clearly understands this as seen on their call to action which reads "Get the blog sent to your inbox." It's a smart way to get new leads while making sure to maintain value by giving out new blog updates.

Another feature the company executes well is customer service, especially where they take advantage of modern geo-location technology by mounting trackers on contractors' vehicles, so that customers know exactly where the contractor is when on the job. It eases the customers' minds and makes it look like the company understands their customers perfectly.

With such innovative technology and profound understanding of their customers, Martell has been able to grow their brand beyond what anyone could've expected, and they have made the homebuilding experience a social thing. They also have photo galleries showing clients' homes under construction which allows people to monitor closely the progress as the house comes to be. It's one of the most shareable contents on their website because clients get to share the images in their own social circles, with friends and family.

Another feature Martell uses for social integration is the Facebook like box; which is updated dynamically every time a user visits their page on Facebook. It's a nifty little widget which shows how many people liked your Facebook page and also displays faces of some of your fans. One advantage to using this feature is the fact that people can join your fan group without having to leave your website. It compels visitors to stay longer on your website and that in itself increases your fan base significantly.

Tip: When creating your own strategy, try to think outside the box like Martell did by giving their clients access to unique photos showing the construction of their homes and allowing them to track their contractors' whereabouts.

Zappos

This is a popular online retailer that focuses on clothing, shoes and accessories. Zappos is known mainly for the great emphasis they put on building strong relationships with their clients. The company's Facebook tab reads: "Let's be in a Like-Like relationship." It's one of the ways they show real commitment to their fans and this helps solidify trust with their customers.

The company's attraction process involves those asking people to Like them and then join their email list. When a visitor clicks the like button, they bring up a sign-up page where people can join the community and get access to products. Because they wait until a visitor joins the community, it gives people a sense of value and it shows they actually care about getting to know their fans and building relationships.

Zappos also uses another interesting strategy where they reveal certain content to fans only. It's actually called "fans-only content" and it encourages people to join in so they can access things like cool fashion images, videos and insider tips. The process is as simple as clicking the like button and the company gets new people coming in every hour, joining the special community to be a part of a fashionable and well-informed group.

Zappos has a custom welcome tab which features comment widgets, where fans can talk about products, and the posts appear on their own pages or profiles telling their friends about Zappos products and what they like most about the company. It is a great strategy for social proof.

As far as engagement strategies go, Zappos doesn't hold back with their "Fan of the week" contest where they have fans send in their pictures with the Zappos box, and other fans get to vote for the picture they like most. The winner gets their photo posted on their wall image where everybody can see. No doubt the company puts their fans first.

Tip: Find out how you can use the power of social media to make your fans feel like stars, and they will love you for it. Shine a spotlight on your followers on all your social media channels and they will be compelled to talk about your brand. It doesn't take a multi-million dollar strategy to be able to do this; just borrow a few ideas from what Zappos and other brands are doing and mold your own strategy to be more effective but still affordable.

Giantnerd

Giantnerd sells equipment designed for outdoor activities such as biking, hiking, snowboarding, etc. This company has in place one of the best examples of social media interaction in the industry. It works by offering fans friendship while also giving them the best value in the process and they've also merged their website with social media in every aspect.

The official company website features a custom social networks which requires a single click to join and makes it very easy for visitors to join. Another cool feature is the incentive program which offers new members a 5% discount on products – they call it the "Nerds save 5%" promotion and it pulls in a significant number of new members.

Giantnerd saw their average order grow by 50% after they put up the like button; a major ROI boost from social media. In addition, they provide a bunch of ways for customers to find information when researching products on their website. For instance if a potential customer wanted to find information on a specific product, they could check out feedback from other social buyers; perhaps log in to the company's WikiNerdia, and get to see all the different products available, including photos and descriptions.

With this great solution for interaction, customers are able to ask important questions about different products by posting on the board for the rest of the community to comment. A lot of studies have shown that people trust their friends and fellow consumers more than they trust the brand, and so it's crucial to have a forum where customers can interact and discuss products as they learn more about the company.

Social media marketing mistakes to avoid

What common mistakes do small-scale business leaders make when implementing their social media strategies? There are quite a few and we're going to look into it so that your strategy comes out solid.

Thinking of social media implementation as a sprint instead of a marathon. A lot of people expect the job to be quick and simple but that's not the case. You can't get into it and commit a month to social media then step back and hope it all works out in the end: the entire plan will fall by the wayside and you won't have anyone to blame but yourself. Give it time to grow and be there to make sure you adjust the details of your plan as needed. Remember you are building relationships –so commit at least a year to engagement and advertising before you can expect to see real traction.

Not having a strategy

This would have to be the biggest mistake anyone could make when running any type of business. Have a clear strategy and understand why you are using it and what you expect to get from it. Also, keep tabs on the movements on your social platforms to make sure you're on track and have what you need to support the totality of your efforts just in case you need to protect the entire campaign from being disjointed.

Not listening

Just because you have good content and can keep your audiences engaged indefinitely doesn't mean you should go out on a relentless rant about whatever you think is important. The core of what you're doing should be to make connections;

and, just like what happens in the real world, (away from the internet) people will like you more if you seem to listen to their rambles and want to help them. If you're constantly talking and not paying attention to the feedback then you'll miss out on a great deal.

Posting bad feelings

This happens more times than you'd imagine. A few CEOs have resulted to using sites like Twitter to air their bad feelings, starting pointless arguments with competitors, workers, etc. some people go as far as posting derogatory language and that's about as low as anyone can get. Try to remember ethics and conduct yourself professionally- that way people will respect you and you won't have to worry about brand image.

Not moderating self-promotion

This occurs more in small businesses where the owners spend most of their time trying to market or promote themselves. Don't forget social media is constantly evolving; so what you're doing now might not appear to hurt your business, but your brand could suffer later on. Look at the forums and find out what the customers are saying.

And don't forget about the reach you have on social media. It can take over two decades to build a business and watch it go down in 20 minutes because someone wasn't paying attention.

Unrealistic goals

You cannot expect social media to run your business entirely. It's not the only way to get results so polish up the other tools you have in your arsenal and see how you can compartmentalize. Whatever plans you come up with, ensure you set reasonable expectations for your team.

Not making the posts relevant to the customer

Nobody wants to receive 20 tweets a day hearing about you. People want messages that are relevant and of value to them. So give them something that's going to be interesting, useful and shareable: but don't send too many messages because you don't want the consumer annoyed. Keep the messages short, succinct and of value to the consumer.

Not responding to fans

Common mistakes here are:

- Ignoring customers
- Not updating content
- Bad design and branding
- Not responding to or addressing comments and complaints
- Spending too much time working on promotional material

Not understanding personal and professional lines

If you're using your Facebook page to post professional material about your business, try not to make it a platform for your other casual or personal posts. Decide whether you want an account to be personal or professional, but don't make it both. LinkedIn is a good platform for conducting business professionally, so you could set up there, and use Facebook for more personal content.

Making casual assumptions

If you evaluate many cases of failure, much of it can be attributed to false assumptions.

Highlight these assumptions and stay away from them:

Researching and monitoring aren't important- On the contrary, it is critical to understand the way your market engages with each other and with your company. The best way to initiate customer engagement and interaction is through social media- while social media provides a good platform for businesses to engage with customers, it's not the only way to interact and it's certainly not good for every type of business, so check out your customer behavior.

It's impossible to measure ROI-There are dozens of tools you can access online for this, so don't operate under that assumption.

A business profile is more important than a personable profile

Many companies start out by making company profiles appear as company portals, and trim them with a lot of complicated information value and relevancy. What this does is increase bounce rates because people check in and then flip out to different profiles and don't even scroll down. To avoid this, start by creating a profile that people will find interesting. Work on getting them in, engage them and then carefully start propagating your message.

Underestimating the resources needed to put it all together

How much do you think it would cost your business to set up and maintain a decent social program? Look at the math to make sure you don't have the wrong idea.

Failing to understand that it's all about building relationships

If you're getting into social media because everybody else is doing it and it feels as if you're getting left out, then you won't have a proper plan to succeed. It's one of the reasons people go and throw out all sorts of profiles on every social platform worth mentioning, trying to sell the brand to everyone, and hopelessly failing.

When you understand that the concept is relationship-building and give it time to grow and mature, then you'll make different choices.

Not integrating with other social assets

The way to get the most out of social media is to integrate it with other forms of digital marketing efforts. Don't leave your Twitter account on an island and hope for the best; link the accounts together and make sure they are all tethered to email, paid ads and search, and the website.

Use this guide to help stay away from some of the more common mistakes companies make on social media, and remember to use images and other visual content to help get people's attention so that you can drive the point.

Tips to boost website traffic from social media
Create the best content for your audience

This all starts with creating content that helps people; and it would be better still if the content excites and thrills. When you publish a great piece of content it helps get people's attention, and more importantly, it gets shared across multiple platforms and that's good for business because it spreads your message and gets people to know your brand and what it represents. So make sure your website has all the right tools to make this work.

Optimize it properly with widgets and any button that you find useful. Facebook and Twitter buttons are a must for any business but if your business focuses more on visuals, then add in a Pin It button to the images. When you publish new content start by going through all your profiles and share the new post with your audience so you can get that first wave of traffic.

Optimize the content

It's important here to remember that only a fraction of your entire audience will actually see the content, and only a fraction of those people will share the content. This fraction is significantly lower on Facebook and Twitter so you may need to work on the content in order to make sure each post gets as many views and shares as possible. That way half your audience won't just be a statistic.

Consider the time you post the content, what day you're posting and the format in which the post goes out. When posting on Twitter, use big images and remember to post your link regularly. Facebook doesn't give you much with link thumbnails so use more images on your content and structure the content in a way that tells a story, as opposed to random thoughts or rants.

Use the analytics tool

Google offers you an effective analytics tool under the "Acquisition" section on Google Analytics so use this tool to get a clear picture of your social engagement. You should be making decisions based on actual data; so whenever you post new content, consider how the last post faired and see how you can make more of an impact. Twitter offers an analytics tool as well, so you could use that to compare notes, or look into other tools available to you. All this information will help make your strategy better for your business.

Share website links while posting content

At this stage your priority should be to boost engagement and build your profile. Talk directly to your customers and answer any questions they may have regarding products or services, so that over time they get to know you and build a relationship with you. Find a balance between sending links and sending content. You don't want your posts to be riddled with links- especially if you're operating outside of Twitter.

There should be a line between sharing content and pushing links. Obviously you don't want your audience to think of your posts as spam, because once that happens it won't be easy to change that perception no matter how good your content happens to be.

Make sure your website is included in all social networks

It should be one of your first moves so make sure when creating a new social program for your business, include the website URL in all social platforms. Have it visible on Google+, LinkedIn, Instagram, Twitter, etc. There should be a website URL somewhere on your company page so don't forget to do that.

Start blogging

Businesses find it challenging to drive content to their social media pages when they can't produce enough new content. The easiest solution here is to stay active on your blog post as a way to maintain a dynamic site and ensure that there's always something to talk about on social media. If you find it difficult to come up with regular written content, use videos instead. If you have a video on YouTube that you can use to increase awareness, embed it to your blog. Do the same with Slideshare, Storify and infographics. If the posts on your social media platforms can point to other useful content on your website, there are higher chances visitors will click through and become new customers.

SEO

You might know this but your Facebook and Twitter pages could actually show up before the company website in a Google search. Make use of the About Us section to direct social media traffic to your website so that you don't miss out on potential traffic.

It's true that prospects will seek out your social media pages before they check into your website. They do this mainly to get a feel of your taste and culture before they decide to spend money on your brand; so ensure you maintain consistency across all the channels.

Google author rank

Google appreciates quality content. When you link up with the content on your Google+, it tells Google that the blog was written by a real person who understands the subject, and the users get the message as well. In order to build trust in your niche you will have to establish yourself as an authority on a specific subject: and visitors will figure it out pretty quickly if you're just winging it.

Review searches

You will have multiple websites doing this professionally but it doesn't stop you from creating a section for reviews on your social media accounts. The goal is to have more people end up on your own pages when they search for reviews of your brand. That way you can then work on getting them to your website, where you've set up tools to ensure visitors want to hang around, and possibly spend money to have what you're selling.

Geo-tagging

Because of the nature of social media and in particular its personalization features, your ability to reach your audience from their distinct location means a lot for the business and the message you're trying to pass over. For this reason, make sure to include geo-graphic location when creating your accounts. It could just land you a few people strictly based on location.

As you can see, there are many ways to get your audience working for you and to boost traffic so get to work and don't take any opportunity for granted. Just a reminder, remember to:

- Blog daily
- Be consistent with your audience
- Optimize posts to increase "stickiness"
- Be patient

The future of social media

A lot has been said about Facebook's acquisition of the popular phone app, WhatsApp. At a price tag of $19 billion, it's definitely a historic purchase, and a few harbingers of doom suggest that it's a sign that we may be going back to the dot com era bubble. But keep in mind that this particular merger is not AOL-Time Warner or some other similar name in the industry that characterized the early 2000s; and in fact, paying attention to cash spent on any of Facebook acquisitions means missing a major point: where Facebook goes, everyone else follows.

Consider, it's Facebook's initial spread that basically made social media what it is today, and since then the company has been expanding the role of social media in the society, and in the process determining what qualifies as the norm in terms of behavior and service. Even with new competitors going head-to-head with Mark Zukerberg, and a chunk of its younger users fleeing to smaller, more streamlined social platforms, Facebook's long shadow is still visible in the social sphere. While the company might not be the embodiment of modern development, it appears Zuckerberg recognizes companies that are, and knows which ones should be integrated into his platform.

Now, considering all that, what can this acquisition -and in deed all their acquisitions- tell us about where social media is heading? We know at the moment that mobile interaction is defining social trends, and this won't stop: so what Facebook is doing, and other social giants as well, is try to figure out what else we're supposed to do with all that functionality.

Aside from mobile purchases, Facebook understands that social communication requires constant growth and evolution. The company may be gearing towards streamlining services and privacy between the sender and receiver, much like WhatsApp has managed to do with a simple and straightforward setup. Even as Facebook creates more capabilities, they still have to offer users a simple individual app experience that works within the larger Facebook umbrella.

Other social media companies may choose to capitalize on that particular trend by working on simplicity, mobile access and brevity. As marketers already understand, these days the reader accesses social posts on a much smaller device, and they have to adjust, so they make shorter posts. This push towards social communication could also send consumers into a more dynamic and interactive mindset, something marketers could use to their advantage by coming up with more gamified experiences. Whatever direction the social giants concentrate on, the services will have to be even more streamlined, and privacy will always be an issue.

Viral Marketing Strategy

Viral marketing is a marketing tactic that depends on people instead of the usual promotional campaigns to relay information to others.

This strategy is normally used by internet marketers to promote their products or services. Like the biological virus where the term was derived, viral marketing relies on "carriers" to transmit the message quickly.

The goal of viral marketing

The primary goal of viral marketing is to spur people to pass along promotional messages or advertising to others. These people essentially become product promoters, passing marketing information to others who, in turn, will spread the message to other individuals – all done for free!

Viral marketing first got noticed when email provider Hotmail.com used it in their marketing campaign. When the company went live online, each email message sent carried an ad for Hotmail along with a link to its website. As individuals were sending emails to relatives and friends, they were also sending out messages that promote the email service. After clicking on the link, recipients can easily sign up for a Hotmail account, and as they send out messages using their new account, the advertisement spreads throughout the world in a short time with very little effort from the email provider.

There are many examples of the primary elements of viral marketing and how they are put into play. The advertising cost is negligible. It uses common tasks to its advantage, such as sending emails. It capitalizes on existing resources, people in particular, to boost their products or services. Without being aware of it, each individual who uses the product becomes its endorser or spokesperson.

When a company goes viral on their ad campaign, their brand gets recognized and their sales go up, resulting in a better payday. The main goal is to send out viral messages that can be passed along rapidly from person to person without investing a lot of time, money and effort.

The tools of viral marketing

Viral marketing takes advantage of existing communications channels such as radio and television. Other strategies ride on blogs, banner ads, as well as social networks like Facebook and Twitter. Hotmail, in its case, used endorsements from other people. The biggest thing about going viral is that it can spread the message like wildfire to more people than traditional advertising.

While there are various strains of viral marketing, they all use the same basic principles.

- Incentive-driven opt-in pages offer free items for providing an email address.
- Pass-along messages can come in the form of interesting emails and funny video clips which people share and forward to others
- Buzz marketing or gossip creates controversies about something which gets people to start talking
- Undercover viral marketing is spawned by strange or false news items and spread by word-of-mouth transmitting the virus like an uncontrolled epidemic. Many individuals have used viral marketing effectively by transmitting their message within

Facebook and other social networking sites. It is a great leap forward from the word-of-mouth concept as it uses the power of lightning-fast Internet to get the message out.

Viral marketing has recently been in the crosshairs of consumers, marketing experts and privacy rights defenders due to spam emails. However, those who have mastered the game use this strategy prudently to avoid drawing fire and ensure that the message will travel far, wide and fast.

The importance of viral marketing

For a business to survive in today's largely competitive environment, it must be able to stand toe to toe against its competition and be able to adapt to the constantly changing landscape. One strategy has come up as a solution for today's business demands and it is called viral marketing. Online or offline, it is essential for business as it can reach your clients faster and it doesn't require a lot of money to launch.

Viral marketing is a type of advertising campaign that relies on individuals to pass on marketing messages to other individuals, so that recognition of a product or service spreads and replicates, yes, like a virus. This approach can create a lot of positive impact during promotional campaigns or product launches.

Here are some reasons why viral marketing is important for the survival of your business.

Viral marketing creates a buzz

Creating a buzz about your product brings a sense of anticipation in your buyers. A successful viral marketing campaign can accomplish this. The louder the buzz, the farther the campaign can spread. Messages that are of great public interest, attention- grabbing and easy to pass along will definitely help the campaign.

It builds more credibility

As more and more people in the entire network talk about and recommend your brand, more credibility is built. This is because your company is endorsed by more and more people to their friends and close associates as your message goes viral, adding points to your credibility rating. The loud buzz that is generated will surely help boost product or service recognition.

It is inexpensive

Viral marketing costs a lot less to launch but is very fast and effective in getting your message out to prospective buyers. It is the least expensive way to market your business because it doesn't require a large advertising budget. Blogging, newsletters, and email marketing are some of the ways to go viral inexpensively.

It keeps your business in the green

Viral marketing helps to keep your business afloat. If your business has already earned more credibility, people will continue to patronize your brand and ensure your business stability.

It can launch your business globally

Through viral marketing, your reputation as a reliable company can reach potential clients across the globe, enabling your company to branch out internationally.

Viral messages are easy to share

Viral product messages are easy to share. Attention-getting videos can be easily embedded into blog posts, web pages and social networking sites.

What viral marketing is not

Many people erroneously believe that viral marketing requires a huge budget to work. Not even close.

    A traditional marketing campaign promotes a brand, singing high praises about its merits, and giving it a lot of exposure and expensive movie star endorsements. With today's consumers being skeptical about nearly everything, this may appear like a hard-sell for a weak product. All that big advertising dollars for so little gain. This is not viral marketing.

What your message should be

The key here is to create an interesting viral message that will appeal to your market. You will naturally want to include your product here. Sure you can, just don't make it too obvious. It shouldn't appear like it's the heart of your message. Release the message virally and wait for sales to come in. Your viral message should be relevant, able to solve a problem and credible enough that people will want to share it.

The 5 rules of viral marketing

One of the most amazing things about viral marketing is the moment when a brilliant idea takes off, it can launch a company to fame and financial success inexpensively. People who are compelled to pass on your message drive other people to action. One individual transmits the story to another, which they pass on to yet another, and so on. This is harnessing the power of the buzz, the word-of-mouse, or viral marketing.

Ingredients for viral marketing success

Success in this strategy depends on how you throw the right ingredient into the mix:

- Free web content which includes blogs, e-books and videos.
- Attention-grabbing information. It could be innovative, bizarre, amusing or features a celebrity.
- A group of people to start the fire.
- Links to your content. This is very important if you want your message to go out. Viral marketing doesn't have to be difficult.

The simple and more engaging your message is, the more widespread its pull will be. Here are some basic rules to follow.

Make your offer appealing

Don't put cash value to your offer. Giveaways like access to online webinars, video tutorials, e-books, special reports are examples of low-cost/high-value items which can spur the recipients to take up your offer and pass the message on to others, increasing the chances of making it viral.

Make your message easy to share

Be sure that your message, whether it's a video clip, an audio recording, an eBook, or any other media, can be efficiently and smoothly passed along to other people with a single click.

Anything that slows down the forwarding of your message such as an opt- in page that captures emails should be minimized.

Take advantage of existing communications networks

You don't need to own a chain of radio or television stations to reach out to people. Make yourself familiar with the popular and immensely effective social networks like Facebook, Pinterest, Twitter, Google Plus and other marketing platforms that will get the job done at no cost.

Make it worth buzzing about

If you want your message to get opened, promote it as the next big thing to make it buzz-worthy. If people think that they are going to benefit from it or look good by using it, your redemption rate will skyrocket.

Keep it short and simple

As was mentioned earlier, the easier your message is to understand, the greater the chances of it going viral. Keep your message free from fluff and go straight to the point. Due to the huge amount of information that bombard them each day, if people have to spend one more minute to decipher your message, then they'll find it easier to click out of the page and move on to other things.

Know your potential audience and how they are going to respond to a particular offer. One of the keys to capturing people's attention is to know what they want and over-deliver. When you provide them with something of value at absolutely no charge, expect a huge avalanche of response to follow. If people are compelled to pass on your message to friends and associates, then your chances of going viral is assured.

The most effective viral marketing techniques

For a message to become viral, that is, to spread and replicate like a virus, it has to be easy enough to share, using as very little effort as possible, such as clicking on a link. The message should also be able to stand out effectively and capture the attention of readers. What's more, it should have some value to users but not necessarily in monetary terms. What is important is it has entertainment or educational value.

That being said, the next question would probably be – what technique should one use for viral marketing? There is no best answer for that question. Below are 7 very effective and proven viral marketing techniques that should be part of your marketing arsenal.

Social networks

Hotmail launched a very successful viral marketing campaign long before social media was introduced. Today, it would be impossible for a business to achieve even a fraction of Hotmail's success without becoming active in social networks such as Facebook, LinkedIn, Twitter, and others. Bottom line is, if properly executed, social media marketing can boost your viral marketing like a rocket sled on rails.

Article marketing

Content is king. It was then, it still is. If you are good in writing articles and can get them to be syndicated, it is not too far-fetched that some of your work can go viral. That is, of course, if they are original, captivating, entertaining or educational, and provides great value.

Videos

You've probably heard of YouTube videos that have garnered hundreds of thousands of views just within a week of getting viral. If you can upload a video that is hilarious, bizarre, educational, or simply grabs the attention of viewers, you might just be the next YouTube sensation.

E-Books

EBook production started nearly the same time as the Internet. EBooks are considered one of the best ways to go viral because they are fast and easy to create and have a large audience reach. People want to share a good reading experience. If the eBook you've written is educational and/or entertaining, original, and a hard-to-put-down page-turner, then people will gladly share it with others.

Newsletters

Newsletters are not just a great way to keep your subscribers constantly reminded of your business name, they also have that strong potential to go viral. You can grab this wonderful opportunity and not leave money on the table. Here's how. Always write a note at the end of your newsletter which encourages the reader to share the newsletter with other people. Surprisingly, most of them will. All they need is a little encouraging to take action.

Like, tweet and share buttons

These buttons provide an excellent and convenient way for your site visitors to broadcast your content via the social networking sites.

There are other forms of content you can use for viral marketing, but in some cases, real success comes from the way you promote your content to your target audience. However, it is truly possible, provided you have an amazing story that you can put in front of your audience, that they will respond positively and willingly share your content.

How to launch a low-cost viral marketing campaign

It doesn't have to cost an arm and a leg to drive laser-focused traffic to your company website. Viral marketing is a low-cost yet effective tool to do just that. Here are some useful tips to help you launch a low-cost viral marketing campaign that will yield positive results.

Write articles that promote your product or service

You can post these articles on your website as well as submit them to article directories. If people find your articles entertaining or useful, they can reprint them on their website, eBooks, e-zine, or newsletter. Don't forget to include your author resource box and the article reprint option below the article body.

If you don't like writing or just don't have the time, there are free or low-cost PLR articles you can use. However, to prevent being de-indexed by Google for dupe content, you should rewrite portions of these articles to alter their content and make them more unique as other people use these PLR articles as well.

Set up your forum or bulletin board

Forums and bulletin boards are useful tools where people can post their comments and links on your site which can help your advertising campaign go viral. You can also embed an affiliate banner or one of your own above the bulletin board's header area.

Most hosting companies include these programs at no extra cost as part of their hosting package. Installing them can be done automatically using the control panel. Just type in your name, password, and other required information and your forum or bulletin board is ready to go. All you need to do is log in and manage it.

Purchase the branding rights to a successfully viral eBook

After branding the eBook with your site URL and links, you can give it away to people at no charge and allow them to pass it along to others. Your eBook will be received or downloaded repeatedly by other individuals down the line until it virally spreads across the internet.

Write your own eBook

Create an eBook and allow people to place their ads in it for free, with the understanding that they will, in return, give away the eBook to their newsletter subscribers and website visitors.

Build your product website

If you have the experience and skill, you can build a website that promotes your product. You can also allow people to download your products for free and provide them with give-away right so they can distribute them freely to other people. This will enable your product and your links to propagate across the internet until your brand gains recognition and, as a result, pull in traffic to your website.

To make this possible, your free give-away product should carry your advertisement or you should require product recipients to directly link to your website. They should also keep your copyright notice untampered as this is where you will include a link back to your website.

If you don't want to spend on paid web hosting, you can also use free websites like Blogger and WordPress to get you started.

How to succeed in viral marketing using Pinterest

There's marketing and there's Pinterest marketing and succeeding in it only requires your understanding of how Pinterest can work to your advantage. This pin board-style of marketing has seen tremendous web traffic since its debut in March 2013. The photo-sharing website has, in fact, already generated more than $54 million in funding from foreign and local investors alike.

There is such excitement in using Pinterest for users when they create images and redefine them as "collections" of events, hobbies and interests and more so when other users "re-pin" them to their own pin boards. Recipes, craft projects, gardening tools, no- rip hosiery, retro fashion, shabby chic furniture, sand art, it's an endless array of everything and anything. Connections, friendships, relationships and collaborations have been established, and continue to flourish, because of Pinterest.

Using Pinterest for business

Business is no exception and has steadily gained a niche in the Pinterest environment. Because it's such a highly visual medium, business has a particularly good opportunity to maximize its marketing strategies when it uses Pinterest. You just have to understand how it works to get information on what kind of content gets shared and why. Women make up the majority of Pinterest users, you have to take note of that, so technology and other traditionally "macho" interests like cars, golf, wrestling and PC games are still in the process of garnering their shares of audiences.

Exposure is obviously what happens as you inevitably progress on viral marketing in Pinterest, that's why you have to keep on being creative. Pinterest is visual, and your content has to be more eye-catching than the other visuals, and your textual content has to be more informative, too, to capture more users of your pin board. While photography is the name of the game here, you have to go the extra mile and choose carefully on what kind of photography is most suitable for your line of business, which is, for instance, shoes.

More than the usual marketing

Viral marketing of shoes is done by big name stores and competing with them will take more than the usual viral marketing because they already do that. Use Pinterest by scouring for great shots of shoes worn by ordinary people instead of celebrities, for example, a pair of Jimmy Choo on a little girl or a pair of Doc Martens on a grandfather.

Create your own images by taking the ordinary a notch higher to make them extraordinary and Pinterest can help you achieve that. Take a seasonal holiday, for instance, like

Valentine's Day. If you're into the costume business, make the occasion to your advantage. Instead of yet overemphasizing that Valentine's Day is meant mostly for lovers, couples and significant others, take on a stand on it and introduce love on February 14 as a universal form of affection between parents and children, between neighbors, between teachers and students or even between friends. Pinterest has hundreds of thousands of images which speak of that kind of platonic love.

Diligent commenting

Riding on a trend using Pinterest is, of course, a trend by itself. If you want to know how to succeed in Pinterest viral marketing all you need to do is actively share your information and connect to other social media sites like Facebook.

Likewise, diligently posting comments on your content, and on others' comments as well, will help you rope in more viewers and subsequently gain you potential customers. Because somewhere out there, someone, or a whole lot of someone's, will be people who not only share your interests but are willing to shell a few bucks to see them come true.

How to succeed in viral marketing using Facebook

Strategy is what you apply when you want to rope in visitors to your website and teaching you how to succeed in viral marketing using Facebook can only mean that there are some factors which you have to take into consideration to achieve success.

A free product is always welcome. Whether the recipient uses it or not, a freebie is exciting to receive. And if the freebie is useful to the recipient, it attains more value and attracts attention to the product itself. An eBook, software, gift certificates, a pair of ear plugs, it could be anything that will be interesting to own or have. No strings attached, no contests, no free trials, no surveys, not even a small fee to sign up to be able to get it, just plain old giveaways.

Getting your message across

Social networks have begun their competitive battle against traditional marketing tools like the telephone, television, print ads and billboards. Because marketing through social media is faster and can potentially reach four times the number of real time users, your first stop is going through your email contacts. On the surface, emailing each one personally and not sending them auto-generated information introducing your product will seem daunting.

But think of it from the recipient's point of view: getting an email which begins with a "Dear James," addressing the recipient in an informal, almost intimate manner, is way better than receiving something that greets the recipient with a generic "Dear Beloved Consumer," that makes even the word "beloved" sound too desperate for a sale.

Set up another account

If you already have a Facebook account but use it primarily for social interaction, register for another account for your business and set up a business fan page to reach out to potential customers. A personal Facebook account will not be effective as a business tool because not all of the people in your personal circle are necessarily interested in your business or have need for the product or service which you offer. Do the same if you have a Twitter account; concentrate on being followed and followed by individuals already in your business niche.

Again, use your Facebook and Twitter accounts to "feel" your readers by actively interacting with them. Ask them questions regularly on topics directly related to your business, share photos and other images with them, get them to invite each other to expand into more networks, because spreading out the buzz about your business will be easier. The adage "the more, the merrier" doesn't hold more true than in this case when you know how to succeed with viral marketing using Facebook.

Blogging your way

Start a blog on your business. If you're not much of a writer, hire people who write for a living to do the blogging for you. Make sure that your blog is updated often and take note of your readers' comments and ensure that you pay attention to their questions, if any, as well as their suggestions. Never underestimate the power of the follow up.

Readers who tune in to your blog may be repetitive but your patience in faithfully answering their queries will encourage other readers to note that your blog cares about them, even when they play like a broken record.

The 7 most effective viral marketing videos

Knowing viral marketing using Facebook and Twitter and still other social network accounts is really just putting out informative but engaging content and images which others can see, relate to and appreciate. And if you have a business which can maximize these visual, cerebral and emotional results, you are halfway into generating more interest and, hopefully, more sales in the future.

Social media has become every business's dream marketing tool and there are more and more viral marketing videos coming up every day because of the proven effect that viral marketing, and videos in particular, has had on consumers over the past five years.

People use the internet for almost anything they need, a condition which most of us did not think possible ten or even 15 years ago. Today, we go online to pay our bills, buy merchandise, connect with long lost schoolmates, meet new friends, participate in conferences, watch films, listen to music and transact business.

YouTube, for instance, has revolutionized the way of discovering new talents (think Charice or Gangnam style dancing), espousing causes (think PETA's anti-fur campaigns showing how animals are methodically slaughtered, without anesthesia, for their skins) and providing blow-by-blow coverage of news (think hostage situations, natural disasters like Katrina, fires and sniper battles).

More than text messaging

Video watchers fall under the 17 to 58 age range with an even distribution of both genders and geography. In some places in the world where access to the internet is minimal, people still find a way to view the news, chat with friends, email relatives, purchase new clothes and write down a recipe by watching videos online in internet cafes or on their mobile phones. Viral marketing using video has, in fact, gained more ground than any other form of marketing, including text messaging.

Attention is what a business needs and there is no better way to capture it than a video uploaded and viewed by the more than ten million people who go online everyday looking for something new to watch. It has to be admitted, even by traditionalists of advertising, that video commercials are more effective than print ads, or even televised ads.

There are certainly more interesting things to watch online than television can ever produce, and because what television airs can almost always be aired online as a video as well, watching television has even become a so-so activity in the past couple of years.

Being unconventional

Video marketing is definitely "it." Videos have this uncanny way of drawing attention to themselves merely by being "unconventional" and that word can have different meanings to different people. While the written word of print ads and texting stimulate the visual senses, videos cover both the visual and the auditory areas and provoke the mind even more.

When watching some of the viral marketing videos the viewer participates in the creation of images that engages the mind to think beyond what is seen. For instance, a video marketing nail art that is done with good lighting, convincing textual content, the latest music and overall engaging approach will persuade even nail biters to grow their nails and try on some polish and eventually have the desire to have nail art done. To watch how a product works through a video online makes the viewer so interested they would want to see how that product works for themselves.

To charge or not to charge

Promoting your business via viral marketing videos is cost effective. It requires very little or no cost to make a video and uploading it on most sites, especially the popular ones, is free. The choice is then yours on whether you want to charge people who view your video or let them watch it for free and let your product speak for itself.

You can categorize your video to ensure that it lands in your business niche and make target marketing easier for your product. Ensuring the correct category where your video will be in increases your product's visibility and availability. When choosing viral marketing videos, make sure that the category it is in can reach out to the most number of people who can be your potential customers.

Viral marketing do's and don'ts

In the frenzy world that characterizes the internet, online marketing has done more for business than all the traditional approaches combined but there are several viral marketing do's and don'ts which you must be aware of to ensure success in generating success for your business.

Relevancy is of prime significance because very few people will be attracted to what you put out if that content is not related in some way to what they are attracted to or interested in. For your content to be relevant, it has to be recognizable as important to the reader. Information about retro icons, for instance, should have updated news about what's going on in the lives of these icons or whether they are staging a comeback or lending their names to certain products (which, hopefully, is one of yours) or simply letting their fans and followers know that they are still alive and kicking.

Getting instant customers

Another one of the viral marketing do's and don'ts is creating marketing content which appeals to the sense of humor of the target audience. So make your content funny in some way that reading or viewing it triggers the laugh button in people. Along with the humor factor, marketing your product in a shockingly attractive manner will certainly provoke people to think about it and develop their own ideas. Controversial topics which may have bearing on your product, for example, can trigger so many responses from viewers that demand for your product becomes more than the supply.

If you are trying to get people to buy your vacuum-packed fresh vegetables, use their photos side by side with photos of vegetables infested with chemical insecticides by choosing those with magnifying glasses superimposed on them. By letting people know that fresh vegetables, your organically grown, chemical free veggies, are available and do exist, by showing the kind of other vegetables there are in their chemical-sprayed appearance, you captivate your viewers into becoming instant customers.

Basic do's

Still another "Do" is responding personally to comments and messages posted by readers or viewers. Yes, it's a lot of nitty-gritty work but a personal reply is always appreciated more than an automated response. "Do" post regularly and frequently sensibly because once you have introduced your product, people would want to know more about it, including new variants or any improvements to it, change of packaging, promos and giveaways associated with it and other updates. Do make use of social networking sites such as Facebook and Twitter but remember to register your business as a separate account. Choose what page your business is most suitable for, and, whether it is on a fan or community page, work your way from there in gathering reader- or viewership.

Just a few don'ts

The "Don'ts" are comparatively few. Don't spam is Rule Number One. Spamming is a nuisance to email inboxes and can be so irritating that the recipient can be induced to homicidal proportions to find their email flooded with spam.

Don't neglect the Terms of Service condition of whatever platforms you are using to avoid future lawsuits or the closure of your site or the upload of your video, two vital conditions which translate to loss of business for you. If the Terms of Service include prohibition of posting photos which can be classified as soft porn, for example, don't be reckless and post half-nude images just to draw attention to your lingerie or intimate apparel product. Yes, you want to connect with people who will be potential customers, but no, you don't want sex addicts, pedophiles and other deviants to flock to your site or watch your video, do you?

When using Twitter as a viral marketing tool, the last of viral marketing do's and don'ts include going overboard on the hashtags and tag every word, or make long descriptive tags, in your tweet. Don't. Go. Overboard. Use them wisely. Highlight keywords which are current, interesting and attention-getting so people can easily find your tweet. And unless you a real mutant like Mystique and still manage to look like the real Jennifer Lawrence, don't use words which only you can understand or find exciting such as #100RandomFactsAboutMe.

The biggest mistakes even experts make in viral marketing

Viral marketing is a powerful business strategy which can generate continuous sales for your business but remember that doing it right to avoid mistakes people make in viral marketing is no less important than putting out great content.

Even the most seasoned marketers can make the same kinds of mistakes over and over again yet most of these are avoidable. For the viral marketing rookie, being informed of them can cut the time, and the regret, not to mention the loss business, it will take to actually experience them.

Timely and updated

Put information in quickly. People don't want to be kept waiting, especially for something they need to use at once. Make sure your server isn't slow or use graphics which take forever to download. Never subscribe to technical arrogance and assume that everyone has Macromedia because people who have plain HTML and text versions installed in their computers are potential customers as well.

See to it that your site or video has these versions readily available. Manually list search engines which people use to view your site. Business people use search engines so much yet often don't see the wisdom in having their own sites listed on the very search engines they use. Learn about Search Engine Optimization (SEO) techniques and use them to strengthen the impact of your content and to stay "in" with the latest in viral marketing.

Choose who you partner with. Don't commit common mistakes in viral marketing by associating with spyware companies and spammers who operate profusely online because if you get involved with them as co-registrants or affiliates, you may be dragged into future lawsuits. Your product may be interesting enough, but having a business relationship with people like those can lose you a substantial number of already existing customers. One questionable mailing can be enough for you to be labeled as a spammer by internet service providers (ISPs), making it hard for you to market online in the future.

Retaining customers

And speaking of customers, your potential ones should not be given the third degree when they sign up with your website or open an account to buy your product or receive your newsletter. Your questions should never be beyond name, age, email address and other contact information of your future subscriber. And don't forget to include asking their permission to use their information for other activities which your business might have such as promotions and events.

Be aware of the right timing, because not being so means that you're either up in the boondocks where they know Eisenhower to still be the American president or you're simply "out of touch" with the rest of the world. If your product mainly caters to specialized markets, for instance, children of school age, and your product is school supplies in general, you do your sales and promotions of these in August before school starts in September and not in December when school is out for the holidays. And remember that although marketing is done most effectively and quickly online, don't fall for the biggest mistakes people make in viral marketing and stop marketing offline.

Chapter 4

It's All About the Customer Base

Knowing Thy Customers

Let's talk about being too big for your britches. Another words trying to be like a big box store. In an entrepreneurial business like online marketing it's all about getting to know your leads and customers on a personal basis.

Now, a huge box store could never do this. Why? Because they have millions and millions of customers. It's not even feasible for them to have a "relationship" with their customers.

On the other hand, this is the life blood of small home-based businesses. I like to call it pressing the flesh! You can really serve a smaller base of leads and customers if you relate to them and share your story. This is so important when it comes to running a small business of any kind. Let's discuss three main points that will really help you catapult your small business into success.

#1 – *Know thy Customer* – Knowing your customer is key. It's also very important that they get to know you. You might ask, how do you do this? It's simple, you communicate with your leads and customers to make them feel comfortable with you and share your experiences. Often times our stories are all the same just different content and experience.

#2 – Be liked by your customers – This is also important, there will always be a certain base of customers that you really resonate with the most. Not everyone is going to relate to you or even like or want what you are selling. Point being here is do things that matter for your leads and provide them value. Be approachable and likable and they will follow you. This is what turns a lead into a paying customer.

#3 – Gain your customers trust and confidence – Always be genuine, truthful and upfront with your leads and customers. They will appreciate it. Don't try to be tricky in your marketing efforts and NEVER be misleading as to what your opportunity can provide. If you do this and can provide real results for your customers than they will trust you and want more.

These are three things that big box stores can never accomplish. They never will either. Their customer base is just way too big and it's impossible for them to get down to this macro level with their customers. However, smaller business models have every opportunity to capitalize on this very simple model.

If you do this and always put your leads and customers first than your results will inevitably be much better. You will see your average customer value skyrocket and they will keep coming back for more. If you apply this simple model in your own business your results will be much better.

Let me provide just a little more insight on how you can do this. Let's use email as an example. Emailing your leads and customers every day is absolutely necessary. Here is where most business owners go wrong with emailing their lists. They don't provide any value to their leads and customers. Providing valuable content to your leads and customers makes all the difference in your marketing efforts. This also builds the three factors I spoke about above. If you provide good actionable value your customers will get to know you, like you and trust you much faster.

Be personal in your emails. Share your struggles in your own business or your life. Provide guidance and position yourself as an expert in the field. This will quickly develop your relationship with your leads and customers and keep them coming back for more.

Effective Marketing to Build Your Customer Base

Ok, so not everyone is a boxing fan but let me tell you this, the Mayweather vs. Pacquiao fight was marketing at its very best. Did you know that this fight paid out the most to an athlete in the history of sports? The cash that was made from this fight was absolutely astounding. Why? Because of the hype leading up to the fight, the huge audience of fans and the skillful use of marketing. This is what made this fight so huge and brought in millions and millions of dollars.

So how can you do this at your level of marketing? Glad you asked! Think of your business as a smaller version of promoting the Mayweather vs Pacquiao fight. You have all the same elements in your own products or services to offer… It's just a different product right?

So I have developed a formula that my wife and I have been using for a while in our own business. This formula is very simple and easy to do from a small business perspective. Remember, your goal isn't to market at the same level of this fight. You wouldn't want to nor could you afford to as a small business. So I offer the same small techniques that we use in our own business to you. This is what has allowed us to scale our business and work with a quality base of loyal customers.

#1 – Build your audience – You can't have a successful business unless you have a loyal following. Not everyone will be a cheerleader for your business but you have to build an audience that is willing to listen to what you have to say. You're probably wondering, how the heck do I build a loyal audience? There are many ways to do this. For starters email marketing is still king, build a loyal list of subscribers and provide them with loads of value. Not just content but actual value that will contribute to something in their lives.

Second is social media. There are many avenues you can approach using social media to build a loyal audience that will continue to follow you. Some of them will become customers today and some will become customers in six months. The point here is you build that audience on social media platforms like Facebook, Instagram, Pinterest, YouTube, etc. Once you have a loyal base of subscribers that knows, likes and trusts you they will be more open to purchasing the products or services that you sell.

#2 – Engage with your audience – This is the part that 98% of marketers online fail at and they fail miserably. Let's look at email marketing for example. Many marketers seem to think they can simply set up an autoresponder, put in a bunch of pre-written messages and make millions. This just isn't the case. Yes, you want to use an autoresponder but you want to engage your audience with broadcasts on a frequent basis. Share what's going on, what are you working on in your business, how can you help them, address your struggles in your business.

This is the very personal engagement that many marketers are missing. Second, reply back to your leads in a timely fashion. These leads are future customers, if they have a question than answer it right away. If you're not doing this you are leaving money on the table. Poor service correlates directly to your monthly income! My wife and I take the time to personally interact with every single customer and lead that has a question within 12 hours! Do this and you will watch your income grow exponentially!

#3 – Convert your audience – Now you need to convert your leads into customers or your customers into reoccurring buyers. Do this by always being on the ball in your business. Answer questions over email or the phone in a timely manner. This will make your lead or current customer feel comfortable with their buying decision. This doesn't mean you have to be a sales person. It's just a conversation. If you approach it this way you will find that it is much easier to convert your leads into sales much faster. I refer to this as soft selling.

You have a conversation and let your prospect talk themselves into the reason they need your product or service. You don't need scripts or sales training. Just be yourself, talk to them like a friend and discuss some of the benefits for them if they buy your product. My wife and I have found this to work very well over the years and ditched the "sales pitch" long ago!

So these are some fundamental things you can apply in your business immediately. Like the Nike commercials always say, "JUST DO IT". You are your own worst enemy in your business!

7 Fundamentals in Our Own Business

Let me ask you a question? Do you think Bill Gates had some pretty solid business fundamentals? Well I am sure we can all answer that question. Of course he did….. Do you think he knew them when he first started in his garage? He may have had a vision but if you would have asked him I can bet you that he never expected to reach the level he did. So why was he so successful? Was it luck? Timing? Business smarts? Well the truth is this, it was probably some of all those things however; he would have never reached the level of success that he did without a strategy and some fundamentals for his business.

In our online business, my wife and I have some very basic fundamentals. I would argue that they are very similar to Bill Gates fundamental but tweaked to an online market.

Fundamental #1: Mindset – Mindset is very important when you are starting or already own a business. This applies to both online and offline businesses. You have to get past the "employee" mentality as I like to call it. There is no one to tell you what to do anymore and all the decisions are made by you.

If you can't shift your mindset to be self-motivated than inevitably your business will fail. It won't matter how set up for success you are or if you have the most successful business model in the world. You have to shift your mind to think like a strategic business owner. You also have to be able to make leaps and take risks in your business. This is what sets successful business owners apart. You will win sometimes and lose sometimes. If you can't wrap your mind around this concept as an entrepreneur than you should probably just stay an employee! Entrepreneurs are adaptive, cunning, deal with pressure and are self-motivated.

Fundamental #2: Content Creation – When I talk about content creation I'm talking about emails, blog posts, videos, Facebook posts, etc. Often time's new marketers are led in the wrong direction when it comes to creating content. Many will offer the advice to "Just post something every day" this is horrible advice. Content is not about quantity, it's about quality. If you can offer your loyal herd of fans quality content at least 3 times a week they will follow you forever. Be creative with your content, have a strategy for your content and most of all BE ORIGINAL.

With the changes that google has done over the past few years it does no good to purchase pre-written PLR articles. These articles have already been posted everywhere on the internet. Google will not look at this as original content and it will actual hurt your rankings in the search engines. So be original, post good valuable and useful content at least 3 times per week and keep your audience engaged.

Fundamental #3: Lead Generation – Lead generation is the life blood of your business. If you don't have leads coming in than you will never sell any products. This sounds very obvious but you would be surprised how many people get this wrong. It's not just about quantity leads, it's about quality leads that fit into your marketing strategy and niche. What good does it do to try and sell a comb to a bald person? This produces non-targeted leads and will result in a lot of money spent with no result. Know your market and generate leads within that market. You should strive to produce at least 20 new leads in your business per day. Use this metric and targeted marketing and you will end up with a slot machine that never asks for money!

Fundamental #4: Follow Up and Engagement – This is the most overlooked piece of marketing in the industry. 98% of every marketer is failing at this simple step. It is so important to build a relationship with your customer base so they get to know, like and trust you. Accomplish this through email, phone calls or Skype calls and even face to face engagement if possible. People buy people, not products. If you present yourself as a leader and have good customer service than you will have leads chasing you. This can take some time when you are new but don't wait on the industry to brand you as a leader. You will be waiting for a very long time. Brand yourself as a leader and present yourself that way in your engagements with leads and customers.

Fundamental #5: Monetization Strategy – Do you have a monetization strategy? Have you positioned yourself to create multiple streams of income? Yet another fundamental that most people fail to capitalize on. My wife and I strive to get customers every single day. But marketing should not stop there. It's one thing to have customers, but wouldn't you like to have repeat customers that buy more expensive products. This is known as a value ladder. If you are not incorporating a high ticket program into your business than you are leaving thousands and thousands of dollars on the table.

To put it simply; would you rather sell 10,000 eBooks at $1.00 a piece or 1 high ticket program for $10,000? Kind of a no brainer right? So your marketing should always have a high ticket element in an OTO (One time offer) that then leads your customers to higher payoff products. This can all start with a $9.95 eBook, then a $50 upsell that leads into higher ticket products that can be $500 or $30,000. You may be reading this and thinking Hmmmmm. Who spends $30K on a product on the internet? It's more common than you may think! So, incorporate this simple strategy into your business and you will see your average customer value go from $9.95 to around $550.00 per customer over their lifetime.

Fundamental #6: Adding the Engine – This is the important part. How do you incorporate all these fundamentals into your business strategy? Your business be it an LLC or

Corporation is like your car. The processes, procedures and business model that you use is like the engine that drives your business every day "Your Engine". This is why franchises are so successful because they have these systems in place for you to follow. The downside to this is the cost of entry. Some franchises can cost hundreds of thousands or even millions of dollars to start up. Most aspiring entrepreneurs simply don't have the capital to fund them.

That's why the internet is so powerful because you can license other people's products and sell them for huge profits. My wife and I use this business model as the engine for our business. Having the car and the engine are two components that you simply can't live without as a business owner. Many entrepreneurs spend so much time and money going from opportunity to opportunity. I like to call it chasing shiny object syndrome! Well you can break that bad habit today and stick to one simple process and business model and stop chasing shiny objects and next best things.

Fundamental #7: Just Add Traffic – Most marketers don't have a traffic problem, they have a strategy problem. They don't have high converting offers to sell or are selling products that have already been saturated in the market. With the business model my wife and I use it's this simple…we just add traffic! That's really it, if you have a quality sales funnel that has a high ticket back-end than you drastically increase your average customer value over their life time. You must provide this "value ladder" to your business and incorporate all of the elements that I've discussed. Follow these fundamentals and incorporate a successful business model into your efforts and you will watch your bank account grow every month!

Now, you have to put this all together in your business model to make it work. Struggling business owners are simply missing an element of this simple formula. Apply these simple things into your business and you can experience levels of growth that you never thought possible. If you don't have what my wife and I refer to as an "engine" than take some time and really research your options.

Now, knowing these 7 fundamentals and applying these to your business is crucial to your success. None of these are hard to apply in your business. None of these fundamentals are really new or a big secret. The problem most marketers have is staying focused on these fundamentals. Many online business owners miss parts of these fundamentals. This is exactly why they struggle in their business.

Getting these fundamentals strategically placed in your business will allow for growth and increase your return on investment in a big way for your business.

Being the CEO of Your Own Life

Let's just face it. You are what you call yourself. You are what you believe yourself to be. My wife, personally, as a military spouse for years, called herself just that. But somehow being JUST a military spouse didn't resonate with how important she really is in the family "Unit"

If you ask the I.R.S. what she is they will say she is the head of the household. But again, something about that term is not as majestic as it should, would, or could be.

So she has renamed herself and so should you. She and I (we), are the CEOs of our own lives. Something about that sounds much more powerful!

As Chief Executive Officer YOU make the final decisions on everything that happens, not only within your family, but within yourself. You are the final decision maker when it comes to your success and your failures, your happiness and your sadness, your loves and your hates, your ups and your downs.

NO ONE else has control over your life. Sure, others can make suggestions, but when it is all said and done, YOU CHOOSE to control your destiny.

Your spouse or your significant other may offer you an idea, but when the rubber meets the road YOU CHOOSE to listen to them or not.

My wife CHOSE to follow her dream of starting her own business as a military spouse and disabled veteran. Little did she realize that action would catapult her to where she is now; coaching military, military spouses and veterans and helping them fulfill their dreams is very rewarding! Yes, she is the CEO of her own LIFE, Master of her own dream, Driver of her own destiny, Creator of her own future; she is what her mom used to call "a shot caller." She calls HER OWN shots!

She realized that this LIFE would not last forever and that if she didn't take charge of her future, then who would? Or would she continue to drift along in the wind like seeds from a dandelion in summer, being blown whichever way OTHERS wanted her to go.

So I am asking you to please claim YOUR title. Look at the three steps below to work your way towards becoming your own CEO and resist hostile takeovers of YOURSELF from outside sources.

Follow your dream – No matter what it takes dig deep, find out what you want, and stop at nothing to find the tools and resources to build YOUR DREAM.

Know your value – It doesn't matter if you are a mom/dad, significant other, college student, or whatever, YOU are the CEO of your own destiny. Act like it!

Handle your business – As CEO your number one business is YOU. Even if you are a mom, dad or have no kids and just work. You can't take care of everything and hold a job if you don't put YOURSELF first. I know this is a struggle for many, however, if you continue to work and focus on this area, it gets better. You can't continue to ignore the important things in life. Is your family important? Of course it is! But, it's time for you to hold your head up and become the CEO of your OWN Destiny!

Getting Outside Your Comfort Zone

Do you think a guy like Warren Buffet has ever been uncomfortable in his business ventures? I wouldn't want to speak for him but I would venture to guess that he has. We all have at some point. In order to reach peak performance in any business it requires you to take leaps!

Here's a recent example from a high end $30,000.00 Mastermind that my wife and I just attended (you read that right, 30K per ticket). Taking your business to the next level has its price, but my wife and I will gladly pay it (but that's a story for another time). Here is an example from this mastermind:

One of the main strategies my wife and I have been using in our business for a long time is hosting sales webinars. We recently attended a high level mastermind where the group was asked, "who's currently using webinars in their business?" Only 4 or 5 hands went up out of about 55 attendees. Those of us that had our hands up were already making multiple 6 and even 7 figure incomes with our online businesses. So what does that tell you?

The next question of course was why they were not doing webinars, and they said things like;

"I'm not ready – I'm still new figuring this stuff out"
"What would I teach? What would I say?"
"I don't have a clue about how to actually set a webinar up, it's too technical for me"

Most knew the webinar strategy they'd just seen had a good chance of making sales, yet they were still unwilling to actually do it. So this is where the mastermind host challenged everyone to drop the excuses, and just get a webinar done. Not over the next few weeks either, but within the next 24 hours. He had to get everyone to first commit to doing it (about 85% said they would), then create their webinar registration link and then blast it out to their lists and Facebook. The intent was to schedule the webinar for the next evening.

He challenged the group to get past those limiting beliefs. He challenged everyone to host their first webinar the following night. "But what about the slides and content, I haven't even done that yet!" one person exclaimed. He replied "Don't worry about that we'll work that out by tomorrow afternoon." People laughed, but he was dead serious.

So at 9 am the next day he asked everyone how they were feeling about hosting their first webinar that evening. Many were nervous, afraid, full of doubt, but there was also some genuine excitement about doing something far outside of their comfort zone, which would take them to the next level in their business.

Here is my point: After being in this industry, seeing both sides of the coin, I can tell you the greatest moments of discomfort have resulted in some of the biggest shifts in my wife and I's income. We have done many webinars with approximately 2,000 attendees, sometimes even more. We usually have 60 minutes to provide value and also promote our business to people that are looking for a change in their lives.

We make sales and it's always our intention to do very well. To be completely honest, we always have similar thoughts to what many of those people at the mastermind had about doing their first webinar in 24 hours. We feel like we need more time, that we are not quite ready yet (just an extra week to prepare would be huge!)

Yet we are wise enough now to recognize these thoughts are coming from a place of wanting to stay within a comfort zone and that these thoughts cannot be trusted. Not if we want to get our business to the next level. So those thoughts are getting ignored.

Now, let's talk about YOU and how all of this applies to you! When was the last time you felt truly uncomfortable? When was the last time you felt you weren't ready to do something?

If it's been too long, then I'm going to guess you have not grown professionally or personally recently. That is not a dig on you, just a simple fact. My wife and I have been there and done that and our business suffered for it. I may be wrong, but if I'm not then here's my advice; Get uncomfortable. Do those things which you know deep down would create massive results, even (especially) if you don't feel ready.

Maybe it's as simple as just getting your first business coach. Maybe it's getting to a live business summit or mastermind when you're not sure if you can afford the airline tickets. Maybe it's creating your first business (LLC or Corporation).

Whatever it is, move in the direction of what scares you because it will probably make you a lot of money once you make the leap.

Chapter 5

The Awesome Discovery Process

Ditching All the Excuses

I have to talk with you about this because I don't want this to be YOU! I have seen this all too often in business and don't want to see you go through this pitfall. What I am about to say might anger a few but will be the push some need to take it to the next step!

Excuses, I hear them all the time. By far the most common excuse I hear from wannabe entrepreneurs for why they don't spend more time and money on growing a new business is this!

I don't have enough time and money, I will say it right off the bat, that's complete crap! Why? Because my wife and I started out with a $3000 loan, the will to succeed and never looked back!

Not surprising though right? I will tell you right now that this is rarely a defendable answer. Rarely is the excuse of, "not enough time or money" a legitimate response. You're probably saying, "Owe sure, your making money in your business. Easy for you to say."

Nope, I am not talking about my current situation or people in my income bracket. I am talking about your situation, and my situation back when I was just like you!

Here's the reason that, "I don't have enough time or money" is a lame excuse: When I ask a follow-up question, "How do you spend your time each day"? Every single wannabe, without exception, has listed tasks that they should not be doing.

Tasks that should be eliminated, delegated or outsourced. Problems that have already been solved and questions that have already been answered. Within the first 90 seconds of the description of their day, I identify at least an hour or more they could reassign to growing their business. In many cases even more than a few hours! This also applies to those who have a 9-5 job!

Look at this list of problems that have already been solved and find at least 3 you can delegate, eliminate or outsource as soon as you're done reading this book.

Household chores, errands, cooking, cleaning, lawn work, home repairs, grocery shopping, dog walking, email inbox management, Facebooking for fun, appointment scheduling, invoicing, book keeping, accounting, tax preparation, filing, tweeting, copywriting, blog posting, web design, site maintenance, customer service, administrative tasks and on and on and on!!!!!!

You can probably find way more than 3 right? In my opinion, if you want to grow a business, you can't afford to be doing ANY of these $3 an hour tasks.... Period!

Ok, so that takes care of the time excuse! What about the money excuse!

Well, most of those tasks, if they can't be eliminated entirely, can be delegated or outsourced for as little as $3 an hour. If you don't believe that you can make more than $3 per hour in the hours you save by outsourcing, well, I have to question your self-confidence.

The choice is yours. Do you want to stay stuck and keep solving problems that have already been solved or do you want to invest in your future? If your future is not worth $3 per hour, I'm afraid there is no one that can help you!

If this reality check made you a touch mad, but gets you off your back side than great. These are just facts that can't be denied and you have to take action. Action takers make money and wannabe's sit on the couch eating chips, drinking soda and watching mindless reality shows on television! Then, talk to their friends about how they wish they could make money with a business venture.

Which one are you?? Action taker or a wannabe!

Our intent is to get you moving. Get yourself in the right mindset to achieve success. At the end of the day your business success depends on one person.

That's you!

The Missing Ingredients

Before I get to the actual ingredient that most marketers are missing lets discuss the components that tie that ingredient together. First of all your marketing should be more about your audience than about the product you are trying to sell.

Second, are your systems working? When I talk about systems I mean emails, webinars, phone follow-ups and product upsells. These systems should be virtually on autopilot. If they are not than "Houston, we have a problem".

Third is to build a herd, a list of loyal subscribers. Do this with email newsletters, webinars etc. Your message should be personality driven to you and your personality. Don't try to be someone you're not! On the same note you should try to appeal to a broad base of buyers. Don't just narrow yourself to a small group of people. In the beginning when you are starting out you can borrow credibility from others to get your message across.

With all of that said, what ties all of this together? The missing ingredient in your marketing soup! That element is economics. Many marketers struggle because they put traffic first. If you put economics first than your new model looks like this.

Economics>>>> Conversions>>>> Traffic

It's reverse engineering your entire marketing plan. The tactical triangle still applies with the 80/20 rule but my wife and I have simply reverse engineered it in our marketing planning! If you start with economics first it will be much easier to find an offer that converts. Then find the targeted traffic to send to the offer.

Fourth, have a good website, don't think about traffic first. More traffic does not mean more sales. If you don't have a good website or offer to promote than your conversions will be almost non-existent. Traffic + conversions = Profit! Once you find the right soup than continue to track, measure and improve your marketing message.

Once you have figured this out you have to know your metrics. Knowing your numbers in your business is super important. When I ask people what their numbers are and they don't know it simply baffles me. How can you run a business without knowing your numbers? In the online business world here are some metrics that my wife and I track.

- Daily earnings per click

- Cost per click
- Weekly average earnings per click
- Cost per sale
- Daily profit and loss
- Average customer value

The most important numbers we track is our daily ROI (Return on Investment). Our second daily metric is how much can we spend to acquire a customer? If you track nothing else than track those two simple things every day. If you don't know your average customer value than there is no way to know if you are over spending with an advertising source to acquire those customers.

So if you are new, your head might be spinning right now! That's ok. Let's look at some business models that put all of this into practical use. Why do 85% of franchises succeed when 90% of self-start up businesses fail? Because these metrics are already in place and there is a system to guide you. A set of procedures that you have to follow. Many people love franchises because they are 90% cheaper in some cases to start and there is a pre-established plan in place to follow.

The downside to franchises is the same positive side. You have to follow rules, this is a big negative in my opinion because I want the freedom to make my own business choices good or bad. Franchises can be very expensive depending on the model but they do work well and most succeed.

Then there was the discovery of ecommerce and info-products on the internet. This exploded the way my wife and I could do business without the large infrastructure of a brick and mortar and employee based business model. Now you could run a business from home.

Information products or opportunity products are a huge part of our daily lives. This is a multi-billion dollar industry and continues to grow like wildfire. I will talk about this more in depth later.

So, I hope this all made sense to you and how you can apply this to your own business or apply it to a start-up business.

Online or Brick and Mortar Business

Let's discuss some of the differences between an online and offline business. Retail vs opportunity products or digital products. A good comparison is (digital delivery) vs (Physical product with physical delivery). There are many types of products on the market and many ways they are delivered. Let's look at a few types.

- Physical products
- Digital products
- Informational products
- Mom and pop services
- Large corporations

Let me drill down into the differences between physical products and opportunity products (Info-products). So what is the difference between the two? Well, they are actually very different and also require much different processes for fulfillment.

Physical products are emotionally driven, a good example is buying an expensive car for $50k. There is logic and a specific emotion behind purchasing a car at that price point. Here is the tough part about selling physical products. Profit margins are generally less and the competition is very high. There is also a lot of overhead that comes with selling physical products. Let's look at a few examples:

- Warehouse expenses
- Employee costs
- Building expenses like rent, heat, lights, air conditioning

Those are just a few that come to mind but will chew up your profit margins in a heartbeat! It takes a lot of resources to own a business that deals with physical products. This is a contributing factor to why startup businesses that sell physical products often fail. They don't do the research and end up finding out that their business could never be profitable due to all of these expenses that they never thought about.

So let's take a look at opportunity products or informational products. These products are delivered digitally and are focused on driving a result. There is far less overhead in these products. In many cases the overhead is nonexistent with the exception of purchasing licenses to sell them. Some good examples to look at are:

- Business courses
- Make money courses
- Relationship courses
- Health and fitness courses

These are just a few examples. There are tons and tons of info-products that you can sell on the market today. So you're likely wondering how to choose an info-product to sell.

Here is some simple advice to guide your decision process. Look for a company that can provide these 4 functions:

- Training, support and solid infrastructure
- Feeder products to assist you in sales for your business
- High ticket back end monetization strategy (Value Ladder)
- Phone sales teams
- Fulfillment process and customer service in place for you

So this is what you should be looking for in your quest to start selling info-products. I ran a very lucrative and successful eBay business for many years. What I found out over time was the physical product line had simply became too competitive for price. With the advent of getting physical products direct from China in bulk it was hard to compete with huge companies to make a profit. Not to mention storage of products, customer service issues and product returns.

This is why I switched to selling info-products. They are simple to sell and have very low overhead when it comes to license rights. I can show you a company right now that licenses 4 info products right now for a few thousand dollars. Now imagine being able to sell that product and not have to worry about delivering the product, customer service, returns or phone sales. That's 90% of your business and all you have to do is focus on selling the product.

I hope you see the power in licensing products using an existing business model. You can cut your cost to about 1/8 of what it would cost you to open an offline business.

Measuring Up In a Business Venture

Let's do a fun exercise that will assist you in finding out where your business stands right now. If you don't run a business than play along! This can be a discovery process for you if you are honest with yourself about where you currently stand in your business right now.

So, how does your business measure up? Are you like a big box store or a struggling new marketer?

Let's find out, and honesty with yourself will make all the difference! Here are the rules: Answer yes or no for each question. A yes is worth 1 point and a no is worth 0 points.

Simple enough right?

Question 1: Do you have a business and marketing plan for the next 6 to 12 months?
YES or NO

Question 2: Are you creating and sharing content at least 2-3 times per week consistently?
YES or NO

Question 3: Are you adding at least 20-50 leads per day into your email list?
YES or NO

Question 4: Are you consistently acquiring new customers with your lead offer (5+ per week)
YES or NO

What is your total score?

If you scored a total of 4 points than congratulations! You have the foundation in place to create a profitable online business!

If you scored less than 4 points your business will struggle to produce profit. You must focus on those questions that you answered NO to.

If you scored 2 or less than you have lots of work to do. But at least you know exactly what to focus your energy on.

So hopefully that was a good discovery process for you to go through. It's very important to answer these questions honestly for your business. Doing this will increase your profitability and guide your business in a profitable cash flow positive direction.

Many people that read this book just need some simple advice to turn some of these simple elements into a YES. I would like to offer the below guidance to you that will assist you in this process. It's simple to do and you just have to focus and get it done!

Tip 1: Get out of your comfort zone, do the things that make you uncomfortable in your business. This could be doing videos, webinars or something as simple as putting your story out there on Facebook for all to see!

Tip 2: Always Fail Forward, no matter what happens don't ever give up on your dream. We all fail at some point in our business decisions. What matters most is how you handle that failure. Will you fail forward and continue on or fail backwards and throw your hands up and quit?

Tip 3: Network with the best, surround yourself with successful people. Have you ever heard of the saying "You can be guilty by association"? Well the same is true with success. Surround yourself by successful people that can mentor, guide and coach you to success. This is known as being "Successful by association". There are few business owners that become successful on their own.

Tip 4: Have a long term vision and plan, know where you want your business to go. Forward plan what you will do every day and stick to the plan. Outsource where needed and never deviate from the plan that you set for your business to succeed.

Tip 5: Be consistent and persistent in your business. Have a system in place for everything that you do every day. Do those tasks that create positive cash flow in a consistent and persistent manner. Never give up and continue to push forward every day. If you do something persistently and consistently for 90 days and it's not working than tweak your strategy and continue moving forward.

Tip 6: Develop your skills of asking quality questions in your business. It's great to ask your coach mentor and friends questions but have quality questions to ask. When you get that one opportunity to ask a top level CEO or successful entrepreneur a question don't waste it on something fundamental.

Tip 7: Embrace your lessons "failures" in your business. It's not always going to be roses, unicorns and rainbows. Embrace those times where it gets tough and you make a wrong choice. Don't continue to look back on it and rehash what you could have done differently. Learn from your lessons and move in a different direction. Just don't learn the same lesson twice!

Tip 8: Be vulnerable in presenting yourself and your business opportunity, products or services. Let people see you for who you are and what you truly believe in. Tell your story and share your experiences with others. Most of all be honest, real and transparent with every aspect of your business.

Tip 9: Most of all HAVE FUN!!!! This should be fun and exciting. Being an entrepreneur is an experience like no other. If you have fun with it and not take everything so seriously you will find that the money starts to come second. Put the customers first and enjoy what you do, it's then that the money just becomes the bonus and icing on the cake!

Discovering Your Why

You may or may not have heard this before. It's important in any business to know your "why." Why are you in business? Do you know why you started a business or do you know why you want to start one now? This is a very important question to ask yourself and also to know! Let's look at this more in depth. Here are some typical answers that I hear frequently.

- I want to make money
- Create stability in my paycheck
- More free time
- Be my own boss
- Spend more time with family and friends

So these are some of the most common answers that I get when I ask aspiring entrepreneurs why they want to start an online business. I am not saying these are not good reasons to start a business but they lack depth in my opinion. Look for more meaning than just the typical self-serving answers.

What I am always a bit disappointed with is I never get the following responses. If I do they are very seldom. These are paramount to the success of your business. Here are some examples.

- To help people

- To show someone how to realize their own dreams
- To provide quality customer service
- To help a charity
- To feel good about yourself knowing you made a difference in someone's life

It is important to note there is nothing wrong with trying to improve your own life with answers like the first set of five. Most people want this same thing if they admit it or not, but here's a little secret that can drastically change the face of your business. Think about the people first, and the money will come naturally.

It's important in any business to profit, that's not what I am talking about. I am talking about being a business owner that truly cares about its customers. If you do this it will show on your quarterly statements. Trust me when I tell you that it will show in a big way.

If you put the customer's needs, wants, desires, pains and struggles as your most utmost priority you will find success quickly.

Make these a priority in your business and provide your customers the solutions that solve their deepest problems. When you do this you put them on a pedestal and there is no better feeling as a business owner to know that you solved someone's pains and struggles in life.

Like I said before, there is nothing wrong with having your own personal goals. You need to have those goals to take your business to the next level. Just be very careful that this does not come off the wrong way in your marketing efforts.

So I challenge you to know the "why" in your business. What drives you to your success? What personal goals have you set? What is your message? How are you perceived by your customers and are you truly passionate about serving their needs.

Take some time to figure this out as a business owner. Put the people first and the money will naturally come on autopilot!

Chapter 6

Getting This Puppy Kick Started

The Art of Personal Branding

Let's look at a case study like Richard Branson. He is among some of the most elite of the elite in the business world and a true example of what an entrepreneur should strive for. Now you may or may not like him but that's completely insignificant. What is your brand in your business? Is it just a faceless name or title?

Let's look at what really makes your brand strong enough to stand up to the challenge. Ask yourself the following questions: What are your core strengths? What are your gifts? What are your talents and what are your attributes? These things all directly impact what your brand will look like and how it is perceived.

Each of us have unique strengths, talents and gifts that come naturally to us. It's important to push our limits and challenge ourselves to do things that may feel uncomfortable or push us into directions that we are not strong in. Let's dig deeper into this!

Effective personal branding quickly demonstrates:

- Who you are
- What you stand for
- Who you serve
- How you will serve

Let's look at some factors that contribute to figuring out effective branding. My wife and I refer to these factors as the 3 C's.

- Clarity: Be super clear on who you are and who you are not. Don't try to be someone else
- Consistency: Be consistent in your message and all of your communications with customers or potential prospects
- Constancy: Always be in front of your target market. You should constantly be showing your brand to them

You are probably reading this and wondering, "How do I do any of this stuff"? Well the answer is very simple! Be yourself and let that shine through in your branding message.

There are many ways to craft your character and make it attractive to your audience.

Let's look at some examples and elements that you can use to put this together:

- Develop your backstory. Everyone has this and it's what makes your brand relate the most
- Use parables

- Define your character flaws. People don't want to see perfect, it's unrealistic
- Polarity – What do you stand for?

Next you have to decide what your identity is. What character does your brand best fit with? Here are some examples:

- The leader
- The adventurer or crusader
- The reporter
- The reluctant hero

We each fit into one of these identities in our character. This all directly correlates back to the beginning when speaking about your own skills, experience and specialized knowledge. Putting this all together creates your unique personal brand.

Each one of us has distinct experiences that have developed our unique skills and knowledge. Ask yourself what skills have you learned, developed and mastered. Has this in essence created your personal brand and who you are?

I challenge you to look at all of these factors that create who you are and mold them into your very own personal brand. Your brand is important and at the very core of your business. At the end of the day it's up to you to figure out how you want your brand to be perceived!

Developing Who Your Ideal Customer Is

Let's discuss target markets and ideal customers. If you take a few minutes and pay close attention to every TV commercial you will see they are targeting an ideal customer. Once you have been in this business for a while it begins to become very obvious.

When you watch an infomercial, the selling strategies are designed to target a certain market or what I like to call an ideal customer, "customer avatar". There messaging is very subtle in most cases but really digs deep into the targeted customers pains, struggles, fears, wants or desires and provides a solution. This is why infomercials have been so successful. So let's dig deeper into the nuts and bolts of this.

Your leads, visitors and customers have one primary question. Do you know what it is? The primary question is, "What's in it for me"? If you can answer that question in a satisfying manner than you're going to make sales, but you have to understand the difference between your broad market category and specific target market niches. I will focus on internet marketing (home business niche) for this example. If you want to target a different niche, you would create a new and relevant lead generation (and product offer) strategy.

Here is the important part. Before you can create a marketing message you must know *who* you are speaking to and *where* they are at in the customer awareness process. If you are not familiar with this process you can see it below.

Unaware> Problem Aware> Solution Aware> Product Aware> Actively Engaged
COLD>> WARM>> HOT

I am not going to go into depth regarding the customer awareness process, but to put it simply, every customer goes through a process or decision point before they make a purchase. Unaware being a completely cold lead and actively engaged meaning they have their credit card in hand ready to make a purchase.

I want to focus on helping you identify who your ideal customer is. I will provide you a guide to follow to help you identify this ideal customer or customer avatar.

- Make a list of all the challenges, problems and obstacles a customer may have that fits to your product. What are their pains? Identify at least 10 "High Stakes" problems.
- What is their primary question they would want an answer to?
- Where do they hang out online? What forums? What Facebook Groups?
- How will you attract this ideal customer? List out some solutions to solve their problems.
- How are you going to serve them and help them reach their specific goals and desires?

Answer these questions and you are well on your way to defining your ideal customer. Remember the goal is to know and understand your customers to the point where the product sells itself to them!

This strategy allows you to really connect with your customers in a unique way and a way like no other. Most of your customers won't even realize that they are being "sold" on your product or service, it's completely subconscious. They will feel like it's a recommendation from a friend or family member or a well-known and trusted leader.

Think of it this way, when you go to the doctor and they recommend a prescription for an illness do you question that? I would say in most cases the answer is no. Why? Because they are the expert in their field and know what they are talking about.

So before you do any marketing, any ad copy or headlines, you need to identify who this ideal customer is. This will allow you to communicate the benefits of your product more effectively to that ideal customer. So let's put this all into action! Use the below as your guide to pinpoint and define your ideal customer.

- What is the gender and approximate age of your customer?
- What are their top challenges, frustrations, pains and problems?
- What is their WHY? What really motivates and inspires them to take action?
- What are their desires, dreams, goals and aspirations?
- Do they have any enemies? Who are those people that drive them crazy?
- Do they have any heroes? Who inspires them? Who do they admire?
- Do they have any interests or hobbies?
- Do they have any fears? What are they? Do they have regrets in their lives?
- Is anyone making them feel guilty? Who do they feel like they are failing and disappointing?

Now ask yourself, what does my product, business, service or opportunity really solve? Then list the ways your customer's life (lifestyle, finances, relationships, day to day life, self-worth etc.) will be different due to your product or service.

Once you have done this and identified who your ideal customer is than its time to shape your advertising message. Come up with a good solid headline that targets this customer avatar. Then target the main body of your message to fit the needs, wants and desires of your target customer.

Branding Yourself with Video

Earlier in this book I talked about the importance of your brand. Let's take this a bit further and move into video branding. This scares the heck out of a lot of people. It's an uncomfortable and unnatural feeling for many people to be in front of a camera. Here is the truth, you have to get over this fear and overcome the desire to stay in a place of comfort.

Your branding video will showcase who you are and what you represent to the world. This video can be a professional video or a simple video shot on an iPhone. The way your video appears to your audience is important, but the content is what really draws followers. So let's look at an outline of what your "Rock Star" video will contain from a content standpoint:

- Introduction
- Background
- Introduce your character (share something personal, dreams, goals, vision, desire)
- What was the "wall" for you?
- Stack up the problems
- Introduce the discovery you made
- Describe the unique solution

- Talk about the shift. What changed and what did you realize?
- Add the conspiracy theory, it's not my/your fault
- Highlight your success or the success of others
- Share the hidden benefits
- Call to Action / Invitation

So there is a pretty simple outline for you to follow to create your very own branding video. But let's dig a bit deeper so you have a good knowledge base on how to get started making your first video.

First, you want to capture your story in an introduction. What is your background and education? What was your life like growing up? Captivate your viewers by telling your unique story. We all have one that relates to an audience.

How did you find this opportunity, product, service, business or solution? What were your unique circumstances that led you to your decision? Get personal here and really share why you made your decision to use this product, opportunity or service.

What got you excited and pumped up about this product, opportunity or service? What potential did you identify and what got you motivated the most to pursue this opportunity that you are trying to pass on to your herd of followers. Why did you start in the first place?

Next you want to really capture your story, recall memories that contributed to your success. What challenges did you face and how did you overcome those challenges. What epiphany did you have through your discovery process?

Can you think of any specific time in this process where you discovered specific skillsets that you didn't know you had?

Describe how they improved your business, your lifestyle etc. What was that skillset and how did it improve these areas. Think of some other crazy, weird or relatable story to tie in. They may not directly correlate but they can be used as metaphors, illustrations or teachings.

Now you craft your personal branding story and your offer. So you might be thinking, how can I capture my prospects attention and keep it long enough to communicate my story, build trust, rapport and sell my offer?

You can use what I call, "open loop story telling" when crafting your sales funnel. Think about one of the challenges you listed from the above questions. Where did this take place (i.e. place, time of year, time of day, weather etc.)? What was your state of mind? Really describe those emotions you were feeling as you were going through that specific challenge.

Think about that moment and identify when your emotions were the highest. What was going through your mind? Then fast forward to when you overcame this specific challenge or struggle. What event or experience occurred where you really knew you had overcame that struggle. How did that make you feel? (Go into detail and really paint this picture).

If you follow this simple guideline that I have laid out you will retain your prospects attention far longer. Studies show that you have 30 seconds to engage your audience in video before they decide to continue watching or move on. Coming up with these short story sequences will be something you can use in product launches, promotions, your follow up sequence and your personal branding. Vivid stories will be engrained into your prospect's memory and they will continue to come back for more.

"Old School" Mindset and How It Hurts Your Future

Before I get started, I know this topic is going to anger a lot of people (In the education field)! I will say that right up front! But, I am willing to take the close minded skepticism in order to drive my point home and hopefully reach a few aspiring minds that can think "outside" the old school box.

So let me explain by started out with my own story… I was raised in a family that had no college education and barely a high school education. My parents were both entrepreneurs and ran their own businesses and did not need the "typical" education that is so often pushed onto our youth today. I did however finish high school as a B-C student but graduated college with a 3.9 GPA. I can tell you that this education did nothing for me up to this point in my life!

Here is what I do know. This is the mindset of 98% of people on this planet. Most people grow up with the mindset that they must get a college education to become successful. So that's what most people do, they graduate high school, get accepted into college, wrack up student loans and enter the work force at $30,000.00 a year. Wow…. Where do I sign up for that!!! When you hear it in those terms does it make sense to you? I mean really, does that even pass the common sense test? MOST people will never see a paycheck of more than $45,000.00 to $50,000.00 per year!

Now imagine for just one second being able to make that much money in one month. It's hard to even believe isn't it? But it's going on all around you every single day. You see, we are conditioned to believe that we have to be educated through attending college and then work for someone else. *You don't have to*! This is very old school thinking and I have noticed a pretty large shift happening over the last few years.

People are starting to realize that they don't have to be a slave to a middle class workforce anymore.

If you have read anything about me and my story you will see that I was trapped in that mindset myself for years. Entrepreneurship is much more than freedom. It's an opportunity to spread your wings and fly and be independent and be your own boss. Now some of these very positive things can be negative without self-drive and discipline. It's not always pixie dust, unicorns, and rainbows!

But here is my whole point... life is too short to be trapped in the rat race. There is so much opportunity out there if you want to grab it by the horns and forge your own path.

At the end of the day it all comes down to breaking those chains and reprogramming yourself from an employee mindset to an entrepreneur mindset. If you can do this than the world is wide open to you for new experiences. All you have to do is take the first steps to get there. Once you are aware of this world that you had no idea existed, you will read this book again and shake your head and say "What Was I Thinking".

I hope this was insightful for you. I know this topic will drum up some controversy but that's ok. It's all about sharing the experience and hopefully expanding someone's mind to another opportunity in life. I encourage you to find YOUR way whatever that is and strive for excellence in whatever you do. Just remember, it's your life and you only get to live it once. It's completely up to you to make it the best life possible.

Pushing Content like a Big Dog

Blah, Blah, Blah... content, content, content. That's all we hear today is content and email marketing is king. I don't disagree with this assessment that many have proclaimed!

Content marketing is without a doubt the number one marketing strategy that still works today. So why are so many people failing at it? Well, that's pretty simple actually... They have a strategy that just plain sucks to be quite honest.

Too many marketers are using content that has been spun over and over and over again. It's old and people are just not interested in it anymore. They have listened to the same blah, blah, blah, over and over again. Now don't get me wrong, it's not easy waking up every single day and sitting in front of a computer screen wracking your brain about what you want to write about. After a while your idea muscle starts to get a bit stressed out!

But I will tell you this, content marketing is an essential key ingredient in your marketing efforts. I would like to share my own content marketing strategy that has worked very well for me. So some of you that are new to marketing may ask, "What is content marketing"? In simple terms, it's a process for delivering valuable content to a group of readers that is designed to attract, acquire and engage a specific target audience. The end objective is to drive potential customers to take a specific action.

Now not all marketing content is a means to convert a prospect into a sale. If you are doing this and have this approach than this is part of the reason you are struggling. Second, if you are recycling old PLR articles over and over again than this is a big mistake. Your audience will soon realize that your number one goal is to sell them something! I have been on blogs and read articles that say the EXACT SAME THING! They are just worded differently! This is not how you want to build your business or brand. Be original and write your own copy that engages your audience.

Remember this! Your content strategy ties all of your marketing together!

- Branding and positioning – Understand your own core message, personal brand and identity.
- Acquire website traffic – This can be in the form of blog articles, search engines, YouTube, Facebook, Twitter, Instagram, guest posts or native ads.
- Lead generation – Use lead magnets, giveaways, check lists, short reports, eBooks, videos, webinars, events and promotions.
- Follow-up – email marketing, blog posts, webinars, videos and Facebook
- Conversions – In 2009 average online buyers consumed 2-3 pieces of content before making a purchase. Since then this number has risen exponentially to about 10 pieces of content.
- Back end sales – Develop relationships and build loyalty with webinars and training. Just continue to pile on more value!

Let's talk a little bit about the style of your content. Your content and how you write directly correlates to your brand and who you are. I am branded to the more coach, mentor, and teach approach which works for me. But here are some other examples:

- Personality driven, story driven or like a soap opera – These create a personal connection and a relationship. They also build trust in your audience.

You make yourself an attractive character but remember that facts tell, but stories sell!
- Value always – Solve problems and provide solutions. Be the one that answers questions. Train and educate and pre-sell your offers.
- Have good sales content – Have a solid call to action, direct offers, good sales webinars and sales videos.

Now let's look at some different types of content you can use in your marketing.

Remember that this all ties back into your marketing strategy. Don't just write content in the dark, have a specific purpose for that content and where you want it to go. So here are some different types of content.

- Round up posts – top 10 or top 100 Lists
- Over the top value resource posts
- Deeply personal "Soul baring" posts
- Educational or problem solving posts
- Controversial posts
- Review posts – products services, software or courses
- Video posts or interview posts
- Blog series

So there you have it, this is a great guideline for you to follow when it comes to writing good quality content 2-3 times per week. If you are reading this and still wondering what to write or report about, here are some steps to further take to help you:

- Identify problems and solutions of your target market (also list out their questions)
- Group them into categories and themes
- Isolate categories or themes for your brand identity
- Brainstorm a master list of topics
- Let it flow to paper

Become more valuable. Research leading blogs, brands, authorities and "gurus" in your niche and find out what the most popular articles, blog posts and videos are.

Make discoveries. Attend, study and invest in yourself. Attend webinars, pick up courses, books, events and mastermind groups.

Putting all of this together may sound very complicated. The fact is this, it's really not rocket science. It just takes some thought process! You have to put that brain muscle that is attached to your spine to work and get the idea juices flowing.

Chapter 7

Some Little Tidd Bits of Information

Spending 15K for Access

So you probably read that headline and are thinking, "you're completely nuts." Who in their right mind would pay 15k to attend a business summit? Let me tell you how business really works. You have to invest in your business and be willing to take actions that grow your business in large leaps. So let me share this quick story with you.

In January of 2015, I spent almost $15,000.00 to attend a mastermind on the small island of Curacao. There was only one speaker at this event that I was super pumped to gain access to and pick his brain. If you are familiar with the TV show Shark Tank than you will know who I am talking about. His name is Kevin Harrington and he is a multi-billionaire and founder of "As Seen on TV."

So why would I pay that much money just to see someone speak? Because the information they provide is of great value. This also gave me the opportunity to corner him and pull out a few extra golden nuggets for our business. When the opportunity presented itself, I did just that. I ended up spending just under an hour discussing our business and how my wife and I could take it to new levels.

He had some great advice and is honestly just a great human being! Many have asked me if it was worth it and my answer is, yes. The ideas, concepts and mentorship that my wife and I received over that single 50 minutes of time resulted in a drastic shift in our business. We went through some exponential growth in our business extremely quickly upon returning from this business trip. It was absolutely amazing. I can comfortably say that I saw a 200% growth rate in our income in 30 days! Now, I am not telling you to go out there and drop $15k on a business mastermind!

But, ask yourself this! Would you be willing to shell out $15k on an idea like that? I can tell you that 90% of the people who read this would say NO. Why? Because they are stuck within a comfort zone in their life or their business. If you are afraid to take risks that could potentially grow a business than entrepreneurship is simply not for you! You have to get out of your normal mindset and take risks. With risk comes reward but with risk there can be failure!

That's why most people don't make these leaps. They are way too concerned about failing. I have had many failures in our business. Product launches that flopped, advertising campaigns that were duds, systems that have failed, etc. The true entrepreneur will pick themselves up, dust themselves off and forge forward.

Let's take programs for example (i.e. Affiliate programs, MLMs, Amway, Empower Network, MOBE, Pre-Paid Legal, etc.). All of these systems work, it's not the system that fails, it's the person running the business that fails. I will give you a good example… I met a guy that was involved in one of these companies. He had seen no success at all and was complaining that this particular company had ripped him off.

So I was very curious about this and ended up in a pretty deep conversation about it with him. I discovered a lot of things from that conversation. The bottom line was this, he was not following what they trained him to do. He was blindly advertising, making all the mistakes there were to make and just not paying attention to how the model worked. He didn't even attend any of the additional free training that this company offered to him.

This is how these companies end up getting a bad name.

People like this guy don't do the proper research or take the time to learn a few things and then they fail. Then they complain on every online forum they can find that they got ripped off after trying it for 20 days! This is not how any business works. If you go into anything thinking there is an easy button than you are going to be very disappointed. Running a business takes a bit of effort on your part. It doesn't matter what kind of business it is either.

So what's my point here? My point is you have to be willing to invest in yourself and your business. My wife and I have invested well over $100k into our own education by attending business masterminds, summits, conferences and so on. But with every one of these came a connection that led to another connection that led to another and another (you get the point). This has been priceless for business and has catapulted my wife and I to heights that we could have never dreamed.

Networking is such an important part of a business model. When you network with likeminded people you get ideas, advice and guidance to enhance your business. You end up reciprocating ideas that help other people enhance their business in the process, so it's a win-win situation. What goes around comes around right!

List Building and Its Importance

Have you ever heard the phrase, "The money is in the list"? If you haven't, than keep reading! If you have, well you need to keep reading too because I am going to share some little tips with you. (Your welcome).

So why is the money in your own list? Well there are many reasons for this. For starters, when you have your own list of leads you can build an audience like a mad scientist! This is so important when it comes to selling products either online or offline.

Many people are involved in the business opportunity niche or the business niche. This is the perfect place to really capitalize on your list building efforts. Many people out there use these programs as a platform to build their lists. The biggest mistake that I see is people pigeon hole themselves to one specific product or service.

It's important to monetize your email list in many directions and NOT with only one single opportunity. Here's an example. If you sign up to sell affiliate products on popular platforms like *Clickbank.com* or *JVzoo.com* there are hundreds and hundreds of options for product choices. Not to mention it's completely free to sign up as an affiliate on these sites. You also have mid-price points of $20 to $49 products to sell for commissions.

You can also use proven paid affiliate programs and license products to cover your huge back-end sales of up to 10K per sale. But here is my point, you have to combine multiple opportunities like the ones above to monetize your list appropriately.

So how do you build a list? Now that you have some products to sell you want to start building your actual list. This requires three things.

- An autoresponder email service (recommend getresponse.com).
- Landing pages (also known as squeeze pages). I recommend the same service as the autoresponder email service since it's a one stop shop.
- A way to track your results. My wife and I use Click Magick because it's reasonably priced and has a lot of tracking options (clickmagick.com).

Up to this point I have given you every tool you need. You now have products, your autoresponder, lead capture capability and tracking services at your fingertips. Now it's time to build your list like a mad scientist.

Now you're probably wondering how to do this. There are many ways to build your list by capturing leads. I have become the masters of solo advertising. Solo advertising is nothing more than leveraging someone else's list to build your own. Then you monetize this list with your offers.

Here is where most people make a mistake when it comes to list building. You can't be scared to drop some cash to build it. Regardless of what advertising platform you use, you must be willing to invest in your business to build your list. You can do this through PPC (Pay Per Click) advertising, solo ads, PPV (Pay Per View) advertising, banner ads, blogs, article marketing, etc. That's an entire different discussion in itself.

Let's look at a simple model of how this all works and how you can build your list like crazy and offer products from the services discussed above. This is a very simple concept that does not require fancy graphs.

Traffic>>>>>> Landing Page>>>>>> Your Product>>>>>> Autoresponder Follow-up

That's it! There is nothing complicated about this, but so many people are doing it wrong in their marketing. Too many people are over complicating this process when it's really very simple to set up.

The Online Magic Formula

When it comes to running your own online business, the formula for success is surprisingly simple:

- Find a popular product that people want
- Create the structure that allows people to find the products you promote
- Turn on your sales engine and count your profits

Yet while it may sound easy, executing such a strategy profitably is much more complicated. After all, if it were easy everybody would be an internet millionaire!

Finding the Right Products:

The key to finding a popular product that people will want is identifying evergreen products. These are products that never go out of demand regardless of how the economy is doing or how many people have already bought them.

These include products that either offer solutions that can never truly be solved or that feed a customer base that is continually filling up with new customers. Examples include dog obedience, weight loss, and make money products.

Internet Search Tools:

Once you have identified an evergreen niche that you will be comfortable working in, it's time to look for info-products that have the highest amount of prospective customers. To do this, you need to use the free search tools provided by the internet.

The first stop should be the Google Product Search. This free site tells you what products within your chosen niche are hot right now. In other words, it tells you the niche info-products that have the greatest number of prospective customers.

The Amazon Bestsellers page is another great place to find niche products with high demand. Plus, you can enroll in the Amazon Associate's program and promote many of the products offered on the site as affiliate products on your web page(s). Then, every time somebody clicks through from your page to Amazon and buys that product, you make a sales commission.

Other places to look for hot products within your niche are the Alexa Internet, "What's Hot" page and eBay Pulse.

Niche Statistics for Info-products:

While Google Product Search and Amazon Bestsellers will tell you what info-products consumers are looking for, that only gives you half the information you need to make your decision about what info-products to promote. The next step is to compile statistical data so that you can make an informed decision.

Researching Niche Statistics Online:

You can find statistics on individual info-products within a niche by using the free Google Keyword Tool. Start by entering some generic, "product niche" terms, such as, "dog obedience training". You will then get an idea of the sort of terms and items people are searching for in that particular niche.

Sources for Niche Data:

One of the best places to find statistical data on your niche to determine its popularity is Google Trends. It will show you whether a particular niche is seasonal or whether it is an evergreen niche that has more staying power.

Using the free Google Trends tool, you can see for example that, "dog obedience training" is an evergreen niche, while searches for, "rose bouquet" tends to peak around Valentine's Day.

Determining Maximum Value:
After you have identified evergreen niches that have lots of potential customers, it's time to find individual info-products within those niches that prospective customers are anxious to buy.

To do this, you must visit websites where you can browse affiliate info-products. Some of the most popular include:

- Clickbank for digital info-products
- Commission Junction for digital info-products
- Market Health for health info-products
- Amazon Associates

Using the Internet's free tools to identify evergreen niches, then select products within those niches that you can promote for profit.

The Death of Multi-Level Marketing

I get questions all the time about MLM (or Multi-Level marketing) and Network Marketing. What is MLM? Well here is the dictionary definition of what Multi-Level Marketing is according to Wikipedia.org.

Multi-Level Marketing (MLM) is a marketing strategy in which the sales force is compensated not only for sales they generate, but also for the sales of the other salespeople that they recruit. This recruited sales force is referred to as the participant's "downline," and can provide multiple levels of compensation.

Now, this form of marketing is completely legal by the way! MLM often times get confused with pyramid schemes when they are NOT the same thing at all. Pyramid schemes are illegal in "most" places in the world.

I have personally never been involved in any of these types of marketing and neither should you. The risk is high and you can get into a lot of trouble by being involved. So stay away from those types of opportunities at all costs.

So let's talk about MLM. I think it's dead! MLM and network marketing is so much different than affiliate marketing. It's based off of the recruitment of others. You are always hunting family and friends, neighbors or whoever you can "convince" to join that particular opportunity.

This concept is dying or already dead. Now, those that have been in it for years to this point have an established base and are of course doing very well, but I have some friends and even established network marketers that I know that have been in this type of business for many years and they are struggling more and more every year.

Many of them are jumping ship and merging over to internet marketing as affiliate marketers. The opportunities are far more stable and they are honest and holistic in every way. So what is a good option to get started in internet marketing? Well there are many options to get started on a very low budget.

Example: If you sign up to sell affiliate products on popular platforms like *Clickbank.com* or *JVzoo.com* there are hundreds and hundreds of options for product choices. Not to mention it is completely free to sign up as an affiliate on these sites. Now you have mid-price point $20 to $49 products to sell for commissions. You can also use a proven paid affiliate program and license their products to cover your huge back-end sales of up to 10K per sale and a phone team is included at no cost to you.

These are not MLM opportunities rather affiliate marketing opportunities. You can leverage other people's products and sell them for a percentage of the final sales cost. This is a very low cost way to start up your own business. If you are interested in MLM or network marketing than this is not the option for you!

I personally prefer to sell products as an affiliate. I have very little overhead and don't have to concern myself with customer support, product fulfillment, phone sales or product creation. I simply leverage other people's products and take a cut of the final sale!

This gives you a lower cost business solution without the high cost or overhead of a traditional business. Let's face it, brick and mortar businesses are very costly and an eBay business is bulky and requires you to have physical products. Been there… done that… and also had a house full of products cluttering our garage. This is a big reason my wife and I made the switch to affiliate marketing.

Making a Hobby into a Business

Many of the world's largest companies were all started as a simple hobby. My first hobby I ever had was collecting sports memorabilia as a kid. Later in life I turned it into a very profitable business on eBay. This little hobby I had was something I enjoyed, it was fun, exciting and I had the thrill of discovering that latest limited edition piece of memorabilia.

Then I branched out to other products and built my eBay business in a massive way. This was a simple hobby that I had turned into a profitable business. I later expanded away from eBay because the competition in that market was very high and the profit margins were too low.

Here is the point, it's pretty easy to turn a current hobby into a flourishing business. Here is another example... I have a close family friend that made custom birthday cards for family and friends during their birthdays, anniversaries, holidays, etc. These cards were simply amazing. I recommended that she scale this hobby to a business and start selling these awesome cards online. The rest is history and her business is doing well and there is not much overhead in it.

This is actually how most business ventures start. There is an idea or concept, then small scale testing, word of mouth orders, and then mass production into the market. This is how you take a hobby and turn it into a business with minimal investment. Pretty cool right?

So you might be thinking.... I don't have a hobby to turn into a business. Well our answer to that is simple! Sure you do, you just don't realize it. If you don't and you want to start a business than it's important that you do something that you enjoy! That's the key here! Do something that you can have a true passion for. If it's helping people, than find an opportunity that allows you to help people. Maybe it's selling products or services! Find what it is you are most passionate about and do that one thing.

Do you know where some of the largest companies began? In their garage! Look at the computer industry for example. Microsoft began with two guys working on what is now a, "computer" from a small garage. Then Bill Gates created one of the largest companies on the planet.

So it's possible with the right desire and drive to take your hobby and turn it into a business. Sometimes it requires a small leap of faith in yourself and the courage to step outside of your comfort zone. This is what usually holds people back from launching a hobby into a business or just taking those first few steps toward starting a business.

Take the time to go through your own life and write down your ideas. What you are passionate about and what you like doing. Maybe you have this special fly fishing lure that you personally made yourself that catches trout like crazy! You can capitalize on this idea and turn it into a very successful business.

There are tons and tons of examples just like that one that people have capitalized on over the years. Look at silly putty for example, it started off as a bi-product that was used to clean walls. It was later repurposed as a child's toy and has made billions of dollars.

Our point here is this, one small idea can result in millions of dollars. Now, we're not saying you're going to be a millionaire, but the possibilities are there if you have the will and desire to make it happen.

Chapter 8

SOME OF MY PRETTY COOL SECRETS AND TIPS

Email or Direct Mail Marketing

Email marketing is still the king when it comes to marketing products and services. Look at a company like Bed Bath and Beyond. They do an awesome job of email marketing and promoting their product with 20% coupons for a purchase and another $10 off when you combine purchases. On and on and on right!

They are very successful doing this over email. But, they have also mastered direct mail in conjunction with email marketing. Let me use my wife as an example, she loves Bed Bath and Beyond and shops there all the time. Why? Because she gets coupons over email and gets them in the mail as well. Seems like at least twice a week, and in-store purchases except expired coupons. That's right, if you have a coupon that you received in the mail and the date expires, you can still use it at any of their stores.

But what does this do? It gives you a perceived value right? Is it a real value? Well that's for you to decide, but it's better than paying the full price right? They are reaching the online user and also the offline user and providing what is perceived to be a huge value, and it is, not saying that it isn't because if you shop there, you would be silly not to apply the discounts that they offer.

I get asked all the time about email and direct mail marketing. Most people say that direct mail is dead and it's the "old way" of doing things. If you look at the model above that I just spoke about using Bed Bath and Beyond as an example you will see that this simply is not true.

They are doing very well with both. Email marketing may be king but I would have to say that direct mail marketing done right comes in at a very close second as a way to market. Here is what scares people... COST! Direct mail is very expensive due to postage, paper and printing. So if you are going to do direct mail it's best that you do small tests with different copy to identify what works best first.

Then scale up your efforts and put more money into what is working! Now, the huge upside for email marketing is it's free. You would of course need an autoresponder service but that's really cheap or there are even free services that you can use. But the overhead is far less in email marketing vs. direct mail marketing. If you have a list of loyal subscribers you can reach out to them for virtually no cost every single day.

Here is the problem with email marketing! People are inundated with emails every single day. So what makes you stand out? You have to stand out from the crowd and offer valuable content. Just like you would with direct mail marketing. Really good email marketers know the formula to market effectively to their subscribers to turn them into cash machines.

I think it's important to optimize both avenues. Do both in your marketing and you will see a drastic change in your income from month to month, but you have to have a plan and a strategy to make it work. If you have an online based business you will have to find a way to pull those offline customers to your website or offer online. This means having an irresistible offer that your customers just have to look at. (They can't resist the temptation to see it, which drives the usual offline customer online).

If you can do this successfully than you will break into a fresh market of customers that will eventually spend their money on your products and services.

Our Simple Facebook Secret

I use to absolutely hate using Facebook. I was part of the Facebook resistance for years and didn't even have a Facebook account. I did mostly traditional marketing like many others. Then, I discovered a simple and cost effective way to capitalize using Facebook to market with. It will almost seem way too simple, but it actually works. I am proof that it works and you can use this technique to build you audience and sell your products and services.

This is not a well-known way to market on Facebook either. Very few people are actually doing this and I'm going to give this little golden nugget to you for free. So take what you discover here and go apply it. Just do a small test with $5 and see what your results are!

Here is the secret formula: You and your story. So many people don't realize how much impact their story can have on other people. We all go through ups and downs in our lives, but this is what makes us relatable to groups of people.

This is such a simple concept and it works. Take about 20 minutes and outline your life on paper. Then organize it chronologically and fill in your story about your life. That's it, that's the secret! From there it's as simple as copy and paste!

Once you have written your story... This should be easy, it's your life and you should be able to put it on paper! Copy and paste this life story into a new post on your business page and run a post engagement ad for $5. You can also boost your post with your followers that have liked your page.

So do you want to know our results from the simple story about my wife and I? Well here are the results! We had 3 sales on that ad and it cost us $20 all total. We traded $20 for 3 sales that totaled just over $1,300.00! That's one heck of a return on investment isn't it!

So I would encourage you to try this very simple strategy yourself. There are not many people out there using it right now and it's a very powerful way to market your product or service. The only thing you have to do is tell your story and incorporate your product or service into it. Just tie it in with your story.

I leave my contact information on the post to include email address, phone number and how to reach my wife and I on Skype. I am giving this audience every way possible to contact me. I don't send them to a product or service to look at. Here is the ultimate goal in marketing... Stop chasing customers and let them chase you! Your story will not resonate with everyone but it will resonate with some people. Those are the people that will turn into customers for you!

So I would encourage you to try this same strategy in your own marketing. Start with a small budget and scale it up if you see results from it. If you don't know how to set up a post engagement ad in Facebook you can go to YouTube and learn how to do it for free. It's pretty simple and once you do it one time you will become a pro at it!

The Price of Scaling Your Business

If you are new to business you may not even know what a mastermind or summit is! That's ok, I will explain it to you. Have you ever attended a live business event before? I have attended many of them to grow my business. Live events are the best way to find new business opportunities and make connections. Most importantly, make connections with like-minded people.

So in 2015 alone I attended 3 separate business masterminds. The masterminds themselves were filled with speakers that shared their business experience and gave out those precious golden nuggets of information. Most important, the masterminds gave my wife and I the ability to network with the speakers and other successful business owners at the events.

These masterminds are really priceless in my opinion. Earlier in this book I wrote about networking with Kevin Harrington who has sold billions of dollars of products on infomercials. These are the caliber of people you will get unlimited access to during masterminds like these.

I often hear people say, why would you spend $10k to attend a mastermind? That's a very simple answer. My wife and I are investing in ourselves and investing in our business to take it to new levels. These events have been critical for the growth of our business and have helped us grow our business every single month.

It only takes one simple strategy shift to take your business from making $500 a month to making $100k per month. This probably seems impossible to you and likely sounds, "to good to be true," but the fact is it's absolutely true and it can be done. You just have to open your mind up to the possibilities and lean forward.

My wife and I don't look at attending a business event or a mastermind as a cost. We look at it as an investment in our own knowledge and an investment into our business. In addition; it can be a huge tax write off as well depending on how your business is set up!

I would encourage you to look into attending a live event if you are just getting started. What you will learn there will increase your knowledge 10-fold in the business world. Now you don't have to go out there and drop 10k on a mastermind right away if you are just getting started. There are many smaller seminars held around the world that are less expensive or even free to attend.

I am very serious about my business and am willing to make these types of investments into ourselves and our business. I would suggest if you are just getting started or have been around for a while to consider this as an option to take your business to the next level. The benefits will far outweigh the costs and you will make some amazing progress much faster in your business.

If you make a small commitment to a free business event you will start to experience success in your business ventures. Attend free events, meet like-minded people, and make connections which will inevitably result in doing joint venture (JV) deals in your business.

Finding a Profitable Business Model Online

What is a profitable business model and how can you identify it when you see it? This is not as hard as you might think! A good business model has some key elements that make it successful. Let's look at some of these elements:

- Solid Front end products at a low price, $7 – $99. These are known as trip wire products that get your customers in the door.
- Back end high-ticket products are so important. These are products that can range from $499 to $30k. These can be coaching programs, event tickets, courses, etc. This is what separates the everyday marketer from the top earners in the industry.
- Follow up with front-end buyers is so important. Having a good email follow up strategy is your key to success.
- Having a really good phone sales team will skyrocket your business. Moving those front end buyers through the pipeline and selling them higher priced products is essential in your business. Let's look at McDonalds for example. When you go to McDonalds and you buy a cheeseburger what is the first thing they ask? Would you like fries and a drink with that (upsell #1) right! Then they may ask would you like to make this a large order (upsell #2). Then they may ask, could we add a desert to your order (upsell #3). This is what increases their average customer value to over $2 per customer in profit. This is why a phone sales team is so important! They serve the same purpose.
- The systems to track your business are also crucial for your business. Having the ability to track sales and track what your customers are buying is important information for you to know.

- Having a mentor or a coach is probably one of the most important parts of your business. This can be a friend, business partner or someone you are paying to coach and mentor you along in your business. If you are paying for a mentor or a coach you have to look at that money as an investment and not an expense.
- Customer service will sink your business if it's horrible. Customers put more stock in the customer support area of your business more than the products themselves. Having a good customer support team will increase your customers coming back for more. You want a team that is friendly, supportive and deals with customer questions quickly.
- Having a solid way to fulfill your product or service is also important. Depending on the product this can be an area that is extremely expensive and bulky. If you are in the info-product business like my wife and I are its way less complicated. But physical products require packaging and shipping and handling.

These are just a few of the things to look into when setting up your business. If you are looking at a brick and mortar business you will have to throw the entire employee dynamic on top of this. This makes business complicated and expensive. That's why I run an internet business! I stay away from many of the pitfalls of a brick and mortar.

You're probably thinking right now…wow, that's a lot of stuff to set up and your right, it is. It can be extremely overwhelming getting all these pieces tied together properly and the upfront costs can be massive. This is why my wife and I chose to merge into affiliate marketing.

What Story are You Telling

Let's discuss your stories and what *you* are writing about. Why do news networks like CNN, FOX and MSNBC do so well? Because they have a good marketing team behind them and they know what sucks us into watching them.

What stories do the best? The stories that do the best are dramatic, negative and often times really sad. Why is this? Because society has conditioned us to react to negative news more than positive news. This is nothing more than a marketing strategy to get more viewers watching!

Do you watch night time drama? There is a lot of it out there. It seems as if that's all that plays on the TV anymore.... Real Housewives, Duck Dynasty, My Big Fat Life, etc. Why is the majority of society attracted to this kind of entertainment? If this applies to you, then that's a question you have to answer yourself. I like the Blacklist as a once a week nighttime drama, but I rarely watch TV. If I do, I watch the Science, Discovery, or History Channels.

Now, I am not bashing these shows at all. If you get some perceived value from it than good for you! By now you're probably wondering… What in the heck does any of this have to do with my business or marketing?

Simple, ask yourself what message you are sending out to the universe! Is your message one that is positive, inspirational and uplifting? Or is it a Debbie downer that's negative, uninspiring and a total bummer?

Why is this important? Your message or your story is what defines who you are to other people. What is your attractive character trait as a business owner? What do you want to be known for and what legacy will you leave behind. I tend to float in the middle with our marketing message. It's not dreary but it's also not all rainbows and butterflies.

There has to be elements of both when you are marketing for your business. Sometimes the truth hurts and it's better to be honest in your message than be a people pleaser because most people will see right through a fake message.

I get asked all the time, how are you successful as affiliate marketers? Quite simply, I am successful because I am honest and sincere in my message. Business is not always rays of sunshine. There are times when you just feel like throwing up your hands and saying, "I'm done". That's the honest truth, and it doesn't matter what business it is. I have talked to many offline business owners that feel the same way when they see their quarterly earnings statements.

The point is your message is so important. Your good days will shine through and so will your bad days. My wife and I have days where we talk about some pretty hard truths in business. Not completely negative, but it shows you some of the reality behind being a business owner. Like I said before, it's a balance between the flowers and sunshine, fire and stone or in other words the good and the bad.

So tailor your story and your message to address both sides. That's the real point I want to drive home here. Give it straight up and unfiltered. People appreciate this kind of message! Why? Because it's honest.

Now, occasionally my wife and I will do a post on our blog as a "testimonial" for a product or service. We will give both sides of the coin in this testimonial. Not just the good, but the bad and the ugly as well. This allows our audience to make an informed decision before they try it themselves.

Honesty always rules supreme when recommending or doing a testimonial on a product or service.

I would recommend that you tailor your story to fit your audience. Your story and how you tell it is your most powerful tool in your marketing arsenal. Use these powers for good and tell your story that ties into your marketing message to gain the trust and confidence of your audience.

Chapter 9

Important Tips to Drive You Further

The Affiliate Marketing Fairytale

There are many "fairy tales" circulating around out there about affiliate marketing, and is what causes businesses to look the other way when it comes to starting an affiliate program. This furthermore discourages people looking to start their very own affiliate marketing business selling other people's products for a commission.

Affiliate marketing is a very lucrative option for a business who has products as well as for partners that are interested in selling those products on a commission basis. Let's look at some of the fairy tales that are circulating around out there about affiliate marketing and how each of these fairy tales can affect you and where you want to go with your business.

Fairy Tale #1: Affiliate marketing or starting your own program is simple to run:

Well, this could not be farther from the truth. As a business owner, running your own affiliate program is not easy. It requires a lot of work on your part unless you are willing to hire an actual affiliate manager. That's more money out of your pocket, which can be a pitfall when it comes to running your own program. Many businesses get into this way too fast, so do your research first!

Now, it's a different experience for an actual affiliate. My wife and I are affiliate marketers and also run our own affiliate program for our own products. The grass is a bit greener on this side of the pasture.

Despite the fairy tales of how easy being an affiliate marketer are, we would be the first to tell you that it requires patients and good old elbow grease to be successful at it. It is work, and work is a "dirty" word in marketing, but in the interest of the truth, it will require some work on your part.

Fairy Tale #2: There are only a few niches that you can be successful in as an affiliate:

This again is another complete fairy tale. You can run a successful affiliate marketing business in any niche as long as it's a good product that resonates with that niche. Let me use this example: There used to be a guy on Clickbank that sold his guide to building chicken coops. This is one of those weird niches that you "would think" would fail, right? Well this guy sold over $100k worth of downloads of this eBook. Now that's impressive!! Proves our point though that any niche can be effective if you have a product to fit what the market is looking for.

Now, it is true that the popular niches like the home business niche and the weight loss niche do very well. These are the largest niches on the market and sell billions of dollars' worth of product every year. So ask yourself, "do you think you could market a product and make a fraction of that for a part time income"? Sure you could!!

Fairy Tale #3: Affiliate marketing is dead and gone! It doesn't work anymore:

This is a complete fairy tale. Let me tell you why! I have been involved in sales for almost 10 years now and by far affiliate marketing has contributed to most of our income generation. It's not old or outdated, it's very alive and well! As long as there are products to sell there will always be affiliate marketing!

However, when Google changed their algorithms, it did have a pretty big impact on affiliate marketers. Google is just not a fan of it and they make no bones about it, but smart marketers like myself found ways around this problem and have since been able to thrive as usual! Where there is a will, there is a way!

Fairy Tale #3: A successful affiliate marketer gets the product on lots of sites:

This is actually the worst thing you can do! You will blow your budget quickly and have very few results to show for it. This is a big mistake that new affiliate marketers make. It's all about quality and far less about quantity. You have to really target your market that you are trying to reach. Would you try to sell a comb to a bald guy (no offense bald guys)! No, of course you wouldn't! So it's important to target websites and advertising platforms that can cater to the niche you are working in. Place your ads there and you will see a far better result!

The Importance of Honesty and Integrity

This is a topic that is near and dear to my heart in our business. Honesty and integrity are so important in your business ventures and will get you a long way. I remember when I was a kid, my dad used to tell me that a hand shake and your word was better than any piece of paper with a signature on it.

Doesn't really seem this way these days does it. With all the scandals in the news and companies going bankrupt due to misappropriation of funding it seems like a dog eat dog world out there. It really disappoints me that some of these companies pray on certain groups of people and rob them of their hard earned money. It sickens me deeply and this is the reason I am overly transparent in our own business.

My grandfather used to say, "listen here boy, if you ever lose your integrity…. you're dead inside" and I believe this to be the truth. Do you remember that feeling you had as a kid when you did something wrong? That pit that entered your stomach and just made you feel sick inside. This is what I would imagine feeling every single day if my integrity was not intact.

Just be honest in your business deals folks! You will find that this will get you way farther ahead than trying to play the trickster. The universe has a way of coming to get those that try to be deceitful and take advantage of others.

Now, you're never going to make everyone happy, that's not what I am saying. If you're in any business you will at some point have a few cheerleaders gunning for you in a negative way. It just is what it is, but here is the thing, if you have nothing to hide behind, than there is no need to worry about it. For example, big companies all have their haters. For many different reasons too! Most are just senseless drama to be very honest!

So don't skate the fine line in your business or ride the razors edge – run your business completely above board and always do your customers right. Your business will flourish if you do this very simple thing.

Here is the problem! We all go through rough spots in our businesses. That's just part of business and it's what you do during these struggling moments that will define you and your brand. Do the wrong things and you can stain your brand forever! Continue to operate with the utmost integrity and honesty and you will find that the tough time moves on fairly quickly.

My wife and I had a very good friend that we'd known for years that ended up in some pretty serious trouble because of this. I won't share the details here or what the circumstances were but at the end of the day he did two things. He compromised his integrity and his honesty with his customers and paid the price for doing so. If you think for one second that you can slide by in the grey area I will tell you that it's simply not worth it.

Take care of your customers and always go above and beyond and provide superior value to them. When you think you have provided enough value than stack on more value. This is what creates your brand as a valuable asset in the marketplace. It also positions you as a trustworthy business and people will come to deal with you directly. Then you don't have to look for customers anymore, they simply come to you!

I know this is a bit "preachy", but it's an important element in the success of any business venture. This is one of my favorite quotes on this subject matter…

"Honesty is a person's most valuable asset. His or her good name, good reputation, and good word depend on the individual's quality of honesty. A business that operates under the principles of profound honesty is elevated within the community. It is respected and treasured. The absence of honesty is a liability to an individual or business."

James H. Merkel & Abdul Wahad Al-Falaij, *On the Art of Business.*

Think about it!!!!!

Taking Charge of Your Website Traffic

Once visitors arrive on your page, what can you do to help them make the decisions you want them to, such as following your CTA (Call To Action)? To answer this question, you have to identify three things about your visitors:

- Why are they on your website?
- How do they make decisions?
- How can the answers to these two questions get them to follow your CTA?

The Decision-Making Quadrant:
One of the best tools for understanding how your visitors make decisions is the Decision Making Quadrant, a tool developed by website guru, Bryan Eisenberg, and was first explained in his groundbreaking book, Always Be Testing.

According to Eisenberg, people make decisions in two main ways:

(1) fast vs. slow and (2) emotional vs. logical. The bullets below present these axes into a quadrant for looking at four different decision-making types online:

- *Fast + Logical* — The Competitive Visitor who wants you to tell them what your offer has that is better than other options.
- *Fast + Emotional* — The Spontaneous Visitor who wants you to tell them why they should use your product or service.
- *Slow + Logical* — The Methodical Visitor who wants you to tell them how your product will improve their lives, along with the details behind your approach.

- *Slow + Emotional* — The Humanistic Visitor who wants you to tell them who you are so that they can make a personal connection.

Which Does Your Webpage Attract?

Look at your existing website and identify which of these four decision-making types it appeals to the most, and which it appeals to the least. What about the other two styles? When those visitors arrive on your page, are they finding what they are looking for?

The Decision Making Quadrant can help you understand your website's current frame of reference, identify its weaknesses and help you make the adjustments necessary so that all four types of visitors get what they want from your page so they can follow your CTA.

Design Elements that Reflect Your Visitors:

The next step is to look at the design elements you can include that will help drive visitors toward your CTA most quickly.

Although web design can be incredibly complicated, the most successful websites share five common principles. Incorporate these onto your pages and you are practically guaranteed to see your conversions increase:

Clarity is King – The moment a visitor arrives on your web page, their brain instantly goes to work trying to understand what they are seeing. To help facilitate this process, you need to give them the answers to these questions as quickly as possible:

- What is this site about?
- What can I do here? Is this something I want?
- What's in it for me?

Craft a compelling value proposition that tells your visitor in clear, precise terms exactly why they should buy from you instead of someone else.

Visual Appeal – First impressions are critical. Keep layouts simple, uncluttered and with attractive images that set a positive tone to set your visitor at ease and put them in the proper frame of mind to make a buy decision.

Strong Visual Hierarchy – Prioritize the parts of your website that are the most important (i.e. the CTA, forms, value proposition, etc.). Visual hierarchy is determined by many factors, including size, color, placement and the amount of white space surrounding a particular page element.

Keep Them Focused – It's critical to conserve your visitors' attention at all costs. Nothing captures attention more than larger than life images, so consider including a single oversized picture of the one thing that is central to your business. Photos of people are also highly effective at keeping visitors engaged. A third focus tool is presenting contrast (i.e. before and after, then and now, etc.).

Limit Focus to One Action per Screen – This goes back to not confusing or distracting your visitor. Don't bombard them with too many images or overwhelm them with content.

Boil down your website to the one action you want your visitors to take – an image, a block of copy, an opt-in box, or whatever it is that most clearly defines what you want them to do — then build the rest of your page around that.

Out of Control Content Marketing

Sometimes I think people tend to overthink their sales pitch. Often the best solution is the simplest.

For example:

- 60% of small business websites don't put their phone number on their home page
- 75% don't have an email address or a link on the front page of their website
- 66% fail to put a contact form on their website so visitors can ask questions, leave comments or request more information

If your website doesn't offer the simplest things your visitors are looking for, then of course it's going to fail.

A Real World Example:
Consider Verve Medical Cosmetics, a small New York-based medical practice whose website was consistently ranking high, but was failing to capture as many of its visitors as it should.

One simple tweak – putting their phone number in the top right corner of their homepage with the message, "Call Us" – and their calls increased 54%, their social media referrals increased 44% and their conversions substantially improved.

Including things like your phone number, email address, contact information, and other trust-building elements are some of the simplest and most effective ways to create a personal connection with your page visitors.

Four Things Your Website Must Have:
Look at your current website. Does it contain these four ways to improve conversions with content?

- Your business' phone number, email address and/or contact information

- A way for visitors to ask questions, leave comments or otherwise interact with your business
- Easy ways for visitors to give your business social approval signals such as Facebook "Likes," Google+ "+1's" or other ways to recommend you to their social media contacts
- Testimonials, awards, security logos, privacy policies and other content that provides social proof that your business is trustworthy and safe.

More Conversions, More Customers, More Profits:
The optimal layout is a laser-focused CTA with appealing images that grab the visitor's attention and hold onto it (*and remember to include the simple things that many small business websites forget).

However, you can still fail to consistently convert visitors into customers if your site's readability is not great.

Fortunately, improving readability is one of the easiest fixes:

- Use large font sizes – The larger the font size, the easier it will be for visitors to read, especially if they are viewing your web page on a laptop, tablet or mobile device. Text should be in at least 14 to 16 point, or even larger if you have the space.
- Consider line height – The space between lines of text is important. If it's too cramped, it's going to be difficult to read. Set your line height at 24 point.
- Contrast – The contrast between your text and the background can determine whether your copy is easy to read or next to impossible to see. Black on white is the starkest contrast. If you are using a

colored background, be sure to choose a color for your text that provides easy visual contrast.
- Narrow Lines – Narrow columns are easier to read than wide swaths of copy. When laying out your text, use newspaper-type columns whenever possible to make it more appealing to your visitors.
- Break Up Copy with Sub Headlines – When viewers see large blocks of copy on your page, they find it exhausting and generally won't read it. But if you break up that same content into smaller paragraphs separated by sub headlines, those same visitors will happily scan your text.
- Bullet Points – Why use a dozen words when two will do? Bullet points give the key information to your visitors as effectively as possible.

Every element of your web page is important and plays a key role in the success of your business. While landing on the Google front page is a great accomplishment, it's not enough to keep your business thriving and successful. Incorporating these techniques will help you convert your visitors into customers so you can make more sales, more revenues, and higher profits.

Innovations That Drive Your Business Faster

In today's world of information and technology blogs have become a viable option to engage people and interact with others. We can share our world of ideas, interests and really connect with an audience that is interested in our content. Blogs have become so popular because they are reasonably easy to maintain. If you are a blog owner you can write short informational stories and then post them to release in a variety of different ways.

Blogs can be released every day, once a week, twice a week or on a schedule that you desire. This content can revolve around whatever the topic of interest is, such as politics, sports, education or maybe even a particular product that you are selling as an affiliate marketer.

One of the problems with blogs today is there are so many of them. There are simply thousands of new blogs published every day with similar content published. The good thing is blogging is free and can be hosted on a variety of hosting platforms. Many of these platforms have really good tools and even free templates called themes that you can use completely free. Choosing something that stands out can make your blog look well thought out and very professional looking.

Free and Profitable Way to Reach out to Your Niche Market:

Having your own blog that is packed full of useful information that also promotes your website or products is one of the most simple ways to engage and attract an audience in your specific niche market. If you always provide top quality content that is valuable on your blog you can build a solid relationship with your base of readers and point them straight back to your website with offers in that niche. This is how you effectively monetize your blog and create a solid profit stream into your business.

Audio Powerhouse – The Podcast King:

Podcasting has also became a very powerful medium to reach a targeted niche audience. Podcasting is nothing more than an audio or video file that is recorded and released on many platforms to provide value to your base of followers. These audio or video files can be created at no cost and most new computers today have the ability to record for this medium. There are many platforms that these audio or video files can be published on for free. iTunes and YouTube are amongst the most popular platforms to use because they are free.

Once you have uploaded your Podcast you can approach your audience in many ways. You can broadcast your content to your list of loyal subscribers through autoresponder services like Getresponse or Aweber to get your message out to the masses. You can also leverage your website or your blog to gain maximum engagement with your audio or video content.

There are many similarities to a blog and a podcast. The key is quality content and creating multiple avenues of engagement to maximize a user's experience and keep them interested. If done correctly this form of marketing can assist you in connecting with your niche market and is a great way to further promote your website. Podcasts can be simple, easy to put together and content driven. There is no need to purchase expensive video cameras, voice recording software and microphones. You can keep it simple and record from an IPhone or simply use the recording software that is already built into most computers today.

The biggest difference between a blog and a podcast is the connection and engagement that is created. Blogs are just published articles where a podcast is actually you presenting the information either live or via recording. This gives your viewers the opportunity to really connect with you and your unique character on a personal and even an emotional level. This can contribute to building a successful brand in the niche market you are working in. In the earlier days of podcasts audio was the most popular medium of choice. Today, video podcasts have become more popular since they build relationships faster because the consumer can connect directly with you on video.

Put Yourself out There – Build Your Character:
Reputation is the cornerstone to creating a business online. With the ability to search for information today it is easy to track down the good and the bad on almost anyone. Building a solid brand for your online business is no different than building a brand for a traditional offline brick and mortar business. Remember, you can bring the normal offline customer online. Be engaged and active in your community by getting out there and pressing the flesh. Look at other organizations online that are similar to yours and become part of their community. You can effectively syphon leads to your own brand this way and build your business.

Always be prepared to sell your brand when you can. Have an elevator pitch ready so you can briefly describe what it is you provide. One of the most effective ways to make connections is to offer tons of value and offer to be helpful. If you spend all your time asking for something I wouldn't expect to see a strong base of supportive followers. Put yourself out there and help someone else, give solid testimonials and offer free lead magnets that will be useful and helpful to your base. Do this and your online presents will explode and people will be open to what you are offering as a suggestion.

Always Be The Professional Character:
Be professional, courteous and helpful to anyone that you engage in your business. This applies to an online or offline business. The fact is, you never know who may end up a customer in the future. When you operate an online business a customer has to connect with you in a different way. They don't see you in a brick and mortar environment while shopping for products in your store. Your customer will

only know your online character so be courteous, professional and consistent. Always offer tons of value and be as attentive to their needs as you can be.

Take a look at what communities you can become a part of online. This is where you can really position yourself as an expert or leader in your niche and build your customer base. You can build your reputation and even position yourself in positions of authority in these communities. This will build your brand and ultimately land people on your website or blog.

CHAPTER 10

MOBILE CONNECTIVITY AND A LITTLE HUMOR

Today's Mobile World

Mobile traffic currently accounts for about 30% of global Internet traffic at any given moment. It is reported that by 2017, people will use mobile devices more than PCs. I think we are already there because based on my own business analytics, over 50% of my site visitors are using a mobile device.

What are people doing while surfing the web on their mobile devices? Buying!

In 2012, purchases made on mobile devices totaled $6.7 billion – that's billion with a "B" – and topped $11.6 billion in 2014 and $31 billion by 2015.

Sadly, businesses have been slow to respond to this staggering shift in consumer buying patterns. According to Jesse Haines, group manager for Google Mobile Ads, only 21% of all major advertisers had mobile-friendly sites.

Although 66% of the top retail brands in fashion, hospitality, jewelry and other areas had mobile sites, one-third of those websites did not allow consumers to actually buy their products from their sites.

The Astonishing Power of Mobile Websites:

Those statistics are staggering. Especially when you consider that mobile websites are the easiest, fastest and most popular ways for your customers to interact with your business.

Mobile websites make it easy for the increasingly mobile consumer to make purchases. Nearly all shoppers polled by Google said they are more likely to buy a product or service if the website is optimized for mobile. 75% said that they would be much more likely to return if they have a positive experience on your mobile website.

Impact on Brick and Mortar Businesses:

It shouldn't be surprising that when people are on the go, they prefer to spend their money at businesses that are nearby, rather than driving halfway across town. That's one of the reasons 65% of people said they used their mobile device to find a nearby business to make an in-store purchase, according to Google.

This is especially critical for brick and mortar businesses that depend on local traffic for their livelihood, such as restaurants and retail stores.

Half of all people using mobile websites said they also use a GPS, Google Maps or another mapping site to find a nearby retail location, according to Nielsen. 44% said they have accessed the mobile website of retailers they usually shop.

Mobile searches for restaurants have a conversion rate of 90%, with 64% converting with the first hour after conducting their search for a restaurant's mobile website, according to xAD and Telemetrics.

The Power of Mobile Searches:
The trend toward mobility is global, not local. While about 8% of all web searches done in the U.S. are conducted from mobile devices, in Africa that figure is nearly 15% and in Asia mobile searches have increased 192.5% since 2012, according to Pingdom.

Locally, about half of all local searches are performed on mobile devices, Microsoft Tag reported. When you mention a location in a mobile ad, search result rates increase up to 200%, according to ThinkNear.

Social Media and Your Online Business:
Optimizing your Internet marketing website for use by mobile devices allows your business to tap into one of the fastest-growing and highly-targetable markets in the history of business: Social media.

Apps like Facebook, Twitter, YouTube and others allow businesses to get their messages in front of exactly the type of consumers who are most likely to buy the types of products they offer. But when these high-converting mobile customers are directed to a website that is not mobile-friendly, 60% will leave without doing anything, according to Google.

Email Applications:
While some pundits have announced the death of email, somebody needs to tell people using mobile devices. That's because about 25% of all people using mobile devices use them to read their emails, according to Return Path. This is especially true for iPad users, who have shown a 73% rise in the number of emails opened on those popular mobile devices.

That's significant because it means your mobile website should be fully integrated with email and offer such functionality as capturing email addresses, automatically responding to email requests and offering consumers pathways to your business via their email inbox.

Mobile-Optimization

Whether you're walking down a busy street, taking public transportation, driving to school or work, or actually sitting at your work desk, you notice something that is unison across all daily activities...everyone has their face firmly pressed into their phone or tablet and is either browsing their social media feed, texting with family or friends, or purchasing a product.

Our world has shifted from a direct to indirect form of communication with one another. This is no secret to anyone, but if you own a business like us, it's critical to your success that you take full advantage of mobile-optimizing your business site in order to reach the instant gratification, short attention span customer.

So what's the difference? Make no confusion about it...

Your online business's web page is different than your mobile-optimized website. A mobile-optimized website refers to reformatting the web page content and images in order to fit and work properly on the smaller screens of phones and tablets. This allows your customers to make quicker and easier buying decisions and interact in real-time by sharing photos, videos, or comments via social media.

The Mobile Customer Experience and Expectations:

If you blow it the first time when someone visits your website that is not mobile-optimized, than there is a very strong chance they will never return. Why? This goes back to the new age customer that has a shorter attention span and demands instant gratification. Whether it's chatting with family and friends, researching or keeping up with business transactions, browsing for pure entertainment, or purchasing products, your website must be mobile-optimized and take no more than a few seconds to upload. In other words, it needs to be able to achieve the same results a customer would expect from doing business in a normal in-person conversation.

Think about it, you've been on a website that took forever to download its images and text, right? How did you feel? Did you leave the site? Did you question the quality of the site? Did you engage with that person, business, or website a second time? If so, and you still had issues, I bet you never visited that site again. Think of it this way, your website must act like a business application on a phone or tablet. A business application allows customers to remove the personal contact, whether in person or by phone, and allows the customer to make decisions, purchases, etc. in a mobile-optimized way.

Positioning Your Business for the Future:
When you mobile-optimize your website you are taking business away from your mobile-unfriendly competitors and fostering loyalty from those with short attention spans and instant gratification needs. The best news is it won't take long for your mobile-optimized website to pay off because according to Google, the vast majority of customers now use their phones to browse the internet, make bank transactions, and most importantly, purchase products. Within just a few short years, there will be more phones than people on the globe; it's no wonder businesses must become mobile-optimized.

Advanced Affiliate Marketing

When choosing affiliate products to promote, you want to pick products that cost more so that you make a higher commission per sale, however, in order to ensure your business is sustainable and remains profitable, you need to have a whole range of products at different price points.

Why is this so important? Because your target audience has:

- Different comfort levels of spending
- If one of your products goes belly-up, you still have dozens of other products to sell at different price points
- Customers that are able to afford all different price points can be pushed up the "value ladder," which means you are able to get them to continue buying increasingly more expensive products.

For example, in the internet marketing niche, eBooks and video courses generally cost between $10-50, which is a low price point that works for the masses. Web hosting programs generally range between $50-200, which is a mid-price point but a necessity in the industry. Then, as an advanced affiliate you need to offer high price points, which include personal 1-on-1 coaching, seminars, and big ticket affiliate products that range from $500-into the thousands.

Advanced affiliate marketers have these types of products in place, not only to diversify their product portfolio, but also so it labels them as an expert in the industry. If you are offering personal coaching and mentorship, and its quality, people are going to recognize you as a leader in the field because your customers aspire to have the same type of success.

*It's important to note that higher dollar products not only satisfy the customer who only wants the best, but it also allows you to sell less product, because you only need a few sales to earn big money. *This is where top affiliates focus their time and energy.*

Two great sources to start deciding what types of products you want to offer are ClickBank and Commission Junction. These are excellent sources because when someone clicks to buy a product, you get a commission.

These advanced affiliate marketing techniques will help you sustain a profitable affiliate business with multiple streams of income. Remember, before getting into any affiliate program, always do your research and read reviews from successful affiliates who have, "been there, done that and got the t-shirt." Start small and build from there.

Puppy, Monkey, Baby Acid Trip

My wife and I can't say we're football fanatics in our household, but most years we still sit down and watch the Super Bowl pre-game (mostly to get the recap of what we missed for the year), and of course indulge in the game, halftime show, its commercials, and probably most importantly, a good reason to eat until your heart rate skyrockets with the end result of a food coma…but anyway….I digress.

So, this year we were most interested in the commercials from purely a marketing standpoint to see what we could learn from the good, bad, and ugly.

…and in this household our jaws dropped and our faces speechless with the debut of Mountain Dew's Super Bowl 50 commercial, "Puppy Monkey Baby," for their latest energy drink.

However, like most everyone watching this acid trip of a commercial, we didn't even know what was being sold until we went back and watched it a second time. The first viewing of it was shock, awe and intrigue as we watched this awkward hybrid of a creature prancing around a living room. The second time we watched it was to see what the heck the commercial was even advertising. Anyone else have this same moment?

So, the point to this amusing story is really this:

As internet marketers, our job is to grab the reader's attention immediately – be direct, demand and do not ask when selling a product, and be consistent in your marketing endeavors, right?

So based on what we're talked about in this book, having to go back a second time to view or read something would seem like a potential failure or even legitimate failure if what you're presenting wasn't interesting enough to go back and read/watch a second time (i.e. you just lost a prospect). Right?

However, in this case, we as internet marketers have something to learn. Although the Mountain Dew, "Puppy Monkey Baby" commercial was a "WTF" moment while 100+ million Super Bowl "goers" tuned in, it caused a trending frenzy on the internet and people couldn't help but go watch a second, third, and even fourth time because of its shock value (whether you thought it was funny, confusing, or just plain creepy) – IT GOT YOUR ATTENTION!

As internet marketers, we have the ability to do the same thing in our own niche. Don't always expect a "LOL" moment or a positive reaction, but if you have the entrepreneur fortitude to take-in all types of feedback; even from the trolls out there that sit behind their computer and type nasty, unproductive messages you just might be looking at $$$$ if you hit the mark.

Remember, "Hitting the mark" doesn't necessarily mean positive. What it means is you've successfully grabbed a viewer's attention and caused them to REACT.

Reaction = engagement (good or bad)!

Elements of a Successful Sales Letter

So, you have your own product or even an affiliate product that you want to promote.

Now what?

Well, for starters, you've completed 50% of your task as an internet marketer.

That's the good news. The bad news (not really, but kind of) is you now need to create a sales page. I say this as "bad news" because many people feel uncomfortable, or don't know enough yet as a new internet marketer how to go about doing this.

But don't worry…it's really not that hard and can be broken down into 5 easy steps that will successfully promote your product to a highly-targeted audience.

Step 1: Define Your Sales Page:

So for newbies, let's first define what a sales page truly is. Think of a sales page as an advertisement for your product. That's really it! The good news if you're new to this element in your internet marketing business; you don't have to have a huge budget to create these. Sales pages are low-cost or even no-cost ways to attract your prospects because you can route them through your squeeze pages for example.

Most importantly, your prospective customer must feel after reading your sales letter that they need to buy your product and buy it now. In other words, when writing your ad, don't "suggest," demand they buy your product.

Step 2: Structure Your Sales Page:

Once prospects find your sales page, it should follow a predictable structure. Remember that your prospects arrived at your sales page by following a link on your squeeze page or by clicking on a URL for your product's niche.

Now, all you have to do is use the copy on your sales page to convince them to do what they already want to do in the first place. BUY!

Step 3: Write an Eye-Catching Headline:
Probably the most important element of the five is writing an eye-catching headline. Why, because this is the first opportunity you have to draw your prospect in. You will likely only have one chance at this.

Your headline should get right to the point and use direct, active and emotional stirring language to engage/connect with your prospect (i.e. what is it that your product is going to do to improve their lives, or why can't they live without your product).

Step 4: Create Scarcity:
Beneath your headline, you want to provide details about your product that are going to make it irresistible to your readers. In the first section, you want to set up a common problem that your prospect may have. Then, introduce your product as the best and only solution for that problem (i.e. scarcity). At the end of your sales letter, incentivize your prospect to purchase your product by creating scarcity.

Examples include: telling your prospect there's only a limited number of your product available, or it's going to be unavailable in the very near future, or come up with another way to motivate your prospect to act immediately otherwise they may risk not having access to your product again.

Step 5: Offer a Bonus to Upsell to a Back-End Offer:

A great way to add value to your sales letter is to include 1-3 FREE bonuses that your customers will receive when they purchase your product. Typically, you want to mention what each bonus is worth so that later you can show how much buyers are getting for their money.

Upsells and back-end offers are secondary offers that are made after your customer already has decided to purchase your product. Usually, after they submit their payment information, they are taken to another screen where you can offer them more; usually higher priced products that are related to your original product.

Following these 5 steps guarantees two things:

- It converts visitors to customers
- It effectively communicates to your audience or customer what you are selling on a multitude of platforms via a letter.

Note: Always create an offer with a 30 or 60-day guarantee in order to remove any risk for the customer.

Chapter 11
Social Media Growth and Secrets to Success

High-Quality Blogs

The objective of guest blogging is to reach the broadest possible audience from the biggest, most popular and most influential blogs in your niche.

If you have been blogging for a while or are a regular reader of blogs, you may already have an idea of which blogs fall into this category. What you are looking for are blogs that are "household words" in your niche subject.

For example, internet marketing is our niche and of course our audience's niche. So what kind of blogs do you think my wife and I use? Well, for starters, as leaders in the internet marketing industry we write our own content and blog about our own content to help other aspiring entrepreneurs and home-based business seekers. But, we also blog about other leading and respected experts in the field, such as Jonathan Budd, Ray Higdon, or Frank Kern to give our audience the broadest range of quality content.

Not only does this provide quality to your audience as mentioned, but it continues to build your reputation in the niche/industry and builds mutually beneficial relationships with other bloggers which you can call on for referrals or testimonials and vice versa.

We practice this regularly in our day-to-day activities. In fact, testimonials are probably one of the most under-rated activities you could be doing to help promote your business.

A good tool to help you as a new blogger is BuzzStream. They help make it easy to find other bloggers within your niche, build relationships with them, and keep track of your interactions with them. This tool also helps you organize your blog contacts any way you like, such as by topic, home country or keyword, and provides you with URLs you can follow to check out the blogs further.

Another option to help find "high value" blogs is to go to blogs within your niche that you enjoy or find useful and see if they list a "blogroll" in the margin. Many bloggers include a list of other blogs that they like on their own blog so that their fans can link to them.

If you know a blog is authoritative, has a lot of regular readers and frequently gets a lot of social approval signals, it's a good bet that the blogs they recommend have a similar status.

If this is a foreign to you and you are still very new to blogging then I recommend you use a tool called Technorati. This is a blog directory that keeps track of the biggest blogs in nearly every niche. It categorizes blogs by niche, topic and keywords and includes a simple search tool that makes it easy to quickly identify the biggest and most influential blogs within your niche.

Thinking Twitter

Who would have thought that Twitter could be used to monetize your business? Most people think of Twitter as a way to keep in touch with friends, follow their favorite public figures, or simply be entertained and informed by the most up to the minute links to interesting articles and blogs.

But there are actually many ways to make money using your Twitter account and other social media accounts you most likely have.

One of the most effective ways is to drive traffic from your Twitter posts to free Cost-Per-Action (CPA) or opt-in pages. Unlike Facebook or Google+, Twitter doesn't have any advertising on it, which means it isn't getting spammed incessantly, thus allowing you to obtain massive amounts of clicks and conversions from your Twitter pages in ways that you couldn't with your other social media accounts.

The first thing you want to do is to figure out where you are going to send the traffic you will be getting from Twitter. What you want are CPA offers or opt-in pages that are going to cost the end user nothing. You can also send them to your squeeze page in which you promote products in popular "evergreen" niches so that you can capture their email address and use it to promote future offers later.

The reality is that you can use this system to send this inexpensive traffic anywhere you want, but your best plan is to send people to your squeeze page. I will be talking more about monetizing Twitter using Click-Per-Action (CPA) networks next.

CPA networks are a great place to start, especially as a new internet marketer to promote a multitude of offers in your business niche, and they are an easy way for you to get paid each time someone clicks on your offer.

As mentioned previously, one of the easiest ways to promote CPA offers is through social media, specifically Twitter. Why, because you don't even need to use your own Twitter account or promote these offers to your own followers if you don't want to.

It's much easier to buy sponsored Tweets from established Twitter account owners who already have thousands of followers. Genius, huh?

So your next question should be, "how do I know which CPA offers to promote?

Well, after you buy your sponsored Tweet (let's take the average going rate of $25), your next step is to find a good CPA offer by researching the estimated payout per click (EPC).

For example, let's say you find an offer from a CPA network that has an EPC of $0.10. Plus, the CPA network pays you $1.30 per email address you send them. Based on experience, this type of offer will give you an average conversion rate of 10% to 15% Click-Through Rate (CTR).

In this instance, for the $25 investment you made in your sponsored Tweet, you got 100 clicks and converted 10 of them. So you made $13, which means you lost $12, which is obviously not a desirable outcome.

But if you got 200 clicks from your sponsored Tweet, you made $26, or a profit of $1. With 300, make $39, or a profit of $14. So you can see the value of scaling up your offer, right? Depending on how many followers the person you buy the sponsored Tweet from, you can easily get 1,000 clicks as long as the offer matches the demographic of the Twitter account.

Remember, this is a great way to short-term cash, but if you want to turn it into a long-term business you need to use the same system to build a list rather than making money off CPA offers only. As always, THE MONEY IS IN THE LIST!

In the above example, instead of sending the Twitter traffic you get from your sponsored Tweet to the CPA offer, you can divert it to an opt-in page where you give away something free. Then all you need to do is buy an eBook as a Private Label Rights (PLR) product for less than say $10 so that you can use it any way you want indefinitely.

Make sense? Go give it a try and test it!

Grow Your Audience Online

So most internet marketers know that the more well-known you are in your niche the more likely your followers will trust you. It's really a no-brainer, however, the real skill to achieving this is through consistent and quality self-promotion. This is so important because although it took my wife and I countless hours when we first started to build our reputation, in the long run it will be easier for you to convince your audience to act on your product recommendation.

The follow-up question I am often asked, "well, how long is this going to take"? My answer….it depends on how consistent you are in your own self-promotion. If you consistently self-promote for several weeks and then take a few weeks off, well, that's not consistent and you will likely never build an audience. You cannot have ups and downs in this part of your business. You must always proactively engage and self-promote in order to build your brand!

I'm going to let you in on a little secret that will help you ten-fold. No expert in their field will tell you they do this all on their own. In fact, many leading experts outsource this type of work to a social media manager. Now, that doesn't mean outsourcing the content you share with your readers.

My wife and I write all our own content, unless we are promoting another leading expert's work in the field, but we have a social media manager to post, edit, etc. on the content we approve for our audience.

Make sense? Why is this key? Well, it saves you valuable time to focus on other tasks that need to get done in your business, so you are not bogged down on the $10-100 p/hour tasks, and rather, so you can focus on the $1,000 p/ hour + tasks in your business.

Now I mentioned the words, "Building Your Brand." So important, and I talked about this earlier in this book! What does this really mean? Well, for starters you need to stop thinking of yourself as just an individual and begin considering yourself as a brand that can be marketed in the same way as any leading company or "brand." Example brands in any industry include: Nike, Starbucks, and H&M.

When you think of these companies you don't think of one individual person. In fact, most of us couldn't even name the CEO of each of these companies. Why? Because they promote their companies as brands not people. This is the BEST WAY to convince people to do what you ask. Be a brand, not a person!

Think Oprah when thinking of people as brands. Oprah is the greatest example of what it is like to be a brand and not a person. You don't even need to say her last name to know who you are talking about, and when you hear her name you think power and influence of authority.

Most of us will never be Oprah, but apply this concept to your own business. Your goal is to create that same kind of brand for yourself so that when you make product recommendations or approach bloggers with a request to write a guest blog, you will be perceived in the same way as the companies and people I have mentioned.

The next best thing you can do to grow your audience is build a list of followers, and the best way to do this is through social media. Your goal needs to be on building a fan base so that you can influence the largest amount of people possible.

So anytime you create a guest blog, you are going to want to have somewhere to direct readers who enjoyed your content and who want to learn more about you. This should be both your blog and website because it gives you the most versatility to promote your brand, collect email addresses for your list, and promote your own products and services.

Ensure you provide links back to your website with every guest blog you publish so that you can constantly grow your pool of prospective customers. Lastly, use Search Engine Optimization (SEO) techniques so that they are ranked at or near the top of the Search Engine Result Pages (SERP) for your niche subject.

My Best Kept Solo Ad Marketing Secrets

Before you can even begin to understand marketing and advertising there are a few fundamental strategy pieces that you must understand. The advertising world can be a very corrupt place in many ways. There are as many bad vendors out there serving Cost per Click (CPC) advertising as there are good ones. I am going to start this section with some basics behind marketing and my own personal success formula to solo advertising.

The Very Basics
Traffic Generation options: Targeted vs. Non-Targeted Traffic

1. ***Targeted traffic*** is just that, you must target the specific niche that you are working in. To do this you must find solo ad vendors that specifically cater to the niche that you are working in.

    *Success Example: There was a little girl in Colorado that was part of a Girl Scout Troop and they were having significant problems selling all their Girl Scout cookies for the year. So this little girl set out to find targeted traffic that would convert. She did her research and decided that her best option was to set up a cookie stand in front of the local medical marijuana store in her home town. The end result was amazing. She was able to sell out of all of her cookies in a matter of hours. This is an example of skillful marketing and targeting a specific traffic source that will convert. The formula for this example would look something like this: Medical Marijuana + Cookies = Profit.

2. ***Non-targeted traffic*** is traffic that will not convert to your offer and is very simply, traffic that is not within the niche that you are promoting.

    *Example: So let's just say we are selling combs and hair products in our business. We would not want to target a market of bald guys right (no offense bald guys)? This goes for any product or service. We wouldn't want to put a banner ad on a Victoria secrets website or a Harley Davidson website for an info-product that shared marketing secrets. That's simply the wrong audience to target and your marketing dollars would be better served flushed down the toilet!

Digging a bit deeper…
Keep in mind, when you hear the phrase, customer avatar, this is simply a detailed profile of your target customer. Once you've got one, you can use it to do things like market to and own a niche where you become "the one to go to," and hone your marketing message so it appeals to a specific someone as opposed to a generic everyone. This is how you successfully target your audience.

Free vs. Paid Traffic Methods

1. **Free traffic methods**, in my opinion, simply do not turn any kind of substantial profit. Why? Thing about it. Posting in forums, chat rooms and other free methods are futile in many ways. Many of these venues have cutoff the ability to lead people to your offers. Many of these methods result in one thing; a lot of time spent with very little to show for it. If you do not classify your time as at least $500-$1000 per hour as a business owner than you are making a very big mistake. Would you pay someone $500 an hour to post in forums and chat rooms? Of course you wouldn't, so why would you do these unproductive tasks yourself?

2. **Paid Traffic Methods**, in my opinion, are the only way to go. These methods are a sure fire

result and they are relatively instant. If you were to place a solo ad, for example, it would be fulfilled within 3-7 days. Now, to be fair here, all forms of paid traffic can come with a heavy cost and risk. With any paid advertising you have the risk of a complete flop, but on the same note, you have the opportunity to capitalize on a huge success.

The key to being successful with paid traffic methods is having a 90 day plan and sticking to it. If you are not comfortable having some wins and losses than paid methods are not for you. The fact is this, you will have some advertising campaigns that do really well and others that don't.

How much can you spend to get a customer?
Customer acquisition is one of the most important parts of your business and knowing what your average customer value is. There is no secret to this, it's a simple formula that looks like this: number of customers (divided by) your profits = average customer value. This is a simple formula and easy to keep track of either daily, weekly or monthly.

Knowing this number does one simple, but important thing for you when you are advertising. This number tells you what you can spend and stay profitable. If you know that your average customer value is $200 than you can spend up to the $200 to acquire one single customer. No one wants to spend that much, but if that's what it takes, then accept it. If you have a good sales funnel in place with high converting upsells than you will do very well.

So what is a solo ad?
In simple terms, a solo ad is a marketing piece used in email marketing in order to get traffic, leads, and eventually

make sales. Solo ads are email ads (i.e. a selling email through which you're promoting your offer) with basic guidelines that have proven successful for me in my business.

1. Click on solo provider's sales pages. Read several to get a feel for the community. Only use this link for learning purposes. It is for your convenience and not meant for recommendations: http://www.soloadsx.com.
2. There are over 400 vendors on this list. You don't have to read 400 pages, but rather, use the link as a tool to search for different sales pages.

Other Sources:

- Do your research on different Facebook groups. You can join solo ads and adswaps, Solo Ads Secret Society, Warrior Forum: http://warriorforum.com and Udimi: http://udimi.com
- It is recommended that you buy traffic from the top 5 English speaking countries, which include the United States, Canada, Australia, New Zealand, and the United Kingdom (T1, Premiere). People from these counties statistically buy the most Internet Marketing stuff. Keep in mind, most solo providers over deliver 10% to 25%.
- Check for a picture or video of solo ad provider (good branding)
- Read a lot of testimonials. Be aware that really high conversions (over 70% or 80%) usually refer to free offers. Testimonials should have realistic numbers. *Note: Visit http://fiverr.com and search

"testimonials." You will see there are many vendors on this website that sell a testimonial for $5. You should study their faces so you can identify solo ad vendors that are giving fake testimonials to boost their business. If you identify this than you will want to blacklist that vendor.

- If a vendor does not work in your niche than move on to a different one. If you are selling a paid offer than you will want to ensure that you completely stay away from vendors that prefer free offers. Their lists are simply full of freebie seekers looking to download everything that you have for free. They will never buy your products!
- Look for these types of statements on solo ad sales pages. These are things that you don't want when running a solo ad. If this is not specifically stated on the page than you will want to ask the vendor directly. (No exit pop-ups, no traffic exchanges, no click rotators, and no safelists). Your unique clicks will be from solo email traffic ONLY - Just proper solo traffic.

Things to understand about Solo Ad Vendors

- The solo vendor business is a business so you should expect good customer support.
- The main objectives of solo ad providers are to sell clicks and run your ad to fulfillment as quickly as possible. Remember, solo ad providers guarantee clicks, but they do not guarantee leads or sales, which has caused a lot of abuse in the business. For example, if you purchase 100 clicks and you only

- get 11 leads, they can say, "it could be your swipe copy or your lead capture page."
- Understand that a solo ad is a very unique way to generate traffic. Just because you purchase clicks for a solo ad doesn't necessarily mean you are purchasing a "real" or "proper" solo ad. A solo ad needs to be seen completely, including the subject line and the entire body. The key to a solo ad is the swipe copy (i.e. your ad) and it can be targeted if the right person sees it, is interested, clicks on the link and arrives to a capture page that is congruent with the ad. Since you are sending out a direct ad, the swipe copy is congruent with the capture page. *Remember, the prospect is interested from the swipe copy, not the capture page. This is what makes a solo ad targeted.
- Initially connect with the provider personally through Skype, the Warrior Forum, or Facebook. I prefer Skype because it's easy to complete the transaction and I also get a feel for what kind of person I am dealing with. I call it the "slicky factor." You know that feeling you get deep in your gut that tells you that something just doesn't feel right about that person.... listen to that feeling.

What to expect once you make the connection...

- The solo ad vendor is going to have questions for you. They will want to know what your offer is and if you have a "swipe," also known as your ad. They should always accept your swipe. Most will reserve the right to make changes to your copy, however, they should tell you what changes they are making before they send the ad out. Do not ever accept the answer of, "I will take care of it for you." Maintain control of your own copy. If they make suggested changes it should be up to you to approve it or not. If you don't like it than you can simply walk away. You don't have to settle for anything, there are hundreds of solo ad vendors out there that are more than willing to work with you on this.

Follow up questions to ask:

- Have you ran similar offers or my offer to your list before and if so, how many times per month have you ran it?
- What is the size of your list that you are sending my offer to?
- When can you run my solo ad and when will it be fulfilled?

Now, there are some quality questions you should ask depending on the responses you get back. For learning purposes, let's just use this crazy example:

The list size is 25,000. The solo ad vendor has ran your same offer to this list 800 times this month and they can run your ad in one day with fulfillment in 72 hours.

Do you see any issues here? You would think that this list is saturated with your offer, correct? (This is a very wild example that I'm using just to prove a point). You should ask some follow up questions in this case:

- How many new subscribers are you adding to your list every day?
- Would you segment your list to those new fresh leads on your list?

Let's say the vendor tells you they are adding 300-400 new subscribers per day to their list and they are also willing to segment to those fresh leads. Did we just turn a negative into a positive? The answer is yes! My point here is this, it's important to ask the basic questions, but more importantly, ask the quality follow up questions.

Before you get to the phone call…

So before you get to a phone call with the vendor, I want to share another missing ingredient that 95% of all marketers just don't do. They don't do their homework by researching the vendor on every social media platform. I probably disqualify two out of every three vendors I research with the above process and then with this last step, so make sure you do your homework and research the vendor.

For example, go to Facebook and search their name. Do they have a business page? Was it created last week? Is there customer interaction on the page? Depending on how you answer these questions, you can identify red flags before you even waste your time engaging with them on the phone. Repeat this process on Twitter, Instagram, Google+, LinkedIn, Pinterest, YouTube, Google, Bing and Yahoo. This will give you some background on the vendor and you will likely disqualify many of them before you ever get to the phone call phase.

*Remember, it's your money and you should protect it at all cost.

JV Rocket and "Tier 1 Solo Ads"

With JV Rocket you can buy a solo ad that will go out to a double opt-in list of 226,000+ subscribers for the price of $2,500. Your ad goes out to customers who have purchased ClickBank products in the "make money" niche such as Get Google Ads for free, Health Biz in a Box, Forced Money, Top Secret Magic Code, and many more.

Many of the top internet marketing and "make money" niche gurus are using JV Rocket to build their lists and directly email their hot offers. $2,500 is a considerable amount of money to risk for most people, so before testing JV Rocket you'll want to make sure you have tested sales materials and a really good funnel. You'll also want to be sure that your offer is a good match for the type of customers who would buy the type of products I just mentioned above.

This doesn't mean that your offers must be similar, but it does mean that the same demographic would order your product. The downside of this solo ad source is that there are no guaranteed amount of visitors you'll get. The upside is, if you have an offer that's on fire and would work well with these type of customers, then JV Rocket can be a goldmine. Just remember, as with any of these ad sources, you're responsible for your business and the risks you take when buying advertising.

Profiting from paid advertising is simple, but not easy. Here's what I mean. It would be easy to blow through $10,000 on JV Rocket. The inventory is there waiting for you to order anytime you want. However, it would be wise to test your sales funnel out by buying solo ads on a smaller scale at $30, $100, or $300 from "Tier 2 Solo Ad" vendors such as the ones on Safe-Swaps.com, SoloAdDirectory.com, or Directory of Ezines.

After you have a tested and proven funnel that works well with the solo ads you've purchased on a small scale, then you may want to consider going big time and ordering what I call, "Tier 1 Solo Ads" using JV Rocket as your source.

When I'm actively running solo ads, I'm usually able to generate hundreds of leads per day. This may change down the road, but as of right now, solo ads are cheap, they're effective and very easy because you don't have to worry about landing page quality score, paying per click or keeping an eye on your ads and paying by the click.

Let's say you buy a solo ad for $300 for 1,000 clicks. You pay 60 cents per click and you know exactly how many clicks are going to come to your site. The vendor who sends you a solo ad sends an ad out to his/her email list, which recommends your freebie or your website. So, in essence, they are transferring their authority over to you. That's what makes it the most effective way of generating traffic, in my opinion. Since the ads are still cheap, it's very effective for anybody who has the money to risk on it.

I realize it's not going to be easy to find solo ad sellers if you have no clue about the world of solo ads right now, but once you find reputable sellers, you want to start connecting with them on Skype. Why? Because I have learned in meeting many different solo ad sellers that a lot of times they will give you great deals on Skype that they don't advertise outside of this platform. You can also find solo ads in one location called soloadddirectory.com. This is a resource I used when I was a newbie marketer.

The key to having profitable solo ads is your sales funnel. You want to have a squeeze page or lead capture page that generates leads through giving away a lead magnet. Then you have an upsell from there, which will be a one-time offer for something that's in the $17-$49 price point. Once your lead has purchased, you then want to begin offering higher price point upsells so you can afford to pay for your solo ads.

Now, you may also want to promote offers on the download page for freebies that you're giving away. That way you can come close to breaking even or you can profit directly from that solo ad before you even get the subscribers on your list. I haven't profited from many solo ads right up front, but I made a profit on the back end from promoting strictly to the subscriber list. That's something you must do.

Remember, a lot of companies in advertising are willing to pay a lot of money upfront and even lose money on the front end. They know they're going to make money on the backend with their follow up marketing, which is what email marketing is all about.

I hope these best kept secrets were of value to you. I've decided to go much farther with just this book and would invite you to see this very process in real time by visiting http://mysolosecret.com

On this page you will be able to watch three, 15 minute videos that walk you through how to make solo ads profitable. There is no obligation, no lead capture page, and no purchase required to attend this training. This training is strictly being offered for free to anyone that purchased this book.

Filthy Rich – Think Like the Wealthy

Being wealthy does not have to be difficult if you have the know-how. In these hard economic times many people are satisfied by just getting by and scraping enough money together to pay the bills.

Wealth and financial freedom are a far-off dream for many people. For them, it means mansions, gated communities, a fast car, private parties or a pool. The truly wealthy have family names like Rockefeller or Morgan.

It can be easy to accumulate wealth. The thing is, not everyone knows how. The twentieth century has brought a boom of first-time millionaires, many of which do not come from family money. They make their first million by employing timeless wealth wisdom and secrets only the ultra-rich used to know. Fortunately for you, there are dozens, even hundreds of little wealth nuggets you can easily apply to your life to expand your portfolio and double, even triple your net worth.

Being smart with money and becoming wealthy is not rocket science, but for many it looks and feels like hard work. The fact of its very simplicity means that more and more people should know and be doing this. But they are not. This is because most people do not know how to make money work for them, not the other way around. This is also because making money involves patience and restraint. Everything about our culture advocates otherwise.

But do you want to end up broke by the time you retire? Do you constantly fend off phone calls from creditors? Do you sigh and shake your head at your bank balance? No one wants to spend their life waiting for payday and watching money flutter away the moment bills come in the mail.

Becoming wealthy is not just about falling into family money, inheriting a trust fund or even having a big income. In fact, many people with huge incomes rarely are truly wealthy. Huge incomes often equal huge expenses and struggling to keep your finances in the black every month does not equal financial freedom. Investing is different from spending.

Someone who has a huge house or houses and a great car may look rich but may not be.

Affluence and wealth can be hard to come by. If you are looking for secrets to getting millions or simply looking for a way to manage your money, this is it. This book will teach you the secrets of the truly wealthy and is a step-by-step guide on how to get there. You will learn everything from gaining financial freedom to basic investing and secret tips from business giants all over the world.

True financial freedom is only a step away, if you know how. Are you ready to start becoming truly wealthy? These gems and secrets are designed to help you turn your resources, whatever they may be, into true wealth. This Chapter can help you whether you follow it step by step or choose a few tactics to start with.

Creating a wealth foundation: Earning financial freedom

Creating the wealth mindset: The wealthy think differently. This is true and an inescapable fact. The other thing is that there is a poor mindset and a wealthy one.

The rich have a different approach to life. They plan, risk and manage their money in a different manner. They also have a positive attitude towards life and opportunities. The first and most important step to true financial freedom is creating this mindset for yourself. This also involves a no-holds barred, honest look at your life and assets.

Creating a starting place is as important as moving forward, so it does not matter if you start with $1 or $1,000,000. It is all about the mindset and the will to move forward to creating your wealth.

Redefine what wealth means for you. Being "rich" simply is a term for many people. Technically, wealth or being wealthy is defined as having an abundance of resources or possessions. The high life does not equal wealth. Having a gigantic mortgage for a beautiful home or a huge car payment does not equal wealth.

Are status symbols your end goal? Does wealth for you mean that ability not to worry about bills or how much is left in your checking account at the end of the month? Does it mean providing comfortably for your family or being free from financial worry?

Does it mean the ability to afford luxury designer goods or getting a membership to the local country club? Being rich or being wealthy can also mean you enjoy a comfortable retirement.

Does wealth mean something totally different to you? Your definition of wealth goes a long way towards setting your goals.

Another important step when it comes to managing your wealth is to set goals. Start with an overall battle plan, such as "By the end of the year, I will have at least $500,000 in savings." Why? You need to be a visionary to be wealthy. A common factor that sets the millionaire apart from the average Joe is this: they know they wanted to be wealthy and they were willing to take the steps to reach their goal.

To reach one goal, you have to make smaller goals and reach them. Every little step you take, every penny you save matters. Use smaller goals as stepping stones. For example, to save that $500,000, one needs to set aside $50,000 every single month, invest or cut down expenses.

Manifest your financial destiny by setting your subconscious towards specific goals. Create dream charts by cutting out pictures of your dream status or words that empower to help fuel your subconscious and get you to wear you want to go. Never underestimate the power of your will and mind. Wealthy people never say they cannot do it, they think of ways so that they can. *Write it down.* Seeing what you want, and getting what you want involve seeing it in black and white.

Know how much you are worth. Take stock of all your assets and income and subtract your debt. Many people go through life financially blind, not knowing how much they are worth or how much they owe and often end up blindsided by money.

The test: Your age x (your average household income from all sources − inheritance) divided by 10 = your net worth. The rich have a net worth often double or triple the amount. The average American has less than half. The goal is to double your net worth.

The truly wealthy consider themselves as the foremost asset. Accordingly, they pay themselves first. They also tend to invest in themselves first, especially when it comes to education. Take classes and groom yourself to be the millionaire, entrepreneur and success you want to be.

Guard your ideas with the passion of the Secret Service. Commodities are now no longer limited to labor, but have expanded to include ideas, imagination and opportunities.

Keep in mind that the average millionaire is not who you think he is. The frugal rich stay richer—if you do not believe this, think of all those high flying celebrities who end up with their homes in foreclosure or selling their tell-all's on TV to pay for all that Cristal and all those houses.

The famous IKEA owner drives a Volvo. HSBC's chairperson famously goes around the main office turning off all the lights long after the employees have left. The stories go on and on. The rich do not live the lifestyle of the rich—they stay rich because they are frugal misers at heart.

Assess your income and what you can do with it. 80% of modern millionaires were able to get there on annual incomes of $55,000 or less. Even meager savings eventually add up to thousands or millions of dollars.

When you look at a job, always know how much the head honcho gets paid because this will later affect your income in terms of promotion, benefits and future potential earnings. If you are gunning for a six figure salary and the current CEO is getting by on $300,000 a year, then maybe the job is not for you.

Find alternative ways to generate income if you are unhappy about your current level of earnings or the amount of the salary you currently have. This can mean looking for other employment with better pay or benefits or finding ways to boost your income little by little. This can mean starting a cottage industry business, learning to invest, buying and selling online or any number of means to add to your nest egg.

Create forms of passive income, the type of income that you receive with little to no effort. Examples of this include: rent from property you own, licensing patents or dividends and returns from investments.

Passive income can come from many sources. Exploiting the business possibilities of the Internet through blogs or sales from eBay or Amazon is one way to add to your income with minimal effort. The truly wealthy prefer passive income anytime. It frees up time for you to do what you want, even while you earn.

Be diverse. Create streams of income, do not rely on one large river. A job that pays $3M is great, but an accident or sudden layoff can cut you off. Think outside your salary. A job paying you $1M a year, plus real estate profits that amount to $1M and another $1M from stock is a far easier and safer thing to manage.

Learn to hold off gratification. A wealthy person knows how to delay gratification and sacrifice *the now* for later. This often comes with a positive attitude towards work and wealth, such as: "If I invest now, I will make 10% more later." The wealthy do not think of now, they think of the future. The present is merely an opportunity.

Change your mentality about spending. Do you really have to have that (fancy car) *now?* The truly rich hold off gratification, knowing that what is trendy, popular or a must have today may not last until tomorrow. Never be frightened of failure.

Be realistic. Growth and wealth do not appear overnight, unless you are lucky enough to win the lottery or find long lost treasure. Investments need time to mature and savings need time to accumulate. Patience will be well rewarded. The wealthy know that scrimping now will lead to better results in the future.

Create a sense of urgency in your life. Do not wait for things to *happen to you.* You may think that you are playing safe by waiting around or looking for the next big deal. This is the financial equivalent of sitting around. Take risks, invest, start the business *now.*

Seize opportunities the moment they happen. The first to get there often wins, leaving the losers in the dust.

Taking stock of what you have right now can have some advantageous surprises. For one, you may find out that you have more than you think. Second, it gives you a clear cut place to start and helps you find balance as well as set goals.

After all, you cannot move forward without knowing where you come from.

Cutting corners where they matter

When it comes to wealth generation, another important factor that is hard to follow is "living within your means." For many people, living in debt has become the norm. It is common for the average person to be buried in debt before they reach the age of 25. A consumer-driven economy based on floating credit also creates the impression that wealth means more products. After taking a hard look at your assets and income, now you have to check your lifestyle and see where you can cut down on expenses.

Write down your expenses. Do not lie to yourself. There is nothing like seeing it in black and white (or red). Keep track of your expenses on a spreadsheet or if you prefer, in a notebook. It gives you a concrete idea of where you are spending too much and where you are spending too little.

If you are looking to save more, write down everything you buy and keep track of it. Do you really need to spend $5 a day on designer coffee? That amounts to $1800 dollars a year just on your morning cup of Joe. Is it paramount to have the latest car every single year when you are hip deep in auto loans?

Cut those credit cards. The average person owns at least seven cards. The average number you need to sustain a good to great credit score? The answer is one or two. One well-managed card does more for your credit score than the dozen overextended cards you have. If you can manage without one, why not cut them all? Your credit score is not just affected by cards, but by other loans you have in your name, like your mortgage or auto loan.

Ruthlessly cut out all the services you do not need and monitor those you do. One millionaire famously counted the sheets in toilet paper rolls because he thought suppliers were overcharging him. He was right.

Before you cut those cards however, understand the utilization ratio: the total credit used versus the total credit available to you. Many people keep multiple cards for fear that one or more lines will be cut, increasing the ratio over time. The goal is to have a very low ratio compared to debt, low balances and even lower interest.

Get a free copy of your credit report. Dispute any outdated items. Keep in mind that items should slide off, not stay on. Focus on judgments, liens and any items that undermine your potential to lenders.

Understand how interest affects your debt. The wealthy understand how interest works for investments, for loans and how it compounds over time. Those who are not wealthy do not.

Compound interest is interest that is added to the principle at certain intervals on the debt. This means that the loan/balance of a certain loan gets higher over time and you end up paying more interest.

Compounding rates differ but can be legally done on a yearly, quarterly, yearly or even daily basis. A loan with a starting principal of $1000 charged with 20% interest per year turns into $1200 at the end of the first year and so on. In contrast, simple interest does not add to the principal of the loan, but is the amount charged for use of that money or loan.

PAY DEBT OFF ASAP. Pay more than the minimum on loans.

Satisfy the interest and part of the principal—the debt amount will lessen over time and the bonus is you pay it off faster. The more you pay now, the less you pay later. Keep records of any and all transactions over the Internet or phone, especially if you are fixing your finances.

Print or save any changes to your account. When calling customer service, ask for the representative's employee number and record the time of the call in the event you need to follow up on a request. Keep exact files and amounts. Keep copies of everything.

Be hyper-vigilant when it comes to cards, loans or mortgages. Look for ways to lower interest, increase payments and keep an eye out for changes that could affect your loans.

Make a budget and stick to it. Think of it as a budge-it. Once you make it, you do not budge-it. Monthly and weekly budgets should be calculated to the penny.

The truly wealthy or those who want to be consider debt to be death to their portfolio. They only allow themselves to go into debt when they need it, and in that case they often refer to it as capital or even better, they often get it from someone else.

Keep the motto in mind when working with debt and get rid of it as soon as possible. Separate your accounts to keep track of your money. Keep a savings account, an investment account and an earnings account.

Know the consequences of forbearing or deferring loans. The breathing room you get is often paid back threefold in capitalized interest or an increased loan principal.

Create an emergency fund or funds. These accounts should contain the equivalent of 3 to 6 months' salary using low risk accounts (savings, certificates of deposits or insured money market accounts) as a safety net not just for your finances but for unexpected events in your life. This prevents you from dipping into your earnings or cashing in other income resources when unexpected and unwanted events happen, such as sudden illness.

Remember that you can grow rich now on money that you are throwing away. To be truly wealthy, you have to know that a simple dollar is an investment goldmine.

On average, millionaires spend more time selecting what to buy than buying the product itself. Why? Because they look for the best bargain before laying their money down—and ask for discounts before making a selection. Apply this principal to your life and watch your expenses go down.

Instead of selecting the first brand-name product you see, take the time to check what exactly you are getting. For example, many commercially branded cereal and grain products have exactly the same nutritional content as their generic cousins, at almost twice the price. Remember that you are paying more for the brand than you are for the product itself.

Millionaires and the wealthy also know the value of patience. Many stay in the first home they bought long after they can afford a more expensive one. Never accept a deal at face value. Negotiate until you feel the terms are in your favor.

The most important thing you should know is that without financial freedom, you cannot be truly wealthy. The most important thing is to create a base: a lower debt to income ratio and leeway to save and put money aside for investing later on.

It also frees up your mind so you can implement the law of attraction. Implementing positive thinking in your life can draw in positive forces and create more and more goodwill and luck. It is hard to think positive when you are constantly worrying about bills or making payments. By thinking positive and creating more positivity in your life, you bring in not just monetary wealth but a wealth in your personal life as well.

Investing and managing your wealth: Becoming truly wealthy

Once you have established a firm financial foundation or put aside a little money, it is time to learn to invest. Many first time investors fall into the trap of waiting, and waiting until they "have enough." The first thing you have to do is nix that notion, right now. You will find out by reading the tips that even measly amounts can add up to great amounts over time.

Others balk at investing because they think "I do not know enough to be a player." That is right. You do not. The truly wealthy understand how money works and never start sentences with the words "I do not know." If you do not understand investing and how it works, it is time to start to do the legwork.

Investing 101

The primary focus of investing is making your money work for you instead of working for your money. Many wealthy people have perfected the art of creating their wealth instead of giving a service. Building wealth also means creating wealth that is sustainable and continues to generate even in the event that you are unable to work.

Learn the difference between having a high income and being truly wealthy. High incomes do not necessarily mean that you are rich, especially if this income comes from only one source.

The myth persists that you can only be truly wealthy if you come into family money or are born into a home of silver spoons, silk sheets and antique furniture. Continue to believe in this myth, and you still have the mindset of the poor.

Many of the middle class believe that a high income job is the end all of their existence and work their butts off to get to a position that pays in five or six digits but end up baffled at how little they have by the time retirement rolls around.

For example, the average high level manager earns $200,000 a year, with benefits but stands to lose that income in the event of layoffs or illness. Although his income earning potential is high, it only comes from one source.

Contrast that with a middle level manager earning $50,000 a year. This middle manager, however, rents out properties in the city for another $500,000 and reaps dividends from stocks and bonds for another $100,000 a year. In the event of illness, death or mass layoffs, half of his earning potential is still secure.

The source of the latter's income is also easily passed on to future generations, securing wealth for the middle level manager's family.

Choose your investment goals as these will decide your allocation strategy later on. A broker or brokerage firm can help you decide on what your plans are, as well as help you begin investing.

Research the different types of investments as well as how risky they are. In general:

Stocks – you purchase partial ownership of a company and as part-owner, are entitled to annual profits. However, many people buy stock to sell when the price is high, not for dividends. The practice of buying low and selling high is relatively low risk but the potential for reward is governed by market and highly emotional changes. Yes, stock is considered an emotional asset.

Bonds – bonds are small loans to companies or governments that the investor pays for. They usually have fixed interest rates and are considered very safe and low risk investments. T-bills, municipal bonds and corporate bonds are some examples.

Mutual fund – this involves pooling money together with other like-minded investors to buy a full portfolio, usually run by firms or money managers. This type of investment is often the starting point for many first-time investors, simply because it provides a more diverse portfolio from the get-go.

REITS – these are companies that deal primarily with the ownership of real estate and manage a portfolio for you. They have the advantage of being diverse and easy to sell—as well as reduce the headache of managing your own property.

Other alternatives – Generally these are the high-risk and high reward securities where the payoff can be huge but the risk is high. Real estate, commodities, FOREX, options and futures fall under this category.

Create an allocation strategy for your savings or income to minimize risk and spread out your investments to guarantee several streams of income versus just one.

Learn about investing and accounting before you start spreading the money around. Consult with brokers or brokerage firm, especially if you have a lot to invest. Take night courses or read investment books to understand what you are getting into.

For example, you have $100,000 dollars to invest. 35% ($35,000) could go to property or real estate, another 30% for stocks, 10% for venture capital, etc. An allocation strategy helps you maximize your investments and also gives you the ability to indulge in some high-risk behavior, if you so wish, without losing all your capital. The financial equivalent of putting all your eggs in one basket, such as investing in all one type of equity, is portfolio suicide.

Account for every cent, every nickel, every dime and quarter. The saying goes you never know the value of money until you have to dig around the couch cushions for it. The truly wealthy know that every penny can be put to good use. Money is stagnant only when you want it to be, or when it flies out of your hands.

Even small amounts matter. Many people say they will invest only when they have x amount, but even a small investment of $1000 can give you great returns in the future. By thinking of returns instead of instant cash or how much you have on hand, you create your wealth through possibilities.

Saving 10,000 a year with a 10% rate of return and seeding that account with an additional 10,000 per year will yield $128,000+ after 10 years. If you start with $5,000, you end up with about $94,000 after said 10 years. That doesn't count the interest the account would generate for years after.

Invest your money as early as you can. The true friend of money is always time and the passage of it. The longer money sits and the more interest it collects, the higher the chances that you will reap thousands of dollars in returns.

A great example for this is the 401(k). Many Americans simply cannot wait until retirement and cash it in as soon as they can. But for what? A faster car, a bigger house or in some cases, that giant flat screen TV everyone else has.

Your 401(k) alone is a savings plan you must NEVER touch. Do the math. If you have an annual salary of $100,000 and contribute 10%, with a 50% employer match rate and no salary increases, you end up with $ 741,184.02 in 20 years. Increase the contribution to 12%, with all other factors constant and the amount rises to $889,420.89. Increase the time frame to 30 years and you end up with $2 *million*.

Buy stock, not product. If you love the product, chances are others will to. So why waste time buying the product when you can make money off the stock. This creates:

a) Passive income and
b) A higher chance of return on investments.

Take Apple. Apple's stock has risen over 12 times in the past five years, quadrupling dividends for investors. How many iPhones or iPods have you bought over the past five years? How much money do you think an average shareholder has made from the products you have been buying? Even with the death of its founder, Steve Jobs, Apple's stock remained strong and rose. Traditionally company stock falls with the death of visible CEOs or front men, but this was not true in this case.

One exception: keep in mind that sales do not make the stock. Activision is a company that markets and makes one of the biggest selling video games in the world, with sales totaling over 400,000 on the *first day* of the new installment release. However, their stock and shares have remained static for around 4 years.

Create assets that will make money for you with a minimum of effort. For example, investing in a restaurant does not require you to show up daily to manage the day-to-day running of the business, only to pay the management firm or keep the standard of a franchise.

Think long term. The truly wealthy do not count on single projects that net huge paychecks, but invest in opportunities that create returns and dividends that last for years. Long term also means the ability of securities to mature. Thinking long term means having the ability to see the future in a sense—and finding projects that affect and create these futures.

Do not wait for business opportunities, create them. Entrepreneurs look at an empty lot and see possibility and a method for them to get rich. Those with a poor mindset simply see an empty lot. The rich look at garbage and see a garbage hauling business, a rust-cleaning service, a recycling center. Those with a poor mindset see only the discarded tires, the dirt and the weeds.

Another great secret is to never care where you money comes from. Many people balk at investing in businesses that are not "sexy" perhaps because they do not want to tell people at parties that they got rich off sewage.

Truly wealthy people spread their money around and reap them in regardless if they were earned because of sewage or flowers. Who cares if it comes up in cocktail conversation?

Always think in terms of specific assets versus their overall value in the market. The truly wealthy do not rely on the ups and downs of the market, but the possible opportunities that stem from them.

For example, the real estate market may be down during the recession but right now savvy investors are buying up foreclosed property in great locations for half prices for later investment.

Know when to hold off, reassess and quit. Investors will say no. But not all of them will. Those with a poor mindset go to the bank for a loan, get rejected and never think about their idea or opportunity again. The wealthy mindset goes to the bank for a loan, gets rejected, and redrafts the proposal and returns to get the approval.

The poor mindset goes into business not knowing the risks of the deal and is baffled when the fallout occurs. The wealthy mindset goes into a deal, knows the risk and gets out if things are going bad. Always follow your gut and do your research. Knowing when to back off from risky or unethical deals will not only save your money but have effects on your financial freedom.

Accept that there will be instances where you will experience some loss, such as when stock goes down or remains stagnant, therefore not providing you with the expected dividends. Accept that this will change as well.

Do not join the bandwagon: just because everyone is putting their money in it, does not mean you should. Get rich quick schemes are simply schemes.

Forget compartmentalizing your money. Every penny is important so do not think of it as a bonus or extra pay. The wealthy put every single cent to good use and are able to account for all of them.

The lesson here is to value every single dollar you earn. One millionaire started by investing $25, that is right, $25 in a mutual fund. He could not afford any more at the time, since he worked a menial job. As his pool grew, so did the amount of his investments. He is now worth multi-millions.

Learn about taxes and how to use them to your advantage, not the other way around.

The truly wealthy know how to make taxes work for them. Never be afraid to learn and ask. Instead of having someone do it for you, learn how to do it yourself.

Finally, never invest if you are not willing to wait. Otherwise, you are throwing your money away like a gambling addict at a poker table.

The truly wealth think of investing as a game that pays out and is fun to play. Never for once think that they got there by simple luck. It takes a lot of research, studying and waiting to get there. The poor make excuses and say, they never have enough time between their jobs, their family and whatever other obligations they have.

The wealthy create the time to invest and invest in their time as well. However, the main difference is this: they enjoy it. They enjoy the time they spend reading investment books. They enjoy reading the reports, watching the stock market and simply *love the game of money*. This is an attitude you need to become successful when you move to invest. This is the attitude that makes winners and makes the wealthy.

Making and protecting your money

The average millionaire or comfortably wealthy person works for himself or owns a business. This is a law that is hard to follow. Most people think a business is a risky proposition simply because there are so many factors that affect the success of a business. A million things can go wrong, but a million things can also go right.

The wealth mindset is one that works for itself, cashing in on your own ideas and labor. The poor mindset works for others, laboring for a minimum cut of the profit.

The idea of working for yourself can be scary. Many first-time business owners fail because they sink everything they have into one venture and never recommit when the road to success gets rocky. The wealthy and the rich stick with their business plan and move forward regardless of the events, and are confident in their success.

Do something that you love, because you will never feel like it is work. The success stories of many entrepreneurs and millionaires always begin with this line "I love…[insert hobby, passion or interest here] so I"

Money always follows passion and the upside is, you will never feel like you worked a day in your life. Ask yourself what you love to do, what you are good at and how important it is to you. Once you know what it is, you will know what venture to begin.

Alternatively, find a need for something you love and fill it. Filling a need or creating a need is an excellent starting point for a business. Curves Gym combined the owner's need for fitness and hatred of being ogled while at the gym.

She provided a women's only gym *without* mirrors, filling a need many women did not even know existed. Women lined up around the street to work out at this gym and it boasts hundreds of franchises around the US today.

Do not be afraid to do something humble—many a business has expanded from humble origins and cottage industries. No idea is too small, no business is "stupid".

Make sure your business fits your lifestyle. If you hate nightclubs, why start one? Why start a golfing business when you have never picked up a club in your life and have no interest in doing so?

Those who cannot run a business, invest in one. It takes the headache out of the management and gives you profit without the effort.

The wealthy know when to expand their business. Those who want to be truly rich run multiple businesses. Take Nigella Lawson, who started with a cooking show and now has a line of products and even utensils. One business, different umbrellas. Different umbrellas, one profit.

The business should never be static, but it should be familiar. Take a cue from top restaurants. They constantly change or update their menus but keep the customer favorites around.

Be the best. There are *no* exceptions to this rule. Provide the best service, the fastest delivery, the highest quality, and the newest products. Follow these rules and the customers will come.

A sub rule to this secret is to always strive to continue to be the best. Once you have set a standard, customers and clients will expect you to maintain it. Many a business has experienced fallout after reaching heights due to declining service or worsening product. Take a cue from timeless products and services that continue to make money over the years. They never balk or shirk when it comes to quality. Even if it means making their customers pay a little extra.

Your business is defined by its employees—especially if you decide to go into any type of service industry. Hire for attitude, train for skill. Never keep an employee who is not worth the salary you pay. Never tolerate stupidity, slowness or excuses. Instead, screen, evaluate and expect change. Millionaires never take slack from their employees. They never hesitate when the time comes to let one go.

Learn to recommit. Every business owner experiences fall out, bad sales or some sort of failure. There will always be a time when you fall into the red. It takes perseverance to go back into the black.

Economize where it counts. Find the best deals for raw product to maximize profit.

The truly wealthy know how to make profit with minimal expenditure. Reduce overhead, especially when it comes to trappings. A huge corner office with the antique desk and leather seats will not mean much when you are scrambling to pay the bills.

Protecting your money

Once you have money, you will take time to protect it by avoiding future catastrophes. Be cautious and always assume the worst. Do not go through life thinking that other people will not take advantage of you or that your money is not important to them. A careless mistake can cost you a fortune. A careless demeanor opens you up to attack. And you will never know where it is going to come from.

Now that you have the money, you have to take the steps to protect it from unscrupulous beings. Many a millionaire's downfall came from lawsuits from hungry money-grubbing relatives or the greed from immediate family. The media is packed with celebrity stories where the 'evil' spouse gets millions in the divorce, millions they never earned simply because the high earner took no precautions.

In the case of lawsuits, anything personal amounts to what you or your companies are worth. Lawyers love public information and can easily figure out what you are worth by accessing public records. Transferring the bulk of your wealth to foundations, trusts or corporations ensures that these stay well out of the public's eye or are untouchable in the event you are attacked.

Protecting your money now ensures that it will continue to benefit you and your family for years and decades to come.

Millionaires and the truly wealthy never put assets in their name and guard their personal assets zealously. They use corporations and protect themselves with liability insurance. Corporate entities are used to operate businesses, partnerships are made with the idea that if all goes to hell, it is time to get out. Use trusts, family partnerships and protect your personal assets and wealth.

Turn yourself into a stealthy, moving target. Never be conspicuous about your wealth and forego the trappings of it. Remember: the bigger, flashier bird is always easier to bring down. The birds that fly low, fly below the radar and detection.

Begin asset protection early to prevent any mishaps. Never let yourself get caught in the trap of beginning asset protection when you are already in heaps of trouble!

There is nothing like being prepared. Besides, transferring assets when you are being sued is illegal and can land you in jail (plus you lose everything). Protect your personal assets from claims and unscrupulous parties!

Create a clear-cut and legal will, even if you are only 32 years old. Make sure you know where your money is going. Many people put off the idea of the will simply because it makes them face their own mortality which is always wrong.

Update and notarize yearly, or anytime you like. A will prevents many a family feud, protects your interests long after you are gone and ensures that money that you share keeps going where you want it to go. Without a will, chaos will ensue, especially if your personal fortune and business assets are worth six digits or more.

For businesses, the equivalent of a will is known as succession planning. Many successful business have failed because an epic predecessor was not able to carefully plan who would succeed him in the event of his death.

Follow the example of Steve Jobs and create a succession plan for your business *before you even get sick or retire*. Many family corporations create a version of this by grooming successors from within the family and stipulating conditions to be met in order to inherit or run the business.

Never enter any partnership, including conjugal ones, without a back-up plan or a clear way out. That is what prenuptial agreements are for. Do not let a future ex-spouse pull a Paul McCartney on you.

Never put all your money into one humungous deal. Diversity is the key to true wealth. Keep in mind that those eggs in one basket are more liable to break if the basket is too heavy.

The final timeless wealth secret. Money is meant to shared, not hoarded. Follow the Rockefeller rule: 10% of your worth is meant to be shared. This creates more for you.

Conclusion

There is no shortcut to instant wealth. Being rich means playing a game that lasts for years. The truly wealthy not only look forward to this game, but also look forward to playing it. By following these timeless secrets, you learn the value of hard work, patience and reap the rewards for years to come.

Never be complacent and put off your wealth creation for tomorrow. True wealth and real wealth starts by making these changes today. Break that piggy bank and start investing *now*.

Wealth creation is both a complex strategy and a waiting game, but by following these tips, you can be on your way to true wealth, a comfortable lifestyle and living your life financially free.

Chapter 12
SOME 8 FIGURE BUSINESS TIPS

Ultimate Traffic Parts 1-3 - Prospect to Customer

People are creatures of habit, and that knowledge can be used to convert visitors into customers. If you pay close attention to when people are triggered to open their wallets, then you can use the same dynamics to develop a strategy to have it work for your sales efforts. Understanding triggers that produce sales is one effective way to develop strategies that can work over a large cross-section of people.

In each part of this chapter we will discuss a variety of different techniques to mine your traffic for sales, explaining what works, the psychological impact of the strategy, and even the how to implement for the best timing and results. The first strategy we will discuss exploits people's tendencies to develop habits and uses that to create sales that get bigger and bigger as they become more involved with you.

The strategic plan

For a habit to work for you, it has to produce the close of a sales call to action. For instance, if you've ever been to the deli, you'll see how this strategy works to make additional sales. You go and you order 1/2 lb. of lunch meat, it doesn't matter which. Odds are, that they will cut up more than you need, never less, and then when they weigh it they'll ask: "Is that okay or do you want me to take off some?" Since you already committed to the order of 1/2 lb. of lunch meat, you'll seem cheap trying to get out of the extra so most of the time you let it go and pay for the extra. Not only that, but when they hand you the lunch meat they ask: "Is there anything else I can get for you?" And, since you've already purchased one item, you are more inclined to purchase another.

This strategy works because you already committed to a purchase, no matter how small, and asking for something on top is taking advantage of the groove you've already slipped into. It may not seem like a lot of extra money going in your pocket, but if you do this to every single sales prospect you encounter, the multiple effect can line your pockets quite nicely.

This strategy works okay with retail sales, but it is dynamite with direct sales on the Internet. The key is to get your visitor to commit to a small sale first and then before they check out, ask them if they want something extra. You will be surprised how fast your orders tend to grow after that.

The psychological triggers

The biggest resistance people tend to have when closing a sale is just the simple act of saying "yes." Once that obstacle is circumvented it becomes much easier to make the sales larger out of pure inertia. Once people are already walking in a specific direction it takes more effort and attention to change directions than it does to just keep going the way you're already headed.

Some people like to call it consistency in action, but it's also about habitual action. Psychologists say that it only takes so much time to create a habit, but it can take more than 21 days to break it and it takes a concerted effort to do so. People generally don't pay attention to their habits and that's why when you identify a trigger it is easy to exploit it to your benefit.

You are actually setting the course without making it obvious to your sales prospect. The minute they agree to even a tiny purchase, you have set the momentum to generate even larger sales, if not immediately – at least, down the road.

How to implement effectively

The trick here is to make the first purchase as simple and as easy as possible. It doesn't even have to be a major purchase. You aren't trying to score a huge sale, you are trying to involve your sales prospect in your business at this point. There's plenty of time to expand their sales later. So, make that first sale as easy and as painless as possible.

This works beautifully online by having a very simple and cheap offer on your home page. It can be anything really, as long as it is a simple process and can produce an immediate effect. Reports and media downloads make very good initial sales online because you can sell them cheap, in mass quantities, and you can also deliver it electronically for an immediate effect. You have a check box to put them on an email or newsletter list too to help you capture their email and allow you to market them for more products later.

With a little research, you can find out what products your customers bought after they bought your initial lead sales package. Then, you can target new customers with that as it's already proven to be a winner. This can lead to larger sales down the road.

However, if you want to implement this strategy immediately, it takes a little more finesse. In the retail, face-to-face world, you would simply do like the deli clerks and offer another product to add to someone's check-out. New home construction companies do this all the time, by calling them "upgrades." You sign for a basic unit and then they start asking you if you want to upgrade the countertops with marble, put in hardwood floors instead of carpet, and so on.

Pretty soon, the price you committed to buying comes out to an exorbitant amount with all the additional things you've consented to buy. And, should you decide you don't have enough money for everything you want, you're stuck with the difficult decision to figure out what you can cut out of your home package. Obviously, the answer is that it's just too difficult to decide what features or options you don't want, instead it's much easier to charge it.

That's why stores also make their payment options as simple and easy as possible. The more payment options you have, the easier it is to close a sale and overrule any objection on a lack of money. Some stores even ante up the ease of purchase by offering their own in-house financing. These financing offers usually start fairly low and come with very little risk on the part of the store, but it can't help to convert sales prospects into bonafide customers.

At any rate, to implement this at the end of a small sale, all you simply have to do is ask, almost as an afterthought, "Oh! Do you want to include this x offer too?" It can be very effective if you are doing this face-to-face and you've already got up to leave and just before departing suddenly realize you forgot to tell them about that extra offer that would go good with his sale.

The key is to be subtle, the hard sell online only makes people mad if you sign them up for extra offers in sneaky, underhanded ways. Always get the customer's approval clearly before charging them for the sale. This can be done at checkout by simply adding an extra page they click through to get to checkout, where other offers are left UNCHECKED but can be selected to add to their original purchase. Make it easy for them to move on and don't confuse them or you'll lose the sale.

Another effective way to implement this technique is called a "one-time-offer" or "OTO". This requires special software that presents the additional product(s) after the first one is purchased but not yet delivered. In this scenario, instead of a download or thank you page, you are delivered to a page which says, "Thank you for your order. Now, because you've just purchased product xyz, we have a special offer for you and don't close this page because you will lose that offer once you do. In other words you will never have another chance to take advantage of this offer."

Then you make an offer for another, usually complementary product at a discount price. This add on sale always increases your overall sales and many people report that up to 50% or more take the OTO. So, imagine you sell the main product for $27 and then offer the resale rights to the product as an OTO for an additional $27, normally $47. So, instead of a $27 sale, you've now made a $54 sale.

Why not offer the resale rights for $54 upfront instead? Because testing has shown that you'll get a lot more sales with the OTO than asking for the $54 at the start. You see, they've already bought the $27 product. Now, it's just a small extra amount and that is more likely to get accepted.

So, let's say you make 100 sales at $27, that's $2700. With the OTO, you make an additional $1350 for a total sales of $4050, assuming a 50% OTO rate.

You can also do the same by offering a complementary product instead of resale rights. You can offer the OTO at a higher price, called an up- sell, or at a lower price, called a down-sell.

To get your OTO offer to truly appear once and only once, you'll need special software. There are a couple ways to do this.

You could hire a programmer at one of the outsource sites like Elance.com or RentACoder.com or you can purchase an already programmed and much more elegant solution like Rapid Action Profits.

If you go with RapidActionProfits, you'll be able to do a lot more as well since they have an add-on system where you can add features as they are developed.

Timing this strategy

There are several different times when this strategy is effective. You can set it up immediately so that a very simple offer is made available on the home page. Make sure to change this offer for repeat visitors. The idea is to start to form a habit by having someone be tempted to buy a small item immediately. So, that's the first time you want to try to slip your visitors into a buying groove.

The second time to use it is after they've already committed to buying a small item and they are checking out. This can be done automatically using software that adds a footer with additional items that might interest your buyer, or an additional page to move through to get to the final checkout.

Mesmerize with something new

In a consumer culture saturated with products for sale everywhere, you have to distinguish what makes your offering better than everyone else's offering. This can be difficult to do if you are selling brooms or something so ordinary that the market has been completely saturated with ads talking about the benefit of brooms or some other item. People become jaded or bored with these ads and can't really justify to themselves why one broom is better than another. After all, they all sweep floors.

That's when you want to try and see your product's unique personality and bring it out into the open where it can be appreciated. Now, that's slick marketing to take something old and make it new again. Not only that, but maybe your product has some benefits that the other products truly don't have. You can polish those up and mention them in your copy too, to differentiate yourself on the market.

The strategic plan

Okay, let's pretend you have a bunch of office supplies you are trying to sell online. You want to get into the mindset of your customers as much as you can. Why would they come online to buy office products? Why are they choosing to buy some products and not others? What is unique about a particular product that can give it a competitive edge? You can even gear your product's unique qualities to the audience you've targeted.

For instance, say you are using Social Ads on Facebook to target a particular demographic of people for your office supplies. Well, Facebook and other social networking sites attract people who want to communicate their identities. So, you may decide to sell office products that can be personalized to suit a person's personality. Whatever the market is, that's the one you are looking to sell to. Keep that in mind.

Try to use strategies that are different from your competitors and that play up your offerings. For instance, if you are selling martial arts courses, you don't want to only list those benefits that everyone else has on their website, you want to make sure you include extra benefits.

While other people may throw out statistics on how many women are assaulted by someone they know, you might opt to go less of the scare tactic route. Instead, you may want to differentiate your courses by stating how easy they are to learn online and how they can help you develop fitness while keeping you safe. So, that way even though there is a whole market of people who may be looking to do martial arts for safety, that's not the only reason. It may be people who are interested in Asian martial arts forms or fitness who you are engaging online.

That's the beauty of online marketing, the audience is very wide open. You are going to have people world-wide who show up to visit your site and you can't assume you know that the sole reason they are looking at your martial arts courses online is because you are afraid for your safety, even if that is the case. You can always add these benefits, but don't forget to add the other benefits too!

The psychological triggers

The key here is that most people need a reason to say yes. That's why salespeople sell benefits and not products. Ask any good salesperson and they will tell you that the benefits and unique characteristics of the product is what eventually sells it, even if the marketer is the one highlighting these qualities. People generally don't buy things they don't need, but they will need a reason to say yes, even if they do need the product.

The reason for this is that people are constantly pressured in this consumerist society to buy, buy, and buy. At some point, they either become jaded or tune out. When they tune out, it's the marketer's responsibility to help them tune back in. The customer may even be in desperate need of your product, but they may not be aware of it – they are so tuned out. It is your job to slowly bring them back in and educate them about why they need your product.

How to implement effectively

Because your customer may not be aware of their need for your product, you will have to give them time to realize it. This is not a fast way to make a sale, but it is a way to convert visitors into customers, eventually. Once they are your customer, they will be so convinced of your product's unique qualities and benefits, they will be hard-pressed to go elsewhere for their needs. So, you are not just converting a visitor, but you are also promoting your brand and establishing familiarity and authority with your products.

So, don't be upset if you don't make a sale right away. This strategy takes patience. You can hit on a few customers who have an eureka moment when you first start listing your benefits, but mostly people need to hear or read things multiple times for it to have an impact.

Then, something can happen in their lives that suddenly shifts their attention back to all those benefits you've been listing on your website or products for years. Maybe they didn't think they needed to supplement their diet, but now they are turning older and people around them are getting forgetful. Maybe they are noticing they are more forgetful too. Suddenly, they remember that one of the benefits of Gingko Biloba, a supplement you are selling, listed the benefits of memory enhancement. All of a sudden, the product is more appealing. And, the thing is you never know when that eureka moment will happen with the visitors to your website, so you have to keep copy up listing each product's unique qualities to help educate them for when the need actually arises.

So, remember to remind your customers often on the benefits of a particular product, even if they've seen the benefit on other pages. Repetition is important with this strategy. You want to be able to slowly, but surely gain the attention of someone who is hearing the same message from various sources until it finally sinks in. That's why when you develop a new product, you don't just want to put one sales page up, but you want to write articles, introduce it to various people at the same time through groups, discussion forums, or even paid reviews. They need to hear about this product over and over again until they finally see a need for it in their lives. When that happens, it's totally up to the consumer.

A great way to implement this strategy and make instant sales is with items that can bring out the inner child in people, like electronics. People love computers, cell phones, flat-screen TVs, and other types of electronic wizardry because it mesmerizes them with technology and also brings out the impulse to play around with their new purchase. Anytime you have a product like that, you can make instant sales and they can be very high priced, in comparison to older products in your inventory. So, even though this strategy can work for any product, in order to get it to work instantly, you want to use it most with products that have an instant mesmerizing effect on people. Things that are tactile and produce an experience of child-like wonder or playfulness are excellent products to use with this strategy.

Software is also something that can be sold quite well with this strategy and allow a person to get a small experience of the larger product either with a free trial or a limited demo-like experience. If your software is for games or like a game, this too can bring out the impulse to play and produce the desired effect to influence your potential buyer to want to possess this new toy.

Timing this strategy

This timing to sell the benefit or the product's unique personality is when they land on your sales page. You should have a sales page that funnels people from a blog, your signature, or other places to where they actually see all the benefits that make your product truly unique. You should set the title of your sales page to include the BIGGEST, and MOST IMPORTANT benefit that you want to highlight about your product or service. Many people don't get past that first title before moving away from the page, so make it count. It should highlight your product's unique nature while being something that is attractive to the majority of people who might land on your sales page.

The second instance of using this strategy is directly underneath the title. Just list every last benefit you can possibly think of for your product or service. Many online marketers think that the longer your sales page is and the more benefits you list, the more likely you will hit one that eventually produces that eureka moment in the customer. Just be sure to ask for the sale several times on the same page too, so that if they do happen to find that reason to buy that overcomes all their objections, they don't have to scroll too far to see the link to buy too.

Lastly, you can also start to keep a file of one-line benefits for each product you are selling. Add that to your signature and rotate them so that your signature changes constantly and people reading your emails see a new benefit every time they read one of your emails. Don't forget to include links to the sales page too here.

Another time to implement it is when you have multiple items in your inventory. You can highlight newer products over the others by showing how this new product has definite benefits over the other ones. The nice thing about new products is that they often can be higher priced and still sell. Think of when a new style of cell phone comes out. These types of electronic products fascinate people with the way they can push buttons, take pictures, send text mails, and endless other features. And, the price is usually quite high for a new cell phone on the market because demand is expected to be high too. So, when you highlight a new product in your inventory, you also have the potential to make higher priced sales too.

The overall timing on this strategy is sometimes up to the customer, not the marketer. You can constantly remind people why your products are unique, but it's up to them to finally connect their need to your product. However, this dynamic shifts when the market environment makes your products far more attractive, like when there is a drought and you happen to have rain barrels.

You may have spent years telling everyone that rain barrels save you money by helping them to store water and use it for their landscaping needs. However, if there is no drought, the fact that people have to buy them and install them without a perceived need, can make them difficult to sell. With the drought, you will see your demand skyrocket, because now you can also add: "Don't let the drought kill all your valuable landscaping, buy a rain barrel." See? Your product didn't change, even your benefit did not change, but the environment for the sales changed dramatically, making the timing perfect for selling rain barrels.

Mine your sales prospect's unconscious desires

In this strategy to turn your Internet traffic into paying customers, you want to concentrate on the person buying, the sales prospect, rather than the product. Your sales prospects can determine what lures will work best for you in converting visitors to customers, but for that you really have to understand your demographics.

If you haven't done some sort of market research in your demographics, you will want to do that. In face-to-face interactions, the demographics are the people you visit to market with your products, but online it is not as obvious who is visiting your site and why. So, you will want to gather some information through surveys, hiring market research for demographics, checking out the statistics of your website logs, and also using social networking to get a better feel for who might be interested in your products.

The strategic plan

To understand the unconscious desires that may be lurking in a sales prospect's mind, you need to interact with them and start to get to know them. Some people do this with surveys, by offering a freebie in exchange for visitors filling out a survey. However, that's not going to give you a full view as many people refuse to fill out surveys. So, the next option is to get the people who visit to interact in a forum or group where you can ask questions, see what people are talking about, and get a general feel for who is showing up to your website.

So, start out by gathering information on anything that might appeal to your customer. In social networking places like Facebook, this is a pretty simple thing to do. You just look through the profiles that people draw up in a network and that tells you a lot about what motivate people who join certain groups on Facebook. But, you also have to direct your market research to your product interest too.

So, say you are trying to find out the subconscious motivations of people who are visiting your pet site. There are the obvious reasons that they are interested in pets and pet products. But, that doesn't determine the subconscious motivation that may get them to buy your pet products. For that, you might want to know more about your visitors. Do they have hobbies? Are they having safety issues? What about where they live, is there something there that might make it more appealing to have pets or more important to have pet products?

At the end of your research into this issue, you may come up with a couple of different ways to implement the strategy, once you have a good idea of some underlying motivations that might be driving traffic to your website.

Then, you simply provide the solution to this unconscious desire by providing services that match your target market's needs. You will want to do that by writing online copy that expresses how it solves their needs, by selling the benefits first. But, if you have done your homework well, you will be pushing a trigger button that gets immediate attention and can result in an instant sale purely from understanding the psychology of why your customers buy.

The psychological triggers

Let's face it, when it comes to subconscious triggers most people are on automatic pilot. Our entire society is set up to keep people in this hypnotic state, so people generally don't question why they do a certain thing or make a particular purchase, they just may have the vague sense they need it. However, there are some subconscious triggers that appeal to almost everyone's egos: sex, money, and power. These are not so hidden, except that when people make a purchase, they may not even be aware that it is exactly one of these triggers that finally sealed the deal.

That's why advertisers showcase pretty girls with their products for men. They may be selling electric shavers, but the woman is the one touching his face on television and going: "Aaah!" Right? Isn't that so? So, was it the features of that particular razor that sold it or the subconscious trigger that insinuated that the person's sex appeal would shoot up dramatically if they used it? Probably the latter. However, if you ask a person why they bought that razor, they will most likely start to tell about the features because the trigger was so subconscious they don't even realize they were influenced by it.

Then, there are subconscious triggers that aren't so universal but are specific to your demographic and your product.

For instance, do you remember the commercials about the elderly person who falls and can't get up? Then, they have the instant communication system around their neck that notifies someone they need help. Okay, so what is the subconscious trigger here? It's the fear of living alone and having no one around to help. That might be specific to the demographic of the elderly people they were trying to sell. But, no matter how memorable the commercial is, most people buying it would probably not want to admit that fear of being frail or even being elderly, for that matter. They might convince themselves that the reason they bought it was because it was convenient or not that expensive.

So, be aware that the unconscious desires can be universal or specific to your demographic. The key is to provide the solution or associate your product with that unconscious desire so that people will feel more compelled to close the deal.

In a way, you will have to be smarter than the people who are buying your products. You may have a product that doesn't appear to have universal appeal, but you want to use this strategy. It's your job to figure out a way to associate that product with either sex, money, or power or some other unconscious desire that may land you a sale.

How to implement effectively

To implement this strategy online, you will not only be targeting sales, but any call to action that can increase the value of your website or blog. In these terms, a call to action may be to buy something, but it can also be to add a comment to your blog, to discuss something in a public forum, to join your email list, or any other action that makes the buyer interact with the site. If you have a lot of activity on your site, this can help you define what is motivating the visits to your site and how to manifest your visitors' unconscious desires, as we talked about earlier.

You will want to use the gathering phase to cull information on your visitor's subconscious desires. Maybe you experience more sales from people who are visiting your site from the Southern United States in the summer than you do from other regions of the country. That tells you that there is something specific to that region that is motivating sales. The fact is that Southern states have a harder time controlling fleas in the summer months and even though you may not live there, your website is worldwide and people have found it and are buying. Well, one of the ways you can influence a subconscious trigger is just to advertise how many Southerners actually buy from your site, but that's not very subtle. It may trigger feelings of belonging and also status too, but it can also make them wonder why they're being targeted.

The key to using a subconscious trigger is to keep it somewhat subconscious. You may get it, but it shouldn't be too obvious to the people who are buying your products or they will resist it.

So, maybe you find out people in the South who have lots of dogs or cats living in the country and like country music or NASCAR.

Voila! You set up your pet site with a referral from a country music star or a NASCAR driver. You don't mention the word "south" at all, even though that's your demographic. You don't say that Southerners have too many fleas in the summer, you just have your celebrity showing how effective it is to treat their pets with your product and what they like about it (the benefits).

The subconscious trigger of identity is very powerful. They will identify your product with where they live, in the

South, and probably think of you more in association with the celebrity. Every time they hear a song or watch NASCAR, subconsciously they will remember that ad and if they happen to be doing it in the summer, you've probably already made a sale.

So, the thing is to be subtle but focused on your product and target audience when you are going to close the deal. That doesn't mean that you can't use this strategy for other things to get your visitors involved in your site and help you determine their needs. As mentioned earlier, a valid action on your site might be someone putting a comment on your blog or adding a post to a discussion group on your site. If your site is a group site with membership levels and more, you can easily use the subconscious desire to belong to stimulate growth in your website and more activity. You can even sell memberships on your site if you target the subconscious desire to belong to a status group very carefully.

The way to do this is to build a core group first, of people who are already online. This gives your site authority. Then, use strategies like Facebook where people join who have similar networks, interests, or because they are friends already. So, you sign up people, and invite them to have their friends join. You can even give them something for their effort, by either using a point system or some free gift. This will help you build a network of people with similar interests who want to buy your products.

Another way to use the subconscious desire to belong is to add different membership levels to your site. This works particularly well for sites that have a great deal of prestige. EBay uses this strategy by offering sellers a Powerseller status on their membership if they happen to have a high number of sales and a 98% feedback rating by the end of several months.

If they do, they are automatically promoted to Powerseller status.

Meanwhile, this motivates people to sell a lot and keep up good customer service on eBay. Similarly, if you own a respected research or non-profit site, you can have people who want memberships to get different perks per membership level and different types of recognition for being a part of your organization. This helps you sell memberships and increases your pool of people.

Timing this strategy

The timing for this is actually very flexible. You can influence people through their subconscious programming at any stage of the sales cycle. It is particularly effective at the beginning when people might be attracted to your website, but not quite identifying it with their needs yet. By carefully triggering those subconscious desires they will associate your website, and products, with the solution to their needs. So, while you can do this anytime, at the beginning it can form a powerful first impression without being overbearing or insulting to the buyer's intelligence.

Another time that is perfect for this strategy is on your membership sales page, since you can trigger the particular subconscious reasons someone might join and help them to seal the deal. For instance, maybe you are a non-profit that deals with environmental cleanup, then you can have on your membership page the different levels and how each level helps you to do more good in the community. You can send them a bumper sticker or some other personally identifying perk to make them proud they belong to such a wonderful organization.

Also, when a deal has already been closed, you might still be able to use a subconscious trigger right before the checkout to get more sales. Like the Amazon list that shows "people who bought this item also bought these" which triggers a status subconscious desire. How can you pass up the other books when so many other people have them? Are they smarter than you? Richer than you? What do they know that you don't know? So, you might get triggered to buy more just to keep up with the Jones.

Spot the flaws first

If you ask a sales person whether an objection to their sales presentation is bad, you'll get the answer: "No." A good sales person knows that with any presentation or marketing, objections will arise. That's a good thing because once an objection is raised by the sales prospect, most marketers can resolve it and dismiss it, leaving the way clear to buying their product. So, objections typically are raised by the customer in most sales transactions, but this strategy is done by the seller and not the potential buyer. That's right, you will be the one raising the objections so that you can just as swiftly dismiss them and get to the closing.

The reason this particular strategy is important in online marketing is because you are not interacting with the potential buyer face to face. They visit your site, find something they like, and like any reasonable customer they will start to think of reasons they shouldn't buy it. That's just what most people do; they resist being marketed. So, if your product has any obvious flaws that's exactly the first objection that will be raised in their mind. Maybe the product is ugly, or it costs too much, or it's gotten bad reviews. Don't wait for the customer to raise that objection in their own minds and click away, instead you raise it first! So, for instance, if you know your product costs more than all the competitors, raise that first by saying: "Our product costs more because it's better than the competition!" And, then go on to use that as a lead into the benefits.

The strategic plan

The strategy is to disarm your buyer by bringing up the objection first, before they even have time to think about it or utter it in their minds. This works whether the product has some faults or not, but it is especially effective with those that have obvious faults. Don't believe that a buyer will miss a flaw with the product or that if you concentrate on only highlighting the good qualities that the bad qualities won't be noticed. Consumers are very sophisticated these days.

Online retailing has made it incredibly easy for them to comparison shop without having to visit multiple stores. Some sites even have reviews of products online that tell them which kinds are the best. Of course, magazines like consumer reports will tell buyers what basic features they can expect from a product and what makes one a better deal than another. It's a bit naïve to think that you will have a totally uninformed consumer drop by your website and not notice anything that is obviously flawed about your product. That doesn't mean you can't bring that up first and either make it a feature or find a way to resolve that objection that satisfies them as fair.

The psychological triggers

When you bring up an objection first it has a couple of effects. First, it makes you appear to be honest and forthright because you willingly brought up the subject first. It also decreases the resistance your buyer may have to the objection because you've reframed it in a way that acknowledges the flaw, but gives them a way to justify it. So, by simply being willing to be upfront, you can undercut the objection before it happens. This is a way of disarming the reaction of the buyer by simply acknowledging the concern upfront.

If, on the other hand, you took the tact of trying to avoid the flaw and hoping they didn't see it, you would appear to be deceitful and the person would lose confidence in the sale. If you brought up the flaw, but minimized it as a valid objection, your buyer will wonder what else is wrong with your product that you don't think is worth mentioning. But, if you bring up the flaw, acknowledge it, and then resolve it for them in a way that they can justify the purchase, you close the deal.

In a way, the buyer is more likely to trust the rest of the presentation because you didn't gloss over the bad features of your product. Since you were honest enough to be upfront, that lends you credibility and that credibility rubs off on the product, whether it deserves it or not. And, when you go on to actually talk about the positive features they are given more weight, because you were honest with the negative ones. While you might think people would be turned off by acknowledging a defect, hiding it under the rug is a worse offense in most people's minds.

How to implement effectively

This is something that you should consider when you have a product or service with an obvious flaw. So, let's say that you are trying to sell used tires. Okay, used tires are obviously not as good as new tires, are they? Well, you can't advertise the tire like new tires. So, you admit – hey, they're used tires. Then, you can go on to say that despite the fact they are used tires and not brand new, they are checked to make sure they have sufficient tread on them, they pass some inspection for holes etc., you offer a guarantee should they not last a certain amount of miles, and you can still offer the same brands that other retail people sell brand new. Oh, and don't forget that if they're used, you save money too because the price is lower for the same name brands.

This works very well if you are selling items on eBay and they are not new or they have some obvious defect. You want to be completely upfront with that defect. It should be the very first thing you discuss, so that there is absolutely no misunderstanding that the product may be perceived to be flawed by other standards. The worse thing that can happen online is that your customer gets a product delivered to them that doesn't match the description on your website. You can expect them to not only never buy another thing from your site, but on eBay and places that allow your customer's to provide feedback, you will get negative feedback and scare other customers away. However, that doesn't mean that you can only sell new products that are in perfect mint condition online.

Far from it! It means that you need to be explicit about the condition of the items that you are selling and very upfront about them.

Another way to implement this is to offer a limited guarantee on the product. That way, if the person is completely unsatisfied, they can return it or get some form of compensation for their troubles. This is one way to dismiss many objections people might have about buying items that aren't new or in perfect condition.

Unfortunately, online, people don't always read every piece of copy you put up about your product. However, they do usually read the very first part of the copy before scrolling down. It seems strange, but that's where you will put the acknowledgement of the defect. If you bury it elsewhere in the copy and get an order and the customer becomes irritated, directing them to the online copy where your flaw is buried two-thirds of the way down the page is going to make them even madder.

On the other hand, if you say, "Yeah, this piece of art is BUTT-UGLY...", it's a great way to get attention and dismiss the worst defect you have on the product. Maybe the piece of art you are auctioning is butt-ugly, however, it's also one of a limited collection of prints made by a celebrated artists and worth hundreds of dollars! The customer scrolling through eBay or your site will initially be shocked to see that you actually admit that this product you are selling has an obvious flaw. They may even find it humorous. It will definitely get their attention, and that will lead them to read the rest of the copy which explains all the other benefits and how you can dismiss the defect as either part of the charm of the piece or as not consequential to its actual value.

Don't be afraid to get down the real nitty gritty details of why the product is flawed. Maybe it's ugly because it has too many loud colors. Maybe it's ugly because it has drab colors. Maybe it's ugly because it's abstract or too primitive. Whatever the problem is, be very clear that you understand that this is something that most people would consider an undesirable trait. Then, go on to dismiss it by building up the positive benefits of the product immediately afterwards. You are dismissing the flaw either by addressing the concern directly or you are going to show that despite this flaw the benefits of the product far outweigh the flaw mentioned.

This strategy is often used by real estate agents when they show houses with obvious flaws. They might point out the fact that the house is a little older than desired by their client, but the location is so good that the money they save in buying an older house can be used to update it and then they have both a good location and a newer home. They might show off the carpet with badly stained carpets and tell their buyers that since the carpets are so badly stained they can ask for a carpet allowance and put in whatever they want after they move it, making it their own.

The trick here is to do this as people are considering buying your product, not as an introduction, but as part of the description of the item. Obviously, this strategy is best left to the actual sales page than as a way to introduce a product to people on online forums or discussion groups. It's for people who already have a good idea that they want to buy in this category and that they may have some decisions to make on whether a flaw that is apparent is a deal-breaker or not.

Timing this strategy

The time to bring up a default is not after you've sold them on the benefits, but before. It should be brought up immediately before the person has time to discover it themselves, but not as an introduction to people who haven't had a chance to discover your site yet. It's like the difference between seeing a house on the market and wanting to visit it and being at the door of a house and opening the door to actually experience it.

If you are imagining the house from afar, if you start to talk about the flaws even before you've visited it, the value of the house plummets and you're less likely to visit the house. You haven't had a chance to experience it so that the better characteristics of the house can outweigh the flaw. So, don't mention these items unless they are already in an area where they have an option to buy and can have a full experience of the product you are offering it.

Then, it's more like you are there with the potential buyer and they are walking through the door as a real estate agent to show them your property that is for sale. If you are walking into a house as a real estate agent, you can say, "the appliances are old, but you can always ask for an appliance upgrade if you like the house."

You don't wait until the person walks into the kitchen, stares at the appliances and then says: "The appliances are outdated!" If you've been in this house before, you should know the negatives, and it should be said as you're opening the door to let them in, preferably before they've even had a chance to see the kitchen. If you bring it up early in the experience (but not before they're actually there with you visiting the products), and in all its gory detail, they imagine something far worse and when they get to the kitchen they might even mutter, "It's not that bad!" That's because you are so upfront with them, that they realize it's not a big deal.

Online, you don't want to put all kinds of objections on your home page, but you do want the sales page to have them if you know there is a problem with the product. If you are doing eBay to make sales and using them as a sales partner, you will want to make sure it is in bold and a title heading at the top of the page. You don't want people to miss it and then end up with something they object to AFTER they've already paid for the item. That will only get you irate customers and negative feedback. So, the best timing is always right up front.

Convert problems into opportunities

If you do spot a problem with your product, you can dismiss it (as in the earlier example), or you can convert it into an opportunity. This strategy is a little more creative than the last one, where you are just being blunt about your dirty laundry. In this one, you are being truthful about the problem, but you are reframing it from a negative to a positive. Once people start to see that you may have a point, that negative really is a positive, then you don't even have to dismiss the objection, it becomes another selling feature.

So, you do have to raise the objection first, and use the strategy's we have already discussed, but you want to resolve the objection on a positive note. If you can be really creative and sell that problem as a feature, it can be a way to disarm and even charm people reading the copy on your website.

The strategic plan

The strategy involves learning how your potential buyers perceive your product and any objections they might raise in their own minds. You don't have to be a mind reader to figure that out. You can simply ask them. You can set up surveys that offer a discount coupon on your products or offers a freebie to get a little market research on particular products. You have to know which objections might be converted into opportunities, and often they may not even be objections that you would think about first.

You can even add a few posts about a product on some group site or your own forums and see what people don't like about the product as well as what they do like. Some of these objections may be specific to your particular product, but others might be pretty generic. For instance, say you are selling tattoo art online. Well, you obviously aren't the only one selling tattoo art designs and you can visit specialty groups and forums and find out what people are talking about. Maybe they think unicorn tattoos are lame, or there is a particular discussion on whether it's such a good idea to have a permanent design on your body or not. Maybe you hear about the bad reactions people got years later from some tattoo they got when they were younger. So, now the objection is that a tattoo is permanent.

However, it also happens to be the opportunity because tattoos are permanent. They don't rub off, they are unique and can highlight your personality or mark a particular moment or event in your life, and you will always have that remembrance. So, even though some people might perceive the fact that a tattoo as permanent as a problem later in life, it's what also makes it so attractive too. All you need to do is educate the person visiting your site on why it is more of an opportunity than a potential problem. For this, you can even suggest that some tattoos now come with ink that can be removed with a laser later.

In the case of tattoos, we have a generic problem that crops up that makes an excellent opportunity. However, there may actually be problems that are specific to your product. In the case of the earlier example of a piece of art that is terribly ugly, would you be able to make it an opportunity? It is possible with a little creativity. Aren't ugly works of art controversial and conversation starters? Maybe it represents a particular time period of style of art that is only recognized by discriminating art buyers. In that case, the fact that it's ugly is the opportunity to express exactly why you were savvy enough to buy the piece anyway. It shows you are a person who understands art and the value of a piece of work.

The psychological triggers

Even though the major part of this strategy is to reframe a negative into a positive, you don't want to try to force something that will never be. You don't want to try to convince the potential buyer of something that is ludicrous or a stretch to believe because people are pretty smart about that sort of thing. So, you are reframing the objection into a positive, but in a way that is believable.

In another way, if you happen to reframe something that would normally appear negative into a positive in a bright and refreshing way, people will be surprised at first. That surprise lowers their resistance to believing the new way the problem has turned into an opportunity. Again, by raising the objection first, you have gotten the upper hand. You have set the stage to be the authority on this particular problem and you have guided the potential buyer to a solution that not only resolves the problem, but presents them with a great opportunity too.

At first, it will stir up feelings of shock that you dared to bring up the problem first, then it will lend you credibility and provide your voice with more authority on the subject. Finally, it will reduce their defenses and make it easy for them to go along with your final assessment of the problem as an opportunity. They will be grateful you actually pointed out something to them they just might have missed.

How to implement effectively

Okay, so you've done some market research and gotten a list of possible objections for your particular product or market. For each product, take out a sheet of paper and create two columns by running a line down the middle of an 8 1/2 X 11 sheet of paper. On the first side list all of the objections that you discovered or thought up, and then start to go through them one by one. You don't want to pick every objection and try to make it an opportunity. What that will do is make people think that there are far too many problems with the product and you're just messing with their minds. If you pick an objection that is not very serious to highlight, because it's easily converted into a positive, it will make you appear condescending instead of helpful.

If you pick something that isn't really an objection, you just think it might be able to be perceived as one, you are going to be raising an objection in your potential customer's mind that might never have surfaced. This will make them stop and think about what other red flags they've missed. So, you don't want to pick a weak objection or one that is non-existent. What you want to do is locate serious objections that people might have to your product and then creatively turn them into a positive. So, be careful which objections you consider to highlight as it can make or break this strategy.

Once you know which objections might qualify for this strategy, the fun starts. You have to be very creative and think up a resolution for each strategy that makes that problem an opportunity. There are some objections that are universal, not specific to your market or to your product. These are things like the price is too high, it takes too long to get it, it's not convenient, or the competition has better or different features.

Don't forget that you can target these objections as well and maybe you want to start with them for every product, just to get the hang of this. Then, you think up a reason for why that objection is really an opportunity. A classic example of this is when you have a product that is really expensive when compared to the competition. You can say it is a good value for the money because it offers more features than the competition too. So, while you pay more than the others, you get more and in the end it is worth more too.

This may be a little more "canned" in online presentation than in a regular face-to-face presentation. If you are meeting a sales prospect in person, you can often hear the objections live and/or anticipate them better from the comments they make. Online, you can't really interact that much with your visitor, so you have to take the strategy of doing your research and then picking just one of the biggest flaws and using that as a lead in for your sales page.

If you have multiple objections you want to resolve, then you can use a table that compares features between your product and other leading brands. Tables are very easy on the eyes of people reading online materials. So, they can see, that price-wise you are more expensive, but then the rest of the features are checked for you and your competitors columns are empty. This gives a very big visual impact and is a way of raising objections and resolving them without having to explain it out in a paragraph. The table is a visual tool that does it for you.

Always, always, always be upfront about any flaw or objection that is going to be a major concern for your customer. If you fail to address it, the potential buyers might bring it up or they might not, but they will surely be thinking about it. If you don't bring it up, it will never be resolved in their minds. An unresolved objection is going to dampen your sales. So, despite the fact that it may seem strange to be bringing up your product's bad points, it's far worse to not acknowledge them at all.

So, what happens if you are in the middle of a sales presentation and the product breaks or it doesn't perform the way you would expect it to? Acknowledge it right away and let people know the reason for that particular problem. Maybe you can bring up the fact that even if the product does not perform the way advertised, there is a guarantee they can use to get a replacement or something similar.

Sometimes people don't want to buy things online because they don't know what they're going to get when it arrives. This is particularly true of diamonds. The biggest objection a person buying a diamond online is how could they be sure the diamond they received was worth the thousands of dollars spent on it? So, many online diamond retailers raise that objection as a valid objection and showcase the fact that their diamonds are appraised by a particular agency. Or, they might discuss how the value is established and how safe the delivery is and any money back guarantees too. Now, the fact that you're buying a diamond online and may not be able to visually see it before it arrives and don't know how to determine worth is an opportunity to have a valid certification of your diamond for free through the website's policies.

Timing this strategy

The timing of this strategy is similar to the last strategy. Always bring up the objection first, before your customer has a chance to do it for you. You can shock them with the declaration of a particular problem. You can even not make it a statement, but a question. Like, "Are you afraid that you don't know if the diamond you buy online is worth what you paid for it?" That lead in will automatically bring people in because it acknowledges a fear that may lurk in the mind of the prospect but that has not be verbalized. Once you verbalize it, many people can relate to that fear and it draws their attention as being relevant to their personal experience.

You come off looking as someone who is sympathetic and understanding for even bringing it up.

Then, when you provide the resolution, "Our diamonds are certified by third-party appraisals that are board-certified to be..." you not only have given them the prospective buyer the solution right away, but also relieved the fear and anxiety experienced with that particular problem. That sense of immediate anxiety and relief can end up leading to an instant sale.

You can do this very well in a targeted email campaign for those people who have subscribed to your email list. Don't spam people with advertisements, but if you are trying out a new product that most people have a problem buying online for some reason, you can use that niche to help you use this strategy by turning that objection into an opportunity. When presented correctly, it can be a way to engage the reader and draw them into your copy far enough for them to find the solution to their problem and associate your product with a new opportunity for themselves.

Engage participation and pride of ownership

People who get involved tend to be more committed to a particular path than those who are just visiting. This is true whether you are doing retail sales or online sales. However, in a face-to-face presentation people are naturally involved because a social interaction is taking place and they usually give you their full attention. Online, people may be surfing the web and be multitasking on their PCs. You don't know if you have their attention or not since you're not directly there to give them eye contact. So, how do you get them involved in your site if you can't reach out through their terminal and put the product in their hands?

Well, the solution is a lot easier than you think since social networking sites are now more predominant. Blogs, discussion groups, forums, and even surveys and games can be a way to engage the person to stop a moment and interact with your site. Once you've engaged their participation, they will start to identify with your site more. Now, if you get them to become a regular visitor who comments on your blog or has tried out some of your products, they start to feel like this is their home. They start to take pride in being part of your site and it can give them feelings like pride of ownership.

The strategic plan

Direct sales like mail marketing use something called an "involvement device" to get people involved over a long distance. That is something that they can touch and feel and that asks for some participation on their part. The one involvement device that comes to mind is some of the advertisements that ask you to peel a sticker from a particular part of the advertisement and place it somewhere else to signal your acceptance of the offer.

It seems very simplistic that having someone place a sticker or add a business card or drop something into a slot could ever increase sales, but it does. Once a person becomes involved in the sales process, they are more apt to pay attention and buy. Any device that engages the reader brings them into the buying process and reduces their resistance to the offer.

You don't just want to use any involvement device, you typically want to use something that ties into what you are selling. That's why Facebook applications are so popular because they are a great involvement devise that typically tie into the product or company and provide a way for people to associate their participation with some company or product.

Then, if there is a link available back to the website, you are already primed to consider this a part of your virtual heritage.

Another type of involvement device is like the advertisements that ask you to draw a picture to see if you qualify for drawing lessons. You find that you get so involved in getting the picture done right, that you can hardly wait to mail it off and receive an offer for classes in the mail. Not only did those advertisers correctly identify people who might have an interest in buying art classes, but they also got them so involved they probably waited by the mailbox to see if they were accepted for this offer. That's very clever marketing!

The key there is that involvement device used was directly related to the product or services being sold. You can still use an involvement device that merely gets a person to participate, and online that would be like getting a comment on a blog. A person has taken some action that has gotten them involved in your community. But, did it make a sale? Not really, it might later, but not right away. So, the best involvement devices are those that are tied directly to the product or service you are trying to market.

The psychological triggers

Have you ever seen a baby find a new toy and become completely fascinated by it? It captures their attention and all their old toys get ignored while they explore this new object. They may put it in their mouths, stare at it intently, shake it, or even smash it on the floor. They get highly involved in just touching it and trying to get as much experience as they can out of it. Well, adults still have that fascination with new toys. And, that's part of the psychology of offering them something new that brings up that childish wonder of exploration.

The other thing is that people love to be challenged and to beat something and identify themselves as a winner. Some of the puzzles, games, and involvement devices can include different levels that differentiate your ability from other people and give you a sense of pride that you made it to a certain level.

Another way to involve people is to make it fun. Who doesn't want to include a little entertainment in their day? In fact, entertainment is one of the most sought after things in our Western culture. If you happen to provide a fun involvement device that also happens to lead them to your product, all the better right? They get to have some fun and you end up with a sale, so in a sense, it's a win-win.

Also, people tend to distrust a product that they can't see, touch, or feel. So in direct retail sales, the involvement device is typically the ability to try on a dress before buying, kick the tires of a new car or test drive it, or even get a free make-over at a make-up department store booth. They want the experience of possessing the item before they actually purchase it.

These types of retail actions are simple ways to involve a person by just allowing them to touch and experience the product first-hand. This becomes a little harder in the virtual world of online sales because your product is not there to have and hold, but you can still produce some very good involvement devices and even virtual "visualize and experience" ads that can lead to bigger sales.

How to implement effectively

Since we are basically concerned with turning traffic from your website into customers, we want to really understand how to create an involvement device online. It's really not that hard, once you understand the concept. What you want to do is put yourself in the customer's shoes and see how you can get them engaged in at least visualizing themselves using your product or service.

In the first strategy, you can simply provide a novel and fun gimmick to your site to get them involved. If you are a dating site, for instance, you might want to add a compatibility test or personality test to your website. Once they complete that, you can sell the service by saying, "Find compatible people who match your personality on our site!" It not only gets them involved right away, but it appeals to ego identity, a large reason people join community sites.

Social networking is great for forming groups of people who can interact with each other. In a sense, the people on your site become the involvement device that attracts more people. If you are trying to sell memberships, you want to highlight who is already on your site and why it is worth it for you to join so you can network with them too.

If you really think about it, your entire website can be an involvement device. It has buttons people can push, drop-down menus they can fiddle with, and maybe videos they can watch. So, you can do the same thing when you are selling a particular product. Just be careful that you don't get too fancy. Some people try to involve their visitors by adding incredible technologies that look great on newer PCs, but can't be opened on older models! You don't want to lose a customer because the involvement device is too complicated or it crashes their system! You want something simple and you want it to appeal to the psychology more than the technology.

When you are marketing people offline, you can also provide involvement devices that lead back to your products online. There are now business cards that are mini CD-Roms that can be loaded into a computer and lead people straight to your website. Just the fascination of seeing something so small, so cute, and so novel, will get people to put it in their machine to see what it does. Once they are on your site, you can involve them further with other involvement devices.

But, what if you're selling engagement rings online? How could you possibly create an involvement device for that? Won't someone want to try the ring on first before buying? Here is where you see the magic of the Internet really shine. You can hire a programmer to build a database of your inventory and an applet that allows them to build a ring online in the virtual world. Thus, they not only get the fun of creating something online, but they get to try out the ring too, in their imagination. It's the closest thing to actually being in a retail store where they can hold the ring in their hands. It may take a bit more programming and sophistication, but if your market demands a virtual try-out there are ways to do this, as many online diamond marketers have proven.

Your call to action can also include an involvement device or a fun game by allowing them some discount for performing a specific function on your site and thus getting access to a coupon code. Once they have that coupon code, wouldn't they want to use it to get the discount? So, you lead the potential buyer from their fun game straight back to your product or service.

Finally, even emails or sales copy can get the reader involved, if you happen to use the person's name in them and help them to imagine what it's like to experience your product. If you have a product that you can personalize, that also will give a person a feeling of pride of ownership before they've gotten the product in their hands. As can be seen, there are a great many ways to use this strategy online to help promote participation and involvement with your website and products.

Timing this strategy

This strategy works best at the very beginning of your sales funnel, or even before. You should have at least a few involvement devices on your website to help you create membership, if you are a social networking site. Otherwise, people lose interest in just writing posts and move on. If you have a fun game, or add a video from YouTube, when they first land on your page your website appears more interactive and alive.

Have you ever seen the sign on the side of the road as your waiting in a traffic jam that says: "You could live here."? That is a simple device that helps you imagine how much time you could save living there, how much nicer your life would be, and how you could own a condo there if you just took the initiative to walk in the door. That's a very powerful involvement device and it wasn't even in a sales brochure. You might not have even been thinking of buying a condo up until then. So, that explains that the timing on this strategy is sometimes even before the person has realized that your company even exists or what your products are.

You can wait for them to somehow stumble upon your site, but why not go out to places where people in your target demographic are and just put a link to your fun, experiential, involvement device there. You don't have to sell the product, you don't have to tell them at the end, they'll be solicited to buy a product. Once they choose to try this out, they will be hooked and you will have created a sales opportunity where none existed.

Once you have the person involved in the product, you can continue to keep them involved by upgrading the experience.

This will create a habit, reducing their resistance to future purchases too. So, if you are using a game, make sure you have various levels. Keep the strategy going continuously and vary it every now and then to keep people involved and buying.

Be authentic to engender trust

In the past, marketers tried to glamorize their products or services in a way that was clearly inauthentic. The type of hype seems to have really jaded a lot of consumers who are pretty savvy these days. They are more likely to turn a deaf ear to outrageous claims or over-the-top commercial images than to pay attention. They do not engender trust. The newer way to generate trust is not to try and pull the wool over anyone's eyes, but rather to be authentic with our product and who you are.

In the age of social networking, more and more people are beginning to learn the value to their social reputation. A reputation that is misrepresented is one that is not trustworthy. If a person is not trustworthy, they do not have enough credibility to sell anyone in such a transparent environment. What will happen is that others in the social network will appear to warn people about the lack of authenticity and their social reputation will plummet along with their sales.

Now, you can be authentic without necessarily being a squeaky, clean, moralist. Authenticity basically means that you have enough integrity to express things exactly as they are. If you are a person who sells diet advice but can't be bothered to control your own diet, that lack of integrity is going to come back to bite you in a social networking situation. However, if you are authentic and say that you could never stay on any diet and didn't see the reason for them, and then you found this diet and it helped you lose 50 pounds, then you are being authentic. Thus, it becomes more and more important to believe in the products and services you are selling, to be able to report on them authentically and engender trust.

The strategic plan

Consistency is the buy word here. If you are consistent in your words and actions, then you become more authentic and can be trusted more. We've all had the experience of seeing someone say one thing and do another. What impression does that leave? You immediately realize that the person is a hypocrite or a con, at worst, or doesn't know what they're talking about, at best. So, to avoid giving off that impression, always make sure that your actions match your words. This goes for the way you describe you, your product, and to how well you keep your promises to the people buying from your site.

One way to establish authenticity is to either bank on your own reputation or someone else's well-known reputation.

You build a reputation through social networking that carefully represents the image you want for your company or product. Or, if you don't want to go through all that trouble, you find ways to associate with people who have already done that, have a high degree of credibility, and then get them to endorse your product or services.

Be clear about whether all your copy, all your products, and your public image are in line with the way you want people to perceive you. If you genuinely believe in what you are selling, that will come through and people will catch your enthusiasm simply from the power of your own self-trust. However, the same is true if you are careful with the copy or the image you are portraying. If you sell diet products and you are 50 pounds overweight, people will notice it, even if not consciously. You don't want to put your image on that website if you are seriously overweight because it shows you aren't being authentic about helping people lose weight.

So, much of this strategy is about being aware. Be aware what image you are projecting. Be aware what topics or writing is subconsciously influencing your potential buyer. Be sure that anything you associate with, whether it be a celebrity or an affiliate be in line with that image you want for you and your products. Secondly, always, deliver more than what you promise and your authenticity and integrity score will shoot through the roof.

The psychological triggers

If you are engaging in online marketing and you are trying to sell products or services without even knowing a potential prospect, the need for authenticity increases. It has taken quite a bit of time for people to begin to trust e-commerce, and many of the reasons for that is because of the potential for being conned online. Visitors will be trying to gage your authenticity from every piece of email, copy, blog, or image they view. They want to know that you are trustworthy enough to deliver what you say you deliver. After all, no one wants to send money and either get nothing, or a very bad product in return. Since, they can't even touch the product they are requesting, it becomes more important they trust the vendor enough to deliver what they promise.

When you go retail shopping, you can look into someone's eyes and get a good feel for whether someone is trying to con you or not. The cues for that behavior may be subtle, but people have a sixth sense about these things. They want that firm handshake, that eye-to-eye contact, that honesty, and that ability to resolve their issues for them. In addition, they like to be able to view a product before they actually buy it. They might want to touch it or try it out first too. Well, when all of that is denied, they have to rely on someone else's word for whether they are engaging in a good transaction or whether they are just throwing money away. In order to relieve that anxiety, you implement the strategy to increase your level of authenticity to promote a sense of mutual trust. But how are you going to do that online when they can't even see your face, much less touch the product?

How to implement effectively

The key is in the subtle cues that are given off by all your interactions with a potential buyer. Make sure that every one of your interactions reflects exactly the image you want for your company, your products, or your services. Things to look for in your copy or interactions that could set off doubts in your buyers mind are things like over-exaggerating your product's benefits or speaking out of context from the image you want to portray. The best way to avoid some of these subtle patterns of speech that can trigger doubts about your authenticity is to pay attention or to avoid marketing anything you don't believe in 100%.

Let's face it, if you are selling acne products and you've either never tried it (because you never experienced a bad outbreak) or you tried it and it failed to work for you, when you go to sell that product, the lack of enthusiasm and belief will shine through the choice of words, the images you use, and any other interaction. It's a part of you and despite the fact that you may try to convince yourself that this is really a product that is worth marketing, because acne products sell well on the Internet, you will find that if you don't believe in it, your words and interactions will take on a subtle tone of over-exaggeration or bland endorsements. Worse, when someone contacts you directly to ask you what your experience was with the product, you may even have to outright lie to save face.

This isn't to suggest that you shouldn't sell that particular acne product, the problem is the way you implement the strategy. If you are endorsing it personally, you are going to want to have some good experiences with the product to remain authentic while selling it. If you are simply choosing acne products as your main market, then you can include it with other acne products that you know do work and simply rate it lower than the others or leave it unrated. That way you maintain a degree of authenticity while being able to promote more products. And, you may find a way to engage your visitors by asking them to rate the products themselves for others. Then, you not only get authenticity from unpaid for reviews, but you didn't have to put up your own reputation in the process.

Forms of this strategy are the celebrity sponsor who tells everyone that they've used your products and like them. Just be sure it is a celebrity that reflects your values and the product's proper image. If your celebrity just got convicted of dog fighting racketeering charges, you would not want them endorsing your pet products.

Social networking also takes this strategy to new heights. If you have a discussion group or forum, and you have a new product, you can offer the product out to the first 10 people who ask for it, in exchange for a review of it on site. Since many discussion groups, social networking sites, and forums have a large audience, you end up picking up a great deal of authenticity by using random people who will give their honest opinion on your products. Just be sure they are good products and good reviews.

Timing this strategy

The timing for this is right in the middle of your sales presentation. Once your sales prospect is engaged and they are a loyal visitor to your site or a subscriber to your blog, endeavor to be consistent and trustworthy in all your interactions. This will help to keep people coming back again and again.

Another time to use this is when you are putting out brand new products. There, you have to attract new sales and banking on your reputation is one way to help spur the belief that this new product is just as good, if not better than your other products. Engage others to review your product too and this will help to spur sales. Capitalize on the authentic image you've already created with your past customers. That's the time to market people who already trust you by making sure they are updated on all the new products that you are selling. This can lead to many repeat sales.

Finally, the best way to establish authenticity is to deliver what you promise, when you promise it. Some people try to do this even better by always delivering more than they promise and earlier than expected. That gives them a little leeway should the post office screw up the timing or something else happens. So, if you want to be perceived as being truly authentic strive to take control of all aspects of your business from delivery to customer support. Failure in any of these areas will reduce your authenticity because it reflects badly on the consistency of the promises you make and what is finally delivered.

If you want to see if your authenticity is being questions, simply send out customer satisfaction surveys on a regular basis or after an online transaction. These are pretty easy to implement on your site and can help you find areas that are not meeting the high standards of consistency that you want to maintain.

You can have these collated monthly for review and/or endeavor to contact people who put in negative feedback immediately, without delay. This helps to reduce the impact of any failure in your consistency and can even increase your authenticity if you manage to resolve a problem that has plagued a customer who didn't know what to do or who to contact to resolve the issue. It also shows you care about your customers.

Enchant with stories

If you've ever heard the story of 1,001 Arabian Nights you know the power of stories to enchant the listener. That's because people are hard-wired to myth for ancient times. They want to hear things spoken in story form and their subconscious has a way of remembering what they hear in story form better than visual cues. If you use stories in your marketing, you will not only capture people's attention, but you will also help them to remember you long after they've left your website.

The other aspect of stories that enchants people is the capacity to create empathy and communion with the story teller. How many of us remember asking our parents to read a bed time story? Wasn't it a special time of bonding for us? The same can be true of stories that you tell when you are trying to establish a rapport with people coming to your website.

The strategic plan

The strategy is to try to capture a person's attention by initiating a story that fascinates them into a longer relationship with you. Obviously, they will not leave until they've heard the punch line or found out how the story ended. The story should have some human elements in it, so that your reader can relate to it on a personal level. If it is just a story of a product, without some human element, it will sound like hype. So, be careful to include your product or service in the story, but don't make it a story solely about that product.

The story should try to stir the reader's curiosity from the get go. It is this sense of "what's going to happen" that will lead the reader, deeper and deeper into your story. It can be a story about some people's experience with your product. It can be a story about the development or discovery of your product. It can even be a humorous story about your product. It really doesn't matter, as long as you are engaging the reader in a deeper relationship and connection with your product or service.

The way you know if the strategy is working is if you can get the reader to read the entire story to the very end, where the sales pitch is. Once they have become so involved in the story line, they will empathize with the actors in the story, identify with the product and their own predicaments, and be very likely to consider buying the product right then and there. That's the power of a good story. It breaks down the resistance to buying, much like a set of benefits does too.

But, in this case, it works more subconsciously than consciously, which makes it a far more powerful strategy in the long run. They may leave your website and three hours later still remember that story and thus, they will also remember your product better. The deeper the impact of a story, the more likely the reader will remember your products when they have a need or are looking for a solution like your story relates.

The psychological triggers

Story telling involves telling jokes as well as long, drawn-out stories with a beginning, middle, and end. They work to lessen the awkwardness of a social encounter, especially between people who have never met before. If you can get a person to laugh at your joke or identify with your story, you become more familiar to them and less of a stranger. The impact of a story is only as good as how well it causes the reader to bond with the storyteller and be drawn into the final conclusion of the story.

Jokes are very easy to reel off at the beginning of a sales encounter, but they are much more difficult to enact well. It takes a certain flare to be able to tell a joke well so that it comes out humorous and not lame. However, jokes are brilliant ways to tell a tiny story in a very small amount of time and have people bond with you through the mechanism of humor and laughter. It builds a warm camaraderie and can help you establish mutual trust from the onset.

However, if you're not good at telling jokes, telling a personal account or story can be another great way to bond with your website visitors. It brings the human element to the forefront of your website and humanizes the technological aspect of being online. It appeals to the subconscious triggers within a person and can be a subtle way to manipulate the unconscious desires or fears they may be experiencing to help them make the decision to buy.

How to implement effectively

Online stories can involve all sorts of media from written copy, to cartoons, or video blogs. If you have a good short story that can be made into a video, you can add that to YouTube to try to make it go viral. It can be a story that relates your product as the solution to an embarrassing event with the title, "Don't let this happen to you!" At the end, you put a link to your website to draw that traffic to your sales page. That's the way to use a video and the power of the Internet to create a sales page story line. It can be very powerful if plenty of people relate to it or find it humorous, as it can be spread across the Internet very quickly if it has mass appeal.

Another way to use a story is through written copy on your website. Maybe the story has a lesson to teach about why your product is the solution to a particular dilemma. Maybe you want to relate a humorous story about your product that is entertaining for the reader. Maybe you want to give the reader the opportunity to experience an "ah-ha" moment that some other customer had when they used your product or service. It really doesn't matter what you write, as long as it stirs the readers curiosity, draws the reader in, and creates a lasting impression. Then, by the time you make your sales pitch at the end, the story has been embedded in their sub consciousness and will have triggered various impulses to buy.

Cartoons or images are like mini-stories that can convey a quick synopsis or be a good lead in for a story. If the image captures a visitor's attention enough, they will probably scroll down and read the story behind it. So, don't think that this is all about copy. Use everything you can to draw a visitor into the copy that eventually has your sales pitch at the end and a call to action to buy your product.

There is one other way to implement this strategy that does not involve actually selling the product. Instead, it could be a story that creates the right environment for your product or educates the reader for why your products are necessary or expedient. This is particularly effective for items that may be so novel that people don't know why they would buy them. There is no conditioning in place or market buzz that has been associated with the item and so they're left not understanding the value of the product at all.

That's when you need a story about your particular industry and how these products were developed to fulfill a particular need. You want to be clear that people understand the results they will get in their lives by paying attention to this particular issue and this sets the environment for making a sales call at the end.

For example, when organic products first came out, only people who were into health foods understood the reasons for buying higher-priced produce or hormone-free meats. It just didn't have a mass appeal and the consumer wasn't really aware that there really was any difference between meat at the local supermarket and meat that was brought up hormone-free and cost much more. Why would you pay that much more for something that you don't understand or value?

So, it took a while for people to realize that our air and water systems are polluted and that farms use all kinds of chemicals as fertilizers on produce that end up in the vegetables and fruits. So, if you happened to be selling some organic product online, you might have a story on the environmental stresses that cause your products to be necessary for a healthy diet. Once you declare the proper environment and frame the value of your product or service, it becomes much more intriguing and interesting to your potential buyer. So, what might not have been something they saw any value in, becomes very important to try so that they too can see the results in their life.

So, while a story is typically something that can relate the potential buyer to a common experience that will help them bond, there are other times when you have to set the stage first before they get why it is a common experience. It may be they have never ever tried anything organic in their lives, so you had to introduce that concept to them from some other area that is familiar to them – our polluted environment.

Timing this strategy

Telling a story that is brief can be done at the very beginning of a sales encounter. It can be done on the home page, in your about me pages, or when you are introducing a new product. Once you've established a nice bond, you can even get into longer stories on the sales page to establish the benefits of your product, especially if it is something new that needs to have the stage set for it to make a dramatic appearance.

You can even use a "joke of the day" type of device to help engage your readers and have it introduce your industry, if not your product. Sort of like the jokes that all relate to screwing in a light bulb. If you happened to be selling light bulbs, this would make an excellent way to establish rapport and humor on your site and eventually sell light bulbs.

Some people like stories so much that they will email them to other people. You can have an "email this story to your friend" feature that is a great way to have people visiting your market for you. In the same way, a YouTube video that goes viral will work marketing magic for you and you don't have to go and post it to too many places. Other people will start doing it for you.

Most stories will do nothing more than introduce the product or establish rapport. Those are the ones you use on other sites and throughout the Internet to establish a presence online. Reserve the longer, deeper, stories for your website where people can become involved in an area that has calls to action to buy your products.

Flaunt your expertise

People love to deal with experts. Experts can be trusted. Experts are "in the know." And, when we deal with experts we feel smart for being able to spot them. So, when you want people to automatically give you more credibility and authority to encourage them to do business with you more, flaunt your expertise.

That's right, no one else is going to do it for you and this is something that is not only all right, on the Internet, but it is easily done. It's called self-promotion and the Internet makes it a very easy thing to do online. If you want people to recognize you for your expertise, you will want to concentrate on your area of expertise and then show off what you know. It's that simple.

The strategic plan

There is a fine line between coming off as an expert and being a pretentious imposter or know-it-all. If you really don't know what you're talking about, that is going to come across sooner or later. So, you do want to know your market niche extremely well. You should do enough research so that you can even anticipate your customers concerns and have solutions ready for them when they come up. You will want to be the person who not only knows your market, but the desires of your customers too. Then, you will want to visit places that can allow you to show off that knowledge without seeming pretentious or an attention hog. Least of all, you don't want to visit just to spam a group with your expertise when it's not even related to the discussion. You should pick the venues that you will be using to show off your expertise very carefully. They should include forums, discussion groups, blogs, your website, and sales page that allow you to add information that gathers attention and solves a problem without it appearing to be a direct solicitation.

This means that you will need to spend some time creating your online image as the expert in residence. You will have to write articles, author eBooks, write in other people's blogs, do guest posts, frequent discussion groups, enter topics into forums, and more. It's not easy being an expert, but its well worth it.

Some people build their image as an expert by collecting titles or degrees. That's perfectly legitimate. If you have a PhD, flaunt it. Put the initials after you name in all your email correspondence and on your website too. There's nothing wrong with having extra initials after your name and you'd be surprised the air of credibility and authority that this gives you.

Use any advantage you have to express your authority on a subject. If you are selling clothing, for instance, you don't want images on your website that show people dressed in frumpy attire. If you are trying to sell office supplies, you don't want people on the site photographed in shorts and sandals. This type of subtle visual statement leads people to question your expertise, not because you yourself are portrayed less professionally, but because you don't associate with people who have authority. People with power generally congregate with other people with power.

If you show up with less than ideal business partners or affiliates, your expertise and authority are questioned, not to mention your judgment.

The psychological triggers

Since we were children, we have been taught to respect authority. We idolized our parents for knowing more than we did and we trusted them to guide us to make the right decisions in life. Later, in school, we are put into an educational system that grades us based on our knowledge of the course material with the teachers being the ultimate symbol of someone with the most expertise in a subject. They were the ones we were supposed to respect and listen to. After we started work, the same rules apply.

Those people who know the system or the game of politics, the experts in the company who deal with the other experts, are the ones that demand our respect and obedience. Through them, we gain our promotions and get the good things in life.

This habit of obedience to authority and recognition of experts as the final say in life never really goes away. It's been impressed upon us since early childhood and, in many cases, a trusted expert becomes the reflection of a trusted parent. We are more inclined to listen to these experts, even feeling a sense of gratitude that there is someone to listen to who can guide us in the proper choices to make. It makes our lives easier and it becomes a subconscious desire to follow authority just as we've been programmed to do. It is so ingrained that some people never question an expert, even if it appears they may not be all that trustworthy. They are so accustomed to having someone to tell them what to do that they actually can feel very reassured just by having someone willing to take up the mantle of authority for them.

Since marketers know that showing your expertise is a great way to make a sale, there is plenty of competition from people trying to sell themselves as experts. It's up to you to differentiate your own knowledge, image, and authority from everyone else so that people are more likely to come to you than the next guy.

How to implement effectively

To become an expert on the web is easy. All you have to do is make sure people know your qualifications and be careful to always project the image of an expert everywhere you go. Unlike a job interview that requires someone who you worked with to offer a reference, you can be your own reference on the web. For that, you want to take the time to develop this strategy everywhere, not just for yourself, but your company image too.

As we mentioned earlier, you will want to mine your personal experience and express that whenever appropriate.

If you have a Master's or a PhD be sure to use those initials after your name when you email, when you add a post to a discussion group or forum, or even when you comment on a blog. It's a very simple matter and it adds loads of authority to your current image. When people see those initials, they will be triggered to defer to you automatically. So, be sure to put ALL initials that represent some degree of expertise next to your name.

If you are doing this for your website or business image, you want to capture your expertise in a single phrase that represent why people should do business with you. This can be like "voted best value for the money by Consumer Magazine." Of course, only add that if it's true!

You don't want to be caught echoing some claim that later points out that you clearly don't have any expertise and are a liar to boot! So, be genuine, but also be sure to take pride in your accomplishments. If you don't have any recognition from others that you can point to, you can still raise the audience's awareness of what makes your business special. Maybe you are the biggest distributor on the East Coast for your particular item. Maybe you make the most unique ukuleles in Hawaii. Maybe you are the oldest company on record for the business.

Believe it or not, people hold a great deal of respect for businesses that can say they've been around for decades. Imagine if you could say that about your online business where most have a habit of disappearing overnight? It creates the image of tremendous stability and also expertise in your area of commerce.

If you still can't think of anything, start by telling your audience why you think your business or staff is special. Maybe you think you have the best group of positive thinkers on staff who find ways to make everyone's day brighter.

Maybe you sell environmentally-friendly profits and for each sale you donate to a green cause. This can make people think that you know about the issues important to them and they can trust you as an expert because you walk your talk.

So ask yourself a few questions to help you establish what makes you or your business experts on your market niche:

- What credentials do I have to prove our expertise?
- Are my workers specially trained or gifted?
- How many years have you been in business?
- What is your satisfaction rating for customers?
- What separates your knowledge from your competitors?
- What image should you be portraying to be considered an expert?
- Am I or my company certified by any outside agencies?

- Who else thinks you or your business is expert in your market niche?
- What do I know that no one else knows?

Once you have the answer to those questions, you can write up articles and feed them to article directories. At the end, in your author's bio box, you can add information on who you are and your status as an expert. Either submit the articles to directories yourself or hire a company to do it for you. These article directories will show up in search engines when someone searches for your company name or your own name. If you have multiple different articles out there under different directories, the search results on a search engine will bring up so many results that you look like an instant expert!

That's one way to get your name out there as an expert fairly quickly. Another way is to visit forums and discussion groups that are within your target niche. Add to the discussions, when you can show off your knowledge and increase your exposure online. If you keep coming back and doing this, at least that audience will begin to equate your name or your company's name as experts in a particular field. And, that also will show up in search results from a search engine.

Writing a book and putting it up on Amazon or some other large distributor will also qualify you as an expert. It used to be that you had to find a publisher to publish your book to really be perceived a formally approved expert. That's not the case anymore. Anyone can self-publish a book and then submit it to online retailers for sale. You can even do an eBook format and offer it for free in various places and build your reputation that way too. Just make sure your books contain reference to your website, your products, and your own credentials.

Finally, you can ask to do guest posts to other people's websites or solicit testimonials for your own website and products. Guest posts on big blogs are particularly effective because it builds traffic as well as allows you to target your particular niche and convert it to sales. And, major bloggers are always looking for guest posters from noted experts so that they can take a break every now and then from posting.

If you are on Facebook, the number and quality of friends and social network that you build can add to your reputation as an expert. If you have a network of 300 people who all are big names in your industry, which automatically qualifies you as a big name too. Its authority and expertise solely by association.

Timing this strategy

The time to self-promote is ALWAYS. It can't be said enough. You might get tired of constantly re-iterating the same catch phrases that note your expertise, but you don't know what new prospects are coming in that will need that reassurance. You want to do it when you are at other people's sites, when you are not selling but rather building a marketing presence online, and when you are selling too.

Almost every interaction you have should echo your expertise so as to trigger that deep-seated desire to obey the call to action later. You don't want to come off as demanding, but simply showing you know your stuff and that they can have a quiet confidence in your history, knowledge, or products can be a great way to trigger the desire to buy.

Prove the product's true worth

In online marketing, you want to get rid of any fears the buyer may have over purchasing your products or services.

People have a big fear of being taken advantage of or buying something that later makes them feel like a fool for being duped into the purchase. There are other people who are always looking for a good deal and demand that they get a high return on their financial investment, no matter what they're buying.

Since you are dealing with consumers who are Internet savvy, you know that they will be able to compare your products or service easily simply by browsing other companies online or doing a quick search through Google. So, you will have to beat them to that and provide whatever comparisons they need to prove your product's true worth. It's far better for you to do it, and limit and frame the results of your research to make your product appear favorably. Than it is for them to do it and figure out that there is at least one product out there that is a better deal for them or has some feature they like better.

This is particularly important if your product has no brand name. Maybe you are selling your own line of products and competing against much better known brands. If you cannot prove your product's true worth in a relatively short amount of time, there's no reason for a sales prospect to even consider buying your product. The fear of being taken will override the possibility of getting a good deal. So, again, you have to make sure they know they are getting just as good a value as the name brands you are competing against, or maybe even a better value.

The strategic plan

When you are targeting value as your main selling point, you want to be able to educate your potential buyer not just about your products, but about the overall market offerings too. So, that means, you have to do a little more research than just being aware of your own value, as compared to other products in your own inventory. Instead, you want to be aware of the product's value when compared to the rest of the market that the sales prospect will eventually want to view.

There are two factors involved here: quality versus price. Price is often not the determining factor for buying a product, unless that product is being compared to the same product somewhere else for a lower price. So, if you have a top selling product available in your inventory, price will determine how good a value someone perceives it to be. Now, however, if you are working with a range of products, and not a specific brand, then you want to concentrate on quality, more than price. The more features, the higher the quality, than the competition and the product becomes a better value, regardless of the price. This may seem odd, but that's because the actual intrinsic value of the product is more, when compared to the rest of the other products on the market.

The psychological triggers

When people see you comparing your own products and are educated about the product's intrinsic value, they equate a better value with a lower price, even if your price is actually much higher than your competition. In other words, it's like a unit price at the grocery store. When people go to compare two different cans of peaches at the store, they look at all the canned peaches and decided which they want to buy. If they are focused solely on price, they will look for the generic brands and not even bother looking at the different types of peach syrups or even the weight by can. Instead, they will gravitate to cheaper brands because that's what they're looking for to start: a deal on the price. Value is not a consideration until after that when they will look at the unit price for that brand to determine which can actually is the better deal by weight. That's when price is a consideration for value only.

However, most people don't buy items this way. They want to go and shop and come home with something they are proud of and feel they got a great deal on too. For that, they would be the buyer that goes to the grocery store and looks at all the canned peaches. They look at the labels and they admire the different ways the peaches are sliced or diced. They look at the types of syrups, light or heavy. They look to see if any are special peaches for some reason.

So, what they are comparing is the value based on the characteristics and features of each brand. Then, when they find a couple of brands they like, they start to look at unit prices. In their mind, the fact that the value is so much higher in one brand than another automatically reduces the expense of them, and that's the first priority. After that price may be a consideration, but let's face it, they will be higher than the generic prices. It's just that the cheaper peaches are simply not worth their money, in their perception.

So, when you are going to show your product's intrinsic value it's important to highlight the features that make it special. If you are comparing it to name brands, you have to show why your product is a better value, not based solely on price, but on the features that it offers or the quality of the product. Otherwise, very few people are willing to spend their money on cheap products just to save a few bucks. They know that after a bit of time, the cheap products break and they will just have to go out and get a new product much more quickly.

How to implement effectively

This is probably the most complicated strategy to implement. It requires you to take the time to educate your sales prospect in a way that they find informative and enlightening, instead of boring. You can do this quickly with a table of comparison with check marks for features, and that tool works very well here. However, what happens when you have features that your customer won't even understand? That's truly the case when you are dealing with technical equipment and people really don't know whether one processor is really better than another. That's when you also have to educate them on why they want that feature too.

That's why you will want to be a little more descriptive here than normal. It can be a bit of a drain for people coming to your site to find a long list of features but it will be necessary to educate the buyer. You can have the short summary in a table and then a bulleted list underneath to indicate what each feature is all about. That way, when someone comes to your website who is knowledgeable on your products, they won't bother to read the bulleted list. The table of comparison is sufficient. Those that don't have that same background will read the list and be impressed that you took the time to educate them on the features and why they are important to them. It shows that you care enough to make them informed consumers.

Another way you can implement this strategy is to have a short story that talks about why the features on your product are a good value. Maybe you are selling purses and your purses are leather and not synthetic. Maybe they have features like a cell phone compartment, an accompanying wallet that matches, and the potential to add your personalize monograph too. When you compare your purse to other purses, you will want to show that the reason these things are important is because they serve a function, they help you to express your identity, and they are durable, valuable, or aesthetically pleasing – even more so than your competitor's purses.

You can even bring up the product's price and compare that to show that even though your products cost more, they are a better value. Or you can show that your products cost less and deliver the same or better value! People still want to know that they are saving money, whether it is through quality or price value.

One way to help you get higher sales is to offer the cheaper product first. The way this works is that people will be so excited by the low price on the cheaper product that when you bring out the higher priced version of that product, they will transfer their excitement to the new product and equate it as a better value. Most of the time, when they hear about all the additional features they get for just x amount of dollars more, they will jump at the chance of getting an even bigger value than they thought they were getting with the cheaper version.

This strategy of offering several versions works well when you are comparing items too. You don't want to compare apples to oranges, so several different versions of the same product in your inventory greatly increase your potential for making a sale. After all, you are giving the customer a choice, it just so happens the choice is still going to mean a sale for you. So, it doesn't matter how you compare them or what features they have, the fact that they are able to figure out for themselves whether it really is price or intrinsic value that will motivate them to buy helps you to make a sale.

This strategy can be turned on its head to still offer a sales opportunity, particularly if you are selling memberships or fundraising for an online charity. In that case, you would not offer the cheapest alternative first. You would show them the most expensive option first. When people balk at that, you would then offer the cheaper alternative. The reason for that is that they are not so much comparing products, but services or donations. When they buy, they're not going to get anything placed in their hands, unless of course you make that an option for the higher priced memberships.

If you are selling packages, like trips to other countries that include hotel, airfare, and sightseeing, you should start with the highest priced package first. Packages include many different benefits and will automatically be perceived to have a higher value than a single item. So, you don't want to start with the cheaper package in this instance. Then, you can offer the cheaper products as an alternative if the higher priced package is rejected.

So, when you are considering implementing this strategy think about the order you want to present your products online. Do you want to highlight the higher priced item first and then offer the lower one or vice versa? You could try it both ways and then see when you make more sales. That's the answer to your problem then. But, be aware, that the order of product presentation will influence people on subconscious levels in the area of proving your product's value.

Timing this strategy

This strategy can be done when people are browsing your product inventories. When they search your site for a particular product, make sure the other products in that inventory show up too. Depending on what they are looking for you can manipulate the order of display to influence them to perceive a higher value.

If you are competing against brand names and using your own generic products, be sure to include that information on your sales page so people know your products are worth it. If you are writing copy ads that are going in printed material, you can compare your products quickly and then put a link to a site where you sell the product.

You can also educate your customer on getting a better value just before they check out. It's like when you go to a fast food place and you order a single item. That's the time when you're told that if you buy a combo package you get a better value. And, most people then buy the combo whether they actually were that hungry or not. The same can be done online, by saying on the checkout, "did you know that for x amount more you could get such and such?" If you have that placed as standard programming in your website, then it will come up and alert the customer that there is a potential for a better value deal and usually bigger bucks for you.

Conclusion

As you can see from these strategies, there are ways to influence a customer who is visiting your site to cause them to buy your products. However, you have to understand your audience, your products benefits, and the correct timing as to when to try each strategy. Once you start to implement some of these strategies on your site, you will see that some work better than others on particular products or at different times. If you pay attention to when you go shopping, you can see instances of each of these strategies at work in your own buying behavior. And, many retailers do train their staff to trigger buying behavior by evaluating the consumer's needs and choosing to interact at particular times with particular phrases that trigger the subconscious to buy.

It's really not magic, but it can seem to be at times. People go about their days mostly unconscious of their own motivations and in sales, this can be a big advantage. They may all come from different backgrounds, but still some behaviors like respect for authority, the desire to play with things, and the desire to bond through stories have their start in childhood programming. These daily habits become so powerful that as adults, we don't even think about why we respect experts, what makes something more fascinating than something else, and why everyone loves a good joke! Yet, that is all part and parcel of being human.

Once you begin to understand your own triggers and why you do certain things, it becomes easier to predict what will trigger other people to close a deal or not. They are no different from you and they will follow their better instincts too. So, learn the psychology, seek to understand the dynamics of human behavior, and then try to find ways to influence people to increase your sales. That's how you turn a visitor on your site into a customer and build life-long relationships.

As you get the hang of using all the tools online available to create that hypnotic spell, you will find it easy to flip from forums to blogs to sales pages and maybe even into third-party vendors like eBay. You will build the confidence you need that you know what works and when and what's the appropriate time to use one strategy over another to make a sale. You will have learned that it isn't difficult to engage people online, it just takes a bit more skill since you are not face-to-face with your potential buyers. But, once you have those skills they can be used all over the Internet to help you gather customers and sales from all over the globe.

Ultimate Traffic Part II - Prospect to Customer
Prime the buyer's greed glands

Greed is a human trait, and maybe we'd like to ignore it because it's not very pretty, but it is a fact of life. People do get greedy and when they do, they tend to lose all sense of reason. That's actually a pretty good time to use this human weakness to help you trigger the impulse to buy your products.

In sales, greed isn't just about charging people the most money you can get out of them, although that is definitely one aspect that marketers use. It's also about providing the trigger so that your buyer believes they are getting a steal, either because of a price differential or the cost versus benefits preview. It's a great way not just to make one sale, but to close on a variety of items.

Closeout and bargain hunting are a form of greed even though it's viewed as frugality. It all depends on if the buyer is buying bargains because that's what they practically need in their lives or whether the impulse to buy is spurred more by overactive greed glands that can't turn down anything resembling a steal of a deal. So, placing these types of deals on your website can help you start to develop a sales strategy that attracts a wide range of buyers.

The strategic plan

It may surprise you to know that the disposable income level of your sales prospects actually define what a good deal is, not the actual value of the product or service you are offering. That's because greed is relative to your economic prosperity, even though high income wage earners are not immune to greed, it just takes a slightly different form.

For instance, when you are trying to sell an item that might be worth $60 to a very well-heeled client, you might want to up the price to $100, and highlight the features and quality of the product, and see if they bite. The reason for this isn't just your own greed, but also the understanding that price to value is relative based on your disposable income.

For someone making over $100,000/year, an extra $40 is not seen as a lot of money and they may be used to paying higher prices due to the markets they shop. They might not even question the price. However, they will assuredly question the quality and want to make sure that the purchase reflects their station in life. The greed here is more about status than money.

On the other hand, if you were to do the same with a person making less than $25,000/year that $100 set point may be enough for them to do some comparison shopping and they'll pretty soon find out that they can buy the same item from your competitor for $40 less. You not only lose the sale, but you lose future sales too from that customer. So, using greed to price your products is tricky. You have to understand your target demographic, and specifically the income level of most of your customers. Then, you can price accordingly.

If you are not sure of the income level, you can always start using this strategy by offering a more expensive option first and then presenting a much less expensive option second. The difference in prices and a clear explanation of the differences in features can be enough to make the greed glands in any demographic start to salivate. It appeals to the high income earners because it triggers their status greed in elevating the higher priced item as the "must have" product, not just because of additional features, but precisely because it is more expensive. It triggers the lower end crowd because the less expensive option will be seen to be a minor sacrifice in features for a large reduction in cost.

The psychological triggers

Where does greed come from? It's said it is one of the original seven deadly sins, but it's probably more a survival instinct. When human beings lived at the mercy of the elements and environment, there were wide disparities between times of prosperity and harsh times when drought, famine, or disease might invade the security of the home. So, the instinct to hoard things and try to get a bigger share than someone else, was basically an innate fear of survival because the future was so uncertain.

That's why even people who are very well off are not immune to greed. It is inbred in our species and helped us, as a species, to survive very bad times, albeit at the expense of others at times. But, the instinct to try to get a very good deal, even one you don't need immediately, is something that appeals to everyone, even if the tactic to implement it is different according to your demographic.

In marketing, the skillful manipulation of price is what triggers this dynamic. Value is something that the buyer determines in a capitalistic system, so that it can fluctuate from person to person. So, the way to engage a perception that your product is a steal is by manipulating the price in relation to the perceived value. Let's be clear, the price itself is viewed as a fixed commodity to the buyer, it is the value that is fluctuating from person to person. If the price is low when compared to the perceived value, even if the price is actually quantitatively high, then it is considered a steal by that potential buyer and the greed glands will kick into high gear.

So, you can either raise or lower the price to stimulate greed, it's that simple. That's the tool you have at your disposal. However, always do it in comparison to your understanding of the customer's perceived value of the product.

How to implement effectively

You may be scratching your head a bit confused about raising a price to stimulate greed. There is a strategy that you can use which shifts the perceived value in the buyer's mind while you do it. It is quite a bit more subtle that lowering a price to stimulate greed, but it can be done, especially for luxury or high-priced markets. Remember that as long as the prices are low in comparison to the perceived value, even if it is quantitatively a high dollar value, it's still considered a steal.

Here is how you might try to implement the greed factor in a high-priced market.

Say you are selling collectible fine china. You have several sets that are obviously worth hundreds of dollars and you are interested in getting a stampede of buyers to your door to generate interest in the product. So, you build a marketing campaign and you talk about how the value of the price of this fine china has increased over time substantially and how rare it is becoming. Now, you're attracting the demographics of luxury buyers who are interested in not only quality goods, but they have a nose for great deals too.

So, you say that in another five years, their investment in the fine china may be worth twice as much again. Be careful with the wording and be sure that they understand that past performance of an investment is no guarantee of future returns. So, here we are very skillfully changing the perception of this product from china to collectibles and an investment, not a household purchase, and we've even shown how the value might potentially increase after the purchase. So, are we going to sell it for the actual value of the product? No way! We are selling an appreciating asset, not a household item.

So, now the value of the product has increased tremendously in the buyer's mind and we can command a higher figure than the actual present day value. But, wait! That's just the start of our greed enhancing program. Now, you say, that while it's true that the china is a great investment and of quality and high value, you can offer the public a great deal by offering it at a discount because you are either going out of business, having an end of year sale, celebrating your business anniversary or whatever! Make up an excuse and make it somewhat believable. Then, cut the price of the set from the higher price to a lower one, but one still substantially higher than what the product's present day value is worth.

Another way to do this is not to cut the value of one set, but offer a discount on volume buying. This would work perfectly if you are selling place settings and you don't know whether they want four, eight, or twelve place settings. However, they may think it's too expensive to buy twelve, until you offer them a discount for buying eight or more. You trigger the greed, and they will start to justify the reasons why having extra sets on hand are a good idea.

Finally, lowering the price of items is always a sure-fire way to attract greedy customers by the boat load. And, you will soon discover that the amount of attention and enthusiasm you get for your sales is completely proportional to the difference in price drops. The lower the price, the more you sell, in other words. The only time when you can't make those sales is when the product is obviously junk and no one wants to buy it, but for the most part if you continue to persuade your customers of the innate value of the product and lower the price, you can spur them into action to close the sale.

Timing this strategy

This is a strategy that can be used even before a customer shows up to your website! Yes, that's right, you don't have to wait for them to show interest in your products, you don't have to wait for them to sign up to mailing lists, you can do it as a mass advertising tool to bring customers in who will be attracted by your specials.

This is an excellent tool for people in direct mail and retail sales. You know that when you put out a special in one of those newspaper inserts or ValuPak envelopes, which you are practically guaranteed new customers as long as the offer is enticing enough to convince them to drop by. Well, on the Internet you don't even have to convince them to gas up their cars and make the trip, you can simply put your link out there and invite them to click on it.

You'll want to include your offer in various third party forums and comment on in discretely where ever you can. Be careful not to spam people, but you do want to advertise it on other places besides your own site.

In order to get the widest exposure, you can offer to give key people in the same niche as you the deal for free, if they review it and write about the value. While that may be a sweet enough deal for some, others will want to get a commission off each product they promote and sell. Then, you can also set up an affiliate program for that special so that they are not only able to promote a great deal to their visitors, but they make money off the deal too. That's the true meaning of greed, when you butter the palms of everyone involved in the deal and make it a win-win-win for everyone.

These types of offers are best as either introductory offers or close-out sales, or end of season sales. There should be a reason why you are able to offer these offers so that people don't become habituated to receiving only sharp discounts from you and get offended when you put up a product at a regular price. And, don't forget the luxury market too when you want to implement this strategy, but instead of money, opt to hype the perceived value so that a lowering of the price still keeps the initial price high.

Impact their emotions

If you think buying is not an emotional experience, you are mistaken! Every word in sales copy is amplified when it triggers an emotional response and can be the difference between copy that excites the imagination of the potential buyer and that which deadens it. When you engage the buyer's imagination they can even begin to imagine what it's like to own the product you are selling and it stirs up the flames of desire for possessing it.

It is true that if you want to sell, you want to sell by impacting the emotions of your potential buyer. Even though you know that the final decision may be justified through logic, the initial way to get by the mind that will think up all sorts of objections to the sale is to appeal to the emotions.

The strategic plan

When you are advertising your products or services you will want to pay close attention to the words you choose. Words are powerful tools on the Internet that you can use to frame the way a person perceives not only the value of your product, but also the experience of possible ownership. Words tell stories that inform your readers about how this product or service solved a problem for some other buyer. Stories can pull a buyer into identifying with the other buyers and help them to visualize their own problems being solved, their lives getting easier or better for having made the purchase.

You will want to pick words that not only tell a vivid story, however, you will also want to use words that influence the buyer's feelings and gives them favorable impressions. It's really not that hard to do. People have a variety of automatic emotional responses to different words. All you have to do is find out which words create the best results and implement them in your sales copy.

You want to create a sales environment that puts people into an emotional mindset. Why? The simple reason is to bypass the logical mind long enough to make the sale. Sure, the final decision to buy will need to be justified with solid benefits, but that's not typically the reason a person ends up making the decision to buy. They may not even be aware that many of their buying decisions are based on how they feel about a product rather than what they think about it. People actually feel thrills when they buy and that thrill acts as a beacon to get them to buy again.

Yet, when they are asked why they buy a particular product, they don't talk about how they feel – that's rather personal! Instead, they list the benefits. That's because when people are asked to justify a purchase, the mind automatically kicks in, even if they made the decision based solely on how they felt at the time of purchase.

The psychological triggers

The brain has two halves and one deals with logic and the other is more intuitive and feeling. The two halves generally don't communicate at the same time in most people. If you have very strong emotions, you're reason is usually blocked from functioning at its highest potential and vice-versa. This can be really useful information in your marketing efforts because if you can get someone to get emotional about your products, you can sell without even really having to work too hard at it.

Not only that, but once an impression is made on the emotional mind, it tends to have a longer memory than the logical mind. It is even well known that feelings can be associated to various stimuli that bring back powerful memories, complete with the emotions, sometimes just by smelling something that reminds you of your childhood. Words aren't just letters strung together that have a logical meaning. They also have a personal meaning. If you can tap into that emotional intelligence and bypass the logical critic most people have standing ready to say no, you will find that you can sell things much faster and retain customers with a higher sense of satisfaction after the sale.

You don't just have to focus on invoking pleasant emotions, because negative emotions can also be powerful motivators to close a sale. Think of people who are in the market to buy GPS systems for their cars. Why would they want to buy that? On an emotional basis, they may be trying to avoid getting lost. So, the feeling you want to invoke is precisely that confused and lost feeling that they dread. And, then offer the GPS system as a solution to never having to feel that way again!

How to implement effectively

The way to implement this strategy is to start making a list of alternative, emotion-packed words that influence your potential buyer in subtle, but powerful, ways. Review your copy for opportunities where you can reach out and literally touch the buyer and comfort or assure them that they are making the right decision to buy.

One word that is very powerful and should be used more in copy is the word "invest" instead of buy. When you buy something it almost has the connotation of being taken for a ride. For instance, when you "buy into" something it means you've been convinced, maybe even despite your feeling it may not be such a good idea. However, the word "invest" has the opposite feeling. It gives you a feeling of security and reaping returns, even if you don't have a logical explanation for why that is so. It's just a good investment.

People in the real estate industry are masters at this game. When a house is small, they call it "cozy." When the walls are painted in odd colors, they call it "custom paint." If it is falling apart at the seams, they call it a "handyman special." These are euphemisms that don't completely hide the meaning, but reframe it to show off the positive aspects of it. They plug into the emotional impact of the words. Cozy gives you the idea of warmth and being hugged by your mother.

Custom paint is a term that can mean anything from a personalized mural complete with the kid's hand prints to a mural vista of the French Riviera by a local artist. It's up to the person reading the ad to fill in the blanks and normally they will fill them in with whatever appeals to them. Handyman special gives you an idea that it's a property that won't last long, being special, and that it only needs little fixes here and there.

So, paying attention to the choice of words is important to implement this strategy. That can be done by pure trial and error or by looking up sales books to find which words carry a positive impact. There are many such words that you see in television ads, like the words "new, improved, easy" and more. Or, you can just start to switch words here and there in your copy and see what impact it makes on your bottom line.

The second way to implement this strategy is to bring out your inner drama queen. You want to be able to exude emotion and have that pour all over your sales copy. Try to write up an offer that really engages someone on an emotional level. Use it in your sales presentations by trying to bring in an emotional content that people can quickly identify with and then use it to manipulate people into a frame of mind that makes them buy.

Especially, you want to focus on framing the benefits in an emotional framework.

This will help your buyer begin to imagine and experience your product more in their feelings. Try to describe the product in emotional language that triggers people into associations that are positive for them. This is the same idea that real estate people use when they advise you to bake cookies or simmer cinnamon sticks in the house before you show it. The scents pull in memories of mom baking in the kitchen and make the sale for you through subconscious emotional associations. Well, you can do the same with words by painting the picture of the emotional trigger for them to be able to visualize it better in their mind.

Obviously, depending on your demographics, the emotional triggers for one group may be different from another. It's your job to figure out which emotional triggers will appeal to the people you are marketing. If you are marketing to hurried, working moms then triggering the image of a crying, babies, and the phone ringing, while dinner burns on the stove, would sell anything that makes this scenario go away. It might be easy to make microwave meals, it can be an answering machine that shows you who is calling and whether it's important. It's not always going to be obvious how to associate the emotion to your product, but it should be relevant to your demographic.

If you were to use that same imagery to try to sell microwave meals for single professionals, they would not relate to it, even if the microwave meal might appeal to them if it had been framed differently. Do you see how the emotion is triggered specifically by the advertising and the target audience? For some, the emotional trigger will strike them right where they live, and for others, it simply leaves them cold. You have to know who you are marketing to, to understand how to trigger the emotions that you want to associate with your advertising copy.

Some emotions are universal because they relate to our childhood. We all equate home with feelings of security (which is good for the real estate market). We all want to feel included and accepted by our family and friends. We all want to feel we are achieving or accomplishing something we can feel proud of. These types of emotions can also be used to mine a larger audience, when you are unsure of your demographics. But, the more targeted your emotional marketing campaign the greater the possibility that it will be a stronger influence to trigger buying behavior.

Timing this strategy

The time to use this strategy is when you are first presenting the product to the public or your website visitor. Don't wait to start to bring some familiarity to the product that the person can begin to identify with it as the solution to their problems. Try to engage all the senses so that they can begin to tie into the sensual aspect of the product – this will lead to the emotional part of their brain and bring forth associated positive memories. Once that first impression is made in the emotional part of the brain, it will be very hard to shake later on.

That's part of the reason that many expert sales people will actually take a sample with them to a presentation, something their potential buyer can touch and experience. It appeals to the emotional side of all human beings and gets them to start imagining what it would be like to own the regular product all to themselves.

Think of how car manufacturers present their advertising for cars. They typically show a convertible car winding down a stunning coastal highway, sea breeze flying through the driver's hair, as the sun beats down on dazzling water and sand. You can practically smell the salt air and taste the spray of sea water in your mouth, and that's the point. They evoke the emotional response by getting you to imagine buying the car. You then become that person with the perfect life that has the wind wiping through your hair in a breezy, freeing, experience while everyone else is stuck in a cubicle hard at work. It's really quite amusing when we analyze how easily our emotions are manipulated, but that's really the case. There are certain desires that most human beings will do anything to experience: love, freedom, joy, and success. Tie those emotions to your product, and you've got a winner.

Go beyond the 100% satisfaction guarantee

Everyone remembers the cheesy 100% satisfaction guarantee that old television infomercials would haul out to get people to believe in their products. Well, consumers are much more savvy now and most people understand this to be more of a trial guarantee that after a certain period expires. In other words, the 100% satisfaction guarantee was usually limited to a few weeks or less, and after that you were stuck with the product. So, in all fairness it was more like a free trial than a 100% satisfaction guarantee. After all, if you're not satisfied and the period for returns has ended, aren't you then still a dissatisfied customer?

So, we're going to tell you how to put in place something that goes beyond the 100% satisfaction guarantee, even though it may seem impossible. Well, it isn't. It is your conviction that the products you offer are of such worth that you can offer a guarantee that goes beyond everyone's expectations and still make money on the product. And, when you have that sort of conviction about the products you sell, the customer begins to believe it too.

The strategic plan

The strategy, on the surface, seems a bit crazy for a business person to implement. What you will suggest to your customers is that if a certain condition is met that you will refund their money or make amends beyond what is expected of you. That means that if you sell a product and it breaks, you promise to refund the money or replace it, even if it's one year or two years down the line.

But, it doesn't just have to be about things breaking, it can also be a usage condition. Say, you buy a subscription to use a particular service and then find you don't use it enough to pay for the membership costs. In this strategy, the way to go beyond the 100% satisfaction guarantee is to offer to refund all the money for the subscription if you don't use the products and services offered by the membership at all within the year. Of course, you would have to have a way of figuring that out.

In a discount club, you have membership costs that give you access to discounts on other products. The idea is that the amount of money you save will easily exceed the membership cost to sign up and you eventually make back your membership fee. But, what if you didn't do that? Would most companies offer you the membership fee back if you found that the use of the club wasn't worth it? Well, if your membership club did this it would set itself above the rest by offering to ensure that whether a member uses the membership they bought or not, they will end up satisfied with the purchase because you will make sure to go beyond the typical business guarantee. Now, add a little perk at the end like a free gift or even a coupon for monies off popular items for having just tried the membership, even if it didn't end up saving you money, and people will flock to sign up.

The psychological triggers

There are lots of people who offer guarantees, but they are only worth the person issuing them. Many times there are clauses in the guarantee that limit the actual worth, such a specific limited time period or meeting a specific condition that is unlikely to happen.

For instance, most tires these days are sold with six year or 60,000 mile warranties. That's a guarantee that should your tire fail before then, it will be replaced for free, right? Wrong! If you look at the fine print, it says that they will replace your tires if the problem is a defect in the workmanship, not for any unforeseen event that might cause your tire fails. Your tires can hit a nail in the road – a far more likely event – and you will have to still pay to replace the tire. And, should your tire fail out of poor workmanship it's still up to you to prove that's the case, instead of it being because somebody slashed your tires or some other environmental danger hit it. It's just not very likely you'll ever use a warranty these days for tires on a manufacturer defect because most tires are made pretty well these days, no matter what they cost.

However, tires are sold based on these guarantees as if the extra money you pay for a really good tire with an excellent warranty is going to give you additional customer satisfaction and security. It really isn't. It's the 100% money back guarantee that really isn't about satisfaction as much as it is about clever marketing, and people realize that.

However, when people are willing to put their money where their mouth is, and put it in writing, that is a very impressive act that creates instant credibility. That means that you will replace or make good on any product, regardless of the reason, no matter what happened or how long it took to occur. Isn't that positively crazy these days? Maybe so, but it also means that you believe above 100% in your company and in its ability to meet the customer's needs. You are betting that your product is so good that people won't need to return it, and that's what you're saying with the beyond 100% satisfaction guarantee.

The person viewing the ad thinks that you are either crazy to make such a good offer or your product is really all you say it is! Otherwise, how could you afford to make this type of guarantee? It raises the perceived value of your product or service and instills confidence in the purchase decision. People know that when they see that over 100% satisfaction guarantee that the likelihood of being taken is very small, and that triggers their confidence in making the purchase. Because you believed in your products, they fell in line and believed in them too. It removes any remaining doubts or resistance to buying the product that a customer might hold in their minds.

How to implement effectively

Implementing this strategy is very easy, it just takes guts. After all, you are basically saying you are willing to show customers that you mean business and that your word can be trusted. If you issue a claim that goes beyond the 100% satisfaction guarantee, you had better be able to back it with action. If you issue it and then go back on your word, you will have a publicity nightmare on your hands and the backlash will be tremendous. So, whatever you promise, be sure you can deliver it and then stick to your word.

This strategy shouldn't be implemented as a standalone strategy. It should always be used as an additional boost to get the customer over the sales finish line. It might be well used for products where there might be some doubts lingering in the minds of the buyer, either because of the price or the novelty. Maybe you are selling a new technology that is designed to do something really novel, but people don't know how helpful it's really going to be. They may read the benefits and even be considering it but the product still needs an additional push to make the customer decide to shell out big bucks to try it. Then, you would trot out the beyond 100% satisfaction guarantee and now those people on the fence will rush to buy.

If you think that you will end up losing too much money refunding purchases or replacing products, you are not realizing that most buyers have short memories. Maybe they buy that high tech air cleaning and filtering system from your store only because they're told if it ever breaks, they can return it for a free replacement. But, odds are when it does break they won't even remember what store they bought it from, much less than you offered them that guarantee. If they do remember, they might think they need the box or the receipt in order to take advantage of the guarantee, and that might or might not be the case. And, then after that, they have to motivate themselves to get back to your store and try to take you up on that beyond 100% guarantee with the product in hand. Most people will simply go out and buy something to replace the broken product and not even think about your offer again.

It's a sad statement on the American consume mind, but most people are not as frugal or careful with their purchases to document the guarantees and keep track of them. It may be a real factor when they are trying to make the decision to buy, but after that it's mostly forgotten unless that guarantee is such a classic aspect of your marketing that you make it over and over again to multiple customers. Then, you will find that people begin to associate that product or your company with that guarantee and they will take you up on it more, but still not at a high rate.

Let's be clear, you aren't just going to offer a good guarantee, you are offering an UNBELIEVABLE guarantee. It's so good, people will think you're nuts for offering it. They may just buy the product to try and prove you wrong. If you are selling subscriptions to a discount club, they might be so intrigued by your offer, and knowing they have nothing to lose, and even maybe something to gain, they will put their money down and see if you are right.

The UNBELIEVABLE part should come when you're not only offer to keep them from losing money on the deal, but also add some incentive to sweeten the deal should the product not meet their expectations. So, for a subscription to a discount club, you offer to give them a free gift at the end of the year AND their money back just for trying the membership, if they find that they don't make up all the money in discounts throughout the year that they paid in the membership fee. What this tells people is that you believe that EVERYONE will save money using your discount club because you're just that fantastic. You're so convinced that's the case, which you're even willing to pay people to try your club out and offer them a free gift should that not occur as you expect.

To figure out which offers need this additional strategy, you should look at your sales numbers. Are some offers languishing while others are going gang busters? Don't fix what isn't broken. Instead, opt for the slow movers to try this strategy as an additional incentive to move those other offers into better performance.

This is definitely a trial and error business when deciding which offers need it and which don't. If you find that after implementing the beyond 100% satisfaction guarantee, your sales jump 200%, then you know that you've got it in the right place. That's the power this strategy has when you use it with offers that may need just that extra boost to get them to go from underperformers to star sellers.

Timing this strategy

Since this is not a standalone strategy, you want to choose other strategies to pull out first. Then, after you have made the case for your product, through selling the benefits, and you notice that you still have the customer teetering on the seat of their chairs biting their nails over the decision, then try the beyond 100% satisfaction guarantee at the very end of the copy. That's right. We want it at the very end of all the selling copy. You may think that's the worst place for it, but it's really the only place for it.

That's because if a person has gotten that far down the sales page and still hasn't made up their mind, then you need to add something to push them over the edge. If you did it earlier, you would not have a chance to implement the other strategies that can help you make the sale instantly. This one works best when there is still some doubt left in the mind of the potential buyer that needs to be removed, and therefore it goes last.

Walk the logic labyrinth

While an emotional trigger will help to stimulate buying behavior, when it comes time to justify the purchase buyers often seek out logic. No one likes to feel that they've been taken on a deal, and so the end result that even if the emotions have carried them away, they will always give a logical reason why they eventually bought the product. That's because people don't admit that it was an emotional response that instigated the buy, they'd rather admit there was a valid reason for the purchase.

Knowing this, that a logical reason may be necessary for some to close a deal, then you want to provide that logical reason just as you would attempt to resolve an objection before it is raised. It doesn't mean that the reason has to really make any sense, it just has to be enough to justify the purchase. It has to answer the question: "Why should I buy this product?"

The strategic plan

Here you are going to aim a very definite reason why a customer should buy your product. It's typically done after an emotional appeal, to seal the deal and give your ad a double whammy. You are going to look at the demographics of your visitors and you are going to try to put yourself in their shoes. What would be the defining reason to buy this product?

There are a variety of reasons that can trigger different segments of the population to agree that to purchase your product makes sense. If you are dealing with people who are budget conscious, you can go after economic reasons. Another possibility is to focus on health as a reason. Maybe they are getting older and more health conscious. Maybe you are selling something to people who are sick. That can be a powerful reason to consider buying your product. Safety is also something is top-most in people's minds. This might work well for some people and not for others. Safety means different things to different people. For mothers, child safety might be the reason that you need to express to close the deal. For elderly people, it might be personal safety when they are home alone.

Aside from very logical reasons like that, you don't have to just concentrate on those. Sometimes some of the best reasons are status, especially if you are selling in the luxury market. In that case, the reason you give might be, "You deserve it!" Is there any logic to that? Not from an intellectual perspective, but from a reasoning standpoint it makes perfect sense to a certain subset of people, particularly the affluent.

Another reason that you can use is that it will enhance your personal or professional recognition. That can be a powerful reason for people who are dating or seeking some sort of career advancement. Again, the reason you choose should fit the demographic of people you are marketing to.

The way this strategy works best is if you can get into the mindset of the people you are marketing to and understand what type of objections they are likely to raise for themselves. If you are not sure what they are, you need to do a little market research with similar products that are selling online. Without understanding some of the potential objections that people might be thinking about when they view your sales page, you will not be able to successfully resolve them in a logical manner, and that's the key to this strategy.

Once you determine the most typical objections, you will be able to think up the proper justifications to overcome them. By doing so, you will eliminate the last bit of resistance in your buyer's mind and close the sale.

The psychological triggers

Our Western culture prides itself on being one of reason and logic. We rely on our intellectual capabilities to justify almost every aspect of our very existence. Since we are young, we are told that civilized people use reason and not emotion to understand their world. While that remains a deep part of our conditioning, the truth is that we react emotionally first and then we attempt to justify our emotions with our thinking minds.

So, when the emotion is felt to make a purchase, we question it.

We have a certain suspicion about salesmen and slick marketing tactics. The emotion stirred up by the copy may be so strong that people are just waiting to find the reason to justify to themselves that, yes indeed, this is a really good purchase. But, without that reason, the sale is not finalized. That's because our conditioning steps is to warn us that anything that seems too good to be true, usually is unless we rationally analyze our course of action.

A good salesman anticipates that as the starting point of a sale's negotiation, not the end. He or she understands that the person who begins to create objections in their mind is actually considering buying the product, but the mental conditioning and inherent distrust built up about deals may be causing them to hesitate. The way they are taught to hesitate is to analyze the situation with their minds. So, those people that are raising objections are already half-sold! Otherwise, they'd simply walk away and never engage in any thought process to defend themselves from a potentially making a poor decision. It's your job, as an online marketer, to understand what objections are typically going to occur at this stage of the game, and resolve them satisfactorily to reduce the resistance to your sale.

How to implement effectively

One can get very creative in implementing this strategy because the mind has a way of creating excuses when it really wants something. Realize that the sale was probably already made on an emotional basis, all you are doing now is closing the sale by engaging the proper reason to assuage our cultural conditioning. So, even though you can go after reasons that make sense and go along with the product, there are plenty of reasons that don't exactly have to tie into the product, but offer some benefit and can be used to walk the logic labyrinth.

For instance, say you are leasing vehicles. Well, you can talk all day long about the wonderful qualities of the vehicles and how leasing is such a flexible option. But, the final reason that may make the most sense from a business perspective may be the potential ability to write off the lease on the company's taxes. You may wonder, where did that come from? Well, if you understood the demographic that is buying your product most, you may discover that it is companies that are leasing vehicles so they don't have to buy their own and maintain them. Instead, they buy a lease and use them only when they are under warranty. Maybe they even have a specific brand that fits their needs best and are already sold on that one model. So, then, you know that other companies who are in competition may not understand how they save by leasing a vehicle, instead of buying. So, that can be a powerful logical argument to overcome objections from new customers who never thought about leasing before.

In this scenario, the reason actually had very little to do with the product's features or quality. It had to do with a competitive edge and the ability to rationalize the purchase as a smart business expense. So, that's how you can get extremely creative with this particular strategy. Don't just limit your reasons to things that tie into the product, but widen your net and cast it into the biggest possible incentive that makes sense for your demographic.

However, if you find that you need to go with standard reasons, there are always reasons available tied to any product. For instance, if you sell clothing, you may want to iterate how practical it is, how it can be thrown in the washer, or even how classic it is that you can mix and match it with many different styles. Whatever you choose, it has to be something of interest to your demographic.

If you are selling technology, you can focus on how it does a specific function better than other products, how it can improve your productivity, how it simplifies a particular task. These are all very logical reasons that appeal to that crowd.

One thing to remember when implementing this strategy is that it is related to the price you set for your product. In other words, if you have a high priced item, you will have to justify it more than a less expensive product. The only time that may not be true is when you are marketing to an affluent demographic. Otherwise, you will always have to justify a more expensive product to someone, even if they are head over heels in love with it.

Take for instance, luxury cars. There's really nothing all that much different from the way one car operates over another. So, they have to be sold on the features and the reasoning they give is that even though it may have the same parts as another car, they are somehow better quality. It may be a car known for its smooth ride, or it may be known for its high safety record, whatever the reason, it's really something that suggests the car outperforms other cars. After all, luxury cars are truly expensive. How would anyone be able to justify ever buying one based on the fact that they needed a car that took them from one place to another? Obviously, that strategy would not work!

Instead, the logic has to include why it is so much better than other cars to justify the high cost. Despite this, it's almost certain that people who buy luxury cars are buying them based on the emotional impact. The feeling of specialness, the luxury of owning one, the way it associates them with a specific class of people is what really sells these cars. But, if you were to ask anyone why they bought a luxury car, they would most likely opt to tell you it outperforms other cars because they have to justify the expense to you and to themselves too.

The funny thing about the way to implement this strategy that it can actually pay to put in technical reasons to sell the product, even if most people have no idea what most of the features are in technical language. Take a look at how personal computers are sold. They will tell you it had this much RAM, hard drive space, and all kinds of technical features that the majority of people don't understand. The higher the price, the more the technical features are listed in one long list.

That's because they are the reasons that people will justify buying a higher priced computer versus a less expensive one, even if they haven't a clue what all those extra features are all about. They only know they have a very smart computer, and likewise, they feel smart opting for a fully loaded personal computer, even if all they want to do is type up a few emails or letters every now and then.

Timing this strategy

The time to implement this strategy is after you've made the emotional sales pitch and the customer is wavering. It almost always comes at the end of a sales presentation, on the side of the box of the software or as an inset for the PC advertisement. It's not the sole reason anyone is expected to agree to buy your product, it's simply put there at the end to remove the last vestiges of resistance to buying the product.

So, for online marketing, it does go in your list of benefits if you have multiple reasons, but you should have one big reason at the end why this is the very best thing a person can do to resolve the problem that led them to your sales page. You can even put it in as an afterthought, as in, "Don't forget, this product does this and this and you should take advantage of that."

Spur their passion for collecting

Everyone associates collecting with antiques and other niche markets. But, the truth is that every market can use the dynamics of the desire to amass collections of things to spur sales. If you don't believe that then you weren't around when the Beanie Babies craze hit the public. Who on earth would have believed grown adults would run around collecting little creatures made of stuffed bean bags? It became a national craze and those little buggers weren't cheap!

The moral of the story there is that if a manufacturer can create a collecting demand for a product that serves no useful purpose, had a unique and sometimes odd look about them, and you can't even eat or invest it, then how much more can you spur the passion for collecting for items that even have additional reasons to buy? Obviously, collecting isn't just for Beanie Babies or antiques, it's for everything and everyone.

The strategic plan

So, even if you are selling bumper stickers or watches, it doesn't matter. You can use this strategy to increase your sales. Don't believe that just because one person has bought one model, it doesn't mean they may not be interested in other models. In fact, people who buy watches, for instance, will often buy several models and collect them for different occasions. Maybe they want a dress watch for when they are at a classy occasions. Maybe they want a fun and flirty one for parties and another more professional-looking one for the office. You can sell them all three! Isn't that a great way to boost your sales?

So, the thing you want to do for this strategy is to target your existing customers. That's right, this is a strategy that is going to bring out the collecting bug in those people that have already shown an interest in your products. In order to get people to start collecting them, you need to start highlighting the collectible nature of your product. Why would someone want to collect them? Who else is collecting them? Can you display them on a shelf? Are they great to own various styles? What are the benefits of collecting your products?

If you ever watch QVC, you will see the way they tout many of their items as collectibles. They will take a call and the person on the other line will tell them how much they love the product and that they've bought several different models! Then, they start listing either their pride in owning such a great collection and how it good it makes them feel, or they start listing all the reasons for why owning many makes sense.

The psychological triggers

You would think that the act of collecting is stimulated because of greed, but it isn't. Collecting falls into its own psychological niche whereby the collector receives a great deal of pleasure and pride from owning many different models of a particular item. It's not because they are unconsciously trying to save up for poor economic times, as in greed, because even things that have no intrinsic function are collected and enjoyed by many people. So, why do people collect things that may not even have any utility in their lives?

If you've ever collected pennies as a youngster, you know that collecting gives one a sense of achievement. Every new penny you find and fit into its pouch gives you pleasure and a feeling of achievement. When the entire collection is done, you can also show that collection off to your friends for them to admire your achievement as well.

In some cases, the history or uniqueness of the collection can also be a source of great pleasure for collectors. That's why people sometimes collect salt shakers in various styles, not necessarily because they need more than one set of salt shakers in their home. Instead, the uniqueness and variety of the pieces bring out great pleasure in the collector who becomes fascinated by each new variation they can add to their collection.

The emotional investment in the collection grows as the collection grows. It becomes a bigger part of the collector's life and may even get a prominent position of display in the home. It becomes a large source of pride. And, once that addiction sets in the collector may not be able to help themselves and be purchasing new items that are far more expensive than when they first started, just to round out their collection. By that time, you almost don't even have to have a reason to sell a collector on a particular piece if the emotional impact of the piece screams out to them "must have!" And, that's the type of enthusiasm and excitement you want associated with your products because it will lead to residual sales that you can count on.

How to implement effectively

It's funny, but this strategy takes a little setup to implement. If you think about it, why did you get into collecting pennies when you were a kid? Would you have done it if they didn't sell those neat little sleeves with all the dates on each slot that you needed to collect to have the complete collection? So, part of implementing this strategy is to simply offer a display case that people can use to track which items they still need to buy to complete their collection and to give a little history of the entire collection.

You can even offer limited quantities of a specific product and increase the collectible status. That way you can even start by charging more for that product, because it is a limited edition. This is one way to manipulate the perceived value while not really changing the intrinsic value due to the collecting strategy.

Always remember to place the bug in your customer's ears that this is a collectible item. You can send them a display case for free with the purchase of more than one item in the collection. You can highlight how other collections you've offered in the past have increased in value in the secondary market. This will give the idea to your customers that they are buying something that will increase in worth and it becomes "an investment."

Remember that what you are trying to build is excitement about each new model, by helping people keep track of what's out there and when a new one comes along. So, giving each model its own unique identity will also stir up interest in collecting different models. This also helps people who may start to push the craze forward when they buy in volume to resell, particularly if you happen to hit a fad. Then, you can expect your collectibles to fly off the shelf like Beanie Babies.

It also doesn't matter if your product is old and outdated, if you are dealing with people who are collectors. If you remember the example of the old TRS-80 computers, many people now collect them as a vintage item. Sometimes even the fact that something is old adds to its collectors appeal, as it becomes harder to find in our throwaway culture. This is why antiques appreciate in value, even though they may not be intrinsically valuable. Old glass bottles or teddy bears are excellent collectibles just for this reason. Bottles break and teddy bears rarely survive childhood. Those that do then become one of the few vintage of examples of that time period and they are sought after by collectors for just that very reason.

Even things with utility can become collectibles with the right framework, due to the uniqueness of each individual item. For instance, when phone cards came out, they each had their own unique designs. After you used the minutes on the card, some people still liked the designs, so they collected them. However, as with anything that is used and collectible, the new, still packaged, and unused item is worth more! That's why even if a person is buying something that has a utility, they may not necessarily even use it if they are collecting it. Think about what a boon it was for those phone companies to sell phone cards that had minutes that were never used! They sold a product with an intrinsic value in minutes that evaporated because people didn't want to ruin the value of the cards. Instead they kept them in the package and sold them as a collectible design and memorabilia.

But, even things that you may not consider to be highly collectible can be collected by somebody. For instance, old tools may seem like they are beyond their appeal, but gardeners may love the idea of having some vintage tools for display in their gardens as a historic and novel motif.

Once you know you have a person who collects one of your items, you know that you have a potential to get them to collect other types of items you sell. For instance, if you find a subset of your customers collecting your watches, maybe they'd also like to collect cuff links. Or if you can find a way to associate another collectible with the first, then you can start cross selling those items. For instance, maybe you have someone who is collecting toy trains. Well, how many other toys do you have that are whimsical and cute enough to be collected? How about all the accessories that you can sell to toy train collectors? Don't they need little mini depots? How about different cabooses? How about books on the history of toy trains or the actual steam engines on which they are modeled? These can be sold as collectibles too.

The nice thing about creating a collection of products and a line of accessories is that you literally have people lining up to buy those items before they're even being put up for sale. That's right. Think about the software games like Mario

Brothers. Those cute little plumbers had all sorts of versions of that game being sold with different complexities to them. You mastered one and you had to get the next one!

That's how you establish a collection, by selling in series. You start with a few models and have some way to collect and display each item in the series. Then, every time you create a new item for your collection, you simply send out notification to all the people who have bought in the past from that collection. You don't have to go out and search out new customers. You don't have to constantly think up new products, just modify an existing one with different models. And, you can even charge more when you create some limited edition collectibles for discriminating collectors.

Timing this strategy

This strategy takes a little planning to have a line of products that can be consistently promoted as the next must have item in your customer's collections. Even though anything is collectible by somebody, obviously some market niches are more wide open than others. You may be able to find someone interested in collecting old drafting tools, but it's highly likely that this isn't a very big batch of people.

So, do a little research on each of your items before you decide to try to employ this strategy. It will take a little planning so that when you are promoting the products, you are promoting in the right series and as a collectible from the start. You will find that some categories of products lend themselves well to this strategy and can increase your sales easily. Things like prints, stamps, coins, vintage items, historical items, and art can be considered to have a wide appeal as collectibles. So, if you sell any of those, you want to focus on developing a collection of products and even create displays that you can send to your customers to promote the collecting bug to take root. As such, this strategy should be implemented by you when you decide to market a particular class of products and should be thought of as a long-range strategy.

It should be cross sold on the backend of a sale anytime anybody makes a purchase from the collection, by suggesting other items within the collection in between the time they have decided to buy one and confirmed the order. This can be just an extra page showing how the history of the collection is developed and other items people purchase with it, or it can be placed as an advertisement on the order form with a discount available for buying more than one in the collection.

Treat them oh so special

Everyone's heard of the posh restaurants that are so exclusive that you have to be somebody to get a reservation and even then, it may be for a seat months away. Yet, the very fact that a restaurant is so exclusive is the drawing card that keeps it booked and turning people away. They can then charge just about anything they want for their meals and many are infamous for providing plates that would make Minnie Mouse think she was on a diet. It doesn't matter though! What matters is how special you feel just showing up to the front desk and getting in. You know you're special and they treat you very, very special too.

When you walk in the restaurant has an ambiance of luxury and opulence. When you sit down, there is fine linen on the table and multiple sets of dinner ware. You are served complimentary bread, still warm from the oven, with perfectly cooled butter pats in ceramic crocks. The menus are custom made and elegant. The centerpiece is fresh flowers, artistically arranged for your pleasure. The people seated in the restaurant are all high class and well dressed. You know that you are seated there because you are part of that special class of people who managed to get a reservation. You're completely sold on the experience and odds are you'll pay several hundred dollars just to have dinner there.

That's the power of exclusivity.

Anything that is so hard to come by and creates an ambiance that is oh so special automatically appreciates in the buyer's estimation. We talked a little bit about this in the previous chapter, but that was for mass produced items that may be artificially manipulated into limited editions. Whereas a limited edition is a version of this strategy, this takes it one step further. You are going to make the scarcity or uniqueness of your item so obvious, and the experience of ownership so special, that people will fall all over themselves to be the ones to have that item in their possession.

The strategic plan

Okay, say you have a product that is so luxurious or outright ostentatious that you think you might have trouble convincing people that it's something they need or want. Maybe the cost to market it is beyond all the other prices of the products in your existing inventory. How can you justify the purchase when it is so obviously out of kilter with what most people expect or even need in their lives?

Well, you begin by informing your customers that you have this very special product. In fact, it's so special it's not just limited, it's downright scarce. Maybe, due to the fact that it is so special and hard to produce, only a certain number can be made or marketed at one time. After they're sold, you'll have to be put on a waiting list and it may be years before you get a chance to even buy one again.

Then you frame the benefits or features of this product by comparing it to the other products in your lineup to show just exactly how special this thing is. Maybe it has a bigger engine, way out of proportion to anything you really need, but that's the beauty of something that is "special." Maybe it is huge when compared to other products in the lineup. For instance, maybe you are selling a home with over 4,000 square feet, way more than you really need. That's what makes it special!

Remember that it can't just be a manufactured limited edition, even though that would be like a watered down version of this strategy. It's more a genuine reason why this product is so special that only a few people are going to get the opportunity and pleasure of experiencing it for themselves.

And, this doesn't have to just be about the product itself. Maybe there is another reason that the product has become clearly special over time. It has increased in value way out of proportion to other similar products because of some unique feature. For instance, maybe you are selling stamps with defects on them. They are special not because they outperform other stamps, but rather because they are highly unique in the stamp world and therefore worth more.

The psychological triggers

Going back to the restaurant example. This strategy holds a tremendous draw across all demographics because of the exclusivity factor. We all want to feel special and be recognized as special people. So, even though going to an exclusive restaurant could never be justified for the budget conscious, it will even attract people from this segment of the population. Why? Well, because the experience is so exclusive that it is seen as a "once in a lifetime" opportunity. And, who is dumb enough to skip that sort of offer? You either take it when it comes up, or you miss out on it possibly for good. It's no contest, most people will definitely try to scrounge up whatever resources they can just to be able to include that special event as a memory in their life.

What's more for items which have a physical nature to them, like exclusive editions of cars or art, you will see people use them as investments. They know that because something is rare, it will always be in demand. As the scarcity continues to drive up the price over time, the fact that they own one of the few remaining items means they might be able to sell it later for more money than they spent on it. Of course, that's not always the case, but many people can justify an exclusive edition of an item with this very logic.

How to implement effectively

Whereas some products are created to be exclusive, you can create an aura of exclusivity even for items that didn't start out that way. So, if you happen to sell used books, you may find that you have several that are out-of-print. Instead of making the book less valuable, the fact that it is now more exclusive gives you a way to market it so that it attracts more attention. You can talk about how it is now out-of-print and a very rare book. You can talk about how the paper it is printed on is indicative of its age or specialness, or even the typeset. Of course you have to educate your buyer so that they understand why you are selling the item as a special buy.

The more detail you give out about what makes this product unique, the more you will start to convince the reader that this is indeed a unique buying opportunity. If you happen to know how many other similar items exist in the world, then this is definitely information you need to relay to the reader to provide proof of exclusivity. For instance, say you are selling a stamp with a defect. You know that there were only so many of these stamps issued before the mistake was caught and corrected. Maybe you know how many people actually own a similar stamp. The thing is you want to include some actual numbers to make it obvious why this is a very exclusive stamp and exactly how much it has appreciated over time.

You can also include this strategy by targeting your collectors for the sale of the exclusive items as well as the limited editions. These are the people who are most motivated to make sure they have all of the models that come out of a specific product, so even though it may be a little more than they're willing to spend, it might just complete their collection or make it ultra-special. So, send out the notice of your exclusive item to your die-hard collectors first to see if you get any bites.

Finally, if you can point out an additional feature that brings your product exceptional value because it will never be created again, then you have a very exclusive item. Examples of this are books signed by dead authors. Obviously, you won't find new ones being created if the author is dead. That means that the signed copy is much more distinguished for its peer of unsigned copies because it also holds memorabilia in the form of a signature from a person of note.

Remember to price your item accordingly. If you say only six copies exist or will be made, you shouldn't come up with a seventh. It destroys your reputation completely as a reputable dealer. It may seem like a great idea to create more because people are paying such exorbitant prices for the few you did sell, but the only reason they did so was because they were convinced it was completely unique and exclusive. If later new ones come off the production line, they are bound to get very angry with you and even potentially sue you for false advertising.

To give the experience of having purchased something completely out-of-the-ordinary, you want to make sure it comes in special packaging. Like a diamond ring comes in a velvet box, you want to make sure your exclusive offers come packaged in high quality materials. Many times people who collect exclusive items won't even remove the packaging and it is more valuable this way. So, to give them the experience of having bought something special also remember to include special packaging.

One way to imprint the degree of specialness on the experience of owning something is to combine it with a certificate of authenticity. This is done with very exclusive prints that may only be sold in very small quantities. Even Franklin Mint will send certificates that come with the package to make sure that if the owner wants to resell the product that they can prove it is truly a Franklin Mint special edition.

Timing this strategy

The time to bring up the actual exclusivity of a product is actually before the sale, although that's not the only time when you will impact the buyer with the fact that they've made a special purchase. You want to be sure to frame the offer to show exactly how special your item is and give that as the reason why the buyer shouldn't delay on their decision to buy. If they hesitate, the opportunity will be lost and they'll never have another chance to buy the same item again!

The other time to make sure the buyer knows they've bought something special is after they've received the item. It should make them feel special when they get it. Otherwise, they will feel ripped off instead of recognized as the smart buyer they want to be. So, always seek to add special packaging, quality materials, and even certificates of authenticity whenever possible. They should have the experience that this is truly a product that stands out as one of a kind and extremely valuable and rare.

Tell them it's urgent

If you let your sales prospect leave to think over your sales promotion, odds are you've lost the sale. The main reason for this is that you didn't include a sense of urgency in your offer, and if you did, the sales prospect might have still hesitated at the end. If you've already raised the objections and resolved them and done some emotional salesmanship, then, why isn't your prospect ready to pull out their wallet now? You may not have relayed a sense of urgency crucial for them to make up their minds while you have them in your sight.

Think of it this way. If you are trying to get immediate action or attention from a crowd of people, you might try saying: "Excuse, excuse me..." into a nearby microphone. Odds, are they will ignore you and go about their business. However, if you were to grab the microphone and yell, "Fire!" you can bet you've instigated immediate attention and action.

Similarly, you want your offers to light that fire under your sales prospects so they don't think they have time to ponder your offer. They must make up their minds right then and there. This dramatically increases the probability that you will close that sale.

The strategic plan

There's basically two themes to this strategy. You are either trying to light a fire at the beginning of the sales presentation or you are trying to overcome a final objection with a sense of urgency.

In the first case, where you are trying to light a fire at the beginning of the presentation, the idea is to make your sales offer dramatic and instantly appealing. That doesn't mean that you have to focus on positive aspects, as fear can also be a powerful motivator to buy. But, you do want to provoke a powerful emotional response that invokes the potential for a huge loss if the person doesn't take immediate action.

No one likes to feel like they are losing something because they weren't bold enough to take action now. You also want them to become engaged in the buying experience so that they want to become the hero of their own drama and resolve that problem that's plagued them and driven them to your sales page. However, if you don't bolster their courage or show them that it is possible, then they might feel strange jumping up to grab your offer, even if emotionally they are ready to do so. So, give them a little push.

One of the best ways to create a sense of urgency to give a time limit to the offer or make it a special "introductory" offer. The time limited offers will work for new and existing customers, whereas the introductory offer is great for people who are new to your site and may need a push to commit to the first sale. Either way, the way this strategy would work is that you are creating an expectation of loss if the person doesn't take you up on their offer at that moment. In the case of an introductory offer, it may be one-time available to people who subscribe to your mailing list. If they don't take you up on it then, later the same offer will be priced much higher.

In the case of the limited offers, the loss expressed may be that you won't be able to even offer the same package at a later date. Once it's sold out, it's gone. Or, once the time limit is reached, you'll no longer offer that package again at that price. Here the loss is expressed as either a price or an opportunity to own a particular product package. So, the sense of urgency is increased dramatically when there is a potential for loss either in monetary or opportunity.

In the second case, you have just sold Mrs. Smith on a great new dishwasher, when she says she wants to go home and think about it or discuss it with her husband. If you let Mrs. Smith walk out and do not resolve that objection with a sense of urgency, you've lost the sale. The second case is much trickier to implement, and we will go over it more in depth in the implementation segment, however, you will want to make sure that you direct a sense of urgency and a personal sense of loss to the potential buyer considering buying your product. Otherwise, once you make it personal, they won't need anyone else's opinion to decide whether the purchase is a good idea or not. Empower them to make their own buying decisions!

The psychological triggers

The species as a whole is programmed to avoid loss and danger, otherwise, we'd have had a tough time staying alive. So, subconsciously we are constantly monitoring our environment for cues that might suggest that we could be in danger or that we will be experiencing a dramatic loss and to flee or evade the problem as quickly as possible.

And, in fact, our nervous system is fine-tuned to make us react much more quickly at signs of danger or loss. You hear the stories of the mothers who have lifted whole cars off their babies who got caught underneath in superhuman efforts of strength and courage. Why? The idea of the loss of their child was so unbearable that nervous system kicked in to give them the boost they needed to overcome that problem. It made them act in bolder ways to take action immediately.

While losing money or an opportunity can't be compared with the potential of losing a child, the same dynamics are at play. It creates a sense of urgency if there is a possible loss of money or opportunity. The greater the potential loss, the more the nervous system kicks in to take immediate action. That's why most financial experts warn that people are risk adverse and shouldn't watch the stock market. If they do and see their investments drop substantially, they pull their money out instead of waiting for the market to correct. That's because the loss triggered a subconscious risk that caused them to take immediate and usually a highly emotional action, rather than to think the other options out.

This works for sales because if you give your prospect time to think about the other options, odds are they'll either think up more objections to your products or decide to buy someone else's product. It may not even be a better product, just better marketed. If they aren't given a reason in every single presentation why they shouldn't walk away and think about, this can be the most damaging of objections to your sales effort because once you are out of sight, it's guaranteed you are out of mind! All that effort for nothing!

How to implement effectively

Your sales copy will have to invoke a sense of urgency since you do not have the prospect in front of you as in a retail store situation. You can do this as boldly or as subtly as you like. You can simply call some offers "introductory" and not say anything about whether the price will change or not, however, just that word implies something will change down the line. Or you can very clearly state that it is a one-time or time limited offer as a more direct way of creating urgency.

However, there are even more creative ways you can invoke a sense of loss that have nothing to do with time. That's what makes them so effective. You aren't necessarily rushing anyone, but the implication is that if they don't rush themselves, they will experience a loss that may be unrecoverable. An example of this would be if you have a product that is giving companies who buy it a competitive edge. So, you can explain how everyone uses it and why it increases productivity and provides that competitive edge. Then, you can suggest all of the major players who have bought your product and how the sales prospect shouldn't delay, so as to remain competitive in their business. Well, there is no actual time frame that you've mentioned or a time limit on your offer, but you've very effectively lit a fire under most business owner's butts due to the potential for loss of business to other well-equipped establishments.

Another way to invoke a sense of urgency is when it's a matter of style or status. When is the best time to get something novel that really sets you above your peers? When the product first comes out. If it is predicted to be a hot seller, then you have to get one before it sells out! This marketing strategy can even help with pre-sales, so that you can reserve orders before the product is even out. If people think the demand will be huge, you can even sell the reservation by asking them to put money down to hold their order and guarantee delivery by a certain date.

This type of logic is also used when marketers say: "Be the first to own this fully loaded cell phone." Or, whatever the product might be. They are hoping to increase your sense of urgency by getting people to jostle for being the first in line to buy their product. After all, once everyone has one then it's not such a big deal anymore and the urgency is lost.

Framing your offer in a way that creates some impulse to take the action to buy when the copy is read is very important to online sales. If you don't get that urgency across, people will drift off to some other site or activity and may even forget where they last saw that offer.

In retail sales, one of the worst objections one can hear is the person who insists that before they can buy something they have to check with their spouse. Why? Well, it puts the marketer in the difficult position of being completely unable to create that sense of urgency to make the purchase while they are still standing there. In those situations, if the marketer doesn't act fast, they will lose the sale for sure. So, that's when they have to get a bit personal. They have to be a little bold too. They might even dare to ask the person if their husband or wife makes all their buying decisions for them? They may want to know if the husband or wife checks with them in all their major purchases too? Or, they might want to know if it's really necessary to get approval for a purchase that may have nothing to do with a spouse.

Now, you would think that getting nosy and personal is going to have a poor reaction. It might, but you know already that if you let that person leave your store with that objection, you've lost the sale for sure. So, what do you have to lose?

Online, the same strategy isn't as important since you aren't face-to-face with a person, but even so, you want to make sure that the visitor understands why it is personally important for them to make that purchase now, without checking in with others. This is easy to do if the products are gender-based like woman's toiletries or men's ties. You make sure your customer is aware that women with taste or men with sense know that it is a great deal that they shouldn't pass up!

Timing this strategy

This is one strategy that should ALWAYS be attempted in conjunction with other strategies. It certainly can't hurt to try and light a fire under your sales prospect's rear end to get them to buy.

Gain trust with your credentials

Now, if you make an offer (no matter how incredibly good it may be), you won't attract sales if no one believes you can deliver what you offered. That's because people need to trust you before they will make a purchase from you. And, if the purchase is something that appears too good to be true, and they don't know you, they simply won't believe you are telling the truth.

Like any relationship, you have to build trust over time by delivering what you promise. So, what can you do for those that have yet to buy and haven't even entered into a commercial relationship with you? Well, you can flash your credentials!

Have you ever noticed that when people find out you are a doctor, they automatically assume you are smarter and richer than the average person? That's because your profession gives you credentials to be a person of integrity and a productive member of society. Education is one way that people flash credentials, by putting the initials to their degrees next to their names. There are certain ways to establish your credentials with your website audience that can be used to get them to trust you more and, thus, help you make the sale.

The strategic plan

The nature of this strategy is to create a tone of authenticity and authority. You want to sound believable, educated, maybe even an expert about a particular topic related to your market niche. When people find someone who they can trust to tell them the truth exactly like it is, then they are more easily influenced into following the advice that person gives.

You will want to invoke associations that enhance your image as a knowledgeable and credible person and reduce the associations to those things that may impinge on your good name. Both of these aspects are looked at quite closely when a customer is trying to make a decision whether you are steering them in the right direction or just trying to make a fast buck.

You will have to pay attention to the language that you use in your sales copy. It shouldn't contain any outrageous claims or even untruthful exaggerations. You want to highlight the benefits of your product or service, but in a manner that comes off as genuine, not hyped.

There are a number of different ways to implement this strategy, to help you build your credibility quickly and effectively, however, the strategy is still the same. You want to remove the objections in your customers mind to the possibility that they are being taken for a ride or influenced in underhanded ways. You do this by seeking to make sure your transactions always have a high degree of integrity from sale to delivery, and that you back everything with your good name.

The psychological triggers

This strategy works because we are conditioned to trust those people who have certain authority over us. As children, our parents are invested with that authority and we're taught to believe everything they say, and more importantly, that they have our good interest at heart. That is where we first learn to trust in an authority figure.

Later, we learn that this same dynamic extends to our bosses, our spouses, and even to people with education or some measure of success in their lives. We assume that if someone has made it to a certain level in society than their word tends to carry weight because they are more experienced and know how to ride the rapids of life. So, we may be automatically triggered to respect an authority figure, but that doesn't necessarily mean we automatically trust them.

Unless you are co-dependent, most people will make other people earn their trust in order engage a healthy relationship. No one wants to be used or abused by people in authority, just because they claim to know better for us. In those instances, we may be triggered, but we can also completely rebel against the idea and dig in our heels and refuse to comply with the direction given. And, that's a perfectly healthy reaction to protect the person from being taken advantage of.

Similarly, online sales people may expound on their credentials all day long and even impress their visitors, but they still have to put their money where their mouth is and act with integrity to gain their trust. If someone hasn't directly interacted with you, than they may decide to ask someone else whether you deliver what you promise. That's called a referral and is another way credibility is built. So, even though you have no direct history with someone it doesn't mean you can't create the atmosphere necessary to get people to trust you enough to buy from you.

You can do that by paying close attention to the image you project online. You have to make sure that it is as authentic to the products and services that you promote. That means that if you sell sports gear and you've never even picked up a tennis racket in your life or played a team sport, you will be completely lacking in credibility unless you get other noted sports figures to become your spokesperson. Then, your business has more credibility even though you personally may have none in that particular niche market.

So, authenticity is the name of the game in Web 2.0 online businesses. You will see this becoming more and more important as social networking takes over the Internet. When people social network, they talk to each other based on friendships they've developed with people they trust.

So, when they go out to buy something they often know at least someone online who can give them a good idea of whether your claims are credible and your business trustworthy. If you scam people, odds are in this Internet age, your online business will not last long. People tend to notify and warn people in their circle of friends quite quickly in social networking sites and can directly impact your bottom line.

How to implement effectively

So, the first thing you want to do is make sure that the copy on your site is truthful. No claims that cannot be supported. If you say free delivery, then keep to your word and don't sneak in a shipping and handling fee. Next, you will want to keep away from marketing clichés that give people the impression of the snake oil vendors of the past. Its one thing to make a claim that may seem unbelievable, but can be backed by hard facts, and quite another just to splatter outrageous claims all over your website without trying to justify them.

That brings us to the next thing you need to do to implement this strategy. That is, you need to handle the customer's objections, which might be in their mind, as efficiently and accurately as possible. If one of the objections is that the price is too high, then don't try to hide that fact, but justify why it is high in a credible way. If the sales prospect may still have problems believing the claims, which are indeed true, then you need to trot out the authority figures, whether you or someone else.

Take for instance a product that is a medical device of some sort and it claims to get rid of acne or some such thing, then you will want to be able to back that claim with either a doctor's credentials or clinical trials. Use the types of credentials that our society agrees gives one authority: degrees, awards, and even personal success. If it is an info- product that shows how you made money on the Internet, you had better be able to pull out whatever evidence to show that you were indeed highly successful using those methods, whether it is bank statements or you annual statement for PayPal.

You can build up an image of an expert on the Internet very quickly. That's because content is so important to drive search engine results. If you know that your market niche is being heavily searched by surfers, you can start to write multiple articles and submit them to article directories to create a bigger name for yourself online. Many of these article directories allow you a resource box that you can put your website address in to bring in traffic from these sites. This serves a two-fold purpose: you become an instant expert on the Internet, and you drive more traffic to your site. It's a great way to build credibility.

If you still have trouble building some credibility, then think about writing free guest posts for sites that already have a big audience and a high degree of credibility. By doing so, you gain traffic and polish up your online image by associating with noted experts or successful online marketers or bloggers. In this way, they lend you some of their credibility for contributing to their site. You can also do mini versions of this by simply commenting on open blogs with informational comments that make you look good. Don't forget to add a link to your site to generate more traffic too!

If you don't have time for all that, you can simply pay someone to endorse your products, as mentioned earlier. You can do this by using celebrity endorsements or simply getting someone in the business with great credibility to write a review of your site or products. Once they give their endorsement, their credibility rubs off on you, virtually overnight! A limited version of this is to pay people to let you advertise on their sites with a link back to your site. They aren't necessarily endorsing you, but the association with their site will reap a similar effect, just watered down somewhat.

Certain geographical regions might lend more credibility to a product than others. For instance, remember when made in Japan made it was junk? Well, when cars started rolling off the Asian assembly lines the fact that they were imported from Japan finally gave them more credibility, not less, but it took time for that impression of trustworthiness to seep into the cultural consciousness. Also, you know that certain places are known for having excellent products – like wine from France and cheese from Wisconsin. If you are selling items that can gain credibility from their place of origin, be sure to mention it! Even your company can gain credibility at times from its place of business, just like the best publishing houses are all known to reside in New York City.

One thing to remember is that if you are the expert on your products, than you know what makes them so special and such a good deal. All you have to do is be able to convey that to your customers in a genuine and friendly fashion for them to start believing it too. And, when the sale is made, don't stop there! Be sure that you pay the same attention to the integrity of the entire sales process so that your customers will know that your word means something and they can expect to get exactly what you promised or you will make good on it. That type of customer service will have them coming back over and over and referring all their friends to you too!

Timing this strategy

You will need to work a little to get this strategy going. It should be planned for even before you have a website up and running and selling products. You should start building your professional image immediately online through social networking sites, building an expert blog, and writing articles if you expect to use your own image to sell your products.

Obviously, your credentials can be added to with every achievement in your life. Be sure to add multiple online profiles that talk about your achievements all with links back to the website when it goes up. Always continue to update your credentials every time you receive some new recognition, award, degree, or have a very successful campaign! The name of the game is to toot your own horn!

You should also have an "About Me" section in all of your websites to make sure people know you are trustworthy. Include that information in the copy too, if you are using this strategy to invoke authority and credibility to sell your products. It should be easy to find this information almost immediately if that's the impact you want to make.

This is a never ending process once you start as your image is what is being used to sell your products, you will want to protect it. You need to constantly monitor your affiliates, your customer service representatives, and your own claims to make sure they are truthful and trustworthy people. Associate with the wrong crowd for too long, and the reputation can shift just like the tail winds of a hurricane. So, keep at it and you can reap a sterling reputation that helps sell your products simply through the virtue of honesty and integrity.

Make it cozy and familiar

As we have already discussed, you can often sell things through the associations you make with it. Now we are going to discuss how linking your product to things that are familiar to your customers can help to breed a cozy familiarity that is appealing. For products that are new, it can even be a way to overcome the resistance to buying if you link the product with something they already know.

One of the easiest ways to do this type of association is to link your products to some cultural phenomena or fad that is currently in the forefront of the mass consciousness. Once it is associated with some fad, by default your product also gains tremendous popularity along with the fad. However, you do have to be careful that when a trend ends, that your sales don't dwindle too. The positive aspects of linking to a popular subject are obvious, but the negative aspects can sometimes be ignored and impact your sales. So, remain aware that you always have to understand that linking your product to other cultural trends works both ways.

The strategic plan

You will want to identify what trends are foremost in the mind of your visitors. They could be cultural, ethnic, behavioral, or simply a shift in the public's awareness. As an example, if you are selling kid's toys and there is a popular television series that has enormous popularity, if you can link your product to this series, you will experience good growth in your sales.

Your product doesn't even have to be directly related to the event that you are exploiting, for it to work. As long as it draws attention – even controversy – to your sales ad. Online controversy is a sure way to gain attention even if it can be explosive. If you understand how to manipulate a controversy to your advantage, you can even use these controversies to sell your products. At the very least, you will increase your site's traffic.

Sometimes an event is a good thing to link your products to, like a historical event. This is actually done around major holidays when all sort of Christmas-themed wares and/or gifts show up in the stores. But, beyond the holidays there are events that can influence your visitors to buy your products: Earth Day for greenies, for instance.

Highly controversial or anticipated events can be great product promoters. The American national elections, for instance, is a giant boom for people who sell items with logos. Now, they can sell T-shirts, bumper stickers, and all sorts of different types of products by linking them to either the Republican or the Democratic candidates. As different controversies erupt over the candidates it can be a gold mine for people who want to show their party loyalties through the products they buy.

But, this strategy isn't just relegated to fads and controversies, it's also about making new products or unusual products more familiar and cozy. An example of this is an ad that was printed in the past selling smoke detectors that look intimidatingly high-tech which compared it to a very sensitive nose. Suddenly, the smoke detector wasn't so odd and frightening, but rather familiar to the average human being. In the process, the smoke alarm is reframed to something that a person can rely on every day to keep them out of danger without being too concerned about the mechanics of it.

The psychological triggers

By associating products with things that already are prominently within the conscious mind of your buyers, it captures more attention from your market. Our minds are constantly filtering out vast amounts of input from many different sources: the media, our friends and relatives, and even the Internet. We have learned to multitask quite well, but at the same time we don't quite pay full attention to everything that comes across our visual screen. So, in order to really grab our attention something has to trigger either a deep familiarity to bypass the filters that throw out garbage inputs, or it has to stir such a controversy that it produces an emotional impact that also busts through your thinking filters.

Human beings are also creatures of habit. They go to sleep on the same side of the bed every night and wake up and brush their teeth in the morning without fail. This type of routine is comforting to people and helps people to manage their lives, their emotions, and their thoughts. Once you've got an established lifestyle that makes you comfortable, you are pretty set in your ways and typically don't want to mess up a good thing. So, why would you switch from your morning cup of coffee to some other beverage? Why would you opt to eat a new toaster croissant, when your old bagels are just as yummy and you've been eating them for years? The fact is that people won't just jump to try new things without first deciding whether they even understand why they'd want to in the first place. The familiarity of the old things are comforting and it takes a lot of momentum to change to something new.

That's why linking new products to old things that are familiar works to sell them better. You're not really selling a new, strange, animal that no one has ever used before, you're selling an improved version of the same, old, classic, and dependable item they've come to know and love. You aren't just asking them to believe you that this new thing will make their lives better, they already know it has and now they can even improve that experience up a notch too. This makes new things that may be difficult to sell because of their strange new offering a much more appealing prospect.

Linking also works on the memory as this is exactly how people recall things in their long-term memory, by linking them to other memories that are more easily recalled. So, even if you don't sell the prospect immediately, your sales ad makes an emotional impact on the psyche that is stored much longer in the memory of the reader and more easily recalled later.

Finally, associating your products with dramatic events or culturally recognized phenomena also lends your products an air of controversy. For those that harbor the inner rebel, they will jump on your band wagon just to be included as part of that anti-culture movement. So, even for those that think they are evading the propensity of human beings to stick with what they know, this strategy can work by linking the product to the thing they know and dislike and then providing it as part of the anti-culture solution.

How to implement effectively

There are various ways to implement this strategy. For a new product that has unbelievable claims because it is so novel, you'll want to link it to something familiar and comforting. These types of items shouldn't be linked with controversy because they're controversial enough.

For existing products that you just want to build a campaign employing this strategy, you can brainstorm all of the current events, cultural phenomena, news items and fads that might be able to be used to sell this product. If you are trying to sell a product with a new feature you can link it to the old product or something familiar to help them accept the new feature.

A more subtle way to associate something that's familiar with a positive framework is to use common items that are held in high esteem to get the message across that this is something worthwhile to possess. For example, the words diamond, gold, and platinum are used in a variety of products and even memberships to link those qualities associated with these items to other products and services. Ever hear of platinum spark plugs? They go for about $60 each. That's what the power of a little clever linking can do for you. It can not only make something seem more familiar, but it also gets some of the same aura of qualities of the items you've associated with it. So, in a sense, you've manipulated the potential buyer's perception of quality by associating it with familiar, but luxurious, elements in nature.

If you can use some of the terms that are being used in the fad to help link your item to the more popular item, it will be easily associated and understood to be linking to it. Like when Star Wars was big, anything that used some of the classic sayings of this blockbuster film was instantly recognized. Yoda sayings in particular were an excellent way to tie into popular culture and still be able to use them in your marketing efforts. Spoofs and take-offs from the saying "The force is with you" were humorous and eye-catching.

The way this strategy can really take off is if you link to something that is in the current news media. If there is a controversy over some news piece, like when women burned their bras, then link your product or service to that particular controversy to get some instant media attention. You don't even have to be for or against the controversy or in women's lingerie. When women burned their bras there were even pizza places baking pizzas shaped like bras, in order to garner attention – and, it worked!

So, while you want to associate with different cultural phenomena, even controversy, it doesn't have to be all that serious. You don't have to take sides, and often it's better if you don't. If you take one side, you lose the other side as potential customers. So, the best way to implement this is to make a social statement without offending people while you are at it.

Timing this strategy

This strategy is reserved for when you are making the pitch for your product or service. You can't really link two things together, if one of the items (your product) remains an unknown. So, there is a bit of a tightrope you are walking here. You want to associate with some powerful symbol in the mass media, but you don't necessarily want it to overwhelm your sales pitch. Remember that the reason you are using the strategy is to sell your product or service, not to promote some cause or movie.

So, this strategy works well as press releases and other mass media items that draw attention, but also talk about your own product too. You can continue to use the same strategy on your sales page, but also list all the benefits of your product and use the strategy to introduce your product first. That way, people who found out about your product from searching for terms related to the mass symbol, will be able to quickly shift from that thing to your own products and services with a great degree of familiarity and comfort. If done correctly, this strategy is a smooth way to lead huge amounts of traffic from other sites to your sales pages.

Connect them with their people

Innate in the human culture is the desire to belong. Whether we want to belong to our families, our heritage, our country, or some other group, the desire is very strong and appealing. And, in sales, when you create an image of a particular brand the people who end up buying that comprise a status group of peers with like-minded values. This can be very attractive to people who seek always to establish a connection that affirms their own identities.

In social networking, the number one reason people are engaged on these sites is their desire to express their identity. Part of that is joining groups of like-minded souls, frequenting places that these people go, and even buying the same things these people buy. So, even though the action may be instigated by their own identity, the final strong desire is a need to belong.

The strategic plan

If you understand this basic need to belong, and you know what products your visitors are buying, you can easily provide the solution for that need by highlighting all qualities that take into account that particular group's identity. In addition, once you understand which demographic your potential buyer belongs to, you also know by association which other products and services would appeal to them. So, you can increase your sales just with this one insight and by facilitating the ability for people to identify with their preferred groups. And, once you have a large grouping of people or products with brands that reflect a certain set of people's values or aspirations, then this will draw even more people to the offer who are completely invested in belonging to that particular group.

So, you do need to do research on the demographics of your visitors. If you are already in business, you will have a good idea what sorts of values and services they are buying into. This will give you an idea of the type of grouping that might be the people they wish to identify with. Of course, just because one belongs to a particular group because of personal demographics, it doesn't necessarily mean that is the group they want to be associated with when buying. It just gives you a starting point.

For instance, in the 2008 United States elections, the Democratic Party was always associated with equal opportunity. They had several candidates running for the party's nomination, from a black man to a woman. The Republicans were seen as less for equal opportunity until they put a woman on the ticket for their vice-presidential candidate. If this were a sale and the product is the presidency, what they are doing is trying to get the swing voters, independents and democrats, to identify more with their party through adding a female as a statement on equal opportunity. They know that the demographic of swing voters are mostly white, older, women who are not happy with Hillary Clinton not being on the Democratic ticket. So, even though that's the demographic, they included a young, white, woman to the description of the ticket to stir up excitement for the Republican ticket, not just from older white women, but from younger voters too.

Similarly, luxury products may be primarily aimed at wealthy buyers, but there is a whole class of people who would like to be associated with the affluent, whether they have the budget for it or not. So, the starting point is the demographic of people who are considered affluent, since they need to be connected to their status group. However, in advertising and marketing, you also have to make it easier for those that want to identify with the group, but lack a key demographic trait to make the switch too.

You can do this either by branding a line of products, with the potential to increase your association as your circumstances change, or by clearly defining the values and qualities of that product with the people who buy it. Then, you continue to cultivate that connection by offering other products and services that those people associate with the grouping of people that they desire to be a part of.

The psychological triggers

There's a number of reasons this strategy is so effective. The most obvious is the natural desire to be accepted as part of a group to increase your chances of prospering, both socially and financially. When times are really tough, that's when people gather together into like-minded groups for the sake of survival. That's what the basic family unit is all about, and that dynamic lasts until the day we take our last breath. A person without friends is a person who more than likely feels worthless. And, a person with many friends who affirm their identity, is a very blessed person indeed.

There are even scientific studies that show that our ability to heal and the joy we have in our lives is directly related to how many social interactions we maintain. People with a wide circle of friends, connections from church, family, and even professional organizations, can withstand the low periods in life much better than those without this type of emotional support in their lives. So, when someone feels they are identified with a particular group and are accepted with in it, it builds their confidence, their self-esteem, and increases their joy in life. Some medical studies even suggest it boosts their immune systems.

All of these things are felt emotionally as a very huge degree of satisfaction, and it's that feeling that is what pulls in prospects when you use this strategy. It makes them feel affirmed, connected, confident, and worthy to be included in the group of buyers who can achieve to own that particular thing you've associated with a status group.

Then, there is the interesting dynamic of camouflage that exists in nature and the human species. When, you don't have what it takes to actually belong to a particular group (like a chameleon that wants to be a part of a particular environment, but is really just a lizard), then the next best thing is to fake it to fool people into believing you actually are a twig, a leaf, or a high-status achiever. Even if you don't really belong to that group, the fact that you are identified with it confers on you the same privileges and status, and sometimes connections, which the others who do truly belong there get. That can heftily increase the probability of enhancing and later confirming an image of success.

How to implement effectively

The key to implementing this strategy in a way that wows your customers is to treat them as if they already belong to the group they desire to be a part of. If they aren't particularly wealthy, but they are looking to buy a luxury car from you, then being treated as such will help to build the desire to make the purchase from you and really belong to the group.

Another way to do this is that when someone buys a brand that is associated with a particular group, like greenies who like conservation and saving the rain forest, then you have a very good idea of what else they would like. You should suggest those items to them, and in fact, you can do it even before the sale is finalized. You suggest products that complement the sale or you can even show how some of the other products you sell also go towards saving the rain forest. You can even ask them to upgrade to be more ecologically conscious.

Let's face it, we tend to like to join cliques of people who can agree with most of our values, even if we don't really have the credentials to belong. Like a person who goes in to buy a luxury car without enough money to finance the purchase, they don't want to be called out for being somewhere they don't belong. Instead, they want to be accepted for the part so much, that they will sometimes even make the sale to prove they belong and can work the part.

You can implement this strategy when you decide to create lists of people to market specific products or brands online. You can have different mailings go to different groupings, each one stating how the new products or services you are offering help them to identify more with their status group. A very powerful technique to then implement is peer pressure. Suggest that other people who bought a particular item also found that they desired other items. You can even purchase marketing lists from people, if you want to include direct mail in your campaigns, that help you to target specific groups, and cross-reference them with other lists or groupings too.

One can't really leave this conversation, without mentioning how social networking has become the cornerstone of this strategy online. Social networking sites like Facebook are set up to neatly get people joining into circle of friends with similar interests. As you start establishing profiles on these sites, you begin to notice that some friends all use the same applications or enjoy putting similar items on their profiles. This gives you great insight into the types of items that they might purchase, if given the chance. While you can't solicit people on social networking sites effectively, you can create links on your profile to offers that are targeted to help these people find a product or service that is branded for their interests.

You can also set up different groups and there you can solicit and market people more than on individual profiles. Social Ads in Facebook are a very finely tuned way to market specific demographics of people and connect them with the offers that help them to identify with their people.

If you can offer your customers something that allows them to flaunt their peer status, this can also help you finalize the offer. This is how education, such as degrees and certificates, are sold. People want to connect with other people who have similar interests and learn and grow more through them. But, when it comes time to use it, they want that sheepskin so they can tell everyone that they are an accomplished member of a specific and special group, and they now have the credentials to prove it.

So, if you are selling items like workshops or online courses, it helps to give out certificates of accomplishment that people can display to others. Online, you can even make up virtual badges and awards that people can post on their electronic profiles or web pages, that show they have become a member of a prestigious group, even if the only qualification is to simply buy a product from you. Then, you can amp that marketing strategy even more by providing a link back to your products, services, or website from the virtual award or badge. This generates more traffic for you and more chances to sell based on this strategy, since it will attract just the sort of people that this appeals to.

Timing this strategy

Since this strategy works through the power of image, you can use it practically anywhere in the sales cycle. You can sell pre-sales by the use of badges or sending specific notices to potential demographics and telling them the reason they were singled out is because they belong on your list. Maybe you were looking for engineers, nurses, or greenies, it doesn't matter. They'll be flattered to be recognized for being a part of that particular social identity and will give your offer serious thought.

You can use it on the sales page in your list of benefits. You can use it as an introductory offer to specific people who meet certain criteria. You can offer it as part of the incentive to join your special forums and groups, to meet up with like-minded folks. Then, you can market those groups quite easily for specific products and services that enhance that image.

You can set up profiles on social networking sites and create articles that highlight your own association with a particular group, making you an expert within the group. Once you create a circle of friends who are totally in line with that social peer group, you can start to bridge them to your website or to an intermediary blog where you can actually market them.

Finally, don't forget that you can add suggestions in emails, on the order form, and even the thank you page after an order is filled out. This strategy is so powerful that the more you use it, the more the buyers actually like it. They never get tired of it because it affirms their personal identities. So, unlike other strategies that needs specific timing and locations, this one is one that can be used anywhere and anytime with astounding results.

Ultimate Traffic Part III - Prospect to Customer

Add a touch of guilt

Most friendships or transactions work on an ideal of reciprocity.

When someone does something for you, you know there is an underlying expectation that the favor will someday be returned. In capitalism, when we go out and buy something, we typically exchange cash for a purchase. So the ideal of reciprocity exists in the commerce system too. Since that is the way we live, it often brings out a feeling of guilt if we take something and don't give something in return. That's the basis of this next strategy that can be used to trigger behavior to help you market and sell your products online.

The strategic plan

In order to trigger a sense of guilt that leads to a purchase, you have to frame your sales offer in a way that brings out the ideal of reciprocity in the sales prospect, in a very subtle way. If you actually try to guilt trip them in obvious manners, this strategy can backfire as no one likes to be manipulated. So, while you are going to actually do things that seem like a "nice extra" to your customer, it's actually going to send out the message: "I've scratched your back, now you scratch mine."

Now, some people are much more guilt-prone than others, even if everyone holds a basic ideal of a fair exchange. On the Internet, in particular, there are hordes of people who want offers for free and have no shame taking them without giving anything of value in return. These people are even as shameless as providing sham email addresses in exchange for free newsletter or reports that they can't get otherwise. Once they receive the free products, they simply destroy the "throw-away" email. And, there's little guilt involved. So, you want to be able to target people who not only feel a little guilt at receiving free offers, but it will also trigger buying behavior too. The most effective way to use guilt is to create an invisible lasso of obligation that literally pulls the prospective buyer to close on your offer.

Then, there are many others who appear immune to your tries to guilt-trip them into buying. That's because of the way people have become quite jaded about returning anything of value for a free offer, and so you have to work harder by repeating free offers, and also you have to vary the offers too. A free newsletter in exchange for an email may have worked in the past, but now it's not as easy to start putting people in a sales funnel as easily. So, you need to be creative in the freebies you give and how they are procured.

You do want whatever you decide to giveaway, whether it is a stamp, a coupon, or an expensive briefcase to have something to do with the product you are trying to sell, even though any small gift in the right setting can help you to sell anything through bribing people into a state of compliance and provide you an interested ear for your sales offers.

The psychological triggers

The pull of a bribe is so powerful that there are even laws against it in social and corporate politics. A bribe is usually something someone gives you with an underlying expectation that in the future you will do something that they want you to do. It is usually done with a basic understanding that you are willing to give favoritism in exchange for a gift. Well, that's really not far from what you're attempting to do here, except it's perfectly legal in some cases. You don't want to violate any ethical or legal provisions, if you are dealing with clients who can't receive gifts, but other than that, it's up to you to decide what you want to give away.

Generally, the bigger a gift is, the more sense of obligation people perceive they have towards you. So, if you are trying to sell something large, like a timeshare, the gift tends to be free weekends at a resort. These are large gifts that prime you into feeling cheap if at the end of your stay, you refuse to sign on the dotted line to buy the timeshare at the resort. However, you'll notice they call it a "free stay" and that the only obligation is that you attend a sales seminar at the end. That really puts the hint in prospective buyer's head that it really isn't free, even if it is labeled free.

People also like to reciprocate in kind. That means, if someone lends you money, they usually want to pay you back with money. On the other hand, if they help you to move your household goods when you buy a house, the underlying expectation is that when they move, you will be there for them too. Money is not the underlying expectation. So, you want to set up the offer so that they understand how they are reciprocating in kind, and then ask them for that sale.

Just in case they don't get it the first time, you can give them multiple gifts and built up the sense of guilt over time.

They will either think you are one of the nicest sites online or that they really should start thinking about buying from you to pay you back before the subconscious guilt becomes overwhelming.

How to implement effectively

In order to see how to implement this strategy, there are many examples in sales you can review. The idea of salespeople taking their clients to lunch or dinner is a form of this strategy that makes the clients more susceptible to closing a sale. Another example is when you get a free newspaper, without obligation to buy. You'll see these stands at different venues like grocery stores. There, a person asks if you'd like a free newspaper. Then, when you go to pick it up, they ask you if you have a subscription and engage you in a sales transaction. It should be pretty obvious that you don't have a subscription, otherwise, you wouldn't bother to pick up a newspaper, but the idea isn't to determine whether you have it, but to engage you in a conversation that leads to them presenting their subscription offers. All for the price of a free newspaper that they hope will guilt you into buying the subscription.

Similarly, you want your freebie to be a segue way into your offers. You also want something that can stimulate the desire to buy as well as guilting people into it. Then, it can be a very powerful strategy.

For instance, sometimes you will get free stands or display cases for people who sell collector's items. The bigger and more elegant the display case, the more likely that you will not only feel pleasure, but also a certain amount of guilt for having received such a nice gift. The combination of these two emotions will lead you to buy more from the company, not only to pay them back but to also show off your collection in that really nice display case.

Charities know how to use this strategy quite well. They will send out mailings asking for donations and include small gifts like stamps, stickers, or even address labels within the mailing. Not only are people more likely to open the mailing to get to the goodies, but they are also more likely to donate too.

Online, you can use the same strategy by offering to give people free information in the form of reports or newsletters. You can even use email to send out weekly messages that can either be entertaining or informational. Just be sure that people have given you permission to be contacted by email so that it doesn't get you into trouble. This develops a relationship with your subscription holders. If your information proves to be valuable or entertaining people will want to read it and then you can market them for other offers.

In order to keep the freebie on target, they generally contain information that is in accordance with your market niche. That way, it not only gives the buyer a sense of guilt but also primes the way for other products like eBooks. You can even advertise other offers within the reports to help set the stage to sell them.

Software sellers know how to use this strategy pretty well by allowing people to download either demo versions or free trials so that the potential customer gets to experience the product for a short time or on a limited features basis. Often, once the trial ends, the person is so hooked on the product they will register to buy it and be grateful for the chance to try it out beforehand.

Another great way to stimulate a sense of guilt is to go the extra mile for your customers. If people feel you are making an extra effort just for them, then they not only feel special, but also more interested in reciprocating in the relationship. You can give them MORE than what they expect to receive and tell them it is a free gift just because. This almost always works to cement a good relationship.

Even the appearance of giving more than what you promised will also stimulate a sense of obligation. For instance, you have a great package that includes various reports, templates, videos, and an eBook. The entire package could be worth $99.95, but instead of selling it for that, you sell it for $59.95 and you let everyone know that you're only charging for the eBook, and everything else is a free gift; A bribe? Of course!

Now, you've not only given something away for free in their eyes, but you also made a BIG EFFORT in providing everything they need to have to solve their problems. You've done all the work of putting all the pieces together for them, and this can also produce a profound sense of obligation as well as connection.

The extra effort can also be something as small as adding something nice to the sale when it is delivered, and letting the customer know it was added intentionally. Some marketers add candy, but this can melt and get sticky in the summer when it is mailed. And, it's not associated with the products you sell, unless you happen to sell candy online. So, try to stick to things that people appreciate and that will help them to think of your products. If you are selling office supplies, you can always add additional freebies to the order like a large paper clip with your URL imprinted on it. It's not only a way of inducing a little touch of guilt, but it also is a way to remind them where to order their office supplies next time they run out.

Timing this strategy

The timing for this strategy is typically before any sales pitch has been made. Although, as we just discussed, it can be used after a sale is completed as well. If you use it before the sales pitch has been made, you may have to do it several times to get the trigger to go off.

The Internet makes it very easy to allow people to sign up to get free articles, videos, or other electronic formats in exchange for an email address. At that point, you are not asking for anything in return, even if the email address is what you are truly after. You are simply giving away things that can help people to connect with you.

If they do get the free item that you've offered them, they might feel more of an obligation to find out more about the rest of your products. So, you can use the free products to remind potential prospects of your other offers. The freebies can even be used as teasers to give people a taste of a larger product and that will entice them with both desire and guilt.

Stir their curiosity

One of the biggest drives that most people have is simple curiosity. It's what makes people seek out new inventions and new adventures. If we didn't have curiosity our culture would stagnate and we'd never have discovered fire or learned how to cook and create recipes. Finding out what happens next when you do something is a very strong motivator for the human species, and it can be used to help you sell your products. All you have to do is put yourself in the position of the buyer and then try to figure out how to tease them into wanting to know more.

The strategic plan

The biggest question in your prospective buyer's mind may be: "Just exactly what is this new product like?" As simple as that may sound, the drive behind that would be curiosity. It's like when you are sitting at a restaurant and you are looking at the menu, trying to make a choice of what to buy. Your inclination is to read the descriptions and become curious about one dish versus another. You may even decide to ask the waitress what the dish is like before you order. Similarly, most people want to have some idea of what the product they are deciding upon is like to experience.

In face-to-face selling, answering that question is easy. You pull out a sample or the actual product and let them try it out. Voila! Instant sale. But, online the curiosity itself has to be used to get the potential customer to imagine what it would be like to experience this product. Or you get them so worked up about finding out for themselves what it's like that they are willing to put their money down to order it just to answer that question for themselves.

So, basically you can either choose to leave the product somewhat mysterious and by nature of what you don't say, sell that product with a trigger of curiosity. Or, you can choose to give exquisite detail of what the product is like with the caveat that the buyer must experience it for themselves to really understand how wonderful the experience really is. In other words, you will constantly allude to the experience with descriptive, powerful, copy without actually making it easy for the mind to grasp. It's always slightly out of focus.

Your copy should also have a similar style even if you decide to focus on a story or stop just short of revealing the secret that you were going to share to your readers unless they buy your product.

And, there are many ways to keep people engaged using a style that triggers curiosity by using phrases like, "wait, there's more..." or "If you think this is interesting, wait until I what I have to say now..."

These types of phrases pull the reader deep into the copy and stir the curiosity to get to the point of the sales page or product.

The psychological triggers

If you ever remember being enchanted by bedtime stories as a youngster, you know that you couldn't wait to know what happened to the hero or heroine at the end of the story. Once you're involved in a story, no matter what it is, you want to know how it ends.

On the other hand, if you tell the reader too much too soon, the story loses its charm. There's no more sense of mystery or excitement. Anything that is too quick to reveal its charm come off as a desperate attempt to seduce the reader in a cheap and trashy way. Often, it turns people off instead of turning them on. However, if you can leave just a little of that story untold and bring the reader in by holding back, then you will find that they have a much higher interest level in the product you offer. So, even though the product hasn't changed, you have triggered a psychological element in the person reviewing the offer that values something that isn't so quick to give itself away.

That's because people value things that are exotic, mysterious, and slightly out of reach. If it is available to everyone and easy too, then people tend to value it less. It devalues itself by making itself appear common, instead of intriguing. So, adding an air of mystery or making something just slightly out of reach can be a great way to not only stir your potential customers' curiosity but also bring up the estimation of value for your product.

How to implement effectively

If you are selling products that have intellectual property rights like books, then you have a perfect market for this particular strategy. That's because what you are selling lends itself quite well to disclosing only some information, but not all of it. That's reserved for people who buy your product.

If you take a look at Amazon.com, they know how to use this strategy to sell their books online. They let you take a "peek" inside the book and show you the table of contents and a sample chapter, sometimes. This is a great way to stir the reader's curiosity, particularly if the chapter ends at a point where it's begging you to buy the book to find out what happens next.

While Amazon's strategy takes a bit of technical know-how, you can do the same with your sales pages. You can give just enough information to the reader to stir their curiosity and then make the offer to have them buy the eBook that you are selling to satisfy their curiosity.

You can also use this strategy on your sales pages. You would tell the reader that you are going to reveal a benefit or payoff somewhere in the sales page that will really be of value to the reader. They will be encouraged to read the entire sales page just to find out the secret that you've hidden in there somewhere.

It's sort of the same strategy as when you are given a clue at the beginning of a sales letter that lets the reader in on a way to save big money on the offer, if they read the entire letter and follow the instructions hidden somewhere in the middle. Here you are telling them that if they take the time to unveil the mystery of how to get an extra discount, then they will be rewarded by saving money!

Not only are you getting people engaged in the copy this way, but you are also raising the probability that they will take the time to comprehend the offer too. That's because you will have captured there attention more and they will be more likely to pay closer attention to your offer. This can really benefit you if what you are selling needs this type of higher level comprehension.

Aside from letting the reader know that there is a secret or mystery that you are willing to unveil in the copy, you can also stir curiosity through testimonials. A testimonial is an account of someone else using the product that you're selling and how they perceived it added value to their lives. This can work very well to stir the imagination and curiosity of people online who don't have the luxury of holding a sample in their hands or downloading a demo copy.

So, say you are selling acne-fighting makeup. Of course, you can include a number of testimonials of how it cleared up the face of people in record time and how it made their face feel silky smooth and grease-less. But, an even more effective approach would be to simply have a video of someone trying it on and showing their confidence and love of life increase just because they used the product. Isn't this what most commercials do? There's the aftershave that after it's used, the man becomes a chick magnet. And, of course, it may sound unbelievable, but many men will be tempted to try the product to see if it really works as well for them.

What's important to remember though is that you don't make any statements that aren't true about your product. In the commercials that show men being swamped by women after they put on a specific aftershave, there is never a statement that suggests that the aftershave itself has the power to draw women like flies. Instead, it is alluded to and hinted at, so that potential buyers get curious as to whether it really would work for them.

Some of the questions you want floating around in the minds of your potential buyer after they read your copy are: "How would it feel for me to experience this product?" or "Will it work this way for me?" In order to get that question to float around and hook into the mind of the potential buyer, you have to leave some of the facts unsaid. You have to allude to things rather than be straightforward where the logical mind can then reject the trigger very easily. Instead, engage the emotions and the desire to experience the product for themselves.

Timing this strategy

There are various times to use this strategy depending on whether you are sowing small seeds of curiosity with leading statements that ask the reader to keep reading to unveil more of your message or whether you have one giant secret you are going to unveil somewhere in the copy.

If you are doing the hidden secret in the copy type of strategy, you need to be upfront at the very beginning of the sales page or offer that there is something hidden deep within the copy that will be of value to them. Maybe it saves them money. Maybe it gives them a free gift. Maybe it provides them with an upgrade for using a specific code. You get to decide what that benefit is and make sure the reader knows that it will be of high value to them, and then you can either tell them what it is or keep leading them into the copy to get them even more curious.

Then after you tell them at the beginning, keep your word and hide that secret benefit somewhere in the copy so that they can have the joy of discovering it for themselves and reaping the benefits.

If you are using this strategy in small bite-sized chunks, then you might spread out small phrases like: "Wait until you hear what comes next..." This will make people keep reading the copy even though no specific benefit has been claimed for reading the next part of the copy. It's just an instrument to stir curiosity. In cases like that, you will do this every so often down the copy of the sales page. It should be interspersed throughout the copy in regular intervals to lead the reader through the copy with a sense of expectation and anticipation characteristic of the state of curiosity.

Lastly, if you are using the strategy of alluding to some experience that the reader must have for themselves, you will want to create a story of a first-hand experience, either through words or a video, without actually saying what benefit they will get from it. Instead, allude to some experience that just has to be seen for themselves to get the full impact and for that they need to buy the product. Then, you will want the entire sales page or promotion to be all about these allusions and then make sure at the end they know where to order the product that will satisfy their curiosity.

Embrace simplicity

It can be a lot harder to write copy that is simple and easily understandable than it is to write complex copy. But, the rewards are worth it. You appeal to a need in most people to be met at their own level. If you talk down to them in tone, they will perceive the copy as condescending and lose interest. If you make it an exercise in grammar school reading, they will also feel slightly insulted or unappreciative. To connect with your buyers, you have to learn to meet them exactly where they are, by embracing a simplicity that appeals to both educated and non-educated alike. And, obviously, that can be a bit of a challenge.

The strategic plan

When you use simplicity as your strategy, you don't just pay attention to the words and tone of your copy, you also have to realize that the marketing offer should be reduced to its simplest elements. You are reaching out to people on a level that feels comfortable to them, and you are also going to make it very easy for them to heed your call to action to buy your product.

If you have words that are too high brow in the copy, odds are you will impress the professors who come across your ad, but turn off the average Joe who just wants to know what you're talking about. So, keeping the words simple, while the content of the conversation in an adult format, can help you reach a wider audience and promote your products better.

In addition, you want to take a close look at the offer you are making. Is there anything about it that can confuse the potential buyer? Is there information in it that you need a specific degree to read? The only time you want to get so excessively technical is when your target audience is a grouping of technically talented people. Otherwise, seek to make the product and its features easy to understand and appreciate.

Some Internet marketers make the mistake of making the offers themselves complicated by asking for one payment now, and then a different payment later – for the same product! So, for instance, they might say that to sign up for membership on a site is $25.00 setup fee, plus a $15/month subscription fee. While it may seem simple, people can get quickly turned off by two different fees or subscription prices. Try to keep your pricing standard so that when an upgrade is requested, the customer knows what they're paying for.

Sometimes the way a product works can be complicated. An example of this is cosmetic treatments like teeth whitening or acne- fighting programs that need customers to follow specific directions to obtain maximum results. While there may not be much you can do to change the number of days of treatment, the steps they need to take with each treatment, and sometimes the products they need to buy for different types of complexions and body types, you can try to simplify those instructions as much as possible.

For instance, in the case of acne-fighting programs, you might want to educate the customer that it takes "3 steps" to follow the regime correctly. Then, talk about the astringent, the blemish cream, and the moisturizing toner separately under each step. This leaves them thinking, "Oh, just three steps." Instead of the opposite reaction which would trigger panic at the complexity of the entire program.

In the same way, if you have the option to overwhelm your customers with choices or to offer a clear and simple choice, choose the simple one. Once a person buys into your featured product they may then be more interested in seeing the full line of products you have to offer later.

The psychological triggers

People are generally lazy and/or lead very complicated lives that make them relish the opportunity to pick up something much simpler. Either way, people deeply appreciate the simplicity of offers that don't take too much effort to understand or overwhelm them with choices they don't have time to make. They would rather have someone else do the hard work for them and then they come in and just be able to sign on the dotted line.

If you think about our modern day culture, this appreciation of simplicity grows more and more as our lives become overburdened with people trying to steal our time and attention everywhere we go. We'd rather not have to pay too close attention to anyone or anything that doesn't make our lives easier, because honestly, they are already seem to be careening out of control!

In particular, the demographic that most appreciates simplicity are parents of small children who are working full-time and/or care giving for others. Even though they may really need a product that simplifies their lives, they may not have time to investigate it. Or, if they are out shopping for themselves, they may give themselves less time and attention than they do to their growing families. In situations like that, you only have a few minutes to capture their attention and sell them on a product.

You see many more of these people who live hurried and time-crunched lives appearing on the Internet than ever before. They don't have the time to go retail shopping and find that Internet shopping saves them time and money. But, just because that's true doesn't mean that they're willing to wade through your complicated offer just to buy your product. On the contrary! They want things to be so simple that you've made up their mind for them, even before they've showed up at your site. They want your offers to show that you've done the research and legwork that is necessary to identify quality products and that you are willing to sell it to them in an easy and fast way online!

If you can deliver that type of offer to them, they are highly motivated to make the purchase right then and there so they can get onto other things that need their attention.

How to implement effectively

To implement this strategy review your copy to make sure it is easily understood. It shouldn't contain large or complicated words, but not read too childishly either. You can make those words sing by using stories, bullet points, or emotional cues to draw your reader in. It's not so much the words you use, but what you are saying with those words that will sell the product for you.

And, of course, the content needs to be sure to be as uncomplicated as possible. Even if your product requires some series of steps to produce results, you will want to sum it up as quickly and briefly as possible to get the message across. Don't try to make the reader have to figure out what your product is all about. It should be self-explanatory from your copy what it is about and why the person should buy it. When you list your benefits, they should be easy enough to understand and appreciate that they need no further explanation or selling.

Finally, a very simple strategy for new potential buyers is to isolate one choice for them in a lineup of products that you've selected as the best choice for your particular demographic. You should be able to feature that item on your website and explain why this product is the one product they need to buy, after visiting your site. Always pick one, very high quality, good value item to promote to your new customers and then tell them all the benefits in simple, easy to read, language. When a person is browsing with little time to review all your lineup, they will appreciate the fact that you've picked the very best item for them to buy without much hassle having to think about it.

Sure, you may have any number of other products on your site, but if you know your visitors and their tastes, then they are relying on you to make their shopping experience as simple as if they had a virtual shopping assistant. They will want you to bring to their attention the best deal that they can get for the types of products that they are looking for.

You should make the offer as simple as possible too. Online, that means you want to give them the option to pay instantaneously using credit cards or even PayPal. They should know that when they click the button to buy, they will be making an order that will be delivered promptly to their home. If you are selling virtual products, you can easily deliver it instantaneously to their computer, and add an element of instant gratification to the sale too.

When you choose a product to feature and the customer is a new customer, you should also make it easy for them to sign up to buy. Nothing deters more customers than a complicated sign-up form that asks for addresses or other information that is not relevant to the sale. All you really need to market to anyone online is a valid email, so choose to keep your registration forms simple and collect only what's necessary to close the sale. Your customers will appreciate that and tend to trust you more.

If you don't know what offers people want, why not ask them? You can set up a simple survey that gives them a coupon or other freebie for participating. It will help you to define the best offers to put forward to your visitors and helps them appreciate the fact that you're listening. Just keep the survey as simple as possible with radio buttons they can click to select and option out of various other options and then give them their freebie immediately after they complete the survey. If it is a coupon for one of your products, you've not only gotten valuable feedback, but you've also motivated them to make a purchase before the coupon expires.

Always have a great introductory offer for new customers, which gives them exactly what they need to leave your site feeling satisfied. Once they get something that meets their needs and you chose it, they are more apt to trust your opinion more when they visit later. By then you will know that they might be interested in other products in your lineup that are not featured or introductory offers.

Timing this strategy

As suggested earlier, this strategy is best used when you are first introducing yourself to new customers. You want to meet new customers at their level and go the extra mile to make their lives easier. You can do this by taking the hassle out of the shopping experience and guiding them to a great choice for them. They will appreciate the fact that you have made their lives easier and that the shopping experience was hassle-free.

You can always use the strategy in your copy on the sales page when you list your benefits too. The easier and clearer you message of benefits is, the more likely that someone will be able to scan them quickly and make up their mind instantly. You can even reinforce the idea of simplicity through the layout of your copy.

You can use bullets and bolding to pick out the relevant words that people can scan on a busy day in the office as they are browsing your site. Maybe they don't want to take the time to read all the copy, but you've made it simple enough for them to get the message they need by isolating the relevant words and information that they can spot quickly by scanning the web page. Then, when they see something that intrigues them more, they can choose whether to read the normal text or not next to it. Either way, this is more in line with today's hectic work schedules and multitasking lives. The easier you make it for someone to get your message and make a choice, the more likelihood they will appreciate you and your products more.

Harmonize to mutual agreements

If you've ever seen two old married people mimic each other due to having been together for so long, you'll have some idea of how this strategy works. You want to be able to harmonize with your potential buyer in such a way that they believe they've known you all their lives and are in complete agreement with everything you say. That way, when it comes time to buy the product, they will be willing to continue this fine partnership by buying your product.

When someone comes across as agreeable, it's mostly because we are seeing traits in them that we like about ourselves. Think of your circle of friends. They are your friends because they harmonize with you. You trust their opinions. You tend to agree with their point of views. You will go a little further to help a friend than you will a total stranger, in most cases. And, you do it because you know they would do the same for you if the situation were reversed. That's what a mutually beneficial friendship is like. It provides a connection of trust and mutuality that cements the relationship.

If you are in marketing, you also want to establish a relationship with your potential buyer, and it's not too different than a trusted friendship. Once you get someone to like you and identify with you, it becomes easier for them to agree with what you are saying. If what you are saying has something to do with a product you are selling, it makes the sale that much easier to achieve.

The strategic plan

What do you do when you want to make friends? You typically try to agree with people, wear the clothing they like, and compliment them. You make yourself generally non-threatening and likable. It's no different for Internet marketing. You will want to present an online image that is likable and also complements the demographic that is coming to visit your site.

Some of the most common ways to be likable is to appeal to generic values of honesty or integrity. In particular, if you are marketing on social networks, you will want to focus on authenticity so that people feel comfortable with you. That means that the image that you present online should match the person you are offline. If later, someone finds out you are not who you say you are, that will be the end of those relationships and in social sites, news like that spreads instantly and can be quite damaging. So, stay on the safe side and present an authentic and honest image and you will be respected and liked for that.

You can influence people to harmonize with you through some subtle subconscious cues too. For instance, if you say something positive and ask the other person to agree with you (and, they most likely would), then you have started harmonizing with the possible be buyer. This can be something as simple as saying: "Lovely day, don't you think?" While it may seem a courtesy, it's actually a very subtle way of beginning the slide down the path of total agreement and mutual trust.

While you are not standing face-to-face with your customers online, you can use the same strategy by using many of the same phrases that will illicit agreement from your visitor. It will have to be something that most people would have a difficult time replying "no" to, otherwise, the first no in their minds is what breaks the spell. You want very innocuous phrases that are tied to statements that are generally positive and produce agreement on the part of the person reading them.

Besides these subtle verbal clues, you can actually make a person agree with you through mirroring their behavior. Although this works best in face-to-face encounters, the strategy can be implemented online in group forums, and social networking sites. So, we'll discuss it next.

The psychological triggers

Infants learn how to mimic their parents and that's how they learn many of their own behaviors. In general, when we don't know how to act in a particular situation, we have been taught to look to others to gain wisdom from the experience of others. Those people we look up to, we also emulate, and this is also a form of mirroring. So, there are basically two foundational behaviors associated with mirroring: learning and socializing.

If you are sitting in front of a new product now, part of what you need to do to make a decision is to learn about it. If you've already got an agreeable authority on the product in front of you (the salesperson), then the likelihood that you will use their knowledge to help make a decision is very likely. But, if you really want to trust this person, they have to be likable. So, the fact that they start to mirror you or lead you into an agreeable frame of mind, will help you make up your mind on whether to close the sale or not.

So, this strategy is used both by the sales person to create a degree of familiarity with the potential customer, and it can also be used to mimic more successful sales professionals by mirroring their actions. It's not just a strategy that works on customers, but it can also be used consciously to create a learning environment for the Internet marketer too. It's always easier to learn something by following proven methods that others have tried and tested, rather than learning everything on your own the hard way.

So, when you do find someone worth emulating, take the time to understand not only the keywords and phrases important for the interaction, but how to handle the environment too. All great modeling comes with a specific environment for learning. Just like people don't learn how to play tennis on a golf course, you don't learn how to implement Internet marketing techniques in a retail store. Go to the experts that are already using these techniques in the specific environment where they should be used. Then, try out the same techniques in the same environment.

That means that you aren't just seeking to emulate a specific person on the Internet who has proven successful with a specific technique. Also take a look at the environment they've established to generate the sales and mimic that as best as you can with your websites and sales pages. That way, you will create a perfect mirroring of their techniques and ambiance.

How to implement effectively

Another word for the mirroring associated with this strategy is also called patterning. In patterning, we are going to try to create mutual agreement through harmonizing consciously with the sales prospect in front of us. For instance, if a person sits down and crosses their feet towards you, you might do the same. If they have a cup of coffee, you would get one too and join them. In this way, you are saying non-verbally to your sales prospect: "I agree with you." And, that translates into the other person thinking: "Gee, this person sure is agreeable."

If you are in social groups online and you are marketing with comments and a backlink to your URL, it pays to be courteous and agreeable. Don't flame other people and in general, choose to agree rather than disagree. You can easily set up reciprocity of good feelings by complimenting the poster or genuinely stating how you agree with the post. Then, add your backlink to your website show other thoughts on the matter that people might be interested in reading. This is one way to drive traffic to your site and get more people viewing your online offers.

Even though you can't solicit a response back from your online visitor, you can still ask some rhetorical questions that lead to agreement. They would be more like the following:

Ninety-five percent of people made three times their money on this investment. Wouldn't you like to be one of those people?

Suffering from allergies makes people miserable. Wouldn't it be nice to know you could go out in the spring and fall and breathe easily? Taking care of pets is important, if we want them to be around a long time. And, wouldn't you want your cat/dog to be healthy and live a long life?

All of these types of rhetorical questions will lead to agreement because they appeal to your readers in ways that are subtle but true. It would take a real contrary person to disagree that they didn't want to make money or stop suffering from allergies. And, if someone is on a pet site that you own, odds are they love their pets and want them to live long and healthy lives. So, if you know the demographic you are attracting, you can generally think up some very easy non-threatening phrases to insert into your web copy that will harmonize with your readership. Once they start harmonizing, it won't be long before you can insert: "And, wouldn't buying this product solve all your problems?" By the time they get to that phrase, they've already been saying, yes, yes, yes, that another yes is due to come out unbidden.

Next, you want to locate people online who are marketing the goods and services that you want to market. These are typically your competitors, although it can be successful affiliates or other Internet marketers who are coaching you. You will want to establish the same attitude and confidence in your products and services that they have with theirs. You want to get into their mindset and use that to help you write copy that sounds similar to their copy, in tone and content.

Remember that you can't just plagiarize other people's online content. Always seek to add your own, although you can paraphrase and keep the gist of what is being said, as long as you don't plagiarize. In some cases, you can even give credit to people and amp up your credibility and aura of success by associating with partners who are willing for you to use their name and words, as long as you credit them. Then, it makes it very simple to emulate someone who is coaching you, if they are also willing to let you use their words online.

If you have such a program available to you, you can sign up and try to get a hold of any books, articles, or information packets that can help you develop a similar pattern of success with their ideas on marketing. Even if the program isn't specific to your market, there are many Internet marketing gurus that have plenty of valuable advice on how to shift your sales upwards and they all deserve an ear now and then. Just choose a couple that you want to pattern and then immerse yourself in their programs and products to understand how they got to be as successful as they did. Then, just mimic those techniques and you have an easy way to get started on the road to Internet marketing riches much faster than if you just did things by trial and error.

Timing this strategy

The timing for this strategy is at the beginning, in the middle, and near the end. At the beginning, you are trying to establish rapport with your sales prospect by finding innocuous ways to connect and harmonize with the other person. In face-to-face interactions this might mean having a cup of coffee with them or chatting briefly about their favorite sports team. Online it would be to project an agreeable image that resonates with your demographic.

Next, you would want to start peppering your copy with rhetorical questions that lead the reader into agreement with you more and more. These should be non-threatening and evoke and emotional response.

Finally, in your call to action, you will ask for the sale by using another leading question that also seeks agreement. It's the final bold move that if timed right will have your prospect quickly reaching to click on the buy button on your sales page.

And, of course, you can use this strategy for your own education by learning how to mimic and pattern yourself off other people's successful sites and strategies. Take what you learn and apply it in the same environment that they implemented it within and that way your tram ride up the mountain of success becomes that much easier.

Put your money where your mouth is

Consumers these days are very smart. They are hypersensitive to marketing gimmicks and paranoid about being conned with slick advertisements. This generation grew up with television and the commercial advertisements that literally ruled the marketplace and human behavior. In doing so, they became inoculated to many of the psychological triggers that were a bit underhanded, but powerful non-the-less. They also can spot a con a mile away, so you have to be extra careful to be as honest and forthright as possible. The payback though is that if you are squeaky clean honest, not just with the good features of your products but the bad ones too, people will tend to value your opinions as a marketer more. You will trigger a deep psychological appreciation of your honest behavior in a sea of dishonest merchandisers. That's why honesty has to be one of the top psychological triggers to implement when you are doing any type of marketing, online or otherwise.

The strategic plan

Honesty is similar to authenticity, except it is a tad more straightforward. You can be authentic about who you are and still misrepresent the products you sell based on your spotless image of personal integrity. Honesty, in this case, is to be truthful – plain and simple. We aren't talking about the truth that you would like to believe, it is about the truth of what the consumer would like to hear. For that, you need to have their best interest at heart, and that's the role of honesty in your life. You have to take into account that even though selling is about making money, if you sell something that ultimately dupes the consumer in any way, it will come back to bite you in the butt in the end. It may take a while, but it will come back eventually. In today's social networking climate, the payback may be sooner than you think.

Social networking sites are great sites to establish a presence and start cultivating a bigger contact list. You build a circle of friends that trust you and will listen to your status updates and newsfeeds. You develop more connections in groups. All these interactions need to have a degree of authenticity and honesty. When you post a link back to your site, you want to be sure it leads to an honest way of doing business. Otherwise, the first person on the network that gets scammed will send out a general message to all their friends to avoid you, and then those friends will turn around and do the same. Once your reputation as an honest person is lost on a social networking site, most of your marketing opportunities are gone too. This is particularly true if you seek to increase the number of friends in your list solely to market them.

There are instances when people send messages or post updates that are viewable by all their friends that certain people are "spammers" and not to accept them as friends. That's all it takes to get you silently blacklisted even if your account remains current with the host site. So, always seek to add value and bring an honest level of interaction to social networking sites in particular.

When you recommend a product, your product or someone else's, be sure they understand the relationship you have with the vendor, what you think of it in detail, and let them know if you are an expert or not. If the product has faults, don't shove them under the rug. It's more than likely the consumers will pick up on those faults as objections and if you leave them unaddressed you've lost the sale. So, always address the faults and either reframe them or make them insignificant. If the fault is major, just don't sell that product. The choice is yours.

The psychological triggers

If you are honest with your sales presentation, people begin to open up more to the possibility of buying from you. It can also be a point of differentiation between you and your competitor. Have they dealt with them and found them less than honest? That's why they should buy from you instead! Honesty is something that is hard to come by and easy to lose. It has to be earned by a continual willingness to put the other person's interest before your own.

People understand the great motivation to lie: self-gain. Lying in this day and age is rampant, from politicians to lovers. People lie to get their way. Just like when you were little and your parents asked you: "Did you do your homework?" And, you lied to get out of having to do it. If our parents weren't particularly invested in teaching us the principle of honesty, that also came across. Like when they said, "Do as I say, not as I do." That basically told you it was okay to lie about your values because it was just a standard used to get other people to do what you wanted them to do. Otherwise, they would have taken the trouble to match their actions where their words went. They would have put their money where their mouth went instead of giving you a mixed message that it's okay to say one thing and do another.

So then when you lie to others you learn that it generally lets you off the hook. You don't have to explain that you really didn't feel like doing your homework or that the product you are selling has faults. That way, if no one objects or tries to verify your story, your lie eases the way to get your way without much effort on your part to be honest about anything. So, it's also a form of laziness. That lack of effort though does come across to people eventually as they do more business with you. They begin to realize that you are the type of person who only does what's in your own best interest and once that message gets through, people pull away in disgust. You become completely untrustworthy. Anything you say after that is suspect. So, while honesty is easy to establish and maintain with a little effort, once you lose it, you lose the necessary trust to continue with the relationship, whether it is personal or business.

And how does all this happen? Here you will be surprised to find out that this interaction on a psychological basis is completely NON-VERBAL. That's right! You may think you have to speak to tell a lie, but your actions are shouting it out loud and clear to your customers. It doesn't even have to be a black and white lie because people are sensitive to being lied to and conned. They will pick up the non-verbal cues of your behavior and add two and two together to figure out that you are not trustworthy. They won't even bother confronting you because, after all, if you are a liar you will deny it. If you are being truthful, you'll deny it. So, they will simply watch your behavior and make a judgment of you and then take their business elsewhere if they decide you aren't trustworthy. Now, though, they may also decide to tell all their friends too before they go.

So, to be perceived as an honest person takes more than just telling the truth. It takes putting someone else's interest above your own, specifically your customer's needs! It also takes a cultivation of behaviors that trigger the association of honesty in your customer's mind. Some of these we'll discuss in the next section.

How to implement effectively

One of the behaviors that suggests a "cover-up" is when you have a website with too many glitzy images and flashing neon fonts. While it may be a way of attracting attention, it also gives off the aura of intentional distraction, like you don't want someone to notice that the product isn't what it is. That's why some social networking sites like Facebook have very clean, crisp, profile images with little extraneous hype or cluttered appearances. This is often referred to as a "professional" appearance and with that moniker comes the suggestion that you are a person of integrity that does an honest business.

So, when you set up your websites, endeavor to portray an honest image versus one of an over-commercialized hyped up sales image that screams "smoke and mirrors." The result will be that the people coming to your site will trust you more because you've kept your profile and site clean, crisp, understandable, and thus it triggers the idea that you are a professional, honest, person.

Next, you want to be sure that products you sell are exactly what you say they are and no less. This goes even for the affiliate offers that you put up. If you associate with dishonest affiliates that reputation comes back to you and can lose you customers. So, you want to investigate your sales affiliates and make sure that they are on the up and up. You should use a redirect page for each affiliate in the event you need to pull an offer because one of your customer complains of dishonest practices. This way, you can change one redirect page and keep all the links on your website still pointing to that page. This is the quickest way to keep control of the affiliates you advertise without having to search through each web page in your site for where you've added a particular affiliate link.

And, it keeps your site honest when you can pull bad offers at the first whiff of trouble.

Make sure your copy doesn't have any small white lies or outright exaggerations. While it may seem unnoticeable to you, people pick up on these very quickly and it can discredit the rest of your offer.

The same is true of your affiliate offers. Make sure they are selling exactly what they say they are selling in the copy.

If you have a product that you think is good, but has an obvious flaw, just be sure to let your customers know the flaw exists. You can use marketing strategies to minimize or reframe the flaw, but definitely mention it. If you don't mention it, the customer will figure it out and keep it as an unaddressed objection in their mind that will kill the sale every time. It's much better to be forthright about the flaws than to ignore them all together.

If you're not sure how the copy reads, why not test it out on someone. Just ask them to read the copy and tell you what they think the ad is really saying. You can even try this approach and use a white lie or exaggeration and see how easily people pick up the deception! If you want to portray an image of honesty, there's no real way to do it other than having some integrity.

Timing this strategy

You have to be honest in all your dealings, not just in the presentation of your website and copy. If you promise to have things delivered within 72 hours, than do everything in your power to keep that promise. Don't try to get orders by lying or it will end up making you look bad in the end. If you run out of a product and need to substitute with another, make sure the customer knows and agrees before you send it out, or provide them a refund.

It's almost always better to provide a refund with no questions asked, even if the person is dishonest and used the product. The reason for this is that a dishonest person will likely try to ruin your reputation, if they don't get their money back. An honest person will deserve the money back, typically. So, in terms of customer service, always make the customer happy regardless whether they are honest or dishonest. On the other hand, you yourself need to be a paragon of honesty to maintain your business reputation.

Blend in with the marketplace

The success of a chameleon depends on its ability to blend in with its environment to escape detection. This strategy is similar in that you want to blend in with the marketplace, not to avoid detection though, but to enhance the probability that your offering will be accepted as a natural part of that environment.

What you really want to do is always take account the needs of the marketplace before you spend too much effort trying to sell a product that has no market. Once you understand what the market prefers, you should try to generate an offer that harmonizes with that need, instead of ignoring it or going off on some new tangent all together.

So, while many life coaches will tell you to follow your dreams, your dreams are limited by the environment in which you find yourself. You can't sell as many copies of a book on crocheting as you can on finances. That's because the market is hungry for good financing information on only a few people crochet these days. So, the environment is rich for growing finance book sales but it is poor for growing crochet books.

Even if you are an expert in crochet stitches, what good does it do to spend your time creating a book few other people will pay to read? Instead, focus on what the market wants and after you've sold enough to raise the capital for the crochet book, then write the book – if it still interests you.

The strategic plan

This strategy is like how you pick a career in life. In that case, the career would be your product and the environment is the job marketplace. Maybe you want to grow up to be a mime, but no one is hiring mimes. So, instead, you focus on a career that can pay you so that you can be a mime on your off hours. Maybe you become a computer technician who does shows on weekends at the local mall. When you make enough money as a computer technician, then you can decide whether to take the mime gig full time and make a go of it.

There is a little twist here though. You aren't just going to pick any career to make money. You're going to pick one that is similar to your actual goal. So, if your real ambition is to be a mime, you get a degree in technical theater. That way, you get to work in the environment conducive to acting and you get to be around people who love to act. Then, you can start to see if there is a way to make money as a mime too. That is the smart way to follow your dreams AND make enough money to live on.

In marketing terms, you may want to sell indoor table top atriums, but your research shows there is no market for them – don't create a website devoted solely to them then! You instead look for a market that is similar and use that to launch your sites. For instance, you may find that people are learning how to grow vegetable and flower gardens in tight economic times. Then, you would devote your site to gardening and have the atriums as one potential product that can be bought off the site.

Always seek to harmonize with the marketplace. If you are trying to sell woman's wigs, don't try to sell them in an environment that won't appreciate them – like in beauty shops where people are paid to cut your hair. Instead, you would seek out cancer groups to advertise and places where people appreciate a fine woman's wig. This is blending into your environment and is important even when you are just commenting on someone else's blog and linking back to your site from there.

The psychological triggers

Have you ever seen anyone walk in with a tie that clashes with the rest of their suit? How about when someone says something totally inappropriate for a conversation? Doesn't that just jar people into silence and staring? It's an immediate turn-off and people will often mock things that are out of place. This is how people will perceive a product that is not timed to harmonize with the marketplace.

Even in the West where the culture of individuality reigns, you will see a look of disgust come across people's faces when something is distinctly out of place or interrupts the flow of an event. That's because our culture works on unwritten rules of social cooperation that are meant to help people work together in harmony, even when everyone is their own individual. There are still social rules in place that people follow to make everyone comfortable and to ease the social underpinnings of a civil society.

When people fall outside those rules, it triggers a social consciousness that degrades the value of that interaction. You are speaking out of turn. You are not following the rules. You are creating disorder in their lives, and they won't appreciate it. More than likely they will either openly mock someone for stepping out of line or they will ignore it completely. Either way, a product that isn't in harmony with its environment is going to receive a very poor public reception, unless that public has been primed for the introduction of a product that steps outside the norms.

If, however, you have a product that falls into the market at just the right time, the public is ready to accept it and the probability that you will close more sales is much higher. So, you want to check what the social environment is like before you devote much of your Internet marketing resources to a product or market that just doesn't have enough juice to justify the effort. It will make your life easier in the long run to go with the flow than it will be to try to fight it.

Then, once you make a bit of money on the markets that are already selling and you still have the desire to try something different – go for it! You will have learned much more about what your market wants, how to play on those desires, and how to make money online selling similar products.

How to implement effectively

To implement this strategy you have to do your homework. Research the marketplace in depth before you commit money, time, and resources to an online sales venture that is doomed to fail because you didn't do this one thing: Harmonize with the marketing environment. With new products, this is even more important because it will have to still meet the needs of the market to sell and you may have fewer ways to determine how it will be received without proper researching consumer trends.

One way to test the environment for a new product is to do a trial offer and see how many people bite. This can be in the form of a popup window or limited time offer. The number of sales on that product will give you an idea of how many people would actually buy the product if you did a full sales page and promotion for it. If it has trouble selling, you can lower the price and try the ad again to see if the price range was off. If it still has trouble selling or even generating interest, odds are the market is not ready for this product or simply can't appreciate it because it is too different.

Another way you can get products to harmonize with the environment is to offer accessories with it that the market loves. Take for instance, cell phones. They were rather new and at first all they did was call people's numbers remotely. Now, they offer cameras, voicemail, special ring tones, web access, and even games. All those people who never had a need to call people from outside their home suddenly found the features appealing to the electronic gizmo culture of our times. Now, everyone carries a cell phone and the more features your phone has the more status it carries.

Maybe you are selling cosmetics online, and so you pair it with some pretty purses or bags. Now you've got two markets: people who wear make-up and people who love to get new purses every season. You've accessorized your offering so that it fits into multiple environments.

You can even just change the marketing perception of an old product to make it fit into a new culture. That's a way of upgrading the image of something that people consider an old-fashioned or traditional and making it appeal to modern tastes. This is one way to get old products to blend into new environments by offering them a new slant.

The diamond ring is an excellent example of this strategy to harmonize with the new environment where people didn't want just a solitaire diamond like everyone else had. They wanted something different. So the diamond industry took their diamond rings and created new concepts so that diamond rings would still be marketable in a changing environment. They started creating right-hand rings for women who were happy being single, but wanted to show off their wealth. They created bands with multiple diamonds and called them eternity rings to celebrate anniversaries. They generally upgraded the old-fashioned concept of a single stone ring to one that was more luxurious and could express a greater degree of individuality for people in our times, whether married or not. And diamond sales went up dramatically because they now had a wider market since they had learned to blend in seamlessly to the new culture of individuality, affluence, and even single people.

You can take the example of the diamond industry and apply it to your own products. What can you do to make your products blend in more with today's fashions, tastes, and cultural biases? Maybe it just means offering products in a variety of colors. Maybe you want to add some accessories like a pouch for a cell phone, if you are selling purses. Maybe you want to remove some items from your inventory or their accessories that stamp your products as being out of step with the times. You don't want to be the person selling typewriters when the entire market was going to computer word processors. It just doesn't make good business sense. Instead, read the signs of the times and unload your inventory and get into something the marketplace wants and appreciates.

Timing this strategy

The timing for this strategy refers more to a cultural sense of time. You want to be take note of what's going on in your society and try to keep ahead of trends happening in your market niches. You want to use that knowledge to predict what might be a good seller and what isn't worth your time marketing. So, much of this strategy is done even before you build a website or offer a product in your inventory. Once it's up there, the only choice you have is to either unload it or accessorize it to get it to match.

You can keep the news of what's happening in the niches you are interested in by subscribing to trade blogs or journals. You should read the latest of what's happening in your world and always attempt to do a trial run for products which may seem like a good

Idea, but you can't locate relevant research to back up that sentiment. So, test it out. Then, the marketplace can tell you whether it's a potential winner or a dud without spending too much time and effort getting an entire campaign up and running.

Exact the facts

Ever hear speeches on a presidential campaign? Many of them are full of rhetoric but short on facts. The reason for that is they try to engage the emotions, but when it comes time to vote, people really want the facts of where the candidates stand. The same is true when you make a buying decision. You may be attracted emotionally at first to the offer, but to close the decision to buy, you have to have a logical reason that is based on sound facts. If the Internet marketer fails to provide exact facts to close the deal, the prospective buyer may feel the offer is vague or not credible. So, it's always a good strategy to exact the facts of any offer to make it as specific and credible as possible.

The strategic plan

What's the best way to be perceived as an expert on some subject? Having the facts about your subject makes you an authority in the eyes of other. With authority comes credibility and with credibility comes trust. And, trust is a major component of any business transaction. When people trust a vendor they are more willing to purchase from them. They have confidence in the products that the vendor sells because they trust the vendor. So, when you seek to be more specific with the facts of your sales presentation, then you invoke an air of expertise and authority. That eventually winds down to more sales, if you can convince people that you really do know what you are talking about more than others.

This strategy works on the facts that you decide to write in your copy. It can be about the social facts that make your product valuable to people or it can be facts about the product itself.

Say you are selling all natural food products. You can focus on the facts that make a natural food product valuable in a conventional marketplace. For that, you would need to compare the facts of conventional products to organic products in a very specific way. You might say (if it were true), "America's conventional food supply is exposed to over 100 chemicals for each pound of food grown on our farms every month." This is very specific in the number of chemicals you can avoid by eating organic foods and the intensity of the exposure. It's extremely specific and can make you look like a very informed expert on the topic of food product safety and health.

That's the way to use this strategy when you are trying to pinpoint social facts that make your product valuable. But, there's also another way.

Say you want to concentrate on the qualities of your product instead to sell it. In the above case of organic foods, you would highlight the qualities of organic foods that make them desirable to the specific market you are targeting, in this case health conscious consumers. So, you would say instead, "In a blind taste test, organic carrots tasted better than conventional carrots 90% of the time."

Now, if you are saying something that is really not true, you will trigger the dishonesty meter of most readers. So, no fibs when you use this strategy or people who are knowledgeable will eventually come across your ad and call you on it. And, you can even get in trouble with Federal guidelines of false advertising if you end up stating facts that can't be backed up with some research somewhere.

That doesn't mean you have to start a research laboratory in your basement just to get some good facts that you can use. You can use any facts by any known experts and just quote them. If they have lots of degrees it helps your product to look very credible too. That's why when new interesting facts come out, you can see it scooped up and used by marketers everywhere to sell their products, when they apply.

The psychological triggers

People really don't trust most advertising these days, particularly if it is just generic hype. But, add a few specific facts and you will see the interest level in your readership soar. The reason for that our culture really values knowledge and expertise. Some people may read your ad and then even try to verify the facts for themselves. Others will be so astounded they take your ad and tell their friends about it to make themselves sound like experts too.

Our minds are much more trained for logical thought than for the intuitive feel of an ad that may work on our subconscious, but rarely makes its way into the conscious mind. However facts speak to the side of us that is constantly searching the environment for new and interesting information. It is easily digested and understood.

Face it, we are in the information age and many children have been born into a world of computers, iPods, televisions, and radios. Testing in school emphasizes facts and the ability to be specific and knowledgeable about certain topics like math or science. We've been programmed to believe that the only way to determine whether something has value is to use the scientific method which involves understanding and testing the facts. This social framework impacts our psychology to give the Western culture a bias that appreciates facts and specificity. The more something seems to be a scientific conclusion with highly specific facts, the more credibility we assign to it. And, for sure, it reminds us of being in a class room where the authority figure, the teacher, knew all the facts and we had to submit to that knowledge to pass the grade.

Similarly, when someone triggers this automatic deferral to authority figures they trigger a deep psychological need to follow the lead of someone else. When that happens they are much more suggestible to your advertising than when they think they have to make up their own mind. Instead, they can rely on your expertise to make up their mind for them.

You also tend to sound more certain and assured when you can rattle off facts that are very specific. It really cements the case that you know what happened and you can be trusted to give an informed opinion. It's like when you are in a court case, the person who has a better recollection of the facts comes off as more believable. If you give a faint and vague recollection of events it leads to doubts in the minds of the jury. It may seem a bit unfair, but it comes across as a person trying to dodge the truth instead of someone who is sure of themselves and the facts of the case.

If you've ever been asked by a woman if she looks fat, you know that the only right answer is no. However, if you hesitate and then say no, it's that moment of uncertainty that kills the reply. There are behaviors that make your words sound unsure and being vague is one way that portrays an image of evasiveness.

Watch a poker game sometime. The best card players have a straight face and bid in the same confident manner no matter what they hold in their hands. That attitude is what comes across the table to make their opponent believe them and to help them make any hand a winning hand. That's the attitude your copy should have too online.

How to implement effectively

The first way of implementing this strategy is to be specific about the product's qualities, without necessarily sounding scientific. As long as you are incredibly specific about what the buyer is getting, it will help them to visualize and imagine owning this thing that they can only see in virtual mode over the Internet.

For example, you are selling designer purses online and you put up an ad on your website. It should go into exquisite detail over what makes this purse special. Maybe it is made of genuine, hand-stamped, leather in a deep burgundy color.

Inside, it has three pouches, one for change, another for makeup and a third for your cell phone. Maybe it has a full metal zipper opening or genuine gold accents. Only you, the marketer, knows what to tell the consumer in detail about this beautiful offer you are making. The more you tell the person who is viewing the offer, the more they will have to imagine it in their mind in greater detail. Now, even though this doesn't work on authority, it works on the bias people have to use their mental powers to imagine the product they can only view in virtual mode online. So, be specific about any feature that can help your visitors touch, feel, smell, or even hear your product in their mind's eyes.

The next way is to research the environment that makes your product valuable and use the facts you unearth to sell your products. If you are selling home security systems, you might want to review crime rates and how they are rising uncontrollably because of poor economic conditions. You can even find out what the national rise in different crimes is like a 10% increase in home burglaries nationwide and use that to sell home security systems.

On tap water filtering systems use the pollution rate of bottle water to make a case for buying a home water filtering system that works at the tap source and that's very effective. It's not hard to find this information and you can even look at your competitor's sites to see what information they've manage to unearth and use it too. You might find information on the average types of contaminants found in sample water supplies and even horrify people with how many hormones and cancer drugs are there without being able to be filtered out by the local water plant.

Next, you can also use the products own unique qualities to be exceedingly specific about the benefits a buyer will get when they purchase it. So, if we continue to use the water filtration example, we would list how many contaminants it filters out and what they are. You can say how water filtering at the tap will help reduce lead too, in case you unknowingly have lead pipes in the house.

You should also use percent's to help you make the case. So, the copy might read: This ABC filters out 72% of harmful chemicals from your drinking water. If you pick a number that isn't a multiple of five it is much more memorable and believable. Ratios are also good too to implement when you are trying to create memorable facts. So, you might say, "Nine out of 10 environmentalists agree that this water filter is the best on the market."

Timing this strategy

This strategy becomes the meat of your advertisement, should you choose to use it. It should be right smack in the middle of your sales page and list all of the scientific facts that can help someone to make up their mind. You can lead people into this sales page with emotional triggers, but once they are there you want to have all the facts ready to help them close the deal. And, those facts need to be easily picked out, easily understood, and memorable. They should be so easy to remember that they can be repeated without having to look them up. It also works well if you do this strategy in bulleted points or tables. There's something about graphs, tables, and bullet lists that make it seem very scientific and to the point. Graphs, in particular, are very visual and appeal to people who may not bother to read your copy, but are impressed with graphics. So, you should include anything in your copy that lends it a very scientific and knowledgeable air that says you've actually taken the time to research your subject. People will be impressed and will be more willing to click on the buy button.

Work up their satisfaction level

In line with the last strategy, you can use people's cultured bias towards mental engagement to create some satisfying offers. To do that, your offers should have some level of intrigue or challenge to them, to give people a sense of accomplishment from having read them. This can take form in a suspenseful story that captures the imagination, but leaves them wondering how the story will end. If they get to the end and are surprised, that will stimulate their sense of intellectual enjoyment and increase the satisfaction level with the ad. On the other hand, if the story is as easy to predict as your choice of breakfast food each morning, then people will feel disappointed that you made it so obvious. Always leave them feeling that there was a bit of mystery or puzzle that needed to be figured out in order to get the jewel in your message.

The strategic plan

An easy and obvious sales pitch actually insults people because people get the feeling they are either being manipulated or they are being talked down to. You do want to make things somewhat easy to follow, but that doesn't mean you want to make the final point easy to predict. It's a bit of a cross between keeping things simple and being too complex to be enjoyable. It's going to have a bit of a challenge, but it shouldn't be beyond the reach of the average person to figure out.

Sometimes getting the right level of challenge in the ad can also be a challenge. Pay attention to your demographic and gear the copy to them. Then you want to speak directly to that demographic taking into account their likes and dislikes. Then, you create an offer that speaks to that level, neither above it nor below it.

Then you want to engage the reader in your copy by leading down the path that can only end in one way, the solution to an intriguing situation or puzzle. They will be so engaged with how it all works out that they will read through your entire sales copy just to see if they got it right. If it's also not obvious, they will be delighted when they get to the end and were able to figure out where you were heading. Or, they will be surprised that they didn't see the answer and be mentally stimulated by the challenge anyways. Either way, the key is to mentally stimulate them by giving them a challenge or puzzle to work on that engages different senses and ways of thinking. Even finding a new perspective from an old story can work and be mentally pleasing to many people.

The psychological triggers

The Myers-Brigg personality test is based on Jungian theory that classifies four different functions of personality: sensing, thinking, feeling, and intuition. Everyone is said to have different components of their personality that makes them use each of these components in different ways. However, the main theory says that all four of these components make up everyone's personality, even if they are utilized differently.

So, what does this have to do with this strategy? The theory can be used to help you design offers that engage people's entire brain function which will include the four components of personality. If you appeal to just the thinking function of people, obviously, the ad won't be as powerful than if you managed to appeal to three out of the four components too. People won't be stimulated enough to remember the copy or to be triggered into buying behavior. That means that you want to mentally engage people on as many levels as possible to really tie into their imagination. You want your ad not just to invoke the senses, but the thinking, feeling, and intuition part of people too.

The more components you manage to stimulate the more pleasurable the ad will be perceived. That's because the person will be stimulated more and the entire brain will be engaged in the experience of reading the ad and imagining the scenario you've invoked. The harder your brain is working the more pleasurable the entire experience is when it finally gets resolved.

Think of it as achieving a level of mastery in any hobby or activity. If you are doing something like a very easy crossword puzzle, you soon bore of the challenge and your attention drifts. Your mind needs more stimulation, and harder puzzles to get the same boost of adrenaline and accomplishment that you had when a previous level was your challenge. As long as the answers are slightly out of your reach, the puzzles remain interesting and stimulating. Eventually, when you complete the entire puzzle you have a really good feeling of accomplishment because you know it took some time and effort to get those results.

How to implement effectively

The copy that you write should appeal to people in this manner. It should be slightly challenging, enough to keep the reader's attention. This can be done through keeping a sense of suspense and mystery until the very end. A surprise ending is also very good to give a person a mental release that is pleasurable. You can even challenge the reader to see if they can figure out what the result is before they see it.

One way to do this is to add quizzes and surveys to your website. People love these types of interactive Internet toys. It's like working a crossword puzzle except there is no wrong answer. And, sometimes these can really work well if your product can be tied to the end result of the quiz.

For example, there are dating sites that make you take a personality test at the beginning to determine who you are most compatible with and then they match you based on the results. The test can be a little long and complicated, but it also offers the potential client a great feeling of satisfaction upon completing it. The interesting way to market this as a trigger is to offer it for free as a "free personality profile" for signing up to the site for a seven day free trial.

The seven day free trial gets extended to a paying membership if it's not canceled in time. The site collects the credit card information ahead of time and then they give out the free personality profile results. So, even though the personality test was challenging and it came back with some results, it was basically an advertisement for a dating site wrapped up in a puzzle/quiz type of wrapper.

To make it really interesting, you can even make a little script that they can plug into their website that has a link back to your site. It's like a badge that shows other people that you took a certain quiz or survey and you got a high score. IQ tests are very popular this way and people love to show off their IQ and then compare it to other people's IQ results. There are many Facebook applications that work on this strategy and if you create one of your own, it can literally bring tons of traffic to your site. If you don't have the skills, but you have a great idea, hire someone to create the application for you and then post it on Facebook. You are allowed to put links back to your site in the applications and it's a great work to market to people in social networking sites.

Some surveys do the same thing. They ask you to take a quick survey and then see how your answers compare to other people's answers. Then, at the end you see an advertisement related to the survey. It gives you a fun way to connect with your visitors and people generally feel very satisfied to have something intriguing and special on the site that stimulates them mentally.

Another way to implement this strategy is to engage the reader in a human interest story with a moral or surprise ending. Sort of like when you were a child and you were told the story of Hansel and Gretal. There's an element of suspense in the story that makes you want to find out if they get eaten or not. What happens to them after all is said and done?

Now, if one of them was wearing a particular sneaker that you were selling and it allowed them to evade the witch because it lit up at night and helped them find their way home, then you can make a case for why the story ended differently. But, you'd want to make it very surprising and a story that engages people's imaginations and all the senses.

To write copy that invokes not just the senses, but also the intuition seems difficult, but it's not. What you do is you basically leave a few things unsaid. You give enough information to set the story, to invoke the thinking and feeling functions, and you describe enough to evoke the senses. Then, to get people to start to use their intuition you leave enough unsaid that they have to place themselves in that spot and wonder: "What would I do in that situation?" It's sort of like the MacGyver series where he takes the gum he is chewing, adds some chemical in the environment and blasts his way out of a prison cell. You're not quite sure how he's going to do it until he actually makes a break for it, but you know all the pieces of the puzzle are there to be able to figure it out. So, you try to figure it out before the ending is given away.

Membership sites use this at times, especially if they are certifying sites. They will say that you can join up at a certain level if you have certain accomplishments under your belt. Obviously, it can't be an easy way to qualify or people everywhere would be certified under their program. So, they list the qualifications that people need to be accepted into the program at a particular level and be recognized as either a professional or a master or whatever. Of course, you have to pay for the privilege even though it was you doing the hard work.

What are the most engaging stories? Aren't they the ones you're not quite sure how they're going to end? Then, when they do end you are surprised and delighted? So, you can create a story for your product, it can be anything from how it was discovered or created to how someone used it to gain success in some endeavor. Some people like to go back in history to find out interesting stories that are not that well known that they can use to help create an "unbelievable but true" type of aura for their product. But, you can also just create a story out of your own imagination that really brings the reader into suspense with how it will all end.

Timing this strategy

You can use the strategy to engage the reader at the start of your relationship with a new customer by using quizzes and interactive challenges to bring the potential customer into your offers in a more enthusiastic manner. You can create applications that work with social networking sites that will bring traffic in from this site. If it works well it might even go viral and you'll have a great way to market people in social networking sites regardless of niche. If you can allow them to add the application to their profile where everyone can see it, it's a great way to introduce your website and products to a new and growing market. You can also use the strategy as the offer if you write captivating stories that have an air of mystery and suspense and end with the hero using your product to save the day.

Cozy up like family

If you've ever been to a foreign land where you didn't know a soul, didn't speak the language, and looked different to everyone on the street, you probably were quite relieved to see some business that you recognized like McDonald's sitting on a street corner. We all love exotic things – for a short period of time- but when we want to come home we want things that are familiar and comforting. This strategy is all about the longing for the familiar and learning how to cozy up to your sales prospects like family.

The strategic plan

Here is where brand names and familiar advertising that rings a bell in your memory become powerful. A brand name uses this strategy because people come to feel connected and rely on brands they are familiar with and tend to avoid those they do not know or trust. So, in essence, the brand becomes a familiar element, like family, and this generates repeat sales and a customer loyalty to that particular product.

But, how do people make a brand name that sticks in the mind of the sales prospect? Lots of money and advertising goes into developing brand names that are easy to remember, show up everywhere, and that will be recognizable and associated with a particular product or company. The strategy though is simply to expose the public to this brand name over and over and associate with the type of advertising that links certain qualities with that brand name.

For instance, when you think of Maytag you think of dependability and washers and dryers. That's because Maytag became such a household brand name and the commercials were always about the poor Maytag repair man who had nothing to do because the appliances rarely broke down. They were humorous and they also got across the fact that you can depend on a Maytag. Even though Maytag is just an arbitrary name, it became associated with a particular subset of qualities and a product to boot.

So, the way to achieve some sort of familiarity to a brand name is to constantly present them in front of people until they start to associate them with the product or advertising. This really isn't as hard as it sounds. And, on the Internet, it can be very easy to do, unlike television and radio ads which can quickly add up into a fortune.

And, you don't have to limit it to a brand name, you can also create eye-catching logos and display them everywhere you want to trigger an association with your website or products. Once people start to associate a symbol with a set of qualities and/or product, it can become a very powerful tool to create familiarity and interest no matter what the environment. That's because an image, unlike a word, bypasses the conscious mind and goes straight to the subconscious. People have images that they associate with certain qualities too and you can mine those cultural biases to associate different qualities of familiarity to your website and products.

For instance, say you are trying to sell flowers online. If you just put up images of flowers or bouquets, you will be showing your product but you won't be making your company or your brand of flowers any more familiar than your competitors. But, if you started a marketing campaign and added a logo with symbols of romance, like a heart or even a kiss, people start to feel your flowers are more familiar because everyone is impacted by these symbols subconsciously. Now, if you use that marketing campaign to tell people to send flowers to the people they love and you make up special "kissable" bouquets, then the idea that you are sharing romance and warmth with people when you send a flower bouquet is even more familiar. It's not just flowers people are sending now, they are sending love. And, what is a more traditional family value than love?

The psychological triggers

In a culture that relies on family and social bonds to survive, there are certain common bonds that create predictable familiarity with different words or characteristics. As an example, if you were to ask people to choose a number between 1 and 10, the majority will pick 7. Why is that? There is some unconscious programming that favors 7 as a random number and people find it the most familiar number to pick. They aren't going to pick numbers they don't like for the most part, and most people like and are comfortable with choosing the number 7 when asked to pick a random number.

What that means for you as a marketer is that you should be aware of these unconscious biases and seek to always use what's going to be familiar and comfortable to the potential buyer. In this case, you would create eBooks with "The Top 7 Tips To Breakthrough Profits" or "Seven Secrets To Light Up Your Love Life." Does it really matter that you can write about eight or that there are hundreds of these tips and secrets out there? Not really. You are marketing to the subconscious mind that favors the number seven.

You should be familiar with the most common choices that people make, whether it be the color that is preferred by most people or genders, and the top features that people want in specific products. That way, when you try to market a product, you can offer these choices to the customer and they will feel as if you got right into their head and picked up what made them comfortable. It will seem like you were listening to them specifically, when you just happen to know what most people find comforting.

Also, repetition is important when using this strategy because the mind takes a certain amount of repetition for it to take some bit of information and store it in long term memory. Without this repetition, you may love the marketing campaign, the product, or the brand, and really connect with it, but you will soon forget it too.

As a marketer, you want to have a certain amount of repetition and exposure to be able to hook into the mind and send out the message that this is important information that needs to be stored in more long term memory.

While some marketers think that to repeat the same campaign year after year is a mistake, it all depends on how successful that campaign is. You shouldn't change an advertising campaign until the sales fall off. That's because even after the novelty of a campaign falls off, you then get into familiarity and comfort. When people are comfortable with a slogan, for instance, it becomes part of the popular culture. Like the slogan: "Got milk?" The dairy association used it to popularize the familiarity of milk and how good it is for you. They even used celebrities with milk mustaches to give it a giggle factor that reminds us of our youth. That campaign is popular and increases the demand for milk, but it also sinks deep into the popular mass consciousness.

In the campaign that asks "Where's the beef?" It was to sell hamburgers of a particular vendor. But, that slogan became so popular and comfortable with the majority of people that it also spun off many other meanings and associations as other people capitalized on its simple, yet effective message. Now, "Where's the beef?" means "Where's the substance?" or "Why am I being cheated?" And, people can ask the same question of other products and it means something totally different. It becomes that familiar a concept and slogan. Ultimately, that makes this slogan highly successful because people recognize it, knows what it refers to and how it can be applied elsewhere. It becomes a part of our modern day culture.

How to implement effectively

One of the first ways to implement this strategy is through mass Internet exposure. You will have to choose something to advertise, but many people use their domain names to link to a mass exposure campaign. It can also be your personal name, a brand name, your company name, but a web URL is memorable and gives instant access to many of your sales offers.

Picking a domain name is tricky these days because all the good ones are taken. To be a memorable domain name that rolls off the tongue it should be a one or two word phrase that also can be easily associated with what you are marketing on that website. Unfortunately, those have all been gobbled up by domain name investors. So, you are probably going to end up with at least three words in your domain name, unless you want to pay an investor for the rights to the domain they own. And, that can be a possibility since a domain name is a valuable piece of your marketing strategy.

You can check out domain names at places like GoDaddy.com and find out how to purchase them there. You will want to buy them with several different extensions like .org and .net to make sure no one attempts to squat on your name for future purposes. Once you own a good domain name that is memorable and easily associated with your products or services, the rest is easy. You just advertise that domain name where ever you go online. And, offline, you can advertise it in your letterhead, your business cards, even on the side of your car, if you're that adventurous.

If you aren't necessarily targeting the domain name, you still want to include it in your advertising in conjunction with whatever brand name, logo, or slogan you are using with this strategy. Then, you want to add it to your signature so that when you post online or send an email, people start to associate these images, words, or URL with your business. It's the small interactions that can have a large cumulative effect later down the line when they are trying to figure out who to contact for a particular solution. If your email is sitting in their inbox after having remained in contact with them over the course of some time, they will associate you with a familiar face and contact you.

That's also the reason that you should use social networking sites and be a member of multiple forums and groups. These types of interactions breed familiarity on a very intimate level over the Internet and they have the potential to reach many more people than just two or three coming into a retail store. Once people begin to associate your name and face with certain qualities, particularly friendship and familiarity, they are more apt to buy something from you or contact you when they have a need.

Timing this strategy

As stated above, you should make an effort to contact people on a regular basis so that your name, brand, logo or products don't fall off their horizon. You may find that by contacting them over a period of time, they will come to know and trust you, even if you don't make a sale every single time. What you are doing is building the relationship so that they start to associate you like family and miss you when you are gone. This can take some time and patience on your part, but the rewards are that you will be turned to when a sales opportunity does come up.

Always have some idea of what elements on your website and sales offers can trigger this association of familiarity. It can be the words you use, the images you display, or even just your name. Once people get really familiar with who you are and what you do, they become more trusting and less resistant to being marketed. So, although the strategy isn't going to reap an instant sale, it will play on the subconscious mind of your targets so that it will reap new and repeat sales very effectively.

Hope for better things to come

Everyone knows what the 2016 elections are all about: Change, safety and making the US great again. That's right because when things are bad, the only thing left to do is to hope for better things to come. For that, we know we need to change the way things are. And, even though there is no definite promise of what will change or how things will change, sometimes people pin all their hopes on something different just because the present moment is uncomfortable. It's just basic human nature and, in fact, hope is a wonderfully positive human emotion.

Hope also helps to motivate many sales too. That's because people typically are looking for solutions to problems when they buy. They aren't necessarily looking for a specific item, they are looking for something that resolves some issue and benefits them. That's why sales pages don't go into great depth on the actual product, but instead they focus on the benefits. And, this is particularly important when you are marketing on the trigger of hope. You have to sell an ideal that things will be better when a person buys your product.

The strategic plan

Since you are trying to trigger the emotion of hope in your prospective buyer, all you have to do to understand how to invoke that is to place yourself in the shoes of someone visiting your site. Maybe it is someone who is aging and unhappy at the many lines and wrinkles on their faces. You know that they are looking for some hope that can keep the signs of aging at bay, even as they continue to get older. You happen to sell cosmetics and some of them are "age-defying" products. While you can't say that it removes wrinkles, since it's not true, you can give the hope and the illusion that it does.

It's not just the words you use to describe your products that can give this future promise of better things to come. In some cases, people have even relied on time lapse photography to prove that their products do produce a noticeable effect of smoothing out wrinkles with continued use. Other than getting a Botox injection, they may decide to spend some money and a little effort to see if your product works, completely on the basis of hope. One thing they do know, doing nothing will not produce any change in their lives. So, hope will spur them to buy when things are bad and doing nothing is worse than taking a risk to see if they can find some solution to their problems.

You are not going to hand out any guarantees that aren't true. There are plenty of ways to create a dream or a fantasy illusion of better things to come, by buying into the product. You can have people who used it give testimonials to convince other people that the product produced some change in their lives for the better. This can help bolster the claim the product is really a "miracle" product.

This strategy helps to create more sales, although it doesn't necessarily deliver everything that the dream or fantasy promises. That's because for some people it will work well and for others not. You can't determine really how many people will use your product the way it was intended or exactly what percentage of people will get good results. So, you can't make any guarantees or assure anyone that it is a 100% failsafe way of changing their situation. You do know, like them, that trying nothing is a sure way to fail though. So why not try something different?

And, that's why you have to remind people of the problem that bought them there. Maybe it was those wrinkles staring them in the face. In that case, you can talk about how devastating it is to see those lines accumulating with no end in sight. You can put up an image of a person with wrinkles and one without to show how different you would feel if you just managed to solve this one problem. So, in order to stimulate hope, you also have to remind people why they need change.

The psychological triggers

People can't live satisfying lives in a situation of despair. Suicides and addiction problems often manifest when people lack hope. So, hope truly is a positive emotion. It helps one to imagine things as they could be, and not as they are. This often spurs people to take action in situations that seem completely unresolvable. If they just focused on what was wrong with their lives and had no hope, they create a self-fulfilling prophecy that keeps them where they are at. While it's important to remind people why they need hope, they have to believe it is possible to do something to create change in their lives or they do not take action.

So, there are two psychological aspects you need to address when you are marketing using a trigger of hope. You have to remind people of how bad things are and you have to make the possibility of a new life possible. While the mind may be completely stumped as to how that's going to occur, you can still tap into other areas of the mind like intuition and feeling that are willing to believe in things it can't see. That's why it's important to have dreams in your life. Without dreams, we can't see our way out of our present predicaments.

Dreams and fantasies inspire us to be something that we currently are not. They give us the confidence to believe that change is possible. They can sometimes even inform us of the steps to make those changes. When we land in the world of dreams and fantasies, that's when the mind's burden of depressing details is overcome and the light of something almost spiritual takes its place. We believe.

How to implement effectively

So, your role as a marketing person is to sell a dream to inspire hope. It's as simple as that. Even if you're not running for president, you can use this strategy to help you sell products based on what they can do to change your customer's lives for the better. To do that, you have to be someone that people have faith in and find credible. You can't just be a homeless person off the street. That would hardly be inspiring. Your story and your image have to inspire confidence and trust, just as your rhetoric will inspire hope.

So, be careful of your own public image and the image your company is promoting too. If you are selling acne medication, it pays to be a dermatologist when using this strategy. If you're not, then get testimonials from dermatologists as well as people who use the product. Your dream of clear skin has to be believable by being promoted by authority figures and experts. So, if you're not one, pay someone to use them as a testimonial.

A great way to incur authority is to add all the alphabet suit of letters associated with your degree of learning next to your name. Even if you aren't a PhD you can still have quite a few certificates and degrees to add distinguished looking letters next to your name. Also, if your product or company has won any awards, this can also help to heighten the image that you are responsible and credible authorities in your field.

Once you have that image in place of being someone "in the know" then you can start to create the dream of a better world. Some areas of the marketplace lend themselves better to this strategy than others. That's because some problems are merely annoying whereas others can invoke despair or a stubborn unwillingness to change on their own, a perfect breeding ground for hope.

Areas that work well with this strategy is the health and beauty industries. People get sick and old. That's a fact of life. Sometimes these things can really depress people who search out a multitude of ways to stave off the effects of aging or to find something to at least make them more comfortable in their illnesses. Even preventative methods like vitamins and exercise programs can create a great deal of hope for people who want healthier lifestyles, but don't know how to achieve it themselves. Once they understand that something is possible, by seeing other people like them who succeeded, they will want to buy this solution to help them overcome their intractable problems too.

And, you can spur that hope by showing the results of those people who bought your products or programs and succeeded in changing their lives completely! Testimonials and interviews are excellent things that can be posted on your site. When you use video for these types of advertisements, people can really engage the same thinking process that the individual in the video went through to make the decision to purchase and ultimately change their lives. And, you can even address objections this way by having the person interviewed explain what they objected to in the offer and how it was negligible or wrong to view it that way (reframe it).

Now, here's the really nice thing about this strategy. There will always be a certain number of people who believe but simply don't have the confidence to take on a program of change on their own. They want to be led by the hand and they are willing to pay to do that from someone they respect or trust. This makes this strategy perfect for services such as coaching, counseling, and consultations. So, you can have a number of products that help people attempt the programs on their own, and then you can also have other services where people can sign up for private consultations or services that will help them to get over any obstacles as they arise.

And, that's not all

You would be able to train other people in the methods and programs that you are selling and create franchises or affiliates of people who are also experts in the system or product. They can pay you to teach them how to sell based on hope and change and they will go out to find new converts. The hope you sell to the affiliates is a hope of riches from mining the same rich vein of despair or problems that people are trying to resolve in mass. The hope you sell to the customers is the actual potential to resolve their problems. In this case, you can't sell an actual solution, just the dream or possibility of a solution, since it will depend on their ability to stick with a program and how it works on them in particular.

Timing this strategy

Keep an eye out for issues that will generate massive despair or anxiety in the public. Right now, home foreclosures and financial concerns are paramount in most people's mind. We hear of suicides and crime going up. This is the perfect time to sell a product that might help people in these markets. Of course, if they are having financial problems they may not have much cash, so you will have to figure out ways they can finance a purchase and still resolve their problem.

As the baby boomers age, you can expect the demand for products that keep them mobile, healthy, and active will increase. This massive demographic is prime for the selling on this strategy. In particular, this demographic has always wanted to do things in new and novel ways, so they are very receptive to change. All one has to do is time their product, service, or program to this growing market and the timing couldn't be more perfect for hope and change.

The timing in this strategy is based on market timing more than timing what you say or do. Of course, you want to know when to apply this strategy in the greater marketplace. For that you have to listen to the social issues going on and what problems are arising for a great number of people. You want to target the demographic with those problems. Then, you want to add websites and offers that appeal to those people based on hope and change. If you do it before you consider the market, this strategy will work, but it will have a greater impact if you time it to coincide with the greater issues going on at large in society.

Big Wealth and the Law of Attraction

With the release of The Secret followed by the outstanding response it has garnered, a lot of people are speaking about the Law of Attraction. The problem is that not half of these people know what they are talking about.

The Law of Attraction is not an enchantment or a potion that will wish all your problems away. There are things that need to be done if you want to experience its richness in your life.

This chapter specifically deals with the implementation of the Law of Attraction in gathering money, but really it is about all its various applications that can help in improving your life.

Sit back, free up your mind from all its clutter, and have a good read.

The Law of Attraction – What it really is and what it is not

Let us begin by understanding what the Law of Attraction really is all about.

It is somewhat amazing to see how much talk there is about the Law of Attraction and how few people actually know about what it is. The Law of Attraction is not a spell that you use and things begin happening that way. It is not that you chant, like begets a thousand times a day and see things happening the way you want. If the Law of Attraction were so simple, we would have already witnessed the world as a much better place by now.

People explain the Law of Attraction in various ways. The common definition you will find will be something like this:-

"If you strongly believe that something should happen, it will certainly happen."

A sentence couldn't be any simpler, but you will immediately realize that this raises more questions than it answers. The question of desires is the most important. Is it only what we desire and think about strongly that will happen? Or will things that we don't desire also happen if we somehow think strongly about them? Then there is also the question of internal conflict of thoughts. At times, there could be situations where we think equally in both ways. For example, we may think that a job could be ours or not. So how do we apply the Law of Attraction in such a case? Or what do we do when we are thinking strongly about something and someone else is thinking strongly about the exact opposite thing? What will happen in that case?

In order to be able to reply to all these questions, it is important to first understand what the Law of Attraction really says.

Notwithstanding the various ways in which the Law of Attraction has been defined, we can break things down in the following four elements:-

- We must know exactly what we want.
- We must begin a thought process for it, and begin vociferously asking the universe to make it happen.

- We must then visualize a situation wherein we already have what we are hankering for, and we must live in that reality.
- At the same time, we must not attach ourselves to what might happen. We must only think about having it. There is no room for apprehension.

In this chapter, we are going to expose various aspects of the Law of Attraction and see how we can apply it in one of the most important areas of our lives – attracting money. Can one really become rich by just thinking vividly about it? We need to understand the law better and learn how to implement it in order to get these answers.

Objective and subjective thinking

Since the Law of Attraction is so strongly based in the thought process, we must first learn what our thought processes really are.

One of the main steps toward understanding the Law of Attraction to a greater degree is to understand what the word "thought" really means. Throughout the description of this law, you will find that it doesn't refer to thinking in the way that we do. We think that we exist, we are in a particular situation, there are certain people with and around us, there are things we are with and so on. Whatever we see becomes real for us, and that becomes a part of our thought. However, this is not the kind of thought process that the Law of Attraction talks about. This is known as objective thinking.

But, in order to see the implementation of the Law of Attraction in our lives, we have to first shun the concept of objective thinking. We have to adopt a higher level of thinking, which is subjective thinking.

Why do we think that our spouse is real? Because we can see them. But this is objective thinking.

With subjective thinking, things will be the other way round. We think our spouse is real and therefore we see them. Now, that is subjective thinking.

Your job isn't real. But because you believe so concretely that it is real, it becomes a reality for you.

Your situations aren't real. However, your firm belief that they are happening makes them real for you.

This is the realm of subjective thinking. When you think subjectively, things are more or less like how you are seeing a dream. When we see a dream, how do we picture ourselves? Is our "dream" self the real us? No, we are the ones who are "seeing" the dream. We are just the frame of reference, the consciousness.

Whatever is happening in our dream is our perspective. That is how thinking works in the subjective world.

In this world, what we see is actually just a manifestation of our thoughts. Now, that doesn't mean those things aren't real. What that means is that those things are present in our consciousness. Just as we might be able to alter things in our dreams, by applying the Law of Attraction, we could alter things in our "real" life as well.

Stop the default processes from ruling your life

We give a lot of focus to things that are irrelevant in our lives, so much so that they actually start ruling our existence. But there are ways in which we can stop them from toying with us.

To a large extent, we allow things and situations to rule over us. How many times in life do we tell, "This situation is beyond me"! "I cannot do anything about it." We do that a lot. Each time that we do that, we are yielding the control of our lives to the situations that are governing us. We do not think even one bit in the way that the Law of Attraction suggests us to do.

And what is that way?

Quite simply put, that way is to think as though we rule the circumstances. The fact is that these circumstances are much in our hands. It is up to us to create situations that are conducive for our development, and not the other way round.

Think about it. Is a financial problem bogging you down? You have probably planned an endeavor but aren't able to do so because of paucity of funds. So what do you do? Most people will think that this is going nowhere and they will bail themselves out. But a person who really believes subjectively will understand that the financial problem lies in the frame of reference and will not worry about it too much. On the other hand, such a person will try to think that he or she could make the situation conducive.

Sounds impractical? It isn't so impractical actually. If you begin to think strongly about having money, what will you do? The Law of Attraction tells you that you have to "visualize" it and actually behave as though you have the money. In that case, you will apply for a loan probably and when you do that, you will be very confident because you believe that the money will be yours. Your confidence will work to your advantage because your potential financiers will get the impression that you have the capability to earn and pay them back. They understand you are a person of merit.

This is what the believers in the Law of Attraction do. They make things conducive to them through an intense thought process. But their thought process is not of this objective world. They think as though they are the center of everything that's happening and that they can have full control over the situations they face.

Pivoting your thought process

So how do you go about developing this kind of thought process, where you think you are the center of the universe and everything just exists in your frame of reference?

In order to create the subjective thought process that the Law of Attraction demands of you, it is very important that you create the right frame of reference. You have to be like the person seeing everything in a dream. Your perceived reality is actually the things that are happening in your frame of reference, which is just another name for your consciousness. But, you need to put a finger on this consciousness. You need to anchor it. This aspect – anchoring your conscious mind – is known as pivoting your thought process.

When you begin pivoting your thought process, the primary requirement is to have a fixed point from where you can begin. Usually, this fixed point is your resolve, your intention, your motive, your purpose. For example, if you really need to start a business, your resolution to do that is your pivot. The stronger you resolve to achieve that, the more profound your pivot will be. That is why people who have stronger resolutions are able to achieve better things than people who don't have a very strong mindset to achieve something.

If you consider your desire as your pivot and see everything from that perspective, everything begins falling into place. You feel as though everything that's happening is happening as a means of bringing you closer to your desire. In the above instance, if your desire to start a business is your pivot, then you feel as though everything happening in your life is taking you one step closer toward realizing your dreams. This includes the positives as well as negatives. If you suddenly meet someone, you feel that somehow that will be connected with your new business, which isn't yet started but you have no apprehensions in your mind about it. You also feel that you're getting fired from your desk job was something that will take you closer to having your own business.

People who believe in the Law of Attraction staunchly build such pivots in their minds. From then on, their entire life is focused on this pivot. This is what drives them and motivates them into coming closer to their goals.

The right mindset about money

We are applying the Law of Attraction to wealth. What is important here is the mindset that we need to make this application.

What does the Law of Attraction tell us about money?

It is actually very important to point out that the Law of Attraction is not just about money. It is a very general law which can be applied to every aspect of our lives. This is a law that helps to enrich ourselves as people, not just financial entities. However, we are endeavoring to see how we can apply the Law of Attraction as regards to attracting money.

That is the reason it becomes vital to know what kind of mindset you must have. If we try to implement the Law of Attraction to this concept, we must realize that a person who is actually trying to attract money should think about it all the time. Since thoughts attract results, this is what must happen.

However, the thoughts mustn't be objective. What are objective thoughts? Now, if you are only thinking about how many dollars you will earn on a particular project, then that is objective thinking. If you cannot think beyond numbers, all you are doing is thinking objectively. You are thinking how much you could make, how much you could save, etc. These are objective thoughts and, if you were to apply the Law of Attraction, you would understand that these thoughts won't attract the money to you.

Hence, you need to think subjectively. Don't think about the money itself, but think about what you must do in order to bring the money to you. Thinking about the quality of your product, for example, is a beautiful step in this regard. When you do that, you are actually improving the sales potential of your product and hence you are bringing in the money.

A person who believes in the Law of Attraction won't think – "I must sell this product because I want to earn money." Instead, such a person would think – "I must be honest in making this product and give it great quality so that I earn money out of it."

A person believing in the Law of Attraction automatically becomes honest because he or she knows what it takes to bring in the money. They don't believe in quick-fix solutions but always go for the long haul. This should be your mindset about money too – Don't think about how to actually bring in the money; think about what you must do in order to let the money come to you.

Wealth manifestation through the Law of Attraction

The five steps you need in order to manifest wealth applying the Law.

Wealth Manifestation through the Law of Attraction. Here are the five things you need to do in order to manifest the wealth that you are expecting through the Law of Attraction.

Believe

The first step is to ingrain the thought of wealth in your subconscious. You have to think staunchly that you will be able to attain the large amount of wealth that you are hoping for.

Visualize

It is very important to actually visualize the wealth. You have to think that the wealth is already in your bank account and now what you will do with it. Begin thinking as if you are planning what to do with the money. You don't have it already, but that's not the point. The Law of Attraction tells that you have to be strong in your belief, and visualization is the best way to do that.

Be grateful

Taking your belief one step forward, you must actually start thanking the universe for granting the wealth to you. Well, it has not already granted you the wealth, but you have no aspersions at all about that happening. You are darned sure that you will get the wealth and so being grateful is the next logical thing.

Listen to your heart

Your heart will tell you a lot of things at this point. It will tell you to do particular things. Do not stifle any of these "voices". Listen to them intently. Act upon them.

You have to make sure that you listen to every voice because any of them could be the one voice that opens the doors of opportunity to you.

Continue your actions

Never give up, never relent. Remember that stopping is a sign of weakness. You don't want the universe to understand that your belief is faltering. You want it to know that you will keep up no matter what. Sooner or later, your supreme confidence is going to bring the wealth at your door.

Is a poor person who thinks positively about money rich?

Does only thought matter? If beggars think about horses, can they ride?

This is a question that irks most people, especially those who hear about the Law of Attraction for the first time. After all, they think, the Law of Attraction speaks about thoughts begetting results, so if they were to think strongly about something, shouldn't they get that realized? In other words, if someone doesn't have a car and thinks strongly about it, they should be owners of the car, right?

Though that does sound very romantic, the problem is that the Law of Attraction does not work in that fashion. It is not about think-think-get-get. There are a lot of under layers here. Firstly, people who think about the Law of Attraction in this manner don't bring a very important thing into the equation – the emphasis of effort. You don't get much without channelizing your thoughts into action.

Let us understand this better with an example. Suppose you have an ambition to open a restaurant. Right now, it's just your ambition. Yes, you are thinking so strongly about it that you can taste it, but that's just about it. Will that make your restaurant then?

The answer is quite obvious – No. The Law of Attraction is not about sitting on your bean bag watching a DVD and expecting your inner desires to manifest themselves. You have to actually let the thought out of your system. You have to let it come out and become action.

When you think strongly about something, there will be an inner voice that will tell you to act in a particular way. If you are looking at opening a restaurant, a small voice within you will tell you to start hunting for good places. The voice will tell you to learn the art of hotel management. The voice will also tell you to begin gathering funds. There are so many things that will be spoken by this still small voice. The important thing is that you have to listen to it. And you have to act upon it.

It is only when you begin translating these thoughts into actions will you be able to do something about realizing them.

So a beggar who merely thinks about a horse won't be able to do something soon. However, if he thinks how he should get the horse and start implementing those ideas, there is all likelihood that he will be atop one soon enough.

What about lotteries and windfall incomes?

What does the Law of Attraction have to say about lotteries and all other kinds of overnight richness modes?

A very commonly asked question by most people is whether they can win lotteries and have other kinds of lucky breaks merely by having a strong belief in them, just as the Law of Attraction would have them do. They think very strongly about winning and so why should they not win? They even think about winning all the time, they buy tickets by the dozen, so the winners should be them, right?

The problem is that these people are in the right premise, but they aren't implementing it in the right way. So, what's the right way? Can you use the Law of Attraction to win a lottery?

Well, for that, the first thing is to think rightly about it. You must not expect a spell to come into action bringing gold coins at your door. This won't happen. But you could align things to work your way. Think positively about winning. When you do that, things automatically begin happening in a way that's beneficial to you. You probably won't become a millionaire overnight, but maybe your strong beliefs will help you win small amounts and be happy about them.

But there are ways in which you can go against the Law of Attraction here. If you expect too much, it's wrong. The Law of Attraction tells you to have a strong belief, but it does not tell you to expect a particular kind of result. Simply visualize what would happen if you are a winner of a particular sum, however, don't force the universe into granting you that sum. In the same vein, if you start getting grumpy if you are not making the kind of income you think you should, you are undoing all your positive belief. Grumpiness is a sign of disbelief and hence it is a sign of weakness.

People who win lotteries think somehow that they deserved the victory. If you were to ask them, they will say that they visualized winning the lottery at some point in their lives and they imagined it so vividly that they felt it was for real.

Try that. Imagine. Visualize your result. Don't go overboard. Don't over-expect. Things will begin aligning your way. But be ready to accept, without grudging, whatever comes your way. It will be better than what you have, if your belief is in the right.

Balancing the inner self and the outer self

If you really follow the Law of Attraction, you have to work at striking the right balance between your inner and outer selves.

One of the most significant applications of the Law of Attraction is to balance our inner and outer selves. Our inner self is our consciousness. It is the way we think and behave. This is where the Law of Attraction begins to take effect. The Law of Attraction starts manifesting itself when we think and that begins in our inner self. Our outer self is characterized by our action. The way we act and implement our thought processes is how our outer self-functions.

If we have to make the best utilization of the Law of Attraction into our life, then it is essential that we learn how to create the balance between our inner and outer selves. It is vital that we put into action what we think. What begins as a thought manifestation must get converted into action.

If you were to just think and sit about getting a new house, it isn't going to happen. Yes, if your thoughts are strong, if your belief is strong, the universe will begin aligning itself toward making things happen. But now, it is you who has to act. If you don't even lift a finger things aren't going to happen. Now, you have to put your outer self into action. This is when the positive energies that have been created start taking shape and things begin happening.

The problem with most of us is that we use our inner self to think and believe. We say so often that we want to do a particular thing but only a few of us actually put our outer selves into action mode.

The Law of Attraction will make things happen. But it will restrict itself to aligning things in a particular way. The rest is your call. It will make you confident about doing certain things, and that is what will influence the people around you and things will happen positively for you, but the main thing for that to happen is that you have to take the initiative and act.

Why doesn't everyone that uses the law of attraction become rich?

A lot of people might think about the Law of Attraction. But only a few of them actually begin climbing the steps of success and really become rich.

If you have been following through so far, you will have realized two things:

- The Law of Attraction is a definite reality; everyone puts it to use.
- However, a lot of people don't really put it to use the right way.

There is no refuting the strength of the Law of Attraction in channelizing the energies of the universe in such a way that things can begin to happen favorably. But the problem is that, the Law of Attraction will only channelize these things. If we don't make use of the energies to achieve what we are hankering after, it's all going to be a lost cause.

For example, if you only think about becoming rich but don't do anything actively in that regard, there's no way that you will become rich. In fact, even if you win through a lottery, you have to make the effort of buying the lottery and tracking the winnings.

The bottom line is clear – the Law of Attraction works but only if you put it to use. These are the things that you must do sequentially:

- You must strongly believe that a particular thing will happen. Your belief should be strong and unwavering, so unshakable that nothing must twist your belief in any way.
- Then you have to visualize this thing, as though it has actually happened with you and that you are enjoying its fruits.
- The next step will be to begin acting upon your inner voice. You will hear your inner voice a lot when you strongly believe in something. Acting upon this is what will bring you closer to realizing your ambitions.

So, if you are planning on becoming rich through the Law of Attraction, the important thing for you is to believe and then act. Without either of them, nothing is going to fall into place.

Conclusion

The Law of Attraction can make you rich. You must have heard it a lot. Now you know what it takes to get there.

Exploit Business Opportunities like the Wealthy

The person who can understand and act upon opportunities is the one that succeeds in life. We speak too much about being there at the right time and the right place, but what does this really mean? What happens to those who aren't there at the right time and the right place? Don't they get their opportunities?

In this chapter we will show you how to understand business opportunities and make the most of them in your life.

Business Opportunities – What are the qualities of a great business opportunity?

How do you make sure that the business opportunity staring at you is good for you? Here are some points.

The first step of any successful business is to find out about the quality of the business opportunity you are planning to start. You should know what you must look for.

The following are a few qualities that you need to check before you start any business. There are more, of course, but these are the ones that you should absolutely not miss out on:

1. The business should have enough targeted customer base. Now, what do we mean by that? Let's say you are planning to start a home-based business. You will need to look for a business that is more in demand. Where need is high and supply is less, you can have a better scope of success. Take the example of SEO opportunities for freelancers. You can do this from home without any high investment. In this niche, the requirement on your part is very high and you are bound to do well if you put in the right effort, because the professionals here are fewer. You need such an opportunity.
2. The business should have a good breakeven point. If your business doesn't have that, then you need to have large amount of working capital. Making a project report that tells how much you will have to put in and how much you will get from the business, and when, is a great idea.

3. Your interest in the business you start is highly important. There are many people who start a business looking at its potential, but don't reach the level they desire, primarily because they don't have much interest in the business itself.
4. Before starting with the business opportunity, see to it that you get proper resources on time, like manpower, guidance, consulting, financial credit if needed, infrastructure, etc.
5. Check before only if your business is over competitive or over in demand, if competitiveness is very high it will be difficult for you to get established in the business soon.

So, in summary, you need to check out all the pluses and minuses of the business opportunity before you plan to start anything. Once you start, it can get very difficult to stop. Being forewarned is being better-armed.

Where to look for business opportunities?

Opportunities don't usually happen; usually you have to look for them.

Now, as you know what to looking for in a business opportunity, you should also know where to find them, get new ideas and more. So just keep on reading – here are some "Best Practice" strategies on how to find best business opportunities.

Method 1 - Search Engines – Your Gold Mine of Information

Search engines are the best place to find the information for any business. You can say search engines are gold mines of information. You could just do a common search on Google or Yahoo! and find out about thousands of business opportunities. But, of course, you wouldn't know which of these are good to have and which aren't, in which case, you might have to read their reviews as well, which again you will find through search engines. Look for specific forums on business opportunities where you will find people talking about them and giving their opinions.

Method 2 – Join Business Forums (Online as well as Offline)
Forums are now a day's very much in demand especially online. There are many business forums having around 2 to 3 million users. Using forums you can discuss get professional help, advice from experts and also from people who are searching for business opportunities. Just Google the keyword of your business with the word "forums" and you will get a list of top forums in that niche.

Method 3 - Classified Ads (Don't Ignore These)
Regularly check newspapers, TV news, online news, online press release where on a daily bases thousands of business opportunities are posted. Just take advantage of this revolution and get great ideas for the best business opportunities.

Method 4 – Get Memberships into Top Clubs
Clubs are one of the best places where people go for entertainment and also share their business experience and resources. Here you can get lots and lots of business ideas and great opportunities. Be social in top clubs and see how you can grow your business with new business opportunities.

Method 4 – Get Information from Government Bodies
Governments do provide many good business opportunities in terms of grants, information help, leads and many

other resources. This source is one of the most trusted sources. Get in touch with your local business regulation bodies to get a long list of business information and ideas.

Successful people aren't born successful; they understand and accept new opportunities

People aren't born with success written all over them. You might be born in a rich household, but that's not a guarantee that you will be rich individually as well. Here's what successful people do – they keep their ear open for any news of new opportunities.

No one is born successful. When we are born we don't even know how to spell successful, knowing its meaning is something quite far-off. When we grow up, we begin chipping away at it in the efforts to turn our lives into successful lives. Some of us do achieve the success that we have thought about, but that doesn't come without a great deal of effort.

One of the most important ingredients in becoming successful is to have a vision, a dream. If you don't know how to dream, you will most probably not achieve anything in life. Some people are afraid to dream, thinking they would be terribly frustrated if they don't achieve their goals. But the fact is that if you don't dream, you probably won't get it. Great people dreamed of flying, going to moon and so on... you see now that we can fly, we can go to moon.

In this age when people are thinking how to build gadgets that can turn objects and even people invisible, it is quite unwise to restrict one's thoughts. What do you dream about? You may dream about having a great business or buying a home or a car of your own. In the light of all the achievements that people have made, do you think all this is as difficult as you think? This shows there is nothing impossible in this world if you do it the right way, if you take initiative and plan it properly.

Just take the example of Bill Gates, my favorite example actually. Practically the whole world today uses his Microsoft products, not realizing that these products belong to a person who was a computer class dropout. Take a look at Facebook. It started as a college project and has today made a revolution in the field of social networking. How can we not talk about Google, which started in a dingy office and today it dominates our online world.

All these successes have been achieved in just a few short years! So what's your excuse?

Don't lose hope, hold on to your big dreams and try to achieve them. The simple steps that you need to take are hard work, and to hit the right time and the right place. Follow this and no one can stop you from reaching your goals. Plan things properly on paper before executing them. Make milestones for yourself and give yourself rewards once you reach them.

Why we should always be on the move!

Success rarely comes to people who wait in the wings for things to happen to them. It happens to people who stay on the move.

I have seen thousands of people fail in their lives due to only one reason, i.e. they don't take action. Let's say you have $10 million but you don't know how and where to use those millions. The amount becomes worthless to you then. So, if you have resources, information and a business plan, make it a point to execute them. Don't just keep them on paper.

Some people work very hard during the initial stages of their business, but if they don't succeed early on, they stop. You must know that success most probably won't come instantly.

You need be dedicated and sometimes work for years to get real success. But some people get demotivated very quickly. Most of these people have not planned for the worst and they don't have back up plans. Keep all these things ready and keep working on your plans and you will see that you will move closer to success.

Failure is not the only reason why people stop working. In some people, overconfidence becomes the primary culprit. These are the people who succeed early on, but then they become overconfident about their achievements, which even makes them complacent. They start thinking they have achieved everything and now they don't need to do much, but the fact is we should never stop and should always be on the move to achieve more and more success.

Then, there are other kinds of people who just keep dreaming, keep thinking they will do one thing or the other, but the fact is they just need to execute those plans. Everyone can dream but only those people who work hard can achieve those dreams.

Identifying great business opportunities and acting upon them!

It isn't enough to just listen to your opportunity's call. You have to act upon it.

There should be a formula to make a great successful business and plan to take action on that formula which should be executed properly by acting upon them.

There are a few things you need to take care of which will help you to take action on your plan.

- Always expect and shoot for the best
- Create your work plan on paper

- Dedicate yourself to work and complete the tasks on time
- Make milestones for your plan
- Make schedules for daily, weekly and monthly task and don't miss them
- Always keep a backup plan which keeps you in the business

Sometimes we work very hard but at the end of the day we are not satisfied with our work. This usually results in poor outcomes. This happens if you work without a plan. So always make a complete plan on paper.

Give yourself targets and gifts too. We always need some kind of motivation to keep our self in business with good standing. Let's say you had to complete a task by tomorrow evening but you complete it in the morning, then give yourself some reward. This rises your opinion of yourself, which is very important.

Plan your tasks with backup plans, say you are not able to complete the task on time for some reason. Ensure that you have something else prepared to cover that time. Fill it in with another task!

Always prioritize your tasks. Sequence them in the order of their importance. There should be a "must-do task" for daily or weekly basis. This gives you a chance to complete your important work at least in a week and don't miss it.

If you don't know how to make a plan, get help from professionals such as accountants and other financial experts, but don't start without a plan. 90% of businesses fail because they don't have a plan on paper. At the same time, implementing the plan is of supreme importance as well.

Does opportunity knock twice?

There is a saying that failure is the first step toward success. Many people stop their efforts when they have failed once. They fall prey to thinking that if they have failed once, they won't be able to do well again. However, opportunities do recur in life; you just have to be ready and grab them when they come again. You should not opt out of accepting these opportunities when they come by you again.

Nine out of ten people who are successful today have faced failure sometime in their lives. Francis Ford Coppola was a washout when his important directorial venture was proclaimed a dud when it was being filmed. However, he continued his efforts unrelenting, and that "dud" is known today as the classic The Godfather. A person of average mindset would have given up when people began to become critical, but he didn't and he gave us one of our greatest cinematic masterpieces of all time.

This is simply a learning process. When we started school in our childhood, we didn't know a lot of things. We learned everything by committing mistakes and fixing them. That's the part that contributes to our success. If you've faced failure before, you will be more successful as you know what to do if you face that kind of conditions in the future.

So it does not matter if we lost the opportunity once or twice, it keeps coming. Let me give you a live example. You were waiting for a bus to go somewhere, and for some reason, you missed one bus, what do you do? Don't you try for another bus to reach your destination or do you return to where you were before? Just as you wait for the bus and catch it the next time it arrives, you wait for opportunities as well. And, just like buses do, opportunities come by you again as well.

If your efforts are correct and meaningful, there is no reason why you should not succeed in them. Opportunities knock several times in life, but you have to be ready to accept them in the right way, and surely you will be able to tackle them as you have learned many things from your past failures.

So never get too depressed, keep trying your best and one day you will be scaling new heights of success.

Using the internet to "discover" your business opportunities

The Internet is one of the best places to discover business opportunities; there are many options available here where you can do research, gather data, research papers and so on. We are going to speak about some of the best methods to find what is more in demand and what people are looking for.

1. You can do research on practically any product or service using search engines. You can find how many competitors there are, what they are promoting, how long they have been in business, what their USP is, at what price they sell at and so on. You can easily get all the needed information from search engines. Simply enter you keyword and you get all the information you need.
2. You can try Google Trends (http://www.google.com/trends), this tool helps you to see what's currently in demand. For an example, you can find out what the trends are from the past or up to the minute today! This tool will let you know how in demand a product is or was in the past.
3. You can try http://pulse.ebay.com, http://www.amazon.com and magazine websites. These websites

give you details of which product or business section is more in demand, which product users are searching for, what people are buying and so on. If you go to magazine websites you can find out which products are highlighted as those websites will only display products or service which are in current demand, so we can use their ideas.
4. You can use the Google External Keyword Tool (https://adwords.google.com/select/KeywordToolExternal) which give you total search volume of a particular keyword which people are searching, for example keyword "weight loss" was searched 20,400,000 times in just one month by American users.

So, you see there are many ways to get information on different business opportunities. Just explore it.

Listening to an opportunity is not enough; you have to put it into action

What you must do when an opportunity comes your way. When you work for someone it makes it easier for you, typically they take all the risk, guide you, and inform you what to do and how to do it. But when you choose to start your own business it's a totally new game. The main part to starting your own business, be it your entrepreneur business or home based, you need to take action, action and action.

You should not only plan on what to do, when to do and how to do, but also implement the plan you have made. As it's your business you only have to take action, no one else will do that for you.

One of the most important reasons for people not achieving success is lack of hard work, or commitment to themselves. You need to execute your plan instantly. Merely thinking about the opportunity at the drop of a hat and trying to implement it isn't going to take you anywhere.

If you work hard and execute your plans as per plan, you will surely get the rewards which you expected and many times much more than expected.

There is a saying that action speaks louder than words. So put your plans into action and see how it gives you returns. You don't get anything just by speaking it out; you need to actually do that. It's not difficult to be a go getter or put your plans into action. Just be confident, be committed to yourself and you will see the results. There is unlimited potential for hardworking people and for those who put their plans in action and not just listen to an opportunity to become successful.

Inspiring people to help you reach your goals

It will be very difficult to plow on without the support of people whom you can trust. The best people are those whom you can inspire. Reaching your goal is not as difficult as many think. You can reach your goal if you follow some of the common techniques from real life. Let me show you one very simple example of a "word of mouth" marketing technique. Let's say you have to buy a T.V, what do you do? Ask your friends what TV is the best? Get reviews online? Get expert advice? Right? Yes, we do all this before buying or taking action. This is really a very simple marketing technique of involving more and more people to help you promote your business. If they like the product or service they will surly promote it to others without any charge as they want to give the best to their friends and family.

Take an example of MLM it's totally based on "word of mouth" marketing. One person joins the network and he invites others to join and then others invite more people and so on. This way, the company reaches its target easily without much marketing and concentrating on quality of the product.

You too can follow the same method, join more and more clubs, more and more events and spread your network. The more networks of people you have, the more easily you can reach your goals. Indirectly you help them and they help you. It's a kind of a win-win situation. You make a friend, which is fun and it helps you to reach your goal.

Can anything be better than this?

So start joining clubs, groups, events, parties, tours and make friends and groups and reach your goals easily without any errors.

Don't stop with just one opportunity

The most successful individuals in the world have been unstoppable. I can say that 99% of people are not satisfied with what they have. Like a person who has a motorcycle will want a car, those who have a car want a luxury car, those who have a luxury car want to have a private jet and so on. This is the nature of humans and that's why we are successful as we always have dreams that keep life moving forward in a positive light.

So when we have so many dreams do you think success can be achieved with just one successful opportunity or business? When we want everything why don't we try to grab more and more opportunities which give us everything we need in life?

The fact is most of the world's richest people have multiple stream of income from multiple businesses. They started with one business and now have multiple ventures to their names. We think that we invested xyz amount and we got good returns, so now everything is fine; but the fact is we always need more and for that we need to have more and more business opportunities.

Burger King started with a single restaurant, now it has franchisees all over the world. This is the power of looking for more opportunities to grow. If you stop at any point you are not going to fulfill the dreams of becoming rich and famous. Diversification is a very important aspect of getting at where you want to reach.

Conclusion

Opportunities come everyone's way but not a lot of people can understand what they should do with them. Most people don't even know where to look for the right opportunities.

But now you have a start. And the right motivation. Go forth and conquer.

Financial Empowerment - Earning the Greenbacks

Financial Empowerment is the buzzword for the new generation. This is the jet- set generation that wants to be self-sufficient in what they have, never have a need for more and keep attracting more even as they sleep.

But what makes them different from others who aren't financially empowered already? What can the have-nots of this generation do to elevate themselves to the status of the haves?

Most importantly, is this upward transition possible?

Here's what it takes in today's world to reach the top economic pedestals of society. This is what it takes to reach the Fortune 500 lists and then stay there.

What is financial empowerment?

Here's a look into what financial empowerment really means. The term "financial empowerment" has many aspects. On a general note, it means being self-sufficient with money, so much so that you don't keep wanting for more. You have your financial coffers full and for any of your needs, you just have to plunge into them and get at the money. A person who is financially empowered is thus dynamic economically as well because he or she is able to use money to attract more money.

This speaks about financial empowerment on an individual note. However, there is also a social aspect to it. Analysts also speak about financially empowering a particular section of people, such as empowering the youth or the seniors or the sick or the women. In each context, it means self-reliance. These particular sections of society are usually dependent on other active and earning classes for their monetary requirements. When economists speak about financially empowering these groups, what they mean is that these groups should be self-sufficient and not have to depend on others.

However, in this chapter we are going to confine ourselves to individual financial empowerment. We are going to speak about how an individual – that is you – can become self-reliant with money. It is a truly great feeling not having to depend on anyone else for your financial requirements and not everyone can do that. But if the right steps are taken, this is very much achievable.

The solutions mentioned in this chapter are going to be simple, but it is in the implementation of them that their true worth comes out. This is what you have to know. No financial empowerment techniques are of any value unless and until they are really implemented in the right away. The approaches must see action.

From here, we begin our journey to financial empowerment. Understand the concepts and implement them and you will see how they start working for you.

Ability v/s Action

Being able is one thing. That creates potential in you, but it doesn't empower you. The empowerment comes through putting your ability into action. There is a wide gulf between ability and action in the world that we live in. There are millions of people out there who are capable of doing something. They might even have the right academic qualifications and some might even have the experience. But then these people aren't putting their talents to the right use. Think about something that can teach excellently, but doesn't put that talent to use. This teacher is instead doing a desk job because according to him or her that's a safer bet. Now, the desk job can only take the person so far because he or she doesn't really like doing that stuff. However, if this person had taken the bigger step of going ahead and teaching – overcoming any limitations in the way, such as stage fright – it is highly possible that he or she would be much better financially stable and empowered today.

We all have various talents, but we fail to discover them and even if we do, we fail to put them to use. J. K. Rowling would not have become the multimillionaire she is today if she had given up her penchant for writing and chased a humdrum "safe" job like most of us do. Imagine Michael Schumacher or Zinedine Zidane's vast bundle of talent hidden behind an office job. Think what Barack Obama would have been if he did not act to implement his immense leadership potential and charisma to rule one of the most developed nations of the world.

The one thing we have to consider is that it is not just enough to be able. It is not enough to be able to swim, cook, dance, write, and jump or whatever. If you want to be financially empowered, you have to use these abilities that are within you and wow the people around you. It is only then that you start taking steps toward your empowerment.

The four fundamentals

If you are looking at financially empowering yourself, you cannot neglect these four important fundamentals. These are the ingredients you need to prepare this recipe of economic freedom. When you are looking at building yourself financially, there are a few things that you must make sure you have with you. These are your allies in your quest for financial empowerment – they are your four fundamentals – without which you will find this journey very difficult. Here we take a look at these four essentials in this chapter, we shall take a detailed look at what they really mean.

Assets

Assets are the material and nonmaterial things that you have with you. These things are valuable because you use them to create more things. However, we are going to bring about a change in your perspective of assets. Normally people think only about monetary assets. But everything that you have, including the love of your spouse, can become an asset.

Education

Education has veritable factors in empowering yourself financially because your career is going to depend on how educated you are. However, education does not just mean academic qualifications – everything that you do in the pursuit of achieving something counts toward your education. Even reading a manual to understand how a particular software application operates will be education for you because you can use it in the future in some other way to enrich what you have got.

Investment

Investing is an asset because this helps you in securing money for the long run. When things are going the way they shouldn't, your investments matter a lot. Even when everything is hunky-dory, your investments build up your financial portfolio like few other things can.

Recreation

You might not willingly take this as a factor for financial empowerment, but the fact is that you need to enrich your mind in order to stay healthier and hence make yourself more stable monetarily. Some forms of recreation can actually directly help in improving your economic standing as well.

The Sum of Five

The Sum of Five is the essential law that helps you to evolve financially so that you keep moving upward. The Sum of Five is a key aspect in financial empowerment. It is a rule, a rule which you apply in order to keep yourself dynamic.

It ensures that you don't remain stuck in the rut when you have achieved a modicum of success, but you keep improving upon it and keep moving northward.

So, what does the Sum of Five state?

The Sum of Five states that if your income is the sum total of the five people closest to you. If the five most prominent people you are dealing with financially make less money than you do, then it is time for you to find some more financial collaborators.

This is the statement of the Sum of Five, but you need not judge it by what it actually says. Look at what it means. What it means is this – When you are involved in a business collaboration with several people, you must take a look at how much the five people closest to you are earning. Here, we don't really mean a number at all. The "five" is irrelevant. You have to look at the people you are dealing with at all times. If the people you are dealing with are making more money than you are, you must continue your efforts till you reach their level. But if they are all making less money than you, it means you have reached a point of stagnancy and now you need to find more people to hobnob with.

You won't be mistaken if you find this law to be a bit selfish. Actually, it isn't that way. We all believe and accept that change is imminent. We say that all the time. Then why do we not change the circumstances that surround us? We tend to live in the same situation for life, without trying to think we should take higher leaps. This is where we make the absolute error.

If we want to progress, it is important for us to improve the situation that we are surrounded with. It is important for us to change the set of people we regularly deal with. There is a saying in an Indian language that says, "A man doesn't really succeed in life unless he leaves his childhood behind." What it really means is that we should not cling to our past more than we should. In life, we continue climbing the rungs of the ladder of success but since we tend to think we have reached our zenith, we never continue moving upward. This is when the downward fall begins.

Understanding the concept of assets

What are assets? Assets are what you utilize in order to start empowering yourself financially. These assets include monetary as well as monetary resources. Most people only consider monetary assets when they speak about assets. They consider things like their bank balance, their property, their cars, their stocks, etc. as assets.

However, there is much more to assets than just these materialistic things.

Here we take a look at assets other than the usual material ones.

Goodwill

Your good name in the market is a veritable asset. It could be your name or the name of your company, your brand, etc. Whatever goodwill your name has accumulated, you could certainly use it in improving your profits, and hence it becomes an asset. For instance, if you launch a new product with the same name of your previous successful product, it already gets a lot of foundation to succeed. That's the reason big name companies sell their goodwill when they give out franchises.

Your qualifications, eligibilities and experiences

Everything that you do in your life is an asset in itself. These are things you can tap into in order to empower yourself in a better manner. For example, if you are a postgraduate, you could use that qualification to pitch in for financing a research plant you want to set up. If you have worked in a particular area, your chances of earning in that area are more.

Your family, friends and other people

Everyone that you come in contact with is a potential asset for you. You are what your family makes you, and that decides your capabilities to a large extent. Also, your friends make you and so do other people that you come in contact with. People are so important to businesses today that there are complete business models that are set up on this concept. Take network marketing, for instance, better known as MLM, where people directly tap into the people they know in order to enhance their income capabilities.

Building your assets

Asset building is your first active step toward financial empowerment. You may have done various things in this journey, but it is in asset building that your journey really gains momentum. Being financially empowered means you have to have enough money so that you don't lack for funds when you need them. You have to be rich enough to have money to cover all your needs and desires. The desires part needs to be seen with more careful attention here, because most people have adequate money to cover their needs. It is when they need to realize one of their dreams that they feel they are lacking in proper funds.

It is necessary that you have the right kind of financial empowerment to chase your goals and intentions. This is where asset building becomes important in your route to financial empowerment. In this context, you try to build on what you can call your own so that you can build more to call your own. There are various ways in which you can begin focusing on asset building.

Proper investments

Investing is the best route to building assets. Find ways to make investments, such as in fixed deposits in banks, money-back insurance policies, stocks or whatever suits your interests. The channel you select for investment should be safe and should guarantee you high returns.

Sniffing out opportunities

Opportunities are all around us, but we don't know how to get at them. Keep your eyes wide open. If there is a business venture that interests you, learn more about it till you know all that there is to it. There are several high-paying opportunities like network marketing that can pay you back a lot without requiring much investment. Keep your mind receptive to such opportunities.

Involve your friends and family

Most of us shut out our near and dear ones when it comes to asset building. We have to understand that assets are not just monetary. There are various other things that can help us build ourselves financially, and toward this end, we have to realize that the role of the people in our lives is quite significant.

Investing in education for your financial empowerment

The journey has begun sooner than you think, but it hasn't ended yet. What we don't really realize is that our tryst with financial empowerment begins much sooner than we think. It isn't when we are 20 and thinking about a career; it is right when we are 3 and attend our first school. In fact, our financial empowerment begins even before that when our parents lovingly and patiently tell us what is what. All those questions, all those attempts at gathering information and, later, education, are nothing but steps toward financially empowering ourselves.

For, what is education if not a way to empower ourselves in every way, including financially? A lot of people tap into their educational qualifications when they are looking for a job, pitching for a promotion, applying for a freelancing assignment or even when applying for financial assistance for a commercial venture. The educational qualification is a kind of abstract collateral; it is something people judge your financial worth with. If you are better qualified they know that you will keep sailing through and hence they don't mind extending a better financial help for your ventures. They don't mind investing in your ventures either because they consider you as a worthy candidate with their money.

That is the reason, it is important to learn as much as possible. After becoming the President of the United States, one of the first things Barack Obama did was to give a clarion call to his people to "go back to school". This does not really mean physically going back to school, but it means continuing to learn something or the other as we did when we were younger.

Come to think of it, when we were at school, we would learn a new thing each day. Are we doing that right now? At school, we enriched our minds each day and became what we are today. But why has this process of "becoming" stopped for some people? Why do some people think that their learning age has ceased? We need to educate ourselves continuously, till the last day of our lives and keep improving ourselves.

When we are more educated, we not only learn better avenues to earn money but we also learn how to manage the money properly so that it keeps growing. No form of education should be intimidating and there is no age when you cannot begin learning something.

Enriching your financial coffers with recreation

How does recreation help in building your financial value? Isn't this like shattering a myth? The common mentality of most people is that when they are getting some recreation for themselves – in whatever form that might be – they are actually wasting time. They think that by giving themselves some amusement, they are actually depriving themselves of the opportunity of being able to earn something. Proverbs like "Wasting time is akin to wasting money" don't help matters one bit. But we should remember that "All work and no play make Jack a dull boy." But, is it only a dull boy that Jack can turn out to be? No, worse things can happen if you deprive yourself from proper routes of recreation.

You have to understand what recreation means first. To recreate means to free up your mind and utilize it in doing something that you really like to do. It means to unwind yourself from your daily rigmarole of work. Since our mind is not a machine, but a living organ with blood and tissues in it, it does need this kind of unwinding ourselves.

But there is a subtle point that you must understand. Every person chooses his or her form of recreation and this is most times connected with what they do professionally. For example, for a person who teaches, reading could be a form of recreation. Now, this is actually helping their profession in various ways. This person is able to expand his or her knowledge and that really helps them in their profession. For a professional sportsperson, looking at someone else's game could be recreation. Now, they could pick up various tips from that and learn.

However, even when you think there are no obvious benefits of your form of recreation on your profession, there are actually several benefits. Consider that you have a desk job. Your mode of recreation is to shoot villains in computer games. How does this help your profession? It actually does, in a very poignant way, because it helps clear the clutter of monotony that your job has created and gives you a chance to do something that revitalizes your energy. You are refreshed and can even return to work the next day in a better mood.

Remember that empowering yourself financially does not mean immersing yourself in money-related thoughts and keeping yourself there all the time. Sometimes, you have to come out of those shackles and think in a liberated manner. This helps you rethink things and you begin looking at the world with a renewed perspective.

The long haul

Financially empowering yourself for the future – Yes, it's possible, but only if you act right now. It may not sound pleasant to a lot of us, but when most of us think of the term "financial empowerment", they tend to think about short-term goals. They think about how they can put in efforts to achieve money in the short term, within just a few weeks probably. One of the biggest mistakes that we do is that we contract our entire lifespan into a few weeks by thinking in this manner. We forget that we have a long life ahead of us and that if you want to be really financially empowered, we have to make sure that we have enough for that period which looms ahead of us.

That is why, when we speak about financial empowerment, it is not going to be much about what you can do that can give you returns today – there is a lot of material on that already – but it is about what you can do so that you stay financially empowered for the longer term. This is actually what must interest each and every one of us. There are some very important ways in which this can be done.

Education

Now, everyone gets basic education and hence if you want to really financially empower yourself, you have to learn something more than the other person. We aren't talking about childhood education here but education that enriches you as a professional. In the Internet marketing milieu, for example, a person who has educated himself or herself to use blogs and article submissions will do better than someone who uses just article submissions.

Investing

People who are in for the long haul will always think closely about investment options. They will think where they can invest so that they can get the best returns. Investment is highly important if you want to financially empower yourself because this is what can help you when the chips are down.

Insurance

Insurance is an assurance that is of value when something goes horribly wrong. There are several unforeseen things that can happen in our lives; one such stroke can wipe out all the financial empowerment that we have achieved for ourselves. Though any loss in the world can never be replenished completely, insurances do provide some respite in such events.

Recreation

Every song you hear, every book your read, every movie you watch, every place you visit enriches your mind in some way. Though you aren't doing these things for gaining knowledge, they are certainly expanding what you know. You are learning new things and anything can be important at any time. Hence, even the way you amuse your mind is essential when you are talking about financial empowerment.

All these things won't bring money right away at your doorstep, but they are definitely enhancing your capabilities. You become a better person, financially and otherwise, when you use these key factors in the right way.

Staying upwardly mobile

How do we ensure that we keep empowering ourselves financially? Our finishing touch will be to speak about how you must remain always moving toward the top. In fact, we have alluded to this already when we spoke about the Sum of Five. When you try to equate yourself with your collaborators and then find better collaborators if you find they are all doing much worse than you, you are staying upwardly mobile. When you mix around with people who have a particular kind of status, it automatically begins rubbing on you. Consciously or subconsciously, you begin taking steps to be with them, and sooner than you think, you are there. You get that one important breakthrough and you get to be with these people.

If you have used the four fundamentals in the right way, and are still constantly using them, then you will keep shaping yourself to be a more significant person financially. You will be going upward all the time and this is what really matters. One thing that you have to keep in mind is that you must broaden your approaches. Once you are set with something, move on to other things. We have spoken about how you must be always aware of opportunities and take them in your stride. Learn how to make the most of them.

Think positive. Think big. When you do that, you usually do big. If you confine yourself to thinking narrow-mindedly, you are going to stay there. A lot of modern philosophers have laid great emphasis on the importance of thought – Stephen Covey, Rhonda Byrne, Paulo Coelho – and you have to understand that there is great truth in this. When you think positively about something, things automatically energize themselves to make that happen. You know this fact in another form already probably – the Law of Attraction. Yes, this law can help you greatly in financially empowering yourself. Get acquainted with it today.

Conclusion

Financial empowerment is quite attainable, even if you have started with nothing. The fact is that most people don't think it can happen to them and hence they stay in the rut.

One of the most important things to materialize the things mentioned in this book is that you have to have the faith in yourself.

Believe that you can make the transition. Believe that you can take that leap.

Wrapping It Up!!

You made it to the end!! I hope this book was an enlightening tool for you. Hopefully you took away some very key concepts to help you in your current business or help you get started in your very first business. Over many years in marketing, I have been very fortunate to learn, grow and profit in this business. There is no reason why you can't find the same success that I've had.

Apply the "hustle" and marketing instincts that will allow you to profit in your business. Remember, there are three components to your success: (1) continuous education, (2) sell, sell, sell and (3) take care of your leads and customers! Find the right opportunity at the right time, get with the right people and you will find that success is abound.

Now, there is one last thing for you to consider. This component has been one of the biggest keys to my success. Having a coach, mentor, business partner or just a friend to bounce ideas off of is vital to the success of your business.

No successful entrepreneur or successful company has been built without the help of a trusted advisor, business partner, mentor or just a friend. This is important for one very simple reason. Just because you think something is a good idea doesn't mean that it is. I can recall many times when I thought I had a good idea for a new product or marketing strategy but my mentor would eventually say, "that won't work." Very irritating at times but it's good to have someone that has been there, done that in your corner. This keeps us accountable as business owners and prevents us from making very costly mistakes.

So I challenge you to put all these resources to good use and apply them in your marketing. Business loves speed and so does money. This is why you have to get off your butt and stop talking about making money and take action. If you do not like your current outcome in life than it is time to change those outcomes with a new course of action. If you implement the information from this book, work hard, remain dedicated to your business, and face challenges head on with action than you to will be well on your way into successful entrepreneurship.

To your ultimate success!!!

Jason and Erika Miller
Jason and Erika Miller
Founders: Patriots to Business
Founders: Jump Start Marketing Concepts, LLC